ATLAS A-Z

LONDON, NEW YORK
MUNICH, MELBOURNE, DELHI

LONDON, NEW YORK
MUNICH, MELBOURNE, DELHI

FOR THE THIRD EDITION
Senior Cartographic Manager David Roberts
Senior Cartographic Editors Roger Bullen, Simon Mumford
Database Editors Cambridge International Reference on Current Affairs (CIRCA)
Systems Co-ordinator Philip Rowles **Production** Melanie Dowland
3D Globes Planetary Visions Ltd., London

FOR PREVIOUS EDITIONS
Cartographic Director Andrew Heritage
Cartography Encompass Graphics Limited, Rob Stokes, Iorwerth Watkins
Project Editor Sam Atkinson **Art Editor** Karen Gregory

First published in the United States by Dorling Kindersley Publishing, Inc.,
375 Hudson Street, New York, New York 10014
A Penguin Company

First American Edition, 2001. Third Edition 2007
4 6 8 10 9 7 5 3
Copyright © 1996, 1998, 2001, 2003, 2004, 2005, 2007
Dorling Kindersley Limited, London

See our complete catalog at **www.dk.com**

Library of Congress Cataloging-in-Publication Data

Atlas A-Z.-- 1st American ed. 2001.
  p.cm
  "Published in the United States by Dorling Kindersley Publishing, Inc."
  Previously published as: Ultimate pocket book of the world atlas & factfile.
  London ; New York : Dorling Kindersley, 1998.
  Includes index.
  Contents: North & Central America -- South America -- Africa -- Europe --
  North & West Asia -- South & East Asia -- Australia & Oceania.
  ISBN 978-0-7566-2872-7 (alk. paper)
  1. Atlases, British. I. Title: Atlas A to Z. II. Dorling Kindersley Publishing, Inc.
  III. Ultimate pocket book of the world atlas & factfile.

G1021 .A623 2002
912--dc21
                                        2001018264 2001047632

Printed and bound in Singapore by Star Standard

For the very latest information, visit:
www.dk.com and click on the Maps & Atlases icon

Key to map symbols

ELEVATION

6000m / 19,686ft
4000m / 13,124ft
2000m / 6562ft
1000m / 3281ft
500m / 1640ft
250m / 820ft
100m / 328ft
0
Below sea level

▲ Mountain

• Depression

BORDERS

——— Full international

- - - - Disputed *de facto*

· · · · · Territorial claim

× × × × Cease-fire line

··········· Undefined

——— State / Province

DRAINAGE FEATURES

——— River

——— Seasonal river

·············· Canal

Lake

Seasonal lake

SETTLEMENTS

◉ Capital city

◎ Major town

○ Minor town

● Major port

COMMUNICATIONS

——— Major road

——— Rail

✈ International airport

◆ Insight; facts, figures and amazing information from around the world

NAVIGATOR

The navigator device can be used to quickly move around the atlas. Using this example, the next map to the north of page 128 can be found on page 120.

4
Atlas contents

North & West Asia 94-95

South & East Asia 106-107

Australasia & Oceania 124-125

Country factfiles 138-359

See overleaf for contents

Factfile contents

Factfile contents

The Political World

Key to Numbers
1. Germany
2. Liechtenstein
3. Czech Republic
4. Austria
5. Slovakia
6. Hungary
7. Slovenia
8. Croatia
9. Bosnia & Herzegovina
10. Serbia
11. Montenegro
12. San Marino
13. Vatican City

The Political World

ARCTIC
OCEAN

Greenland
(Denmark)

Arctic Circle

Alaska
(US)

CANADA

ATLANTIC
OCEAN

Aleutian Islands (US)

PACIFIC
OCEAN

UNITED STATES
OF AMERICA

Bermuda (UK)

Midway Islands
(US)

Puerto Rico (US)
DOM. REP.
ST KITTS & NEVIS
ANTIGUA & BARBUDA

Hawaii
(US)

MEXICO

BELIZE

BAHAMAS
CUBA

DOMINICA
ST LUCIA
BARBADOS

Tropic of Cancer

MARSHALL
ISLANDS

WALLIS & FUTUNA (France)

GUATEMALA
EL SALVADOR
HONDURAS

JAMAICA

HAITI

ST VINCENT &
THE GRENADINES

Palmyra Atoll (US)

NICARAGUA
PANAMA

COSTA RICA

VENEZUELA

GRENADA
TRINIDAD & TOBAGO

NAURU

KIRIBATI

*Tokelau
(NZ)*

Cook
Islands
(NZ)

COLOMBIA

GUYANA

French Guiana (France)

Equator

TUVALU

SOLOMON
ISLANDS

*Galapagos Islands
(Ecuador)*

SURINAME

VANUATU

Niue (NZ)

French
Polynesia
(France)

*Pitcairn
Islands
(UK)*

ECUADOR

P E R U

BRAZIL

FIJI

TONGA

*American
Samoa (US)*

BOLIVIA

CHILE

PARAGUAY

Tropic of Capricorn

New
Caledonia
(France)

SAMOA

NEW
ZEALAND

PACIFIC
OCEAN

ARGENTINA

URUGUAY

CONTINENTAL KEY

North & Central
America

South America

Africa

Europe

NW/SE Asia

Australasia
& Oceania

Falkland Islands (UK)

CHILE

South Georgia &
South Sandwich Islands
(UK)

ANTARCTICA

Antarctic Circle

The Physical World

Spitsbergen
Franz Josef Land
Severnaya Zemlya
ARCTIC
New Siberia Islands
Novaya Zemlya
Greenland Sea
Barents Sea
Kara Sea
Laptev Sea
Arctic Circle
Denmark Strait
Norwegian Sea
Yenisey
Lena
Kolyma
Cherskiy
Iceland
Scandinavia
North European Plain
Siberia
Sea of Okhotsk
British Isles
North Sea
Volga
Ural Mountains
Ob'
Lake Baikal
Amur
Sakhalin
EUROPE
Baltic Sea
ASIA
Bay of Biscay
Alps
Danube
Caucasus
Lake Balkhash
Altai Mountains
Gobi
Manchurian Plain
Hokkaido
Azores
Iberian Peninsula
Black Sea
Aral Sea
Tien Shan
Yellow River
Sea of Japan (East Sea)
Honshu
Madeira
Atlas Mts
Mediterranean Sea
Anatolia
Caspian Sea
Hindu Kush
Plateau of Tibet
Kyushu
Canary Islands
Syrian Desert
Iranian Plateau
Indus
Himalayas
Yangtze
East China Sea
Taiwan
Tropic of Cancer
Sahara
Zagros Mts
Thar Desert
Ganges
Mount Everest 29,035ft (8850m)
AFRICA
Arabian Peninsula
Deccan
Philippine Sea
Sahel
Nile
Red Sea
Arabian Sea
Bay of Bengal
South China Sea
Me
Cape Verde Islands
Niger
Lake Chad
Ethiopian Highlands
Horn of Africa
Sri Lanka
Malay Peninsula
Philippine Islands
Equator
Gulf of Guinea
Congo
Congo Basin
Great Rift Valley
Lake Victoria
Somali Basin
Seychelles
Sumatra
Borneo
Celebes
East Indies
New Guinea
ATLANTIC
Kilimanjaro 19,340ft (5895m)
INDIAN
Java
Java Sea
Angola Basin
Zambezi
Timor Sea
OCEAN
Namib Desert
Mauritius
Réunion
Great Sandy Desert
Tropic of Capricorn
Kalahari Desert
Mozambique Channel
Madagascar
OCEAN
AUSTRALIA
Nullarbor Plain
Cape Basin
Ninetyeast Ridge
Darling
Mid-Atlantic Ridge
Cape of Good Hope
Southwest Indian Ridge
Southeast Indian Ridge
Tasmania
Kerguelen
South Indian Basin
SOUTHERN
Antarctic Circle
OCEAN
ANTARCTICA

The Physical World

OCEAN

East Siberian Sea

Beaufort Sea

Chukchi Sea

Queen Elizabeth Islands

Ellesmere Island

Baffin Island

Baffin Bay

Greenland

Brooks Range

Mackenzie

Bering Strait

Mount McKinley (Denali) 20,322ft (6194m)

Great Bear Lake

Great Slave Lake

Hudson Bay

Labrador Sea

Arctic Circle

Bering Sea

Gulf of Alaska

Aleutian Islands

Coast Mountains

Coast Ranges

Rocky Mountains

NORTH AMERICA

Great Lakes

Appalachian Mts.

Grand Banks of Newfoundland

Mid-Atlantic Ridge

Vancouver Island

Great Plains

Mississippi

North American Basin

Northwest Pacific Basin

Hawaiian Islands

Mid-Pacific Mountains

Polynesia

Micronesia

Gulf of Mexico

West Indies

Caribbean Sea

ATLANTIC

Tropic of Cancer

PACIFIC

Galapagos Islands

OCEAN

OCEAN

Solomon Islands

Fiji

New Caledonia

Coral Sea

Tasman Sea

North Island

South Island

New Zealand

Southwest Pacific Basin

East Pacific Rise

Easter Island

Peru Basin

Andes

Amazon

Amazon Basin

SOUTH AMERICA

Equator

Brazil Basin

Cerro Aconcagua 22,831ft (6959m)

Gran Chaco

Pampas

Patagonia

Argentine Basin

Tropic of Capricorn

Falkland Islands

South Georgia

Cape Horn

Tierra del Fuego

Drake Passage

South Sandwich Islands

Antarctic Peninsula

OCEAN

Antarctic Circle

Time zones

-2   -1   0   +1   +2   +3   +4   +5   +6   +7   +8   +9   +

ARCTIC

ATLANTIC
OCEAN

Greenwich Meridian

INDIAN
OCEAN

11:00   12:00   13:00   14:00   15:00   16:00   17:00   18:00   19:00   20:00   21:00

The
World's
Regions

North & Central America

ATLANTIC OCEAN

Sargasso Sea

St Pierre & Miquelon (France)

Bermuda (UK)

Virgin Islands (US)
British Virgin Islands (UK)
Anguilla (UK)
ST KITTS & NEVIS
ANTIGUA & BARBUDA
Guadeloupe (France)
Montserrat (UK)
DOMINICA
Martinique (France)
ST LUCIA
BARBADOS
ST VINCENT & THE GRENADINES
GRENADA
Netherlands Antilles (Neth.)
TRINIDAD & TOBAGO

Turks & Caicos Islands (UK)
DOMINICAN REPUBLIC
Puerto Rico (US)
HAITI
Aruba (Neth.)

BAHAMAS

CUBA

JAMAICA

Cayman Islands (UK)

BELIZE
GUATEMALA
HONDURAS
EL SALVADOR
NICARAGUA
COSTA RICA
PANAMA

Gulf of Mexico

Great Lakes
Lake Superior
Lake Michigan
Lake Huron
Lake Erie
Lake Ontario
St Lawrence

UNITED STATES OF AMERICA

Appalachian Mountains

Ohio
Missouri
Arkansas
Mississippi

Great Plains

Rio Grande

MEXICO

Sierra Madre Occidental

Mount Whitney 14,495ft (4418m) ▲
Death Valley -282ft (-86m) •
Colorado

PACIFIC OCEAN

Galápagos Islands (Ecuador)

Clipperton Island (French Polynesia)

Tropic of Cancer

Equator

SOUTH AMERICA

Andes

Equator

0 km   1000
0 miles   1000

A B C D E
5 6 7 8

Western Canada & Alaska

RUSSIAN
FEDERATION

Wrangel I.

ARCT

OCEA

◆ In 1867 William Henry Seward negotiated
the purchase of Alaska from Russia for
the price of $7,200,000, which amounted
to around two cents per acre (0.4 hectares).

Attu I.

Bering
Sea

Arctic Circle

Bering Strait

Rat Is.

Aleutian Islands

St. Lawrence I.

Nunivak I.

Yukon

Brooks Range

Prudhoe
Bay

ALASKA
(part of USA)

Mt McKinley
20,322ft (6194m) ▲

Fairbanks

Umnak I.
Dutch Harbor ○
Unalaska I.

Alaska Range

Anchorage ○

Kodiak I. ○ Kodiak

Valdez ○
Cordova ○

YUKON
TERRITOR

◆ The Aleutian Islands span some 1200 miles
(1800 km) and by crossing the 180° line of
longitude, form both the most easterly
and westerly extents of the USA.

WHITEHORSE ○

Rocky

Gulf
of
Alaska

JUNEAU ○

B

CO

PACIFIC

Ketchikan ○

OCEAN

Prince Rupert ○

Queen Charlotte Is.

*Queen Charlotte
Sound*

◆ On July 9, 1958 a massive landslide
dropped 40 million cubic yards
(30.6 million cu m) of rock into Lituya Bay
creating a wave 1720 ft (524 m) high.

Port Hardy ○
Vancouver I.

VICTORIA

0 km   400

0 miles   400

A   B   C   D

NAVIGATOR

137
96 | 18-19 | 20
26

Greenland
(Danish external territory)

◇ Despite an area of 769,900 sq miles (1,994,000 sq km) the northerly province of Nunavut has only 13 miles (21 km) of highway.

160° 140° 120° 100° 80° 60° 80° 40°

I C

N

Queen Elizabeth Islands

Ellesmere Island

Axel Heiberg Island

Bathurst I.

Devon Island

Lancaster Sound

Melville Island

Resolute

Somerset Island

Baffin Bay

Davis Strait

Beaufort Sea

Banks Island

Viscount Melville Sound

Prince of Wales I.

Amundsen Gulf

Victoria Island

King William I.

Inuvik

Kugluktuk

N U N A V U T

Arctic Circle

IQALUIT

Baffin Island

Hudson Strait

Great Bear L.

N O R T H W E S T

Southampton I.

T E R R I T O R I E S

Mackenzie

YELLOWKNIFE

Thelon

Great Slave L.

Rankin Inlet

Hudson Bay

QUEBEC

Hay River

Fort Smith

ISH MBIA

Fort St. John

A L B E R T A

Fort McMurray

L. Athabasca

M A N I T O B A

C A N A D A

O N T A R I O

rince eorge

Grande Prairie

EDMONTON

SASKATCHEWAN

Saskatchewan

Flin Flon

Thompson

Churchill

◇ Some 7% of Canada's 3.5 million sq miles (9.2 million sq km) land area is devoted to grain production yielding around 26 million tons (tonnes) of wheat every year.

Kamloops

Leduc

Red Deer

Prince Albert

Saskatoon

Yorkton

L. Winnipeg

Vancouver

Calgary

REGINA

Brandon

WINNIPEG

Kelowna

Lethbridge

Estevan

U S A

F

E

G

100°

80°

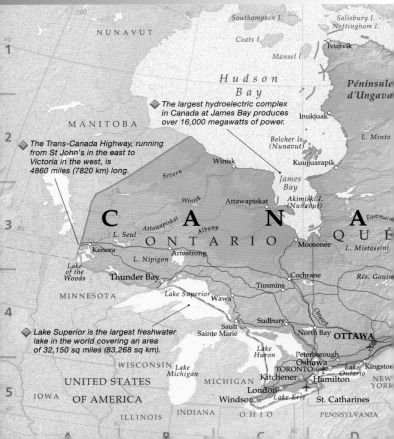

NUNAVUT

Southampton I.

Salisbury I.
Nottingham I.

Coats I.

• Ivujivik

Mansel I.

H u d s o n
B a y

Péninsule
d'Ungava

MANITOBA

◆ The largest hydroelectric complex
in Canada at James Bay produces
over 16,000 megawatts of power.

Inukjuak •

Belcher Is.
(Nunavut)

L. Minto

◆ The Trans-Canada Highway, running
from St John's in the east to
Victoria in the west, is
4860 miles (7820 km) long.

Kuujjuarapik •

Severn

Winisk •

*James
Bay*

Winisk

Attawapiskat •

Akimiski I.
(Nunavut)

Eastmain

C A N A
A
QUÉ

Attawapiskat
L. Seul •

Albany

L. Mistassini

O N T A R I O

Kenora •

Armstrong •

Moosonee •

L. Nipigon

Rés. Gouin

*Lake of
the
Woods*

Thunder Bay •

Cochrane •

MINNESOTA

Lake Superior

Wawa •

Timmins •

Ottawa

◆ Lake Superior is the largest freshwater
lake in the world covering an area
of 32,150 sq miles (83,268 sq km).

Sault
Sainte Marie

Sudbury •

North Bay •

OTTAWA

*Lake
Huron*

Peterborough •

WISCONSIN *Lake
Michigan*

Oshawa •

UNITED STATES

MICHIGAN

TORONTO •

*Lake
Ontario*

• Kingston

IOWA

OF AMERICA

Kitchener •

Hamilton •

NEW
YOR

London •

St. Catharines

ILLINOIS

INDIANA

Windsor •

Lake Erie

OHIO

PENNSYLVANIA

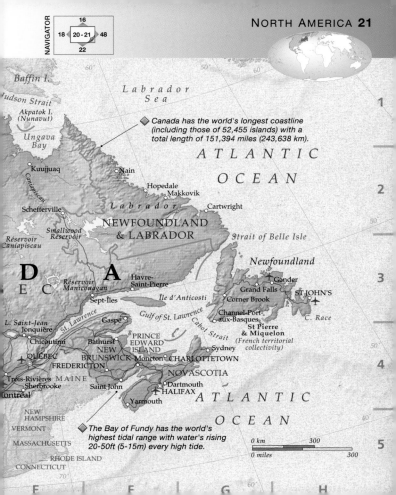

Baffin I.

Hudson Strait

Akpatok I.
(Nunavut)

L a b r a d o r
S e a

Ungava
Bay

Canada has the world's longest coastline
(including those of 52,455 islands) with a
total length of 151,394 miles (243,638 km).

A T L A N T I C

O C E A N

•Kuujjuaq   •Nain

Caniapiscau

•Hopedale
•Makkovik

•Schefferville   *L a b r a d o r*   •Cartwright

Smallwood
Réservoir

NEWFOUNDLAND
& LABRADOR

Strait of Belle Isle

Réservoir
Caniapiscau

Newfoundland

D   *Réservoir*   **A**
E   *Manicouagan*
C

Havre-
Saint-Pierre

+Gander

Grand Falls•   •ST JOHN'S

•Sept-Îles   *Île d'Anticosti*

Corner Brook•

Gulf of St. Lawrence

Channel-Port-
aux-Basques•

C. Race

L. Saint-Jean   Gaspé•

St. Lawrence

St Pierre
& Miquelon
(French territorial
collectivity)

•Jonquière

St. Lawrence

•Chicoutimi   Bathurst•   **PRINCE**
                                  EDWARD
                  NEW   **ISLAND**

Cabot Strait

•QUÉBEC   **BRUNSWICK**   •Sydney
                              Moncton• **CHARLOTTETOWN**
FREDERICTON

•Trois-Rivières **MAINE**   **NOVA SCOTIA**

•Sherbrooke   Saint John• •Dartmouth
ontreal   +HALIFAX
                  Yarmouth•

A T L A N T I C

NEW
HAMPSHIRE

O C E A N

VERMONT

The Bay of Fundy has the world's
highest tidal range with water's rising
20-50ft (5-15m) every high tide.

MASSACHUSETTS

0 km   300

RHODE ISLAND   0 miles   300

CONNECTICUT

USA: The Northeast

◆ The Chicago River
originally flowed into
Lake Michigan, but was
reversed in 1900 by
the completion of
a canal.

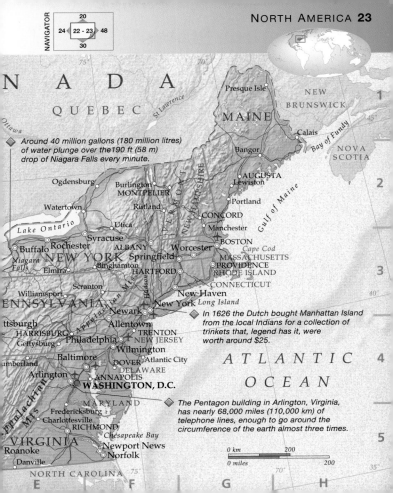

75°   70°

C A N A D A

QUEBEC

St Lawrence

Presque Isle

NEW BRUNSWICK

45°

MAINE

Calais

Ottawa

Bangor

Bay of Fundy

NOVA SCOTIA

◆ Around 40 million gallons (180 million litres)
of water plunge over the 190 ft (58 m)
drop of Niagara Falls every minute.

Ogdensburg

Burlington
MONTPELIER

AUGUSTA
Lewiston

Watertown

Rutland

Portland

Gulf of Maine

Lake Ontario

Utica

CONCORD

Manchester

Buffalo   Rochester   Syracuse

ALBANY   Worcester

BOSTON

Cape Cod

Niagara
Falls

NEW YORK
Elmira

Springfield

MASSACHUSETTS

Binghamton

HARTFORD

PROVIDENCE
RHODE ISLAND

Williamsport

Scranton

CONNECTICUT

40°

New Haven

P E N N S Y L V A N I A

Newark

New York   Long Island

◆ In 1626 the Dutch bought Manhattan Island
from the local Indians for a collection of
trinkets that, legend has it, were
worth around $25.

ttsburgh

Allentown

HARRISBURG

TRENTON

Gettysburg

Philadelphia

NEW JERSEY

Cumberland

Baltimore

Wilmington

DOVER   Atlantic City

A T L A N T I C

Arlington

ANNAPOLIS

DELAWARE

WASHINGTON, D.C.

O C E A N

MARYLAND

Fredericksburg

◆ The Pentagon building in Arlington, Virginia,
has nearly 68,000 miles (110,000 km) of
telephone lines, enough to go around the
circumference of the earth almost three times.

Charlottesville

RICHMOND

Chesapeake Bay

VIRGINIA

Newport News

0 km   200

Roanoke

Norfolk

0 miles   200

Danville

NORTH CAROLINA

75°   70°

35°

USA: Central States

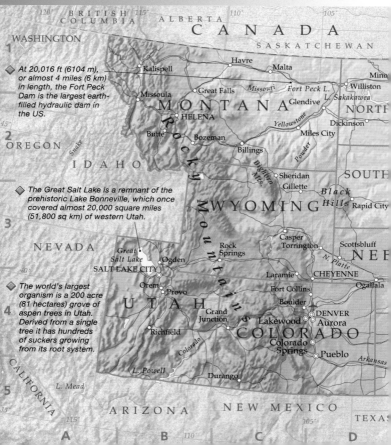

At 20,016 ft (6104 m), or almost 4 miles (6 km) in length, the Fort Peck Dam is the largest earth-filled hydraulic dam in the US.

The Great Salt Lake is a remnant of the prehistoric Lake Bonneville, which once covered almost 20,000 square miles (51,800 sq km) of western Utah.

The world's largest organism is a 200 acre (81 hectares) grove of aspen trees in Utah. Derived from a single tree it has hundreds of suckers growing from its root system.

USA: The West

Hells Canyon is the deepest in the US, with cliffs up to 7900 ft (2408 m) high.

CANADA

BRITISH COLUMBIA

ALBERTA

MONTANA

IDAHO

WASHINGTON

OREGON

Missouri

Great Salt Lake

Pocatello

Idaho Falls

American Falls Res.

Twin Falls

Snake

BOISE

Caldwell
Nampa

Baker

La Grande

Hells Canyon

Snake

Lewiston

Bitterroot Range

Coeur d'Alene

Spokane

Columbia

Walla Walla

Pendleton

Richland
Kennewick
Yakima

Blue Mountains

Ellensburg

Burns

Bend

Goose Lake

Alturas

Klamath Falls

Cascade Range

Medford

Cascade Ranges

Springfield
Eugene

Albany

Corvallis

SALEM

Portland

Vancouver

Longview

Columbia

Astoria

Newport

Coos Bay

Bandon

Crescent City

Coast Ranges

OLYMPIA

Tacoma
Seattle
Bellevue
Everett

Bellingham

Port Angeles

Aberdeen

Vancouver Island

Great

Redwood

NAVIGATOR
24
18 26 - 27 32
134

At Black Rock Desert on October 15, 1997, ThrustSSC, driven by Andy Green, became the first land vehicle to break the sound barrier by achieving a speed of 763 mph (1228 km/h).

Death Valley is not only the lowest point in North America at 282 ft (86 m) below sea level, it is also the hottest, with a maximum air temperature of 134°F (57°C) recorded in 1913.

The Golden Gate Bridge, completed in 1937, has 80,000 miles (129,000 km) of wire in its two main cables, weighing a total of 22,200 tons (tonnes).

USA: The Southwest

◇ The Colorado River has cut down some 6242 ft (2000 m) into the Colorado Plateau to form the Grand Canyon, exposing rock strata over 2 billion years old.

◆ Meteor Crater was formed when a meteor about 150 ft (46 m) across struck the desert at about 40,000 mph (64,372 km/h) creating a bowl shaped depression 4,150 ft (1,265 m) wide and 570 ft (174 m) deep.

◇ The first atomic bomb was tested at Trinity Site near Alamogordo on July 16, 1945 yielding an explosive force equivalent to 20,000 tons (tonnes) of TNT from around 2.2 lbs (1 kg) of plutonium-239.

NEVADA · UTAH · COLORADO

L. Powell

Grand Canyon

Painted Desert

Farmington

L. Mead

Colorado Plateau

Los Alamos
SANTA FE

Gallup

Flagstaff

Albuquerque

Prescott

ARIZONA

Colorado

NEW
MEXICO

CALIFORNIA

Glendale Scottsdale
PHOENIX Mesa

Sonoran

Roswell

Yuma

Desert

Casa Grande

Alamogordo

Artesia

Carlsbad

Tucson

Las Cruces

Douglas

El Paso

Rio Grande

Baja California

Golfo de California

MEXI

PACIFIC

OCEAN

0 km   200
0 miles   200

K A N S A S

Ponca City
Enid
Tulsa
Broken Arrow
OKLAHOMA
Arkansas

Borger
Amarillo
Pampa
OKLAHOMA CITY
Shawnee

Canadian
Norman

ARKANSAS

Clovis
Red River
Lawton
Red River

Vernon
Wichita Falls
Paris

⬥ On January 10, 1901
the Lucas Gusher blew
oil 100 ft (30 m) into the
air, flowing at 100,000
barrels a day until it was
eventually capped nine
days later.

Lubbock
Denton
Fort Worth
Arlington
Longview

Brownfield
Dallas

Hobbs
Abilene
Tyler

Sweetwater
Jacksonville
Toledo Bend Res.

Big Spring
Brazos

Odessa
Midland
Colorado
Waco
Neches

Pecos
San Angelo
LOUISIANA

T E X A S

Bryan
Beaumont
L. Travis
Houston
Port Arthur

Edwards
AUSTIN
Pasadena
Plateau
Texas City
San Antonio
Galveston
Freeport

Del Rio
Victoria
San Antonio

Eagle Pass

G u l f

Laredo
Corpus Christi
o f

Kingsville
M e x i c o

C O
Padre Island

Rio Grande
Brownsville

USA: The Southeast

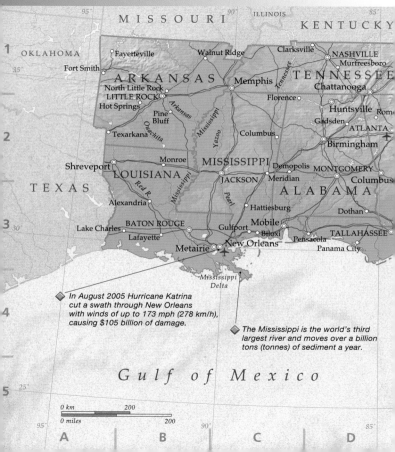

MISSOURI
ILLINOIS
KENTUCKY
OKLAHOMA
Fayetteville
Walnut Ridge
Clarksville
NASHVILLE
Fort Smith
Murfreesboro
ARKANSAS
Memphis
TENNESSEE
Chattanooga
North Little Rock
LITTLE ROCK
Florence
Huntsville
Rom
Hot Springs
Pine Bluff
Gadsden
ATLANTA
Texarkana
Columbus
Birmingham
Shreveport
Monroe
MISSISSIPPI
Demopolis
MONTGOMERY
LOUISIANA
JACKSON
Meridian
Columbus
Alexandria
Hattiesburg
ALABAMA
Dothan
Lake Charles
BATON ROUGE
Gulfport
Mobile
TALLAHASSEE
Lafayette
Biloxi
Pensacola
TEXAS
Metairie
New Orleans
Panama City
Mississippi Delta
Gulf of Mexico

In August 2005 Hurricane Katrina cut a swath through New Orleans with winds of up to 173 mph (278 km/h), causing $105 billion of damage.

The Mississippi is the world's third largest river and moves over a billion tons (tonnes) of sediment a year.

0 km 200
0 miles 200

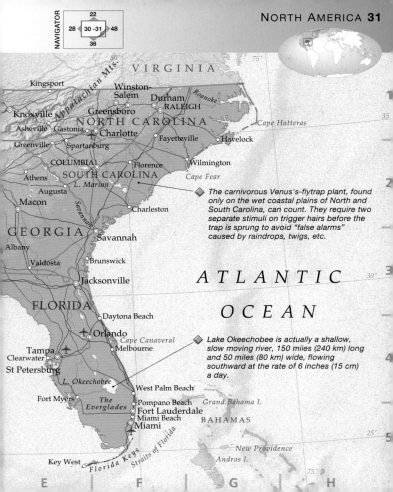

80°

75°

V I R G I N I A

Kingsport

Winston-Salem   Durham
RALEIGH

Roanoke

1

Knoxville

Appalachian Mts.

Greensboro

N O R T H   C A R O L I N A

Cape Hatteras

35

Asheville   Gastonia   Charlotte

Greenville   Spartanburg

Fayetteville   Havelock

COLUMBIA

S O U T H   C A R O L I N A

Florence

Wilmington

Athens

L. Marion

Cape Fear

2

Augusta

Savannah

Macon

Charleston

The carnivorous Venus's-flytrap plant, found only on the wet coastal plains of North and South Carolina, can count. They require two separate stimuli on trigger hairs before the trap is sprung to avoid "false alarms" caused by raindrops, twigs, etc.

G E O R G I A   Savannah

Albany

Brunswick

Valdosta

A T L A N T I C

30°

3

Jacksonville

O C E A N

F L O R I D A

Daytona Beach

Orlando   Cape Canaveral

Melbourne

Lake Okeechobee is actually a shallow, slow moving river, 150 miles (240 km) long and 50 miles (80 km) wide, flowing southward at the rate of 6 inches (15 cm) a day.

Tampa

Clearwater

St Petersburg

L. Okeechobee

West Palm Beach

4

Fort Myers

The Everglades

Pompano Beach
Fort Lauderdale
Miami Beach
Miami

Grand Bahama I.

B A H A M A S

25°

5

Key West   Florida Keys

Straits of Florida

New Providence

Andros I.

75°

E   F   G   H

Mexico

◆ Large examples of the Saguaro cactus, found in the Altar Desert, can take nearly 150 years to grow to their full height of around 50 ft (16 m), and can hold several tons (tonnes) of water.

◆ Gray whales have one of the longest migrations of any mammal, traveling some 12,500 miles (20,000 km) every year from the Arctic Ocean to their winter breeding grounds in the Golfo de California.

◆ The cliff divers of Acapulco must time their dive from the 125 ft (38 m) cliff at La Quebrada to coincide with the incoming swells to avoid being dashed on the rocks in the shallow inlet.

NEW MEXICO

UNITED

ARIZONA

Tijuana
Mexicali
Ensenada
Desierto de Altar
Ciudad Juárez
Rio Grande

1

30°

I. Ángel de la Guarda

Hermosillo
Chihuahua
Sierra Madre

I. Cedros

Baja California

Golfo de California

Yaqui
Conchos

M

2

Ciudad Obregón
Gómez Palacio
Torreón

Los Mochis

E

Culiacán

Durango

25°

La Paz
Fresnillo
Zacatecas

Tropic of Cancer

Mazatlán

3

Aguascalientes

Sierra Madre Occidental

Islas Marías
Tepic

Guadalajara

Puerto Vallarta
L. de Chapala

4

20°

P A C I F I C

O C E A N
Islas Revillagigedo (part of Mexico)

5

0 km   200
0 miles   200

A   115°   B   110°   C   105°   D

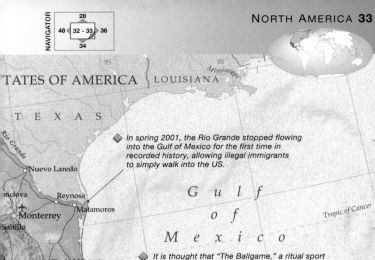

TATES OF AMERICA — LOUISIANA

Mississippi

90°

95°

T E X A S

Rio Grande

Nuevo Laredo

onclova — Reynosa

Monterrey — Matamoros

Saltillo

In spring 2001, the Rio Grande stopped flowing into the Gulf of Mexico for the first time in recorded history, allowing illegal immigrants to simply walk into the US.

G u l f

o f

M e x i c o

Tropic of Cancer

25°

85°

1

Ciudad Victoria

It is thought that "The Ballgame," a ritual sport played by Maya and Aztec civilizations, and a forerunner of soccer, often ended with the losing team being sacrificed.

Cancún

Mérida

20°

3

riental

San Luis Potosí — Tampico

Ciudad Valles

Río Verde

Dolores Hidalgo

eón — Poza Rica

apuato — Querétaro

Tulancingo

Pachuca

Xalapa

Isla Cozumel

Yucatan Peninsula

Campeche

Bahía de Campeche

BELIZE

Morelia

Cuernavaca

MEXICO CITY

Puebla

Tehuacán

Veracruz

Coatzacoalcos

Minatitlán

Villahermosa

ruapan

C

O

Balsas

Oaxaca

Tuxtla

GUATEMALA

4

Sierra Madre del Sur

Acapulco

Golfo de Tehuantepec

Tapachula

EL SALVADOR

HONDURAS

15°

5

100°

15°

95°

90°

Central America

MEXICO

95°

90°

85°

1

Belize City

Usumacinta

Flores

San Ignacio
BELMOPAN

BELIZE

Islas de la Bahía

GUATEMALA

Gulf of Honduras

15°

Huehuetenango
Quezaltenango

Cobán

Lago de Izabal

Puerto
Barrios

Puerto Cortés

San Pedro
Sula

La Ceiba

Trujillo

2

Zacapa

HONDURAS

Patuca

GUATEMALA CITY

Santa Rosa
de Copán

Comayagua

Juticalpa

Co

Escuintla

La Esperanza

TEGUCIGALPA

Santa Ana

SAN SALVADOR
EL SALVADOR

San Miguel

NICARAGUA

Choluteca

Somoto
Jinotega

Gulf of Fonseca

Estelí

Matagalpa

3

Chinandega
Corinto

León

Juigalpa

MANAGUA

Lago de Nicaragua

Granada
Rivas

San

PACIFIC

OCEAN

10°

◆ Unique freshwater species of shark and swordfish have
evolved in the long period since Lake Nicaragua was cut
off from the Pacific Ocean by a belt of volcanic cones.

Península de Nicoya

Liberia

4

◆ The strongest living creature is the Rhinoceros Beetle
found in the jungles of Costa Rica, which can support
up to 850 times it's own body weight, equivalent to
a human carrying about 70 tons (tonnes).

Alajue
Puntarenas
SAN JOSÉ

5

0 km   200

0 miles   200

A

B

90°

C

85°

D

◆ The Blue Hole in Lighthouse Reef, a submerged
cave some 1000 ft (300 m) in diameter and
400 ft (120 m) deep, was originally explored by
Jacques Cousteau, co-inventor of the aqualung.

80°

Greater

75°

HAITI

Antilles

1

JAMAICA

slas Santanilla
part of Honduras)

Bajo Nuevo
(part of Colombia)

C   a   r   i   b   b   e   a   n

2

15°

Cayos Miskitos

Coast

S   e   a

I. de Providencia
(part of Colombia)

3

I. de San Andrés
(part of Colombia)

Islas del Maíz

uefields

◆ Gatun Locks on the Panama Canal are
110 ft (33 m) wide and 1000 ft (303 m) long,
took four years to build and required
2 million cubic yards (1.5 million cu m)
of concrete.

OSTA
RICA

Limón

Gulf
of
Darien

4

10°

tago

Colón

PANAMA

PANAMA CITY

Panama
Canal

Penonomé

Balcanica

Isla del
Rey

COLOMBIA

David

Santiago

Golfo
de
Chiriquí

Chitré
Las Tablas

Golfo
de
Panamá

5

80°

75°

E   F   G   H

The Caribbean

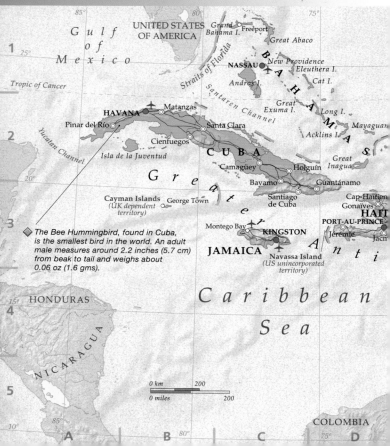

Gulf of Mexico

UNITED STATES OF AMERICA

Grand Bahama I. ○ Freeport

Great Abaco

B A H A M A S

NASSAU ● New Providence
Eleuthera I.

Straits of Florida

Andros I.
Cat I.

Tropic of Cancer

Santaren Channel

Great Exuma I.

Long I.

HAVANA ○ Matanzas

Mayaguan

Pinar del Río ○

Santa Clara

Acklins I.

Yucatán Channel

Cienfuegos

C U B A

Isla de la Juventud

G r e a t e r

Camagüey

Holguín

Great Inagua

Bayamo

Guantánamo

Cayman Islands
(UK dependent territory) ○ George Town

Santiago de Cuba

Cap-Haïtien
Gonaïves

A n t i l l e s

◇ The Bee Hummingbird, found in Cuba,
is the smallest bird in the world. An adult
male measures around 2.2 inches (5.7 cm)
from beak to tail and weighs about
0.06 oz (1.6 gms).

Montego Bay

KINGSTON

JAMAICA

Jérémie

PORT-AU-PRINCE

HAITI

Jacm

Navassa Island
(US unincorporated territory)

C a r i b b e a n

HONDURAS

S e a

N I C A R A G U A

0 km   200

0 miles   200

COLOMBIA

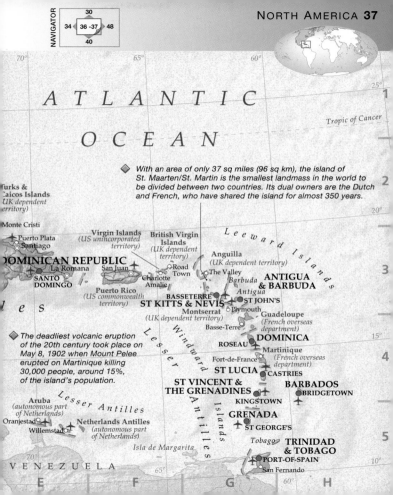

70°   *65°*   *60°*

A T L A N T I C

O C E A N

Tropic of Cancer

25°

◈ With an area of only 37 sq miles (96 sq km), the island of
St. Maarten/St. Martin is the smallest landmass in the world to
be divided between two countries. Its dual owners are the Dutch
and French, who have shared the island for almost 350 years.

20°

rks &
icos Islands
UK dependent
rritory)

Monte Cristi

Puerto Plata
Santiago

DOMINICAN REPUBLIC

SANTO
DOMINGO

La Romana

San Juan

Puerto Rico
*(US commonwealth
territory)*

Virgin Islands
*(US unincorporated
territory)*

Charlotte
Amalie

British Virgin
Islands
*(UK dependent
territory)*

Road
Town

The Valley

Anguilla
(UK dependent territory)

L e e w a r d I s l a n d s

Barbuda

**ANTIGUA
& BARBUDA**

Antigua

BASSETERRE
ST KITTS & NEVIS

Montserrat
(UK dependent territory)

ST JOHN'S

Plymouth

Guadeloupe
*(French overseas
department)*

Basse-Terre

les

L e s s e r A n t i l l e s

ROSEAU

DOMINICA

Martinique
*(French overseas
department)*

◈ The deadliest volcanic eruption
of the 20th century took place on
May 8, 1902 when Mount Pelee
erupted on Martinique killing
30,000 people, around 15%,
of the island's population.

Fort-de-France

ST LUCIA

CASTRIES

**ST VINCENT &
THE GRENADINES**

KINGSTOWN

BARBADOS

BRIDGETOWN

Aruba
*(autonomous part
of Netherlands)*

Oranjestad

L e s s e r A n t i l l e s

Netherlands Antilles
*(autonomous part
of Netherlands)*

Willemstad

W i n d w a r d I s l a n d s

GRENADA

ST GEORGE'S

Isla de Margarita

Tobago

**TRINIDAD
& TOBAGO**

PORT-OF-SPAIN

San Fernando

V E N E Z U E L A

15°

4

10°

5

70°   *65°*   *60°*

E   F   G   H

ATLANTIC
OCEAN

Greater Antilles

Lesser Antilles

Caribbean Sea

Isthmus of Panamá

Jamaica

Hispaniola

Puerto Rico

Trinidad

French Guiana (France)

SURINAME (claimed by Venezuela)

GUYANA (claimed by Suriname)

Tumuc Humac Mountains

VENEZUELA

Orinoco

Carpní

Guiana Highlands

Represa Balbina

Rio Negro

COLOMBIA

Cauca

Magdalena

Meta

Putumayo

Napo

Içá

Ucayali

Marañón

ECUADOR

Chimborazo▲
20,702ft (6310m)

PERU

Andes

Lake Titicaca

BOLIVIA

Altiplano

Amazon Basin

Amazon

Juruá

Purus

Madeira

Madre de Dios

Beni

Japurá

Tapajós

Serra do Cachimbo

Xingu

Tocantins

Araguaia

Serra do Roncador

Serra Formosa

Chapada dos Parecis

Planalto de Mato Grosso

Pantanal

B R A Z I L

Brazilian Highlands

Planalto da Borborema

São Francisco

Represa de Sobradinho

Serra Geral

Equator

20°

10°

40°

50°

60°

70°

80°

10°

10°

A   B   C   D   E

1   2   3   4

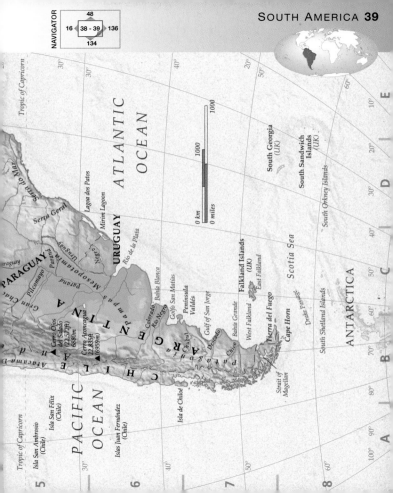

Northern South America

Caribbean Sea

Ríohacha

Santa Marta

Gulf of Venezuela

Coro

Less

Barranquilla

Maicao

Maracaibo

CARACA

Cartagena

Valledupar

Ciudad Ojeda

Cabimas

Maracay

Sincelejo

Lago de Maracaibo

Barquisimeto

Valencia

Acarigua

Montería

Mérida

Valera

Guanare

San Juan de los Morros

Cauca

Cúcuta

Barinas

San Fernando

Magdalena

San Cristóbal

Bucaramanga

Arauca

Apure

VEN

Bello

Barrancabermeja

Arauca

Medellín

Quibdó

Itagüí

Tunja

Yopal

Puerto Carreño

PACIFIC OCEAN

Manizales

Pereira

Meta

Orinoco

Armenia

Ibagué

BOGOTÁ

Buenaventura

Villavicencio

Guaviare

Cali

Neiva

COLOMBIA

Popayán

San José del Guaviare

Ne

Pasto

Mocoa

Florencia

Mitú

Esmeraldas

Tulcán

A Puaricos

Ibarra

QUITO

0° Equator

Caquetá

Manta

Santo Domingo de los Colorados

Portoviejo

Ambato

Guayaquil

Riobamba

Putumayo

Milagro

ECUADOR

Golfo de Guayaquil

Cuenca

Machala

Loja

PERU

The first coffee seedlings were brought to Colombia in 1804 by Jesuit Missionaries; today Columbi produces over a million tons (tonnes) of coffee beans every year.

Nestling between snow capped peaks, at 9350 ft (2850 m) Quito is the second highest capital in the world.

Antilles

GRENADA

Isla de Margarita

Carúpano

TRINIDAD & TOBAGO

Cumaná

Barcelona

Maturín

Tucupita

El Tigre

The Serpent's Mouth

Orinoco

Ciudad Guayana

Ciudad Bolívar

Embalse de Guri

ZUELA

Caura

Paragua

Caroní

Salto Ángel

Guiana Highlands

Cuyuni

Bartica

Rockstone

GEORGETOWN

Linden

New Amsterdam

PARAMARIBO

Nieuw Amsterdam

St-Laurent-du-Maroni

Sinnamary

Kourou

CAYENNE

GUYANA

W.J. van Blommesteinweer

SURINAME

French Guiana
(French overseas department)

Essequibo

Courantyne

Maroni

Orinoco

Guiana Highlands

Acarai Mts.

Amazon

Amazon

B   R   A   Z   I   L

Basin

ATLANTIC OCEAN

◆ The Guyana shield is one of the Earth's oldest surfaces, formed around 4 billion years ago.

(claimed by Venezuela)

◆ Angel Falls (Salto Ángel) plunge 3121 ft (951 m) to form the world's highest waterfall.

(claimed by Suriname)

(claimed by Suriname)

◆ The European Space Agency launch facility at Kourou takes advantage of the Earth's spin near the Equator to gain 10 percent more payload than an equivalent launch at Cape Canaveral in the US.

Equator

◆ 2.47 acres (one hectare) of Amazon rain forest can contain more than 750 types of trees and 1500 plant species, amounting to around 900 tons (tonnes) of living plant material.

0 km   200
0 miles   200

60°

10°

1

2

3

4

5

60°

55°

5°

E   F   G   H

Peru, Bolivia & North Brazil

VENEZUELA

COLOMBIA

GUYANA

Guiana

Boa Vista

Equator

0 km   400

0 miles   400

ECUADOR

Rio Negro

Represa Balbina

Putumayo

Napo

Amazon

Manaus

Iquitos

Amazon

Marañón

Moyobamba

Amazon Basin

Piura

Tarapoto

Jurua

B   R   A

Chiclayo

Saña

Pucallpa

Purus

Trujillo

Chimbote

Porto Velho

Huaraz

Huánuco

Rio Branco

Madre de Dios

Huacho

La Oroya

Puerto Maldonado

Riberalta

Callao

Guapore

LIMA

Huancayo

Beni

PACIFIC OCEAN

Ayacucho

Cusco

Pisco

Ica

Puno

Trinidad

Nazca

BOLIVIA

Arequipa

Lake Titicaca

LA PAZ

Cochabamba

Montero

Santa Cruz

Tacna

Oruro

Lago Poopó

SUCRE

Puerto Suárez

Potosí

PARAGUAY

Uyuni

Tupiza

Tarija

◆ Lake Titicaca is the largest lake in South
America at 3220 sq miles (8340 sq km)
and with an altitude of 12,500 ft (3810 m)
it is also the world's highest navigable lake.

CHILE

ARGENTINA

BOLIVIA'S TWO CAPITALS

La Paz - legislative and
          administrative capital
Sucre - legal capital

50°   40°

French Guiana
(French overseas department)

Highlands

Macapá

Ilha Caviana de Fora

The Amazon River is 4195 miles (6751 km) long with a peak flow of 7 million cubic feet (198,229 cu m) of water entering the Atlantic Ocean every second.

ATLANTIC

Amazon   Belém   *Ilha de Marajó*

Santarém

OCEAN   Equator   1

São Luís

Paranaíba   *San Fernando de Noronha (part of Brazil)*

Fortaleza

Represa de Tucuruí   Imperatriz   Teresina   Mossoró   2

Pajós   *Xingu*

Carolina   Campina   Natal
                                            Grande   João Pessoa

Z   I   L   Juàzeiro do Norte   Recife

res Pires   *Araguaia*   *Tocantins*   *Represa de Sobradinho*   *São Francisco*   Juàzeiro   Maceió   3

Mato Grosso   Aracaju   10°

Taguatinga   Feira de Santana

Brazilian   Salvador

Cuiabá   Itabuna

Anápolis   **BRASÍLIA**   *Highlands*   Vitória da Conquista   4
Goiânia

Montes Claros   Governador Valadares

Uberlândia

Uberaba   Divinópolis   Belo Horizonte

Campo   Ribeirão Preto   Vitória
Grande
Paraná   Marília   Nova   Campos   20°   5
Londrina   Campinas   Iguaçu   Juiz de Fora
        Sorocaba   Taubaté   Rio de Janeiro   *Tropic of Capricorn*   30°
            São Paulo

F   50°   40°   G   H

Paraguay, Uruguay & South Brazil

BOLIVIA

Gran Chaco

Tropic of Capricorn

General Eugenio A. Garay

Mariscal Estigarribia

PARAGUAY

Pozo Colorado

Pilcomayo

ASUNCIÓN

Lambaré

San Juan Bautista

Pilar

Fuerte Olimpo

Concepción

Paraguay

Coronel Oviedo

Villarrica

Caazapá

Encarnación

Dourados

Campo Grande

São José do Rio Preto

Presidente Prudente

Marília

Bauru

Ourinhos

Londrina

Maringá

Ciudad del Este

Paraná

Iguaçu

Guarapuava

Ponta Grossa

Curitiba

Joinville

Blumenau

Florianópolis

Lajes

Pelotas

Erechim

Passo Fundo

Carazinho

Caxias do Sul

Santa Maria

Canoas

Porto Alegre

São Borja

Uruguaiana

Uruguay

Artigas

Salto

Paysandú

Fray Bentos

Mercedes

Trinidad

Las Piedras

Durazno

MONTEVIDEO

San Carlos

Rivera

Tacuarembó

Negro

URUGUAY

Melo

Chuy

Mirim Lagoon

Bagé

Lagoa dos Patos

Pelotas

Rio Grande

ARGENTINA

Rio de la Plata

Serra do Mar

◆ Formed by river deposits washed down from the Andes and Brazilian Shield, the Gran Chaco is virtually free of stones. It is composed of sand and silt sediments that are up to 10,000 ft (3050 m) thick.

◆ The Itaipú hydroelectric scheme is able to produce more power than 10 average nuclear reactors; it supplies 24% of the electrical power consumption of Brazil and 95% for Paraguay.

B R A ... A

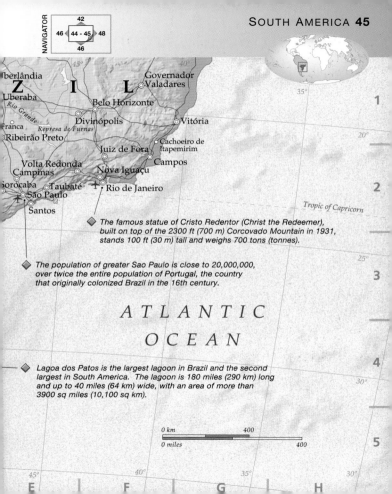

Z
I
L
berlândia
Uberaba
Rio Grande
Franca
Ribeirão Preto
Represa de Furnas
Divinópolis
Belo Horizonte
Governador Valadares
Vitória
Cachoeiro de Itapemirim
Juiz de Fora
Campos
Volta Redonda
Campinas
Nova Iguaçu
Sorocaba
Taubaté
São Paulo
Rio de Janeiro
Santos

The famous statue of Cristo Redentor (Christ the Redeemer), built on top of the 2300 ft (700 m) Corcovado Mountain in 1931, stands 100 ft (30 m) tall and weighs 700 tons (tonnes).

The population of greater Sao Paulo is close to 20,000,000, over twice the entire population of Portugal, the country that originally colonized Brazil in the 16th century.

ATLANTIC

OCEAN

Lagoa dos Patos is the largest lagoon in Brazil and the second largest in South America. The lagoon is 180 miles (290 km) long and up to 40 miles (64 km) wide, with an area of more than 3900 sq miles (10,100 sq km).

Tropic of Capricorn

0 km   400
0 miles   400

Southern South America

The world's tallest, active volcano is the Guallatiri volcano in northern Chile. It stands 19,918 ft (6071 m) tall, and last erupted in 1987.

The driest place on earth is the Atacama Desert in Chile with an average rainfall of 0.004 inches (0.1 mm) per year. Until recently some places had received no rain for over 400 years.

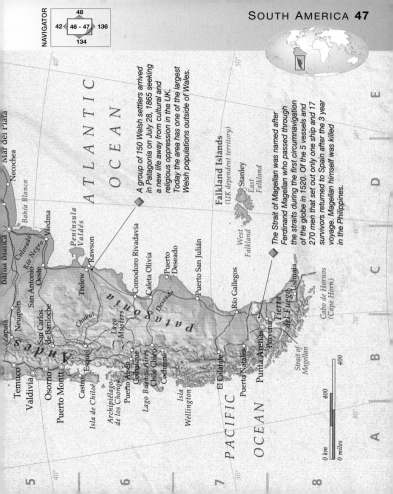

A group of 150 Welsh settlers arrived in Patagonia on July 28, 1865 seeking a new life away from cultural and religious oppression in the UK. Today the area has one of the largest Welsh populations outside of Wales.

The Strait of Magellan was named after Ferdinand Magellan who passed through the straits during the first circumnavigation of the globe in 1520. Of the 5 vessels and 270 men that set out only one ship and 17 survivors returned to Spain after the 3 year voyage. Magellan himself was killed in the Philippines.

The Atlantic Ocean

◇ The North Atlantic Deep Water Current is an oceanic "river" that carries around twenty times more water than all the rivers of the world put together.

◇ The Gulf Stream travels across the Atlantic Ocean at up to 110 miles (170 km) a day.

Labels on map:

Barents Sea
Svalbard (Norway)
Arctic Circle
EUROPE
Black Sea
Red Sea
Tropic of Cancer
Nile
Port Said
Scandinavia
Baltic Sea
Danube
Mediterranean Sea
AFRICA
Sahara
Greenland Sea
Jan Mayen (Norway)
Faeroe Is. (Denmark)
North Sea
British Isles
Rotterdam
Alps
Atlas Mts.
Gibraltar
ARCTIC OCEAN
Denmark Strait
Iceland
Azores (Portugal)
Mid-Atlantic Ridge
Madeira (Portugal)
Canary Is. (Spain)
CAPE VERDE
Greenland (Denmark)
Ellesmere I.
Baffin Bay
Davis Strait
Baffin I.
Labrador Sea
Newfoundland Basin
Bermuda (UK)
Hudson Bay
Arctic Circle
Great Lakes
St. Lawrence
Grand Banks
New York
NORTH AMERICA
Sargasso Sea
West Indies
Caribbean Sea
Gulf of Mexico
Tropic of Cancer
Mississippi

Africa

ATLANTIC OCEAN

Caspian Sea

Black Sea

Caucasus

EUROPE

ASIA

The Gulf

Tropic of Cancer

Arabian Peninsula

Gulf of Aden

SOMALIA

Syrian Desert

Cyprus

Red Sea

ERITREA

DJIBOUTI

SOMALILAND (not internationally recognized)

ETHIOPIA

Ethiopian Highlands

Shibeli

Mediterranean Sea

Nile

EGYPT

Blue Nile

White Nile

SUDAN

Sudd

UGANDA

Lake Turkana

Sicily

Libyan Desert

Uele

CENTRAL AFRICAN REPUBLIC

Congo

TUNISIA

Atlas Mountains

Ahaggar

Tibesti

CHAD

Iberian Peninsula

Ceuta (Spain)

Melilla (Spain)

MOROCCO

ALGERIA

LIBYA

NIGER

Sahara

CAMEROON

Madeira (Portugal)

Islas Canarias (Spain)

WESTERN SAHARA (disputed)

Tropic of Cancer

MALI

NIGERIA

Niger

EQUATORIAL GUINEA

SAO TOME &

MAURITANIA

Sahel

BENIN

TOGO

GHANA

Gulf of Guinea

SENEGAL

Senegal

Niger

BURKINA

CÔTE D'IVOIRE (IVORY COAST)

GAMBIA

GUINEA-BISSAU

GUINEA

SIERRA LEONE

LIBERIA

COMOROS

Mayotte
(France)

MADAGASCAR

Tropic of Capricorn

INDIAN
OCEAN

Mozambique Channel

▲ Kilimanjaro
19,341ft (5895m)

TANZANIA
BURUNDI
DEM. REP.
CONGO

RWANDA

Lake Nyasa

MALAWI

Lake
Tanganyika

MOZAMBIQUE

ZAMBIA

Zambezi

ZIMBABWE

SWAZILAND

LESOTHO

ANGOLA

Bié
Plateau

BOTSWANA

Kalahari
Desert

SOUTH
AFRICA

Orange River

GABON

Cabinda
(Angola)

NAMIBIA

Namib Desert

Cape of
Good Hope

ATLANTIC

OCEAN

Ascension I.
(St Helena)

St Helena
(UK)

Tropic of Capricorn

Tristan da Cunha
(St Helena)

Gough Island
(Tristan da Cunha)

0 km   1000   1000
0 miles   1000

Northwest Africa

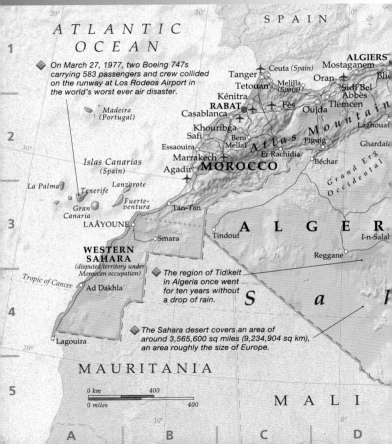

SPAIN

ATLANTIC
OCEAN

◆ On March 27, 1977, two Boeing 747s
carrying 583 passengers and crew collided
on the runway at Los Rodeos Airport in
the world's worst ever air disaster.

*Madeira
(Portugal)*

Tanger   Ceuta *(Spain)*   **ALGIERS** Mostaganem
Tetouan   Melilla   Oran   Sidi Bel
                (Spain)   Abbès   Bli
Kénitra   Fès   Oujda   Tlemcen
RABAT
Casablanca   Laghoua
Khouriga   Beni   Figuig   Ghardaïa
Safi   Mellal   Atlas Mountain
Islas Canarias Essaouira   Béchar
(Spain)   Marrakech   Er Rachidia   *Grand Erg*
        Agadir   **MOROCCO**   *Occidental*

La Palma *Tenerife* *Lanzarote*
    Gran *Fuerte-*
    Canaria *ventura* Tan-Tan
        LAÂYOUNE   A L G E R
            Smara   Tindouf   I-n-Salal

WESTERN   Reggane
SAHARA
(disputed territory under ◆ The region of Tidikelt
Moroccan occupation)   in Algeria once went
                            for ten years without
Tropic of Cancer Ad Dakhla   a drop of rain.   S a l

                    ◆ The Sahara desert covers an area of
                    around 3,565,600 sq miles (9,234,904 sq km),
                    an area roughly the size of Europe.
    Lagouira

M A U R I T A N I A

    0 km   400
    0 miles   400   M A L I

A   B   C   D

ITALY

GREECE

Sicily

Crete

MALTA

Mediterranean Sea

◆ The hottest place on earth is Al 'Aziziyah, Libya, where on September 13, 1922, an air temperature of 136°F (57°C) was recorded.

Annaba ✈ Bizerte
TUNIS
Constantine
Sétif
Kairouan
Batna
Sousse
Biskra
Gafsa
Sfax
Chott Melghir
Tozeur
Gabès
Zuwārah
Az Zāwiyah
Al Baydā'
Darnah
Banghāzī
Al Marj
Tubruq

Ouargla
Touggourt
Médenine
TUNISIA
TRIPOLI
Al Khums
Gharyān
Mişrātah
Yafran
Khalīj Surt
Ajdābiyā

Surt

I A

Grand Erg Oriental

Great Sand Sea

Birāk

Sabhā

Awbārī
Murzuq

L I B Y A
Libyan

Al Kufrah

Tropic of Cancer

Tassili-n-Ajjer

a

r

a

Desert

Ahaggar

Tamanrasset

Tibesti

◆ Libyan oil is especially prized because of its low sulfur content, which means it produces much less pollution than other fuel oil.

N I G E R

C H A D

EGYPT

Northeast Africa

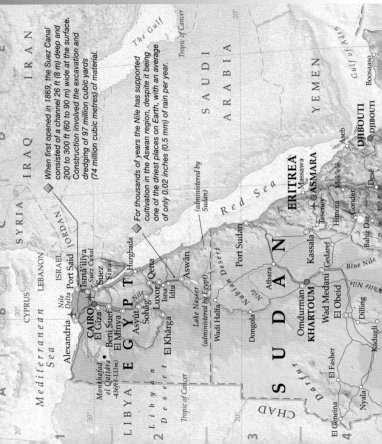

When first opened in 1869, the Suez Canal consisted of a channel 26 ft (8 m) deep and 200 to 300 ft (60 to 90 m) wide at the surface. Construction involved the excavation and dredging of 97 million cubic yards (74 million cubic metres) of material.

For thousands of years the Nile has supported cultivation in the Aswan region, despite it being one of the driest places on Earth, with an average of only 0.02 inches (0.5 mm) of rain per year.

The Gulf

Gulf of Aden

Tropic of Cancer

IRAN

SYRIA

IRAQ

JORDAN

LEBANON

ISRAEL

CYPRUS

SAUDI ARABIA

YEMEN

Red Sea

DJIBOUTI
DJIBOUTI

Boosaaso

Aseb

ERITREA
Massawa
ASMARA

Mek'elē

Dese

Gonder

Bahir Dar

Himora
Tesenei

Gedaref
Kassala

Blue Nile

Mediterranean Sea

Alexandria

Nile Delta

Port Said
Ismā'iliya
Suez Canal
Suez

Sinai

Hurghada

EGYPT

CAIRO
El Gîza

Beni Suef
El Minya

Asyūt

Sohâg
Qena
Luxor
Isna
Idfu

Aswân

El Khârga

Nile

Lake Nasser
(administered by Egypt)

Wadi Halfa

Dongola

Monkhafad
el Qattâra
-436ft (-133m)

Libyan Desert

LIBYA

Tropic of Cancer

Nubian Desert

Port Sudan

(administered by Sudan)

Atbara

Omdurman
KHARTOUM

Wad Medani
El Obeid

Dilling

SUDAN

Darfur

El Fasher

El Geneina

Nyala

Kadugli

CHAD

White Nile

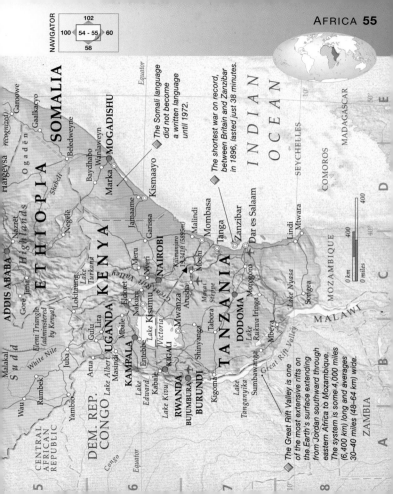

SOMALIA

Garoowe

Gaalkacyo

Haangeeysa (recognized)

O g a d ē n

Beledweyne

Wanlaweyn

MOGADISHU

Marka

The Somali language did not become a written language until 1972.

Baydhabo

Shabeele

Kismaayo

The shortest war on record, between Britain and Zanzibar in 1896, lasted just 38 minutes.

Equator

Jamaame

Garissa

INDIAN OCEAN

MADAGASCAR

SEYCHELLES

COMOROS

MOZAMBIQUE

Malindi

Mombasa

Tanga

Zanzibar

Dar es Salaam

Lindi

Mtwara

400

400

0 km

0 miles

ETHIOPIA

ADDIS ABABA

Nazrēt

Highlands

Goré Jima

Negēlē

Malakal

Rumbek

Wau

Yambio

S u d d

White Nile

Juba

Arua

Gulu

Lira

Masindi

Lokichokio

Elemi Triangle (administered by Kenya)

UGANDA

KAMPALA

Entebbe

Mbale

Kabale

Lake Albert

Lake Edward

Lake Kivu

RWANDA

KIGALI

BURUNDI

BUJUMBURA

DEM. REP. CONGO

CENTRAL AFRICAN REPUBLIC

Congo

Equator

KENYA

NAIROBI

Meru

Nakuru

Eldoret

Kisumu

Nyeri

Lake Turkana

Lake Victoria

Mwanza

Great Rift Valley

Moshi

Arusha

Kilimanjaro (5,895m)

Masai Steppe

TANZANIA

DODOMA

Shinyanga

Tabora

Morogoro

Iringa

Lake Rukwa

Mbeya

Songea

Lake Nyasa

Lake Tanganyika

Kigoma

Sumbawanga

Great Rift Valley

MALAWI

ZAMBIA

The Great Rift Valley is one of the most extensive rifts on the Earth's surface extending from Jordan southward through eastern Africa to Mozambique. The system is some 4,000 miles (6,400 km) long and averages 30–40 miles (48–64 km) wide.

0 km   400

0 miles   400

Tropic of Cancer

¹

WESTERN
SAHARA
(disputed territory
under Moroccan occupation)

◆ Mauritania and Madagascar are the
only countries in the world not to use
a decimal-based currency. The basic unit
of currency, the ouguiya, is divided
into five khoums.

Nouâdhibou

CAPE
VERDE

Ilhas de Barlavento

Santo
Antão
São
Vicente São
Nicolau
Sal
Boa Vista
Fogo Santiago
Maio
Ilhas de Sotavento

PRAIA

Saint Louis

ATLANTIC
OCEAN

DAKAR

SENEGAL

BANJUL

GAMBIA

Bignona

BISSAU

◆ Gambia is only around 20 miles (32 km)
wide and 300 miles (483 km) long;
its unusual shape and size are down
to territorial compromises arising from
19th-century Anglo-French rivalry
in western Africa.

GUINEA-
BISSAU

Boké

CONAKRY

SIERRA
LEONE
FREETOWN

Bo

◆ Monrovia, named after the fifth US President
James Monroe, was founded in 1830 by the
American Colonization Society as a settlement
for freed American slaves.

Tubmanburg LIBERIA

YAMOUSSOUKRO

MONROVIA

Buchanan

Zwedru

◆ A Ruppell's Griffen Vulture collided with a
commercial airliner at 37,000 ft (11,277 m) above
Côte d'Ivoire to earn the posthumous distinction
of the highest flying bird ever recorded.

Harper

Bîr
Mogreïn

'Erg Iguîdi

Kâghet

El Hank

Er

Fdérik Zouérat

Choûm Ouarâne

Atâr

S

Akchâr

Akjoujt

El Mreyyé

NOUAKCHOTT

MAURITANIA

Rkîz

Aleg Senegal

Kaédi Kiffa

Aoukâr

Nioro

S

Kayes

Ségou

BAMAKO

Niger

Bani

Mbaké
Diourbel
Kaolack

Gambia

Gaoual Labé

GUINEA

Kindia

Niger Bougouni

Siguiri

Kankan

Bobo
Dioulass

Odienné

CÔTE
D'IVOIRE
(IVORY COAST)

Lac
Kossou

Gagnoa

Abidja

20°   10°

A   B   C   D

1   2   3   4   5

ALGERIA

LIBYA

◆ In the late 1960s and early 1970s a series of
catastrophic droughts caused the Sahara Desert
to advance southward up to 60 miles (100 km) into
the Sahel region. The loss of human life by starvation
and disease was estimated in 1973 to be 100,000.

Tropic of Cancer

'Chech

a *h* *a* *r* *a*

Tibesti

○Taoudenni

Ténéré
du
Tafassâsset

20°

Tessalit

'Erg I-n-Sâkâne

Adrar des
Ifôghas

Azaouâд

Assamakka

Massif
de l'Aïr

Ténéré

C H A D

○Araouane

M A L I

Lac
Faguibine

Gao

Agadez

Grand Erg de Bilma

○Tombouctou

Ansongo

Lac
Niangay

○Hombori

N I G E R

Tahoua

Nguigmi
○

Zinder

Gouré
○

Lake Chad

Mopti

Maradi

S *a* *h* *e* *l*

BURKINA

NIAMEY

○Sokoto

Katsina

Hadeja

Sokoto

OUAGADOUGOU

Gusau

Kano

Maiduguri

Koudougou○

Féda-
Ngourma

Zaria

Kandi

Longola

Kumo
○

BENIN

Kainji
Reservoir

Kaduna

Wa

Natitingou

N I G E R I A

Tamale○

Sokodé

Ilorin

Jos
Plateau

GHANA

Oyo

Ogbomosho

ABUJA

Benin

○Abomey

Ede

Enugu

unyani

Lake
Volta

Ibadan

Benin
City

Gotel
Mountains

C.A.R.

Kumasi

Nsawam

Sapele

Onitsha

Aba

Calabar

Asamankese

LOMÉ

PORTO-
NOVO

Lagos

ACCRA

Bight of Benin

Mouths
of the Niger

Port Harcourt

C A M E R O O N

Gulf of Guinea

EQUATORIAL
GUINEA

◆ Lake Volta is one of the largest man-made
lakes in the world covering 3283 sq miles
(8502 sq km), or 3.6% of Ghana's area

Black Volta

White Volta

Red Volta

Niger

Benué

Niger

Parakou

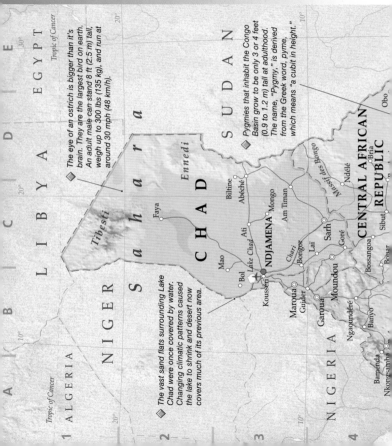

The eye of an ostrich is bigger than it's brain. They are the largest bird on earth. An adult male can stand 8 ft (2.5 m) tall, weigh up to 300 lbs (135 kg), and run at around 30 mph (48 km/h).

Pygmies that inhabit the Congo Basin grow to be only 3 or 4 feet (0.9 to 1.2 m) tall at adulthood. The name, "Pygmy," is derived from the Greek word, pyme, which means "a cubit in height."

The vast sand flats surrounding Lake Chad were once covered by water. Changing climatic patterns caused the lake to shrink and desert now covers much of its previous area.

E — D — C — B — A

EGYPT

LIBYA

ALGERIA

NIGER

NIGERIA

SUDAN

CENTRAL AFRICAN REPUBLIC

Tropic of Cancer

Sahara

Tibesti

Ennedi

CHAD

Massif des Bongo

Faya

Biltine
Abéché
Mongo
Am Timan
Ati
Mao
Lake Chad
NDJAMENA
Bol
Kousséri
Chari
Bongor
Laï
Goré
Sarh
Ndélé
Bria
Sibut
Bossangoa
Bozar
Obo

Maroua
Guider
Garoua
Moundou
Ngaoundéré
Banyo
Bamenda
Nkongsamba

Southern Africa

ATLANTIC OCEAN

DEM. REP. CONGO

Cabinda (Angola)

Cabinda

Uíge

Ambriz

N'Dalatando

LUANDA

Malanje

Lucapa

Saurimo

Ndola

Mufulira

Sumbe

Lobito

Benguela

ANGOLA

Cuanza

Kuito

Huambo

Zambezi

Chingola

Kitwe

Luanshya

ZAMBIA

Menongue

LUSAKA

Lubango

Namibe

Tombua

N'Giva

Cubango

Choma

Rundu

Livingstone

Zambezi

Lake Kariba

Chitungwiz

ZIMBA

Cunene

Etosha Pan

Tsumeb

Grootfontein

Okavango

Victoria Falls

Okavango Delta

Maun

Bulawayo

Francistown

NAMIBIA

Ghanzi

WINDHOEK

Kalahari

Mahalapye

BOTSWANA

Limpopo

Swakopmund

Walvis Bay

Rehoboth

Desert

GABORONE

Lobatse

TSHWAN (PRETORIA)

Tropic of Capricorn

Mmabatho

Soweto

Johannesburg

Keetmanshoop

Kroonst

Lüderitz

Karasburg

Orange R.

Kimberley

Vaal

MASERU

LESOTHO

BLOEMFONTEIN

Middelburg

Drakensber

SOUTH AFRICA

Beaufort West

East Londor

Bellville

CAPE TOWN

George

Port Elizabeth

Cape of Good Hope

◆ The Okavango River pours some 14.4 billion cubic yards (11 billion cu m) of water into the Okavango Delta each year. It drains away through a maze of lagoons, channels, and islands covering around 5800 sq miles (15,000 sq km) before eventually disappearing into the sands of the Kalahari Desert to the south.

◆ The Kalahari Desert is the largest continuous sand surface in the world. Iron oxide gives a distinctive red color to the sand, which is over 200 ft (60 m) deep in places.

SOUTH AFRICA'S THREE CAPITALS

Tshwane (Pretoria) - administrative capital
Cape Town - legislative capital
Bloemfontein - financial capital

0 km   400
0 miles   400

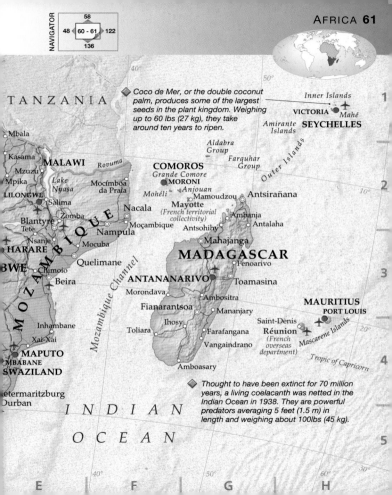

Coco de Mer, or the double coconut palm, produces some of the largest seeds in the plant kingdom. Weighing up to 60 lbs (27 kg), they take around ten years to ripen.

Thought to have been extinct for 70 million years, a living coelacanth was netted in the Indian Ocean in 1938. They are powerful predators averaging 5 feet (1.5 m) in length and weighing about 100lbs (45 kg).

Europe

Arctic Circle

Limit of winter pack ice

ICELAND

Lofoten

Norwegian Sea

Faeroe Islands
(Denmark)

Shetland Islands

Outer Hebrides

British Isles

Orkney Islands

Vänern

Vättern

North Sea

Ireland

IRELAND

Isle of Man
(to UK)

Britain

DENMARK

UNITED KINGDOM

Celtic Sea

NETHERLANDS

North

Oder

English Channel

BELGIUM

GERMANY

Channel Is
(UK)

LUX.

CZECH REPUBLIC

Loire

FRANCE

Seine

Rhine

SWITZ.

LIECH.

AUSTRIA

Bay of Biscay

Massif Central

Alps

Po

SLOVENIA

ATLANTIC OCEAN

Garonne

Pyrenees

Rhône

Mont Blanc
15,771ft 4807m

SAN MARINO

CROATIA

PORTUGAL

Duero

Iberian

MONACO

ANDORRA

ITALY

BOSN. & HERZ.

Ebro

Tagus

SPAIN

Peninsula

Corsica

VATICAN CITY

Madeira
(to Portugal)

Guadalquivir

Strait of Gibraltar

Balearic Islands

Sardinia

Tyrrhenian Sea

Sicily

Gibraltar
(UK)

M e d i t e r r a n e a n

Canary Islands
(to Spain)

A t l a s   M o u n t a i n s

AFRICA

MALTA

0 km   800
0 miles   800

A   B   C   D

Barents Sea

North Cape
Ostrov Kolguyev

Arctic Circle

Ob'

Irtysh

Ural Mountains

Kola
Peninsula

White
Sea

Northern Dvina

SWEDEN

FINLAND

Gulf of Bothnia

Lake Onega

R U S S I A N

Lake
Ladoga

F E D E R A T I O N

Åland

Gotland

ESTONIA

LATVIA

Baltic Sea

LITHUANIA

RUSS.
FED.

European Plain

Central
Russian
Upland

Volga Uplands

Volga

Ural

Aral Sea

Syr Darya

BELARUS

POLAND

Pripet
Marshes

Dnieper Lowlands

Vistula

Bug

Dniester

UKRAINE

Don

Dnieper

Ural

Amu Darya

Carpathian Mountains

Dniester

SLOVAKIA

MOLDOVA

Sea of
Azov

Caspian Sea

HUNGARY

Crimea

Caucasus

ROMANIA

SERBIA

Danube

Black Sea

El'brus
18,510ft
(5642m)

BULGARIA

Balkan
Mountains

MON.

MACED.

TURKEY

ALBANIA

Aegean
Sea

Anatolia

A S I A

Zágros Mountains

GREECE

Peloponnese

Euphrates

Tigris

Sea

Crete

Cyprus

E F G H

The North Atlantic

◆ At 840,000 sq miles (2,175,600 sq km), Greenland is the largest island in the world. However, 650,000 sq miles (1,638,400 sq km) of this is a massive ice sheet so heavy that the central land area has sunk to form to a basin more than 1000 ft (300 m) below sea level.

◆ The Jakobshavn Glacier, often moving 100 feet (30 m) a day, is among the world's fastest glaciers, and calves around 1350 icebergs every year.

Arctic Circle

70°

Devon Island

Ellesmere Island

Nares Strait

N U N A V U T

Qaanaaq

Innaanganeq

Knud Rasmussen Land

Savissivik

Qimusseriarsuaq

Hudson Bay

Baffin Bay

Kullorsuaq

C A N A D A

Baffin Island

Péninsule d'Ungava

Davis Strait

Limit of summer pack ice

QUEBEC

Hudson Strait

Frobisher Bay

Cumberland Sound

Qeqertarsuaq

Qeqertarsuaq

Qasigiannguit

Sisimiut

Kong Frederik IX Land

Greenland

(Danish external territory)

Ungava Bay

Maniitsoq

NUUK

Kong Christian IX Land

Gunnbjørn Field 3700m

NEWFOUNDLAND & LABRADOR

Paamiut

Ivittuut

Kong Frederik VI Kyst

Ammassalik

Denmark

Labrador Sea

Qaqortoq

Nanortalik

Limit of winter pack ice

Faxaflǿ

Nunap Isua (Kap Farvel)

ATLANTIC OCEAN

0 km   800
0 miles   800

A   B   C   D

ARCTIC OCEAN

Lincoln Sea

Kap Morris Jesup

Wandel Sea

Nord

Kong Frederik VIII Land

Kong Christian X Land

Greenland Sea

Daneborg

Kong Oscar Fjord

Ittoqqortoormiit

Kangertittivaq

Kangikajik

Strait

Limit of winter pack ice

ICELAND

Siglufjördhur

Húsavík

ureyri

Seydhisfjördhur

REYKJAVÍK

Selfoss

Surtsey

Zemlya Frantsa-Iosifa

Novaya Zemlya

Kvitøya

Svalbard (Norwegian dependency)

Nordaustlandet

Kong Karls Land

Spitsbergen

Barentsøya

Longyearbyen

Edgeøya

Barentsberg

Storfjorden

Bjørnøya (Norway)

Nordkapp (North Cape)

Barents Sea

♦ With temperatures ranging from 59° F (15° C) in the summer to -40° F (-40° C) in the winter, vegetation on Svalbard consists mostly of lichens and mosses; the only trees are the tiny polar willow and the dwarf birch.

♦ Greenland's deeply indented coastline is 24,430 miles (39,330 km) long, a distance roughly equivalent to the Earth's circumference at the Equator.

Jan Mayen (Norway)

Norwegian Sea

RUSSIAN FEDERATION

Arctic Circle

FINLAND

NORWAY

SWEDEN

♦ Even though only one twentieth of Iceland's potential geothermal power has been harnessed, around 89% of houses are heated geothermally.

Gulf of Bothnia

Faeroe Islands (Denmark)

Tórshavn

Shetland Islands

Scandinavia & Finland

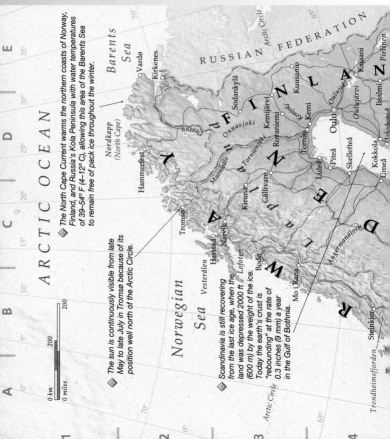

◆ The North Cape Current warms the northern coasts of Norway, Finland, and Russia's Kola Peninsula with water temperatures of 39–54° F (4–12° C), allowing this area of the Barents Sea to remain free of pack ice throughout the winter.

◆ The sun is continuously visible from late May to late July in Tromsø because of its position well north of the Arctic Circle.

◆ Scandinavia is still recovering from the last ice age, when the land was depressed 2000 ft (600 m) by the weight of the ice. Today the earth's crust is "rebounding" at the rate of 0.3 inches (9 mm) a year in the Gulf of Bothnia.

ARCTIC OCEAN

RUSSIAN FEDERATION

Barents Sea

Vardø
Kirkenes

Nordkapp
(North Cape)

Sodankylä

FINLAND

Kuusamo

Iisalmi
Kajaani
Pielinen

Oulujärvi
Oulujoki
Oulu

Hammerfest

Muonio
Ounasjoki
Deatnu
Kemijärvi
Rovaniemi
Kemijoki
Kemi
Tornio
Torniojoki
Tornionjoki

Piteå
Skellefteå
Kokkola
Umeå

Tromsø

Harstad
Narvik
Lofoten
Kiruna
Gällivare

Boden
Luleå

Vesterålen

Bodø

Mo i Rana

Norwegian Sea

Ångermanälven

Steinkjer

Trondheimsfjorden

Arctic Circle

0 km   200
0 miles   200

The sauna is a Finnish institution with some 2 million sauna facilities to serve a population of just 5 million.

The 10 mile (16 km) bridge and tunnel link across the Oresund sound is one of the largest infrastructure projects in European history. It connects the Danish capital Copenhagen to the Swedish port of Malmo.

The Low Countries

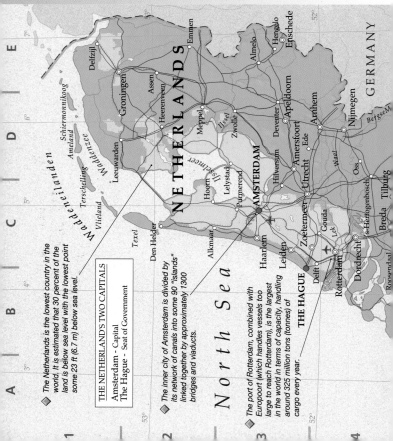

THE NETHERLAND'S TWO CAPITALS

Amsterdam - Capital
The Hague - Seat of Government

◆ The Netherlands is the lowest country in the world. It is estimated that 30 percent of the land is below sea level with the lowest point some 23 ft (6.7 m) below sea level.

◆ The inner city of Amsterdam is divided by its network of canals into some 90 "islands" linked together by approximately 1300 bridges and viaducts.

◆ The port of Rotterdam, combined with Europoort (which handles vessels too large to reach Rotterdam), is the largest in the world in terms of capacity, handling around 325 million tons (tonnes) of cargo every year.

GERMANY

NETHERLANDS

North Sea

Emmen
Delfzijl
Hengelo
Enschede
Almelo
Assen
Groningen
Heerenveen
Apeldoorn
Arnhem
Schiermonnikoog
Ameland
Waddenzee
Terschelling
Leeuwarden
Meppel
IJssel
Zwolle
Deventer
Ede
Nijmegen
Waal
Vlieland
IJsselmeer
Amersfoort
Utrecht
Oss
's-Hertogenbosch
Tilburg
Texel
Hoorn
Lelystad
Hilversum
Gouda
Breda
Den Helder
Purmerend
AMSTERDAM
Alkmaar
Zoetermeer
Lek
Dordrecht
Haarlem
Leiden
Delft
Rotterdam
THE HAGUE
Roosendaal

BergseM

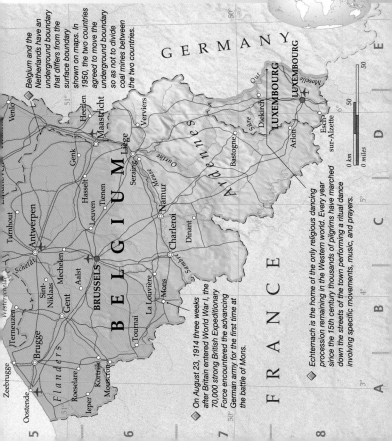

GERMANY

LUXEMBOURG

BELGIUM

FRANCE

Venlo

Heerlen
Maastricht
Verviers
Liège
Genk
Seraing
Hasselt
Leuven
Tienen
Namur
Bastogne
Diekirch
LUXEMBOURG
Arlon
Esch-
sur-Alzette
Moselle

Turnhout
Antwerpen
Charleroi
Dinant
Mechelen
Aalst
BRUSSELS
La Louvière
Mons
Tournai

Sint-
Niklaas
Gent
Zeebrugge
Brugge
Oostende
Roeselare
Ieper
Kortrijk
Mouscron

Terneuzen
Westerschelde
Schelde
Flanders
Sambre
Meuse
Ourthe
Sûre
Our
Ardennes

Belgium and the Netherlands have an underground boundary that differs from the surface boundary shown on maps. In 1950, the two countries agreed to move the underground boundary so as not to divide coal mines between the two countries.

On August 23, 1914 three weeks after Britain entered World War I, the 70,000 strong British Expeditionary Force encountered the advancing German army for the first time at the battle of Mons.

Echternach is the home of the only religious dancing procession remaining in the Western world. Every year since the 15th century thousands of pilgrims have marched down the streets of the town performing a ritual dance involving specific movements, music, and prayers.

The British Isles

After the surrender of the German fleet in 1918 and its internment in Scapa Flow, over 50 ships were scuttled by the German crews on June 21, 1919, to prevent them falling into British hands.

With a depth of 788 ft (240 m) and a length of about 23 miles (36 km), Loch Ness contains the largest volume of fresh water in Great Britain.

Midges have the fastest wing-beat of any insect, and are able to flap their wings at around 63,000 beats per minute.

The Giant's Causeway comprises approximately 37,000 dark basalt polygonal columns packed together; they were formed by volcanic activity some 55 million years ago.

ATLANTIC

OCEAN

North Sea

Faeroe Islands

Shetland Islands

Lerwick

Orkney Islands

Kirkwall

Thurso

Isle of Lewis

Stornoway

Outer Hebrides

North Uist

South Uist

Barra

The Little Minch

Isle of Skye

The Minch

Ullapool

Loch Ness

Inverness

Moray Firth

Elgin

SCOTLAND

Grampian Mts.

Ben Nevis
4406ft (1344m)

Aberdeen

Dundee

Perth

Firth of Tay

EDINBURGH

Firth of Forth

Southern Uplands

Forth

Stirling

Glasgow

Greenock

Loch Lomond

Mull

Oban

Jura

Islay

Isle of Arran

Ayr

Fort William

UNITED KINGDOM

NORTHERN

Newcastle upon Tyne

Sunderland

Dumfries

Newcastle

p

e

◈ Seven percent of Ireland's barley crop goes into the production of Guinness stout.

◈ The River Severn has the second highest tidal range in the world, as much as 50 ft (15 m), often giving rise to a tidal bore. In September 1996 one such wave carried a surfer for 5.7 miles (9 km).

France, Andorra & Monaco

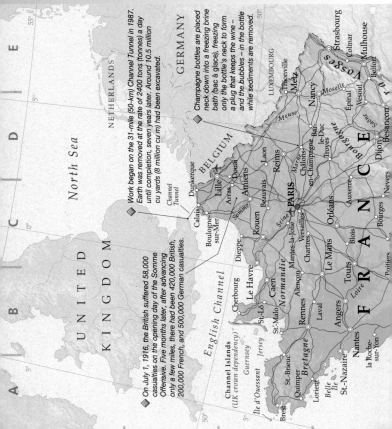

Work began on the 31-mile (50-km) Channel Tunnel in 1987. Earth was removed at the rate of 2400 tons (tonnes) a day until completion, seven years later. Around 10.5 million cu yards (8 million cu m) had been excavated.

Champagne bottles are placed neck down into a freezing brine bath (bac a glace), freezing only the bottle's neck to form a plug that keeps the wine – and the bubbles – in the bottle while sediments are removed.

On July 1, 1916, the British suffered 58,000 casualties on the opening day of the Somme Offensive. Five months later, after advancing only a few miles, there had been 420,000 British, 200,000 French, and 500,000 German casualties.

The word denim comes from "de Nîmes," this being the town where the fabric was originally produced.

One of history's great leaders, Napoleon Bonaparte was born on August 15, 1769, at Ajaccio in Corsica.

The lowest point in Andorra is Riu Runer at 2756 ft (840m) above sea level.

The Tour de France bicycle race is typically held over some 20 day-long stages covering around 2200 miles (3600 km) for the coveted yellow jersey.

Spain & Portugal

0 km 100
0 miles 100

ATLANTIC

OCEAN

Ferrol
A Coruña (La Coruña)
Gijón (Xixón)
Avilés
Oviedo
Santiago de Compostela
Galicia
Lugo
Cordillera Cantábrica
León
Pontevedra
Vigo
Ourense (Orense)
Miño
Emb. de Ricobayo
Palencia
Valladolid
Viana do Castelo
Chaves
Póvoa de Varzim
Braga
Bragança
Vila Real
Zamora
Matosinhos
Guimarães
Duero
S **P**
Porto
Vila Nova de Gaia
Douro
Aveiro
Viseu
Salamanca
Ávil

◇ Port has been produced in the Duoro Valley under strict regulation since the 1750s. Brandy is added to the grape juice to fortify and strengthen the wine.

Coimbra
Covilhã
Sistema Central
Figueira da Foz
PORTUGAL
Castelo Branco
Tagus
Plasencia
Caldas da Rainha
Tagus
Santarém
Portalegre
Cáceres
Sintra
Mérida
Guadiana
Cascais
LISBON
Badajoz
Setúbal
Alcácer do Sal
Sierra Morena
Beja
Córdoba

◇ Portugal is one of the world's largest producers of cork and has regulations protecting cork trees dating back to 1320.

Sines
Guadiana
Sevilla
Guadalquivir
Lagos
Algarve
Andalucía
Cabo de São Vicente
Faro
Olhão
Huelva
Antequer
Málaga
El Puerto de Santa María
Cádiz
Marbel

◇ Gibraltar was seized by a combined Anglo-Dutch fleet under Admiral Rooke in 1704. British sovereignty was then formalized in 1713 by the Treaty of Utrecht, and Gibraltar eventually became a British colony in 1830.

Algeciras
Gibralta (UK)
Ceuta (Sp
MOROCCO

NAVIGATOR
72
48
74 - 75
78
54

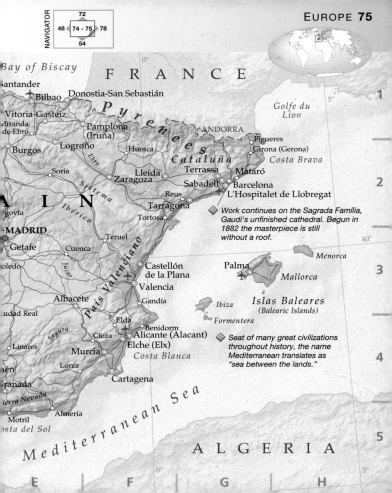

Bay of Biscay
FRANCE
Santander
Bilbao
Donostia-San Sebastián
Vitoria-Gasteiz
Miranda de Ebro
Pamplona (Iruña)
Pyrenees
ANDORRA
Golfe du Lion
Logroño
Burgos
Huesca
Figueres
Girona (Gerona)
Costa Brava
Cataluña
Ebro
Soria
Lleida
Zaragoza
Terrassa
Mataró
Sabadell
Barcelona
L'Hospitalet de Llobregat
Reus
Sistema Ibérico
Tarragona
Work continues on the Sagrada Família, Gaudí's unfinished cathedral. Begun in 1882 the masterpiece is still without a roof.
Segovia
Tortosa
MADRID
Getafe
Teruel
Cuenca
País Valenciano
Menorca
Toledo
Júcar
Castellón de la Plana
Palma
Mallorca
Valencia
Albacete
Gandía
Islas Baleares (Balearic Islands)
Ibiza
Formentera
Ciudad Real
Elda
Benidorm
Segura
Cieza
Alicante (Alacant)
Elche (Elx)
Seat of many great civilizations throughout history, the name Mediterranean translates as "sea between the lands."
Linares
Murcia
Costa Blanca
Lorca
Jaén
Cartagena
Granada
Sierra Nevada
Almería
Motril
Costa del Sol
Mediterranean Sea
ALGERIA
0°
5°
40°
1
2
3
4
5
E
F
G
H

Germany & The Alpine States

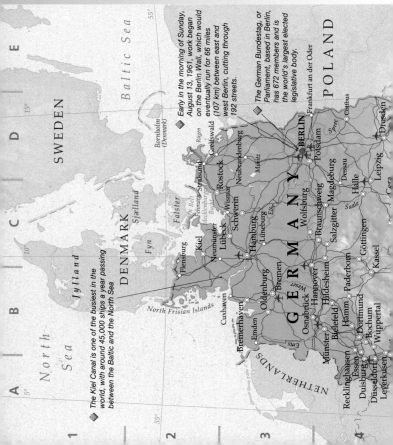

The Kiel Canal is one of the busiest in the world, with around 45,000 ships a year passing between the Baltic and the North Sea.

Early in the morning of Sunday, August 13, 1961, work began on the Berlin Wall, which would eventually run for 66 miles (107 km) between east and west Berlin, cutting through 192 streets.

The German Bundestag, or Parliament, based in Berlin, has 672 members and is the world's largest elected legislative body.

At 528 ft (161 m) the spire of Ulm Cathedral is the tallest in the world.

Born in Salzburg on January 27, 1756, Wolfgang Amadeus Mozart was already writing music by the age of five, and at eleven he produced his first opera.

The glass roof over the Olympic stadium in München (Munich) measures 914,940 sq ft (85,000 sq m) making it the biggest structure of its kind in the world.

St Gothard tunnel is 10.14 miles (16.32 km) long, making it the second longest road tunnel in the world.

In April 1998 a violin made by Italian master Stradivari at Cremona in around 1680 sold at Christie's in London for £947,500.

San Marino formed in AD 301 is the oldest, and, at 24 sq mi (61 sq km), one of the smallest, republics in the world.

Brindisi
G. di Otranto
Lecce
Gallipoli
Bari
Altamura
Taranto
Golfo di Taranto
Potenza
Crotone
Catanzaro
Ionian Sea
Benevento
Napoli
Salerno
Torre del Greco
Golfo di Salerno
Isola di Capri
Cosenza
Isola Stromboli
Reggio di Calabria
Stretto di Messina
Isola Vulcano
Messina
Isole Eolie
Isola Lipari
Isola d'Ustica
Cefalù
Palermo
Catania
Siracusa
Ragusa
Sicilia (Sicily)
Caltanissetta
Salso
Agrigento
Trapani
Marsala
Isole Egadi
Isola di Pantelleria
Strait of Sicily
Isole Pelagie
Malta Channel
Gozo
VALLETTA
MALTA
Mediterranean Sea

Tyrrhenian Sea

Mediterranean Sea

Sardegna (Sardinia)
Nuoro
Oristano
Cagliari
Alghero
Iglesias

TUNISIA

Mt Etna began some 300,000 years ago as a submarine volcano and has since grown to a cone with a base 30 miles (48 km) wide and 10,958 ft (3340 m) high.

The medical school at Salerno is the oldest in Europe, established during the 11th and 12th centuries.

The George cross that appears on the Maltese flag was awarded to the islanders by King George VI of Britain for their heroism during World War II.

0 km   100
0 miles   100

BELARUS

LATVIA

LITHUANIA

◆ Warsaw was home to the world's first public library, opened in 1747.

KALININGRAD
(part of Russian
Federation)

Courland Lagoon

SWEDEN

Baltic Sea

Bornholm
(part of Denmark)

◆ Hitler's demand in 1939 that Gdansk be returned to German control precipitated the invasion of Poland which ultimately led to World War II.

Gulf of Danzig

Elbląg

Gdynia
Gdańsk
Grudziądz
Bydgoszcz
Toruń
Włocławek

Słupsk
Koszalin
Człuchów
Piła
Noteć

POLAND

Białystok

Narew
Bug

Olsztyn
Ostrołęka

Mazury

WARSAW

Wisła

Płock

Lublin

Ostrowiec
Świętokrzyski

Radom

Łódź
Warta

Kielce

Wisła

Pomeranian
Bay

Zalew
Szczeciński
Szczecin

DENMARK

GERMANY

Gorzów
Wielkopolski

Warta

Poznań

Zielona
Góra

Odra

Kalisz

Wrocław
Odra

Legnica

◆ In November 1989 the so-called "Velvet Revolution" saw Czechoslovakia split into the Czech Republic and Slovakia.

0 km   100
0 miles   100

UKRAINE

Dniester

Rzeszów
Tarnów
Kraków-Biała
Bielsko-Biała
Śląski
Ostrava
Olomouc

Wodzisław
Rybnik

Laborec
Prešov
Poprad
Košice
Rožňava
Martin
Žilina
Banská
Bystrica
Ózd
Lučenec
Miskolc
Trenčín
Nitra
Váh

Nyíregyháza
Debrecen

R O M A N I A

Mureş

Tisza

Great Hungarian Pln

Szolnok
Kecskemét
Szeged
Békéscsaba

BUDAPEST

SLOVAKIA

Carpathian Mts.

Sudeten

Elbe
Kladno
PRAGUE
Pardubice
Plzeň
Tábor
Jihlava
Stratonice
Brno
Prostějov
Telč
Strakonice
Telč
České
Budějovice

CZECH REPUBLIC

Morava

Přeštany
Trnava
BRATISLAVA

H U N G A R Y

Danube

Győr
Tatabánya
Székesfehérvár
Veszprém
Balaton
Szekszárd
Pécs
Baja
Kaposvár
Drava
Nagykanizsa
Zalaegerszeg
Szombathely
Sopron

A U S T R I A

ITALY   SLOVENIA

CROATIA

BOSNIA -
HERZEGOVINA

SERBIA

Adriatic
Sea

◆ Built in 1357, Charles Bridge was the
only crossing point of the Vltava in
Prague until the 19th century.

◆ With a surface area of around
231 sq mi (598 sq km) Lake Balaton
has an average depth of only 11 ft (3.25 m).

◆ The Great Hungarian Plain (Alföld) stretches south from Budapest
to the borders of Croatia and Serbia and east to Ukraine and
Romania. It covers an area of 20,000 sq miles (51,800 sq km)
and is almost completely flat.

Southeast Europe

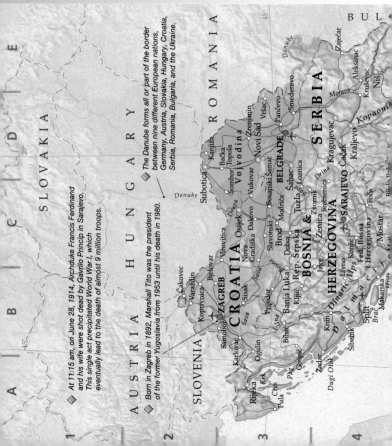

◆ At 11:15 am, on June 28, 1914, Archduke Francis Ferdinand and his wife were shot dead by Gavrilo Princip in Sarajevo. This single act precipitated World War I, which eventually lead to the death of almost 9 million troops.

◆ Born in Zagreb in 1892, Marshall Tito was the president of the former Yugoslavia from 1953 until his death in 1980.

◆ The Danube forms all or part of the border between nine different European nations; Germany, Austria, Slovakia, Hungary, Croatia, Serbia, Romania, Bulgaria, and the Ukraine.

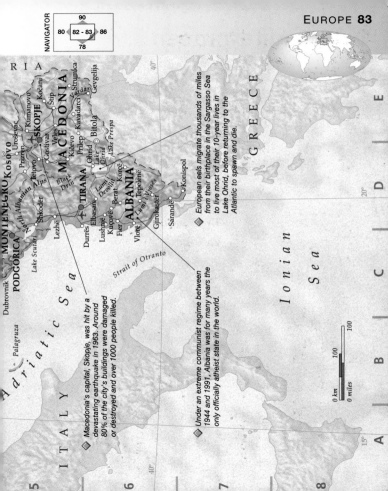

European eels migrate thousands of miles from their birthplace in the Sargasso Sea to live most of their 10-year lives in Lake Ohrid, before returning to the Atlantic to spawn and die.

Macedonia's capital, Skopje, was hit by a devastating earthquake in 1963. Around 80% of the city's buildings were damaged or destroyed and over 1000 people killed.

Under an extreme communist regime between 1944 and 1991, Albania was for many years the only officially atheist state in the world.

The Mediterranean

ATLANTIC

OCEAN

UNITED KINGDOM

NETHERLANDS

BELGIUM

GERMAN

Thames

English Channel

Seine

Rhine

LUX.

E U

U

Loire

FRANCE

Danube

LIECH.

SWITZ.

L. Geneva

A

L

P

S

Po

SA
MAR

Bay
of
Biscay

Dordogne Massif
Central

Rhône

Garonne

Apennin

Genoa

MONACO

Livorno

Pyrenees

Marseille

ANDORRA

Golfe
du
Lion

Corsica

VATICAN
CITY

PORTUGAL

SPAIN

Tagus

Iberian
Peninsula

Guadalquivir

Ebro

Barcelona

Balearic Is.

Valencia

Sardinia

M e d i t

Tyrrher
Sea

Gibraltar
(UK)

Gibraltar

Strait of Gibraltar

Oran

Algiers

Tunis

Tell Atlas

TUNISI

Sfax

Madeira
(Portugal)

MOROCCO

Atlas Mountains

ALGERIA

Chott el Jerid

Trip

Canary Is.
(Spain)

Grand Erg
Occidental

Grand Erg
Oriental

A F R

S a h a

I

a

0 km   400

0 miles   400

50°

10°

10°

1

2

40°

3

30°

4

5

A   B   C   D

10°   0°   10°

POLAND

UKRAINE

CZECH REP.

ROPE

AUSTRIA

SLOVAKIA

HUNGARY

SLOVENIA

Hungarian
Plain

CROATIA

MOLDOVA

Carpathians

ROMANIA

BOS. &
HERZ.

Dinaric Alps

SERBIA

Danube

Danube
Delta

RUSSIAN
FEDERATION

Sea
of Azov

Crimea

BULGARIA

MONTENEGRO

Balkan Mts.

Black Sea

Caucasus Mts.

Adriatic Sea

Rhodope Mts.

ITALY

ALBANIA

MACEDONIA

Bosporus

GEORGIA

Pindus Mts.

Naples

Aegean
Sea

Lesbos

TURKEY

Anatolia

Ionian
Sea

GREECE

Piraeus

Izmir

Peloponnese

Kos

Lake
Van

Taurus Mts.

Sicily

Rhodes

MALTA

Crete

Cyprus

SYRIA

Euphrates

Tigris

rranean

Sea

LEBANON

Haifa

ISRAEL

IRAQ

Anti-Lebanon

Syrian Desert

ASIA

Gulf of Sirte

Nile
Delta

Port Said

Suez Canal

JORDAN

SAUDI
ARABIA

LIBYA

EGYPT

Arabian
Peninsula

CA

ra

a

Libyan
Desert

Nile

Red Sea

Bulgaria & Greece

Sofia's skyline is dominated by the gold domes of the Alexander Nevski Memorial Church which took craftsmen and artists some thirty years to build between 1882 and 1912.

Built between 447 and 438 BCE, the Parthenon survived almost unscathed for over 2000 years until, in 1687, a gunpowder magazine beneath the building exploded causing considerable damage.

ROMANIA

SERBIA

ALBANIA

MACEDONIA

BULGARIA

Balkan Mountains

Rhodope Mountains

Pindus

G R E E C E

TURKEY

Black Sea

Thracian Sea

Marmara Denizi

Vóreíes Sporádes

Danube

Vidin

Dobrich

Varna

Kamburya

Razgrad

Shumen

Ruse

Pleven

Lovech

Vratsa

Gabrovo

Sliven

Yambol

Burgas

Stara Zagora

Kazanlŭk

Yazovir Iskŭr

Plovdiv

SOFIA

Pernik

Pazardzhik

Velingrad

Haskovo

Khaskovo

Blagoevgrad

Petrich

Serres

Drâma

Xánthi

Komotiní

Kavála

Orestiáda

Alexandroúpoli

Samothráki

Thásos

Akrotírio Pínes

Akrotírio Drépano

Límnos

Mitilíni

Lésvos

Kílkis

Thessaloníki

Kalamariá

Thermaïkós Kólpos

Kateríni

Véroia

Kozáni

Flórina

Lake Prespa

Lake Ohrid

Ioánnina

Igoumenítsa

Kérkyra

Kérkyra

Prévez

Peneiós

Tríkala

Kardítsa

Lárisa

Vólos

Olt

Danube

Iskŭr

Tundzha

Maritsa

Struma

Vardar

Akrotírio Palioúri

A B C D E

1 2 3

20° 25°

40°

TURKEY

Aegean Sea

Chíos

Sámos

Dodekánisa (Dodecanese)

Ikaría

Mýkonos

Kykládes (Cyclades)

Tínos

Ándros

Náxos

Amorgós

Íos

Astypálaia

Páros

Sýros

Santoríni

Mílos

Mirtóo Pelagos

Kýthira

Ródos

Ródos (Rhodes)

Kárpathos

Kos

Kritikó Pélagos (Sea of Crete)

Iráklio

Kríti (Crete)

Chaniá

◆ Only about 100 of the 2000 or so Greek islands are permanently inhabited.

◆ The Minoans developed the first Hellenic civilisation 4000 years ago, based at the luxurious palace of Knossos. Unfortunately in 1400 BCE this civilization came to an abrupt end, destroyed by a tidal wave.

Agrínio

Chalkída

Évvoia

ATHENS

Korinthiakós Kólpos

Pátra

Kórinthos

Peiraiás

Tripoli

Pelopónnisos

Spárti

Kalamáta

Ionian Sea

Kefalloniá

Zákynthos

Iónia Nisiá (Ionian Islands)

◆ The first Olympic athletics festival was held at Olympia in around 776 BCE.

◆ The Corinth Canal was completed in 1893 after 11 years of work. The canal is 4 miles (6.3 km) long, 80 ft (25 m) wide and 26 ft (8 m) deep. The central section runs along a 260 ft (79 m) deep cutting through solid rock.

Mediterranean Sea

LIBYA

0 km   100

0 miles   100

A   B   C   D   E

The Baltic States & Belarus

◆ Rich oil shale deposits in northern Estonia are quarried, crushed, and heated to produce almost 7,000 barrels of oil a day.

◆ Low salinity and the shallow coastal waters cause pack ice to accumulate at the head of the Gulf of Bothnia and off Finland during most winters; occasionally the ice becomes banked up in pressure ridges that are almost 50 ft (15 m) high.

FINLAND

SWEDEN

RUSSIAN

Gulf of Bothnia

Gulf of Finland

Narva Bay
Kohtla-Järve
Narva
Loksa
Rakvere
Narva
Lake Peipus
Lake Pskov
Tapa
Paide
TALLINN
Paldiski
ESTONIA
Tartu
Võru
Valga
Vihtsu
Viljandi
Gulf of Riga
Hiiumaa
Vormsi
Haapsalu
Pärnu
Saaremaa
Kuressaare
Burtnieku Ezers
Valmiera
Cēsis
LATVIA
Madona
Rēzekne
Jēkabpils
Daugavpils
Navapolatsk
Kolka
Riga
RIGA
Ogre
Talsi
Jelgava
Dobele
Birži
Rujiena
Western Dvina
Ventspils
Venta
Saldus
Radviliškis
Panevēžys
Utena
Kuldīga
Mažeikiai
Telšiai
Kelmė
LITHUANIA
Ukmergė
Liepāja
Plungė
Šiauliai
Venta
Neris
Kretinga
Šilutė
Tauragė
Jurbarkas
Kaunas
Klaipėda
Neman
Gusev
Mariampolė
KALININGRAD
(part of Russian
Federation)
Kaliningrad
Chernyakhovsk
Coudand
Lagoon

Gotland

Baltic Sea

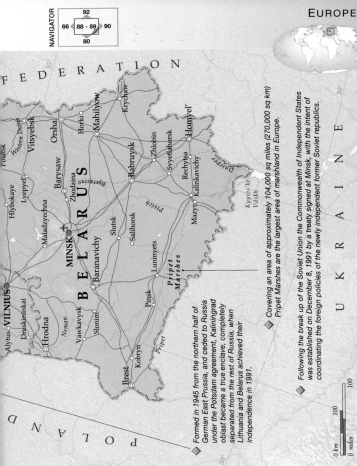

F E D E R A T I O N

Polatsk
Western Dvina
Vitsyebsk
Orsha
Horki
Mahilyow
Krychaw
Hlybokaye
Lyepyel'
Barysaw
Zhlobin
Homyel'
Maladzyechna
Zhodzina
Byarezina
Babruysk
Svyetlahorsk
Rechytsa
Dnieper
B E L A R U S
Kalinkavichy
Slutsk
Salihorsk
Mazyr
Dnipro
MINSK
Baranavichy
Prlpsch
Kyyus'ke
Vdskh
Druskininkai
Vawkavysk
Luninyets
Pripet Marshes
VILNIUS
Alytus
Neman
Slonim
Pinsk
Hrodna
Kobryn
Pripet
Brest

P O L A N D

U K R A I N E

Formed in 1945 from the northern half of German East Prussia, and ceded to Russia under the Potsdam agreement, Kaliningrad oblast became a true enclave, completely separated from the rest of Russia, when Lithuania and Belarus achieved their independence in 1991.

Covering an area of approximately 104,000 sq miles (270,000 sq km) Pripet Marshes are the largest area of marshland in Europe.

Following the break up of the Soviet Union the Commonwealth of Independent States was established on December 8, 1991 by a treaty signed at Minsk, with the intent of coordinating the foreign policies of the newly independent former Soviet republics.

0 km 100
0 miles 100

Ukraine, Moldova & Romania

POLAND

BELARUS

Pripet

Pripet Marshes

◆ On April 25, 1986, engineers accidentally initiated an uncontrolled chain reaction in the number 4 reactor of the Chornobyl' nuclear power plant. The resulting explosion released 8 tons (tonnes) of radioactive material in the world's worst ever nuclear accident.

Kovel'

Luts'k

Korosten

Rivne

L'viv

Zhytomyr

SLOVAKIA

Ternopil'

U K R

Ivano-Frankivs'k

Khmel'-nyts'kyy

Vinnytsy

◆ Vlad Dracula or Vlad the Impaler was the real life prince upon whom Bram Stoker based his famous Count Dracula. Dracula was born in Transylvania in 1431 in the town of Sighisoara.

Uzhhorod

Kam''yanets'-Podil's'kyy

Chernivtsi

Dniester

Satu Mare

Suceava

Botoşani

Rîbniţa

Bălţi

MOLDOVA

Baia Mare

Oradea

Dej

Transylvania

Dubăsari

HUNGARY

Cluj-Napoca

Iaşi

CHIŞINĂU

Arad

Alba Iulia

Târgu Mureş

Piatra-Neamţ

Tiraspol

Timişoara

Deva

Sighisoara

Bacău

Tighina (Bendery)

ROMANIA

Sibiu

Basarabeasca

Reşiţa

Carpaţii Meridionali

Focşani

Siret

Râmnicu Vâlcea

Braşov

Galaţi

Reni

Drobeta-Turnu Severin

Târgovişte

Buzău

Brăila

Tulcea

SERBIA

Piteşti

Ploieşti

Craiova

BUCHAREST

Corabia

Giurgui

Danube

Constanţa

Eforie Sud

Olt

Mangalia

BULGARIA

RUSSIAN

FEDERATION

30°

35°

40°

◆ A monument in central Kiev stands as testament to the 7–12 million Ukrainian peasants who died during the Great Famine of 1932–33.

Shostka

Chernihiv

Chornobyl'

Sumy

Kyyivs'ke Vdskh.

KIEV

Kaniv's'ke Vdskh.

1

50°

Bila Tserkva

Lubny

Kharkiv

A I N E

Cherkasy

Poltava

Donets

Syeverodonets'k

Kremenchuts'ke Vdskh.

Kremenchuk

Slov''yans'k

Luhans'k

Oleksandriya

Pavlohrad

Horlivka

Kostyantynivka

Kirovohrad

Yenakiyeve

Dnipropetrovs'k

Makiyivka

Krasnyy Luch

Pivdennyy Buh

Kryvyy Rih

Nikopol'

Zaporizhzhya

Donets'k

3

Kakhovs'ka Vdskh.

Mariupol'

Mykolayiv

Melitopol'

Berdyans'k

Kherson

Dnieper

Kakhovka

Odesa

Sea
of
Azov

◆ In 1872 an ironworks was founded at Donets'k by British industrialist John Hughes (from whom the town's pre-Revolutionary name Yuzovka was derived) to produce rails for the growing Russian transportation network.

Karkinits'ka
Zatoka

4

40°

Kryms'kyy
Pivostriv

Kerch

RUSSIAN

45°

Yevpatoriya

Simferopol'

Black
Sea

FEDERATION

Sevastopol'

Yalta

0 km   100

0 miles   100

5

◆ Odesa was one of the major flashpoints in the Russian Revolution of 1905, and was the scene of the mutiny on the warship Potemkin, when sailors protesting against the serving of rotten meat eventually threw the officers overboard.

E   35°   F   G   H   40°

European Russia

The port of Murmansk remains ice free throughout the winter thanks to the Gulf Stream, whereas St. Petersburg 600 miles (965 km) to the south on the Baltic Sea is ice-bound between December and May.

Arctic Ocean

Norwegian Sea

Barents Sea

Karskoye More

Kara Sea

Novaya Zemlya

Ostrov Vaygach

Ostrov Kolguyev

Kol'skiy Poluostrov

Beloye More

Murmansk

Arkhangel'sk

Mezen'

Pinega

Severnaya Dvina

Vorkuta

Usa

Pechora

Ukhta

Syktyvkar

(Ural Mountains)

Arctic Circle

RUSSIAN FEDERATION

Kama

Kirov

Kotlas

Vologda

Yaroslavl'

Ivanovo

Cherepovets

Rybinskoye Vdkhr.

Onezhskoye Ozero

Petrozavodsk

Onega

Ladozhskoye Ozero

Velikiy Novgorod

Tver'

MOSCOW

Smolensk

Velikiye Luki

Pskov

Sankt Peterburg

Gulf of Finland

FINLAND

SWEDEN

NORWAY

Arctic Circle

Gulf of Bothnia

Baltic Sea

ESTONIA

LATVIA

LITHUANIA

BELARUS

Dnepr

SIBERIA

0 km 400

0 miles 400

1

2

3

4

The Ural Mountains form the traditional boundary between Europe and Asia, extending some 1550 miles (2500 km). They were formed over 280 million years ago as the East European and Siberian plates moved together.

From August 1942 to February 1943 German armies laid siege to Volgograd, formerly known as Stalingrad. The Germans themselves were eventually surrounded and lost almost 250,000 men.

Caviar is the processed eggs, or roe, of sturgeon that live in the Caspian Sea and Volga River. Overfishing and poaching in recent years has seen the price of the finest Caviar rise to around US $1800 for 2.2 lbs (1 kg).

Running from the Black Sea to the Caspian Sea the Caucasus Mountains include Mt El'brus, which at 18,511 ft (5642 m) is the highest point in Europe, and still uplifting at the rate of 0.4 inches (10 mm) every year.

KAZAKHSTAN

UZBEKISTAN

TURKMENISTAN

Aral Sea

Perm

Izhevsk
Naberezhnyye Chelny
Vyatka
Ufa
Orenburg
Orsk

Nizhniy Novgorod
Cheboksary
Kazan
Ul'yanovsk
Tol'yatti
Saransk
Samara
Balakovo
Penza
Saratov
Tambov
Mikhaylovka
Ryazan
Vladimir
Tula
Orël
Volgograd
Astrakhan'

Bryansk
Voronezh
Belgorod
Rostov-na-Donu
Elista
Makhachkala

Donets
Don
Volga

UKRAINE

Krasnodar
Stavropol'
Cherkessk
Nal'chik
Vladikavkaz
Grozny

Caspian Sea

Sochi
El'brus 18,510 ft (5642 m)
Caucasus

GEORGIA
AZERBAIJAN
ARMENIA

TURKEY
IRAN
IRAQ

Black Sea
Sea of Azov

Ural'skiye Gory

North & West Asia

A R C T I C

Franz Josef Land

Severnaya
Zemlya

Svalbard
(Norway)

Novaya Zemlya

Kara Sea

Nort

Norwegian
Sea

North Cape

Barents
Sea

Khe

Arctic Circle

Gulf of Bothnia

Lake
Onega

Northern
Dvina

R U S S I A N

Centra

Lake Ladoga

West Siberian

Ob'

Yenisey

Plain

Ob'

Irtysh

Chulym

Ang

North
Sea

Baltic Sea

Volga

Central Russian
Upland

Irtysh

Ishim

KALININGRAD
(Russ. Fed.)

Volga

E U R O P E

Don

Ural

KAZAKHSTAN

A

S

Aral Sea

Ozero
Zaysan

Danube

Caucasus

Caspian Sea

Lake
Balkhash

Ili

Tien Shan

Black Sea

GEORGIA

UZBEKISTAN

KYRGYZSTAN

ARMENIA

AZERB.

TURKMEN.

TURKEY

Lake
Van

Amu Darya

TAJIKISTAN

SYRIA

IRAQ

IRAN

AFGHANISTAN

Tibetan
Plateau

Mediterranean
Sea

LEBANON

Tigris

H

i

m

a

l

a

y

a

s

ISRAEL

JORDAN

Euphrates

KUWAIT

Ganges

Tropic of Cancer

BAHRAIN

The Gulf

QATAR

U.A.E.

Nile

Red Sea

SAUDI
ARABIA

OMAN

20°

AFRICA

YEMEN

Arabian
Sea

Bay of
Bengal

Gulf of Aden

Socotra (Yemen)

A   B   C   D

O C E A N

120°

140°

160°

180°

80°

1

New Siberian Islands

Ozero
Taymyr

Laptev Sea

Siberian Lowland

Kotuy

Anabar

Olenëk

Lena

Yana

Indigirka

East Siberian
Sea

Wrangel Island

Long Strait

Chukchi
Sea

Bering Strait

Kolyma

Arctic Circle

2

Siberian Plateau

F E D E R A T I O N

Velikaya

Bering
Sea

60°

b

Chona

e

Lena

r

Amga

i

a

Vitim

Lake
Baikal

Argun

Amur

Zeya

Sea of
Okhotsk

Kamchatka

Aleutian Islands

3

I

A

Sakhalin

Kurile Islands

(administered by
Russian Federation,
claimed by Japan.)

40°

4

Gobi

Yellow River

Yangtze

Sea of
Japan
(East Sea)

East
China
Sea

P A C I F I C

O C E A N

Tropic of Cancer

20°

Mekong

South
China
Sea

0 km   800
0 miles   800

5

E   120°   F   140°   G   160°   H   180°

Russia & Kazakhstan

NORWAY
DENMARK
SWEDEN
GERMANY
Arctic Circle
ARCTIC
Barents Sea
Zemlya Frantsa Iosifa
FINLAND
Murmansk
KALININGRAD
(part of Russian Federation)
POLAND
LAT. EST.
LITH. Pskov
BELARUS
Sankt-Peterburg
Velikiy Novgorod
Arkhangel'sk
Novaya Zemlya
Karskoye More
Nori'lsk
UKRAINE
Cherepovets
MOSCOW
Vologda
Vorkuta
Salekhard
MOLDOVA
Bryansk
Yaroslavl'
Syktyvkar
Tula
Ryazan'
Nizhniy Novgorod
Kirov
Perm'
Ob'
Zapadno-
Sibirskaya
R U S
Voronezh
Kazan'
Izhevsk
Ural'skiye Gory
Serov
Ravnina
Rostov-na-Donu
Volgograd
Samara
Ufa
Yekaterinburg
Nizhnevartovsk
F E D E
Sochi
Stavropol'
Ural'sk
Orenburg
Chelyabinsk
Ob'
Nal'chik
Astrakhan'
Rudnyy
Kostanay
Petropavlovsk
Krasnoyars
GEORGIA
Groznyy
Orsk
Omsk
Tomsk
ARM.
Makhachkala
Kokshetau
ASTANA
Novosibirsk
Kemerovo
AZ.
Aktau
Caspian Sea
K A Z A K H S T A N
Pavlodar
Barnaul
Novokuznetsk
Karaganda
Semipalatinsk
Ust'-Kamenogorsk
Aral Sea
Zhezkazgan
Balkhash
Kyzylorda
Ozero Balkhash
TURKMENISTAN
UZBEKISTAN
Shymkent
Taraz
Taldykorgan
IRAN
KYRGYZSTAN
Almaty
CHINA

A   B   C   D

OCEAN

80°

180°

70°

60°

Ostrov
Vrangelya

Vostochno-
Sibirskoye
More

Pevek

Anadyr'

Severnaya
Zemlya

Ambarchik

Bering
Sea

Novosibirskiye
Ostrova

More
Laptevykh

Ossora

Poluostrov
Taymyr

Ozero Taymyr

Tiksi

Ust'-Kamchatsks

Poluostov
Kamchatka

Olenëk

Magadan

Petropavlovsk
-Kamchatskiy

Srednesibirskoye
Ploskogor'ye

Okhotsk

S I A N

Yakutsk

Sea of
Okhotsk

Sibir
(Siberia)

Suntar

R A T I O N

Sakhalin

Kuril'skiye Ostrova

Komsomol'sk-
na-Amure

Kansk

Bratsk

Skovorodno

Yuzhno-
Sakhalinsk

Ozero
Baykal

Blagoveshchensk

Khabarovsk

Irkutsk

Chita

Amur

JAPAN

Ulan-Ude

C H I N A

◆ *The Trans-Siberian Railroad, completed in 1916, runs*
5866 miles (9440 km) between Moscow and Vladivostok.
Crossing eight time zones, the journey takes eight days.

Vladivostok

0 km   500

0 miles   500

MONGOLIA

100°

110°

120°

130°

E   F   G   H

Turkey & the Caucasus

ROMANIA

Black Sea

BULGARIA

◇ An average of 50,000 commercial ships pass through the Bosporus a year, along with thousands of ferries and smaller passenger boats. The strait is three times busier than the Suez Canal and four times as busy as the Panama Canal.

Edirne ● Kırklareli

GREECE ● Tekirdağ

Çanakkale Boğazı (Dardanelles)

Çanakkale

Lésvos

Ayvalık

Chíos

Manisa ● Uşak

İzmir

Aydın

Sámos

Bodrum

Dalaman

Ródos

Kárpathos

Krití

Megísti

Mediterranean Sea

Sinop

Zonguldak *Küre Dağları* Kastamonu

İstanbul Karabük

Marmara Denizi

İzmit Adapazarı Çankırı *Kızıl Irmak*

Bursa

Balıkesir Eskişehir ● ANKARA Kırıkkale

Kütahya

Afyon *A n a t o l i a* Nevşehir

Denizli *Tuz Gölü* Niğde

Isparta Konya

Ereğli

Antalya *T o r o s   D a ğ l a r ı*

Antalya Körfezi

Samsun

Ordu

Canık Dağları

Çorum

Tokat

T U R K

Sivas

Kayseri

Kahramanmaraş

Adana Osmaniye

Tarsus

Mersin Gaziantep

İskenderun

Antakya

TURKISH REPUBLIC OF NORTHERN CYPRUS (recognized only by Turkey)

Girne (Kyrenia)

Gazimağusa (Famagusta

NICOSIA × ×

Paphos Larnaca

Limassol

CYPRUS

LEBANON

RUSSIAN FEDERATION

Caspian Sea

◆ An earthquake struck Armenia in 1988, killing 55,000 people and devastating the country's infastructure.

C a u c a s u s

Gagra
Sokhumi
Och'amch'ire
P'ot'i
Bat'umi
K'ut'aisi
Enguri

GEORGIA
T'BILISI ◦ Rust'avi
Hopa
Quba
Trabzon
Rize
Gäncä
Mingäçevir
Sumqayıt
BAKU
Vanadzor
Gyumri
Kurä
Doğu Karadeniz Dağları
Kars
ARMENIA
AZERBAIJAN
YEREVAN
Sevana Lich Nagorno-Karabakh
Erzincan
Erzurum
Büyükağrı Dağı (Mount Ararat) 16,853ft (5137m) ▲
Xankändi
AZERBAIJAN
Naxçıvan
Aras
Länkäran

E Y

Elazig
Muş
Van Gölü
Van
◆ Azerbaijan has substantial oil reserves located in and around the Caspian Sea. They were some of the earliest oilfields in the world to be exploited.
Güney Doğu Toroslar
Malatya
Tigris
Diyarbakır
Siirt
Adıyaman
Batman
Kurdistan
Şanlıurfa
Mardin

I R A N

◆ The salty water of Lake Van inhibits all animal life except the Darekh, a small fish that has adapted to the harsh conditions.

◆ Atatürk Dam, one of the largest dams in the world, was completed in 1990. The reservoir behind the dam covers an area of 315 sq miles (816 sq km) and often requires interruptions in the flow of the Euphrates River to maintain water levels.

S Y R I A
I R A Q

0 km   200
0 miles   200

The Near East

◆ The Euphrates is 1700 miles (2470 km) long and drains an area of 171,000 sq mi (443,000 sq km). Although less than 30 percent of the river's drainage basin is in Turkey, about 95 percent of the river's water originates in the Turkish highlands.

◆ Lebanon only has one permanent river, the Nahr el Litani, which runs for 110 miles (175 km).

◆ Manufactured by a secret process, Damascus steel was much prized in the preindustrial era as an extremely hard metal used for high quality sword blades.

TURKEY

Tigris

Al Qamishli

Al Ḥasakah

Al Jazīrah

Dayr az Zawr

Euphrates

IRAQ

Ar Raqqah

Buḥayrat al-Asad

SYRIA

Tudmur

Ḥalab

Idlib

A'zāz

Orantes

Ḥamāh

Ḥimṣ

Anti-Lebanon

DAMASCUS

Al Lādhiqīyah

Ṭarṭūs

Tripoli

LEBANON

Baalbek

Zahlé

Litani

BEIRUT

Saïda

Soûr

Mediterranean Sea

CYPRUS

0 km   100

0 miles   100

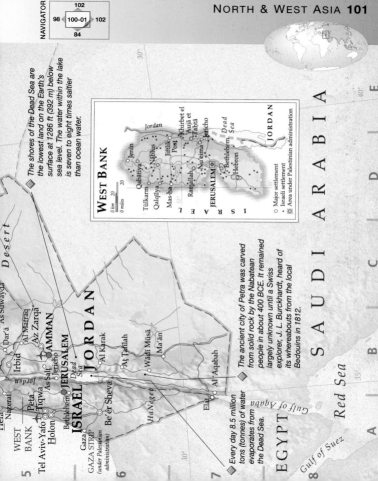

The shores of the Dead Sea are the lowest land on the Earth's surface at 1286 ft (392 m) below sea level. The water within the lake is seven to eight times saltier than ocean water.

WEST BANK

0 km   20
0 miles   20

- ○ Major settlement
- ● Israeli settlement
- ▣ Area under Palestinian administration

Jordan
Jenin
Qabatiya
Tūlkarm
Nāblus
Jiftlik
Post
Khirbet el
Auja et
Tahta
Qalqilya
Mas-ha
Ramallah
Nu'eima
Jericho
JERUSALEM
Bethlehem
Hebron
Dead Sea
JORDAN
ISRAEL

The ancient city of Petra was carved from solid rock by the Nabatean people in about 400 BCE. It remained largely unknown until a Swiss explorer, J. L. Burckhardt, heard of its whereabouts from the local Bedouins in 1812.

Every day 8.5 million tons (tonnes) of water evaporates from the Dead Sea.

SAUDI ARABIA

JORDAN

EGYPT

Red Sea

Gulf of Suez

Gulf of Aqaba

Desert

WEST BANK

Nazerat
Tel Aviv-Yafo
Holon
Tiqwa
ISRAEL
Bethlehem
JERUSALEM
GAZA STRIP
(under Palestinian administration)
Be'ér Sheva
HaNegev
Elât
Al 'Aqabah
Irbid
Dar'ā
As Suwaydā'
Al Mafraq
Az Zarqā'
AMMAN
Salt
Jericho
Dead Sea
Al Karak
At Tafīlah
Wādī Mūsā
Ma'ān
Jordan

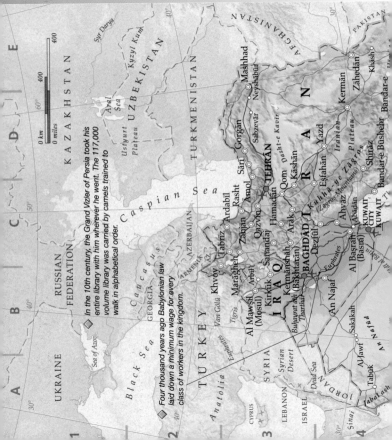

◆ In the 10th century, the Grand Vizier of Persia took his entire library with him wherever he went. The 117,000 volume library was carried by camels trained to walk in alphabetical order.

◆ Four thousand years ago Babylonian law laid down a minimum wage for every class of workers in the kingdom.

RUSSIAN FEDERATION

UKRAINE

KAZAKHSTAN

UZBEKISTAN

TURKMENISTAN

AFGHANISTAN

PAKISTAN

Syr Darya

Kyzyl Kum

Aral Sea

Ustyurt Plateau

Caspian Sea

Mashhad

Neyshābūr

Gorgān

Sabzevār

Sārī

Āmol

Dasht-e Kavīr

Kermān

Zāhedān

Khāsh

Bandar-e

IRAN

Yazd

Eşfahān

Kāshān

Qom

TEHRĀN

Iranian Plateau

Shīrāz

Kūhhā-ye Zāgros

Zagros Mountains

Bandar-e

Bushehr

Āhvāz

Ābādān

Dezfūl

KUWAIT

KUWAIT CITY

Al Başrah (Basra)

Black Sea

Sea of Azov

Caucasus

GEORGIA

ARMENIA

AZERBAIJAN

Ardabīl

Rasht

Qazvīn

Zanjān

Tabrīz

Khvoy

Marāgheh

Sanandaj

Hamadān

Arāk

Kermānshāh (Bākhtarān)

BAGHDĀD

An Najaf

Arbīl

Kirkūk

Al Mawşil (Mosul)

IRAQ

Euphrates

Tigris

Van Gölü

TURKEY

Anatolia

SYRIA

Syrian Desert

Euphrates

Buḩayrat ath Tharthār

LEBANON

ISRAEL

CYPRUS

Dead Sea

JORDAN

Sakākah

Al Jawf

An Nafūd

Tabūk

Jabal at

Sīnai

0 km 400

0 miles 400

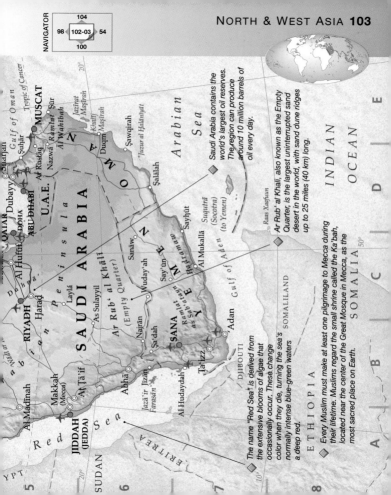

Saudi Arabia contains the world's largest oil reserves. The region can produce around 10 million barrels of oil every day.

Ar Rub' al Khali, also known as the Empty Quarter, is the largest uninterrupted sand desert in the world, with sand dune ridges up to 25 miles (40 km) long.

Every Muslim must make at least one pilgrimage to Mecca during their lifetime. Muslims regard the small shrine called the Ka'ba, located near the center of the Great Mosque in Mecca, as the most sacred place on Earth.

The name "Red Sea" is derived from the extensive blooms of algae that occasionally occur. These change color when they die, turning the sea's normally intense blue-green waters a deep red.

Central Asia

◆ Since 1960, the Aral Sea has shrunk by 40 percent, becoming extremely saline and consequently losing all but one of it's once-abundant fish species.

Aral Sea

Ustyurt Plateau

Turan Lowland

UZBEKISTAN

Köneürgenç ○ ● Nukus

Daşoguz ○ ● Urganch ○ Uchquduq

Caspian ● To'rtko'l

○ Zarafshc

TURKMENISTAN *Aydarko' Ko'l*

Türkmenbaşy ○ ● Navoi

Hazar ○ ● Balkanabat *Turan* ● Buxoro

Sea ● Bereket ● Seýdi ● Samarq

Serdar ○ *Garagum* Qarshi

Baharly ● Türkmenabat

Gökdepe ┼ *Garagum Kanaly* ● Atamyrat

Abadan ○ ● Mary Bayramaly ● Saýat

AŞGABAT ● ● ○ Äqcha

Kaka ● *Murgap* Sheberghān

Tejen *Darýa* Mazār-e Sh

◆ The desert of Kara Kum (Garagum) occupies over 70 percent of Turkmenistan, severely limiting human settlement across much of the country.

Bālā Morghāb ● Meymaneh

Serhetabat ● *Darýa-ye Morghāb*

I R A N *Harīrūd*

Herāt ● **AFGHANISTA**

◆ The Kara Kum (Garagum) Canal, the world's longest irrigation canal, stretches some 683 miles (1100 km) and is known as the "River of Life" as it irrigates large areas of arid land.

Farāh ●

Gereshk ● Ka

Zaranj ● Kandahār ●

Dasht-e-Mārgow

Darýa-ye Helmand

0 km 200

0 miles 200

Syr Darya

Ozero Balkhash

K A Z A K H S T A N

1

BISHKEK
Kara-Balta
Tokmak
Tyup
Karakol
Talas
Ozero Issyk-Kul'

SHKENT   Chirchiq
Namangan
KYRGYZSTAN
Tien Shan
2
Olmaliq
Angren   Dzhalal-Abad   Naryn
Qo'qon   Andijon
Khujand   Osh
roteppa   Farg'ona
Sulyukta   Khaydarkan
Zeravshan
Kokshaal-Tau Shan

40°

◇ *Mount Communism was so named for being the highest point in the former Soviet Union, rising to 24,590 ft (7495 m).*

USHANBE   *Surkhob*   TAJIKISTAN

Norak   *Bartang*
Danghara   Murghob   C H I N A   **3**
eppa   Kulob   *Pamirs*
rmez   Farkhor   Khorugh
ölm   Feyzabad   *Pamir*
Kondoz
Baghlan

Hindu Kush
hkhomri
Asadabad
ABUL
◇ *Until recent years, people living in remote areas of Afghanistan were immunized against smallpox by having dried powdered scabs from victims of the disease blown up their noses. This treatment was invented by the Chinese in the 11th century, and is thought to be the oldest form of vaccination.*
4
Ghazni   Jalalabad
Gardiz

Indus

◇ *Despite an area of 251,771 sq miles (652,090 sq km), Afghanistan has a limited road network and no railroads whatsoever, making access to much of the country extremely difficult.*

K I S T A N   I N D I A   **5**

70°   80°   30°

South & East Asia

Black Sea

Caspian Sea

Aral Sea

Syr Darya

Lake Balkhash

Irtysh

Yenisey

Uvs Nuur

Lake Baikal

Hovsgol Nuur

MONGOLIA

Altai Mountains

Iranian Plateau

The Gulf

Gulf of Oman

Hindu Kush

Tien Shan

Takla Makan Desert

Altun Shan

Kunlun Mountains

Gobi

Yellow River

A   S   I   A

Plateau of Tibet

CHINA

PAKISTAN

Indus

Sutlej

Thar Desert

Jumna

Ganges

Himalayas

NEPAL

Brahmaputra

Mount Everest 29, 035ft (8850m)

Salween

Mekong

BHUTAN

Xi Jiang

Yangtze

Rann of Kachchh

Gulf of Khambhat

INDIA

BANGLADESH

Deccan

Western Ghats

Eastern Ghats

MYANMAR (BURMA)

Irrawaddy

LAOS

Red River

VIETNAM

Hanoi

Arabian Sea

Laccadive Islands (to India)

Bay of Bengal

Andaman Islands (to India)

Andaman Sea

Mekong

THAILAND

Gulf of Thailand

CAMBODIA

Tônlé Sap

MALDIVES

Gulf of Mannar

SRI LANKA

Nicobar Islands (to India)

MALAYSIA

SINGAPORE

Sumatra

Java

Equator

INDIAN

OCEAN

0 km   1000

0 miles   1000

40°   60°   80°   100°

40°

20°

80°   100°

1

2

3

4

5

The *Altai Mountains* provide one of the last refuges for the endangered snow leopard. There are thought to be only 600 animals left in the wild.

RUSSIAN FEI

KAZAKHSTAN

The *Turpan Depression* is the lowest and hottest place in China. Temperatures can exceed 117°F (47°C) around the lake of Aydingkol Hu, which lies 505 ft (154 m) below sea level.

0 km   400

0 miles   400

Zapadnyy Sayan

Yenisey

Ulaangom   Uvs Nuur

Ölgiy   Hyargas   Mörö
            Nuur
Hovsgöl
Nuur
Har Us Nuur   Hangayn   Tsetse
Altay   Nuru
Hovd   M O N G

Ulungur
Hu
Karamay   Gurbantünggüt
        Shamo
Kuytun   Altay   G
Yining   Shihezi   Bayanhongo
        ÜRÜMQI   Qitai
        Turpan   Hami
Ozero Issyk-Kul'   Xingxingxia   Dalain H
KYRGYZSTAN   Tien Shan   Bosten Hu
                              GANSU
Tarim He   Korla
Kashi   Tarim Basin   Lop Nur
TAJIKISTAN   XINJIANG UYGUR   Ruoqiang   Qilian Sha
Yengisar Shache   ZIZHIQU
Yecheng   Taklimakan   Altun Shan   Qaidam
(claimed   Shamo   Pendi
by India)   Qinghai H
AFGH.   Moyu   Golmud   Dular
        Qira
        Kunlun Shan   C H I
PAKISTAN   Karakorum Range   Qingzang Gaoyuan   QINGHAI
        Indus   AKSAI CHIN   (Plateau of Tibet)   Bayan Har Sh
        Kashmir (administered by China, claimed
JAMMU   by India)   Tongtian He   Mekong
AND   Yushu
KASHMIR   Rutög   Amdo   Qamdo
DEMCHOK/DÊMQOG   XIZANG   Tanggula Shan   Nagqu   Salween
(administered by China, ZIZHIQU   Siling Co
claimed by India) Gar   (Tibet)   Tangra   Nam Co   Damxung
        Zanda   Yumco   Nyima   Nyainqêntanglha Shan
                    Brahmaputra   LHASA
INDIA   Himalayas   Lhazê   ARUNACHAL
        NEPAL   Gyangzê   PRADESH
                                    (claimed by China
            Mount Everest
            29,035ft (8850m)   BHUTAN   INDIA

Although forming around 20 percent of China's landmass, Tibet is sparsely populated, supporting only 1 percent of China's 1.3 billion population.

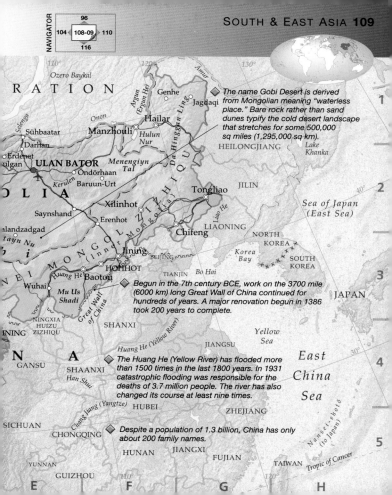

The name Gobi Desert is derived from Mongolian meaning "waterless place." Bare rock rather than sand dunes typify the cold desert landscape that stretches for some 500,000 sq miles (1,295,000 sq km).

Begun in the 7th century BCE, work on the 3700 mile (6000 km) long Great Wall of China continued for hundreds of years. A major renovation begun in 1386 took 200 years to complete.

The Huang He (Yellow River) has flooded more than 1500 times in the last 1800 years. In 1931 catastrophic flooding was responsible for the deaths of 3.7 million people. The river has also changed its course at least nine times.

Despite a population of 1.3 billion, China has only about 200 family names.

Whereas European languages such as English or French use an alphabet of 26 letters, the Chinese language uses a system of over 50,000 characters or symbols.

The "Yongle dadian," an encyclopedia of the Chinese Ming dynasty, had 22,937 chapters in 10,000 volumes. More than 2000 Chinese scholars worked on the book for 5 years before it was finished.

Tangshan, China, suffered the deadliest earthquake of the 20th century on July 28, 1976. One quarter of the population was killed or seriously injured, with an estimated death toll of 242,000 people.

Tiananmen Square in Beijing is the largest public square in the world covering an area of 100 acres (40.5 hectares).

RUSSIAN FEDERATION

Ozero Baykal

Amur (Heilong Jiang)

Shilka

Argun (Ergun He)

Onon

Selenga

Xiao Hinggan Ling

HEILONGJIANG

Qiqihar

HARBIN

Lake Khanka

Mudanjiang

JILIN

Jilin

CHANGCHUN

Chongjin

Hunjiang

NORTH KOREA

Sea of Japan (East Sea)

Hamhúng

Fushun

SHENYANG

LIAONING

Fuxin

Jinzhou

Haicheng

PYONGYANG

Namp'o

Dandong

Dalian

Korea Bay

Bo Hai

Anshan

Yingkou

TIANJIN

BEIJING

HEBEI

Datong

Great Wall of China

Handan

Shijiazhuang

SHANXI

TAIYUAN

Yellow Sea

Korea

40°

SOUTH KOREA

SEOUL

Taejon

Taegu

Pusan

Qingdao

Zibo

JINAN

SHANDONG

Huang He

NINGXIA

YINCHUAN

SHAANXI

Qilian Shan

Qinghai Hu

Qaidam Pendi

XINJIANG UYGUR ZIZHIQU

MONGOLIA

NEI MONGOL (Inner Mongolia)

A   B   C   D   E

1   2   3   4

90°   100°   110°   120°   130°

50°

40°

Li is the family name for over 87 million people in China.

By far the biggest tidal bore in the World is the Ch'ient'ang kian (Hang-chou-fe) in China. At spring tides the wave attains a height of up to 25 ft (7.5 m) and a speed of 13-15 knots (24-27 km/h).

Parcel Islands
(disputed by China, Taiwan and Vietnam)

Spratly Islands
(disputed by China, Malaysia, Philippines, Taiwan and Vietnam)

(China and Taiwan claim all of each other's territory)

The Giant Bamboo is the fastest growing plant in the world, able to grow at the rate of 3 ft (90 cm) a day.

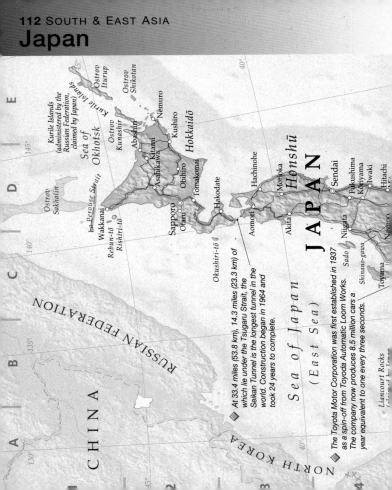

Kurile Islands
(administered by the
Russian Federation,
claimed by Japan)

Ostrov Iturup

Ostrov Shikotan

Kurile Islands

Sea of Okhotsk

Nemuro

Kushiro

Ostrov Kunashiri

Abashiri

Kitami

Hokkaidō

Asahikawa

Obihiro

Tomakomai

La Pérouse Strait

Wakkanai

Ostrov Sakhalin

Sapporo

Otaru

Hakodate

Hachinohe

Honshū

Morioka

Sendai

Rebun-tō

Rishiri-tō

Aomori

Akita

Fukushima

Kōriyama

Iwaki

Hitachi

JAPAN

Niigata

Nagano

Okushiri-tō

Sado

Shinano-gawa

Toyama

Sea of Japan

(East Sea)

RUSSIAN FEDERATION

CHINA

NORTH KOREA

Liancourt Rocks

At 33.4 miles (53.8 km), 14.3 miles (23.3 km) of
which lie under the Tsugaru Strait, the
Seikan Tunnel is the longest tunnel in the
world. Construction began in 1964 and
took 24 years to complete.

The Toyota Motor Corporation was first established in 1937
as a spin-off from Toyoda Automatic Loom Works.
The company now produces 8.5 million cars a
year equivalent to one every three seconds.

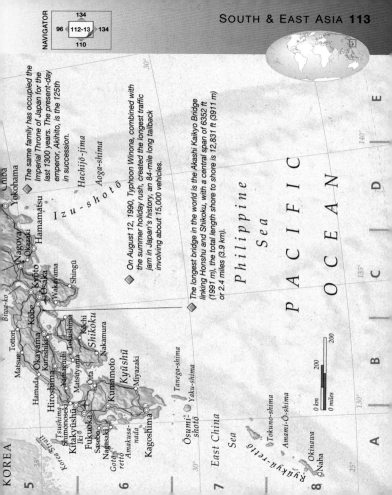

The same family has occupied the Imperial Throne of Japan for the last 1300 years. The present-day emperor, Akihito, is the 125th in succession.

On August 12, 1990, Typhoon Winona, combined with the summer holiday rush, created the longest traffic jam in Japan's history, an 84-mile long tailback involving about 15,000 vehicles.

The longest bridge in the world is the Akashi Kaikyo Bridge linking Honshu and Shikoku, with a central span of 6352 ft (1991 m), the total length shore to shore is 12,831 ft (3911 m) or 2.4 miles (3.9 km).

30°
140°
135°
130°
25°
30°
35°

Chiba
Yokohama
Hachijō-jima
Aoga-shima

Izu-shotō

Nagoya
Okazaki
Kyōto
Kōbe
Ōsaka
Hamamatsu
Wakayama
Shingū

Biwa-ko

Matsue
Tottori
Hamada
Okayama
Kurashiki
Hiroshima

Tsushima
Iki

Shimonoseki
Kitakyūshū
Fukuoka
Sasebo
Nagasaki

Gotō-rettō

Yamaguchi
Matsuyama
Takamatsu
Kōchi
Shikoku
Nakamura
Tokushima

Ōita
Kumamoto
Kyūshū
Miyazaki

Amakusa-nada

Kagoshima

Ōsumi-shotō
Tanega-shima
Yaku-shima

Philippine Sea

P A C I F I C   O C E A N

East China Sea

Ryūkyū-rettō

Tokuno-shima
Amami-Ō-shima

Okinawa
Naha

KOREA

Korea Strait

0 km   200
0 miles 200

A   B   C   D   E

5
6
7
8

Southern India & Sri Lanka

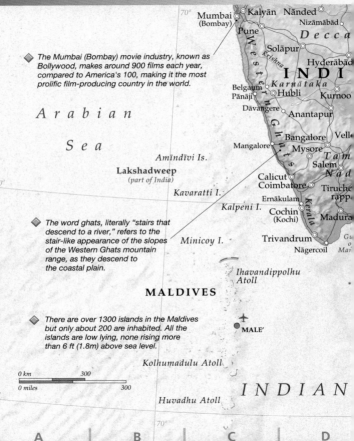

◆ The Mumbai (Bombay) movie industry, known as Bollywood, makes around 900 films each year, compared to America's 100, making it the most prolific film-producing country in the world.

◆ The word ghats, literally "stairs that descend to a river," refers to the stair-like appearance of the slopes of the Western Ghats mountain range, as they descend to the coastal plain.

◆ There are over 1300 islands in the Maldives but only about 200 are inhabited. All the islands are low lying, none rising more than 6 ft (1.8m) above sea level.

Arabian

Sea

Amīndīvi Is.

Lakshadweep
(part of India)

Kavaratti I.

Kalpeni I.

Minicoy I.

Ihavandippolhu Atoll

MALDIVES

✈

● **MALE'**

Kolhumadulu Atoll

Huvadhu Atoll

INDIAN

Mumbai (Bombay) ◉ Kalyān Nānded
Nizāmābād
Pune ◉ *Decca*
Solāpur ◉ Hyderābād
Western ◉ **INDI**
Krishna *Karnātaka*
Belgaum ◉ Hubli ◉ Kurnoo
Panājī ◉
Dāvangere ◉ Anantapur ◉
Ghats Bangalore ◉ Vell
Mangalore ◉ Mysore ◉ *Tam*
Salem ◉ *Nād*
Calicut ◉ Tiruche
Coimbatore ◉ rapp.
Ernākulam ◉
Cochin ◉ Madura
(Kochi)
Trivandrum ◉ *Gu*
Nāgercoil ◉ *Mar*

70°

10°

0°

0 km   300
0 miles   300

A   B   C   D

70°

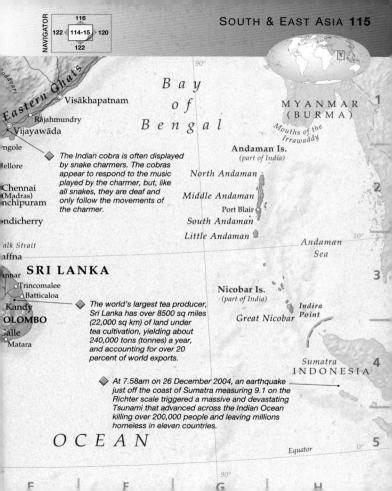

90°

B a y
o f
B e n g a l

Eastern Ghats

odāvari

● Visākhapatnam

● Rājahmundry
● Vijayawāda

ongole

●ellore

● Chennai
(Madras)
anchipuram

●ndicherry

alk Strait

affna

SRI LANKA

annar
○Trincomalee
○Batticaloa

● **Kandy**
OLOMBO
alle
● Matara

MYANMAR
(B U R M A)

Mouths of the
Irrawaddy

Andaman Is.
(part of India)

North Andaman

Middle Andaman

Port Blair ●

South Andaman

Little Andaman

Andaman
Sea

10°

Nicobar Is.
(part of India)

Great Nicobar

Indira
Point

Sumatra
INDONESIA

Sumatra

OCEAN

Equator

0°

*The Indian cobra is often displayed
by snake charmers. The cobras
appear to respond to the music
played by the charmer, but, like
all snakes, they are deaf and
only follow the movements of
the charmer.*

*The world's largest tea producer,
Sri Lanka has over 8500 sq miles
(22,000 sq km) of land under
tea cultivation, yielding about
240,000 tons (tonnes) a year,
and accounting for over 20
percent of world exports.*

*At 7.58am on 26 December 2004, an earthquake
just off the coast of Sumatra measuring 9.1 on the
Richter scale triggered a massive and devastating
Tsunami that advanced across the Indian Ocean
killing over 200,000 people and leaving millions
homeless in eleven countries.*

90°

E   F   F   G   H

North India, Pakistan & Bangladesh

XINJIANG UYGUR
ZIZHIQU

SAI CHIN
ministered by China,
imed by India)

◇ The northern ranges of the Himalayas contain the highest
mountains in the world, with average heights of more than
23,000 ft (7000 m) and many peaks higher
than 26,000 ft (8000m).

C H I N A   QINGHAI

MCHOK/DÉMQOG
ministered by China,
imed by India)

◇ Cerrapunji, 4232 ft (1290 m) above sea level, has an average annual
rainfall of 503 inches (1279 cm), although this is monsoon rain and
the winter is a virtual drought. The highest ever seasonal rainfall
was 901 inches (2290 cm).

XIZANG ZIZHIQU
(Tibet)

◇ In the kingdom of Bhutan, all
citizens officially become a
year older on New Year's Day.

ARUNACHAL PRADESH
(claimed by China)

H i m a l a y a s

Mount Everest
29,035ft (8850m)

areilly

NEPAL

● KATHMANDU   ● THIMPHU

Gangtok   ● BHUTAN

Guwāhāti

Uttar
Pradesh

● Biratnagar

Dispur

Kohima

Lucknow

Saidpur

Kānpur   Vārānasi   Patna

Ganges

Jamalpur

Brahmaputra

Sylhet   Imphāl

muna

Allahābād

Bihār

Rājshāhi

BANGLADESH

Tropic of Cancer

I A

Gaya

West

DHAKA

Jabalpur

Dhanbād

Comilla

Ranchi

Bengal

Khulna

M Y A N M A R
(B U R M A)

radesh

Kolkata
(Calcutta)

Chittagong

Raipur

Mouths of the Ganges

Orissa

Mahānadi

Cuttack

Bay
of
Bengal

◇ The heaviest hailstones
on record, weighing about
2.25 lbs (1 kg), are
reported to have killed 92
people in the Gopalganj
area of Bangladesh on
April 14, 1986.

Eastern Ghats

ver   Varangal   ● Visākhapatnam

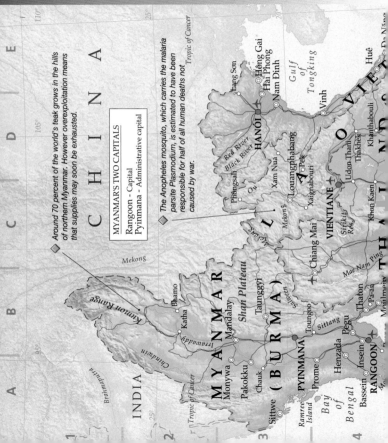

Mainland Southeast Asia

Around 70 percent of the world's teak grows in the hills of northern Myanmar. However overexploitation means that supplies may soon be exhausted.

MYANMAR'S TWO CAPITALS

Rangoon - Capital
Pyinmana - Administrative capital

The Anopheles mosquito, which carries the malaria parsite Plasmodium, is estimated to have been responsible for half of all human deaths not caused by war.

C H I N A

M Y A N M A R

(B U R M A)

INDIA

Bay of Bengal

LAOS

VIETNAM

THAILAND

Mekong

HANOI

VIENTIANE

RANGOON

PYINMANA

Mandalay

Chiang Mai

Lang Son

Hông Gai
Hai Phong
Nam Dinh

Vinh

Huê

Gulf of Tongking

Tropic of Cancer

Red River
Black River

Phôngsali

On

Xam Nua

Louangphabang

Pek

Xaignabouri

Udon Thani

Thakhek

Khanthabouli

Khon Kaen

Sirikit Rés.

Bhamo

Katha

Shan Plateau

Taunggyi

Toungoo

Pegu

Sittang

Thaton

Pa-an

Salween

Irrawaddy

Chindwin

Monywa

Pakokku

Chauk

Prome

Henzada

Insein

Bassein

Sittwe

Ramree Island

Prome

Mae Nam Ping

Kunlun Range

Brahmaputra

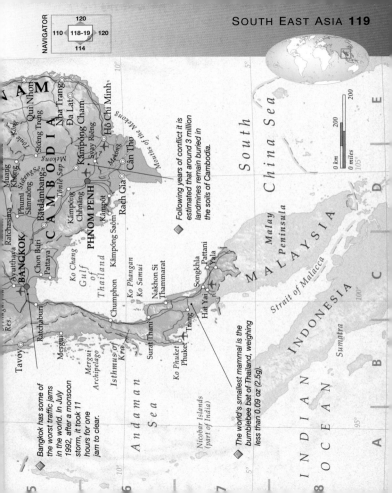

N | A | M
Qui Nhơn
Kông
Tônlé Srêpôk
Stœ̃ng Trêng
Muang
Không
Phumi Sâmraông
Bătdâmbâng
C A M B O D I A
Tônlé Sap
PHNOM PENH
Kâmpóng Chhnăng
Kâmpóng Saôm
Kâmpôt
Nha Trang
Đà Lạt
Hồ Chí Minh
Kâmpóng Cham
Svay Riêng
Cân Thơ
Mekong
Mouths of the Mekong
Rach Gia

Ayutthaya Ratchasima
BANGKOK
Chon Buri
Pattaya
Ratchaburi
Res.
Tavoy
Mergui
Mergui
Archipelago
Isthmus
of
Kra
Ko Chang
Gulf
of
Thailand
Chumphon
Surat Thani
Ko Phangan
Ko Samui
Nakhon Si
Thammarat
Trang
Ko Phuket
Phuket
Hat Yai
Songkhla
Pattani
Yala

Malay
Peninsula
M A L A Y S I A
Strait of Malacca
I N D O N E S I A
Sumatra

South
China Sea

A n d a m a n
S e a

Nicobar Islands
(part of India)

I N D I A N
O C E A N

◆ Following years of conflict it is estimated that around 3 million landmines remain buried in the soils of Cambodia.

◆ Bangkok has some of the worst traffic jams in the world. In July 1992, after a monsoon storm, it took 11 hours for one jam to clear.

◆ The world's smallest mammal is the bumblebee bat of Thailand, weighing less than 0.09 oz (2.5g).

0 km   200
0 miles   200

10°
5°
105°
100°
95°
5°
10°

E
D
C
B
A

5
6
7
8

Maritime Southeast Asia

MALAYSIA'S TWO CAPITALS

Kuala Lumpur - Capital
Putrajaya - Administrative capital

◆ The Rafflesia plant has the largest flower in the world. The bloom, 3 ft (90 cm) in diame attracts insects by imitating the foul smell of rotting flesh.

◆ In August 1883 a devastating volcanic eruption destroyed most of the island of Krakatau and triggered a tsunami that claimed around 33,000 lives.

120°
Luzon Strait
Babuyan Channel
130°

Philippine

Tuguergarao
Ilagan
Luzon

aguio
Dagupan

geles
Cabanatuan

ANILA
Lucena

tangas
Naga

Mindoro

Legazpi City

ndoro Strait
Sibuyan Sea

Calbayog

Roxas City
Tacloban

s
Iloilo
Cadiz
Cebu

Peurto
Princesa
Bacolod
City

Bohol Sea
Butuan

wan
Iligan
Cagayan de Oro

Sulu Sea
Mindanao

amboanga
Davao

Sulu Archipelago
Davao Gulf

General
Santos

Celebes Sea

Kepulauan
Sangir

Sea

◆ The Philippines take their name from Philip II
of Spain, who was king when the islands were
colonized during the 16th century.

PHILIPPINES

P A C I F I C

Yap

*Kepulauan
Talaud*

◆ Indonesia is the world's largest archipelago
with almost 14,000 islands stretching 3100
miles (5000 km) between the Indian
and Pacific oceans.

Northern
Mariana
Islands
(to US)

1

Guam *(to US)*

MICRONESIA

Babeldaob

PALAU

O C E A N

3

Equator

wau
Manado

Gorontalo
Gulf of
Tomini

Palu
*Sulawesi
(Celebes)*

Kepulauan
Banggai

Kepulauan
Sula

Kendari

Parepare
*Pulau
Buton*

Makassar

rres Sea
Sumba

*Pulau
Sumba*

Pulau Morotai
*Pulau
Halmahera*

Molucca Sea

*Halmahera
Sea*

Sorong
Sea

Maluku (Moluccas)

Wahai

Ambon
*Pulau
Seram*

*Pulau
Buru*

Ceram Sea

Kepulauan
Kai

Banda Sea

*Pulau
Buton*

E N E S I A

Tenggara

Flores

Kupang

*Pulau
Alor*
DILI
EAST TIMOR

Timor

Timor Sea

Savu Sea

Kepulauan
Leti

*Jazirah
Doberai*

*Pulau
Biak*

Sungai Mamberamo

Jayapura

Pegunungan Maoke

Papua
(Irian Jaya)

New
Guinea

Kepulauan
Tanimbar

Pulau Yamdena

Arafura Sea

Digul

PAPUA

NEW
GUINEA

Torres Strait

10°

A U S T R A L I A

120°

130°

140°

1

2

3

4

5

The Indian Ocean

ASIA

Lake Baikal

Yenisey

Ob'

Lake Balkash

Aral Sea

Caspian Sea

Volga

Black Sea

Caucasus

Iranian Plateau

Tigris

Euphrates

Kuwait

Arabian Peninsula

Red Sea

The Gulf

Gulf of Oman

Dubai

Mina' Qabus

Aden

Gulf of Aden

Ethiopian Highlands

Horn of Africa

Socotra (to Yemen)

AFRICA

Equator

Mombasa

Tropic of Cancer

Karachi

Indus

Indus Fan

Murray Ridge

Arabian Sea

Arabian Basin

Mumbai (Bombay)

Himalayas

Brahmaputra

Ganges

Ganges Fan

Kolkata (Calcutta)

Bay of Bengal

Andaman Islands (to India)

Nicobar Islands (to India)

Sri Lanka

Colombo

Ceylon Plain

Yellow River

Yangtze

Mekong

Tropic of Cancer

Hong Kong (Xiangang)

South China Sea

Gulf of Thailand

Irrawaddy

Andaman Sea

Sumatra

Singapore

Equator

Borneo

East Indies

Java Sea

Kepulauan Mentawai

Cocos Basin

Investig

Mid-Indian Ocean

British Indian Ocean

Chagos-Laccadive Plateau

Chagos Trench

Laccadive Islands (to India)

MALDIVES

Carlsberg Ridge

Great Fracture Zone

Mid-Indian Basin

Mid-

Somali Basin

SEYCHELLES

Masca

Aldabra

◇ With no part of the Maldives over 8 ft (2.4 m) above sea level, they are under great threat by global warming. There are over 2000 islands yet the total land area is only 115 sq miles.

120°

100°

80°

60°

40°

Australian
Basin

Exmouth
Plateau

Tropic of Capricorn

AUSTRALASIA
(to Australia)

Perth
Basin

Fremantle

Naturaliste
Plateau

Diamantina Fracture Zone

Wharton
Basin

East Indiaman Ridge

Broken Ridge

Ninetyeast Ridge

(to Australia)

SOUTHERN Ridge

Limit of winter pack ice

Limit of summer pack ice

Antarctic Circle

ANTARCTICA

Every cubic mile (4.3 cu km) of
seawater holds over 150 million
tons (tonnes) of minerals.

Amsterdam Island

Île St-Paul

INDIAN

OCEAN

Southeast Indian Ridge

SOUTHERN

OCEAN

South Indian Basin

Osborn
Plateau

Mid Indian Ridge

Kerguelen Plateau

The largest animal ever seen alive was a 113.5 ft (35 m),
170-ton (tonne) female blue whale.

Crozet
Basin

French Southern &
Antarctic Territories
(to France)

Kerguelen

Banzare
Seamounts

MAURITIUS

Réunion
(to France)

Crozet
Islands

Heard & Mcdonald Islands
(to Australia)

Farafangana

Plateau

Madagascar
Basin

Madagascar
Plateau

Prince Edward
Islands
(to South Africa)

E n d e r b y   p l a i n

Antarctic Circle

Mayotte
(to France)

Mascarene
Plain

Atlantic-Indian
Basin

MADAGASCAR

Natal
Basin

Davie Ridge

Mozambique
Channel

Durban

0 km   1500
0 miles   1500

Australasia & Oceania

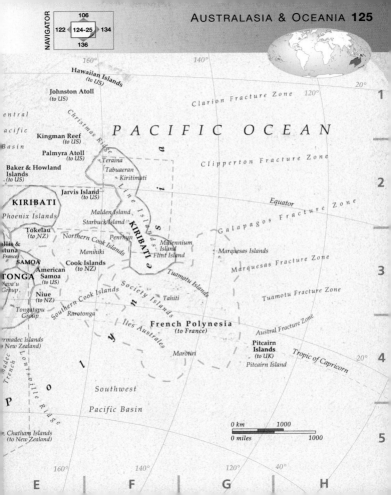

Hawaiian Islands
(to US)

Johnston Atoll
(to US)

Clarion Fracture Zone

120°

20°

1

entral
acific
Basin

Kingman Reef
(to US)

Palmyra Atoll
(to US)

Baker & Howland
Islands
(to US)

Christmas Ridge

Teraina
Tabuaeran
Kiritimati

Clipperton Fracture Zone

PACIFIC OCEAN

Line Islands

2

Jarvis Island
(to US)

KIRIBATI

Phoenix Islands

Equator

Galapagos Fracture Zone

Tokelau
(to NZ)

Malden Island

Starbuck Island

KIRIBATI

Marquesas Islands

His &
tuna
France)

Northern Cook Islands

Penrhyn

Manihiki

Millennium
Island
Flint Island

Marquesas Fracture Zone

SAMOA

American
Samoa
(to US)

Cook Islands
(to NZ)

Tuamotu Islands

TONGA

Society Islands

ava'u
Group

Niue
(to NZ)

Southern Cook Islands

Tahiti

Tuamotu Fracture Zone

Tongatapu
Group

Rarotonga

Iles Australes

French Polynesia
(to France)

Austral Fracture Zone

20°

rmadec Islands
o New Zealand)

Marotiri

Pitcairn
Islands
(to UK)

Tropic of Capricorn

4

ermadec Trench

Louisville Ridge

P

Southwest
Pacific Basin

Pitcairn Island

P
o
l
y
n
e
s
i
a

* Chatham Islands
(to New Zealand)

0 km   1000
0 miles   1000

5

160°   140°   120°   40°

E   F   G   H

The Southwest Pacific

130°   140°   150°   160°   170°

Guam
(US unincorporated territory)
HAGÅTÑA

MARSHALL ISLANDS

Yap
Marianas Trench

Caroline Islands

Chuuk Is.

MICRONESIA

Pohnpei
PALIKIR

Kosrae

Majuro

Ratak Chain
Ralik Chain

KOROR

PALAU

Equator

◇ The Pitohui bird has a poison on its feathers and skin similar to the poison arrow tree frog, making it the only known example of a poisonous bird.

PAPUA NEW GUINEA

Bismarck Archipelago

New Ireland

INDONESIA

Mt Wilhelm
14,793ft (4509m) ▲   Madang

New Guinea

Bougainville I.

New Britain

New Georgia Islands

PORT MORESBY

Lae

Solomon Sea

HONIARA

Santa Cruz Is.

SOLOMON ISLANDS

Arafura Sea

Torres Strait

Arnhem Land

Gulf of Carpentaria

Coral Sea

Banks Is.

VANUATU

◇ Found only in the rain forest of New Guinea, Queen Alexandra's Birdwing, with a wingspan of 11 inches (280 mm), is the largest butterfly in the world.

Coral Sea Islands
(Australian external territory)

New Caledonia
(French overseas territory)

PORT VILA

AUSTRALIA

NOUMÉA

Îles Loyauté

Great Barrier Reef

BAIRI
Tara

NAURU
Banal

Melanesia

A   B   C   D

10°

0°

10°

20°

180°   170°   160°   150°

International Date Line

1

PACIFIC OCEAN

10°

◆ In 1994 the International Date Line was repositioned around Kiribati territory bringing Millennium Island 14 hours ahead of GMT, making it the first landfall for sunrise at the dawn of the new millennium.

Kingman Reef *(administered by US)*   **Palmyra Atoll** *(administered by US)*

Teraina
Tabuaeran
Kiritimati

2

Baker & Howland Is. *(administered by US)*

Jarvis I. *(administered by US)*

Line Islands

Equator   0°

KIRIBATI   *Phoenix Islands*   **KIRIBATI**

Tungaru (Gilbert Islands)

◆ Samoa is home to the world's smallest spider, the Patu marplesi, which spans a mere 0.017 inches (0.4mm).

3

TUVALU

FONGAFALE

Tokelau *(NZ dependent territory)*

Vostok I.   *Millennium I.*   10°

Flint I.

American Samoa *(US unincorporated territory)*   *Northern Cook Is.*

Wallis & Futuna *(French overseas territory)*   *P o l y n e s i a*

SAMOA   **PAGO PAGO**

Vanua Levu   **ÁPIA**

French Polynesia *(French overseas territory)*

Îles de la Société

FIJI

Vava'u Group

Niue *(in free assoc. with NZ)*   **Cook Islands** *(in free assoc. with NZ)*

PAPEETE

4

Viti Levu

SUVA

Ha'apai Group   **ALOFI**   *Southern Cook Is.*

Tahiti

TONGA

NUKU'ALOFA   **AVARUA**

International Date Line   *Rarotonga*   Tropic of Capricorn

| 0 km | 500 |
| 0 miles | 500 |

20°

5

180°   170°

E   F   G   H

Western Australia

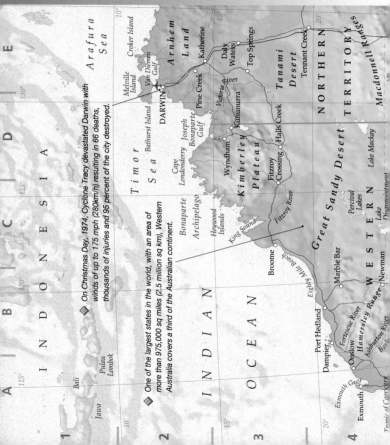

On Christmas Day, 1974, Cyclone Tracy devastated Darwin with winds of up to 175 mph (280km/h) resulting in 66 deaths, thousands of injuries and 95 percent of the city destroyed.

One of the largest states in the world, with an area of more than 975,000 sq miles (2.5 million sq km), Western Australia covers a third of the Australian continent.

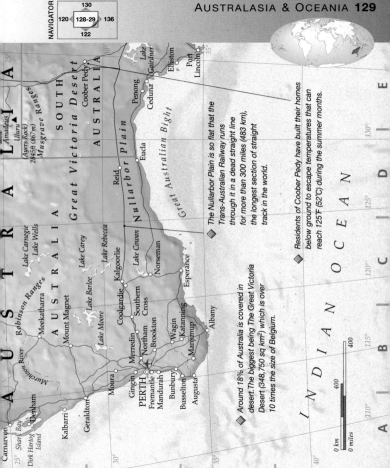

AUSTRALIA

SOUTH AUSTRALIA

Great Victoria Desert

Musgrave Range

Uluru ▲
(Ayers Rock)
2845ft (867m)

Amadeus

Lake
Gairdner

Coober Pedy

Penong

Ceduna

Port
Lincoln

Elliston

Nullarbor Plain

Reid

Eucla

Great Australian Bight

Lake Carnegie
Lake Wells

Robinson Ranges

Meekatharra

Mount Magnet

Lake Barlee

Lake Carey

Lake Rebecca

Lake Moore

Kalgoorlie

Lake Cowan

Coolgardie
Southern
Cross

Norseman

Esperance

Murchison River

Kalbarri

Geraldton

Moora

Merredin

Gingin
Northam
PERTH
Fremantle
Mandurah
Bunbury
Busselton
Augusta

Brookton

Wagin

Katanning

Manjimup

Albany

AUSTRALIA

Carnarvon

Denham

Shark Bay

Dirk Hartog
Island

INDIAN OCEAN

0 km   400
0 miles   400

◆ The Nullarbor Plain is so flat that the
Trans-Australian Railway runs
through it in a dead straight line
for more than 300 miles (483 km),
the longest section of straight
track in the world.

◆ Residents of Coober Pedy have built their homes
below ground to escape temperatures that can
reach 125°F (52°C) during the summer months.

◆ Around 18% of Australia is covered in
desert, the biggest being The Great Victoria
Desert (348,750 sq km²) which is over
10 times the size of Belgium.

Eastern Australia

◆ The venom of the Sea Wasp, Marine Stinger, or Box Jellyfish can kill a person in between 30 seconds and four minutes.

◆ Australia's Great Barrier Reef is the world's largest area of coral islands and reefs, running for about 1,240 miles (2,000 km) along the coast of Queensland.

◆ Koalas feed only on nutrient-poor eucalypt leaves and consequently have evolved a low energy lifestyle based around sleeping for 20 hours each day.

PAPUA NEW GUINEA

INDONESIA

Torres Strait

Cape York

Cape York Peninsula

Coral Sea

Coral Sea Islands
(to Australia)

Great Barrier Reef

Great Dividing Range

Cooktown

Port Douglas

Cairns

Tully

Hinchinbrook Island

Townsville

Charters Towers

Bowen

Whitsunday Group

Mackay

Rockhampton

Bundaberg

Biloela

Emerald

Clermont

Barcaldine

Longreach

Winton

Hughenden

Cloncurry

Mount Isa

Selwyn Range

Gregory Range

Flinders River

Normanton

Gilbert River

Mitchell River

Princess Charlotte Bay

Gulf of Carpentaria

Burketown

Wellesley Islands

Groote Eylandt

Wessel Islands

Arafura Sea

Arnhem Land

DARWIN

Pine Creek

Katherine

Daly Waters

Top Springs Roadhouse

Barkly Tableland

Tennant Creek

Tanami Desert

NORTHERN TERRITORY

QUEENSLAND

AUSTRALIA

Alice Springs

Macdonnell Ranges

Uluru (Ayers Rock)

Tropic of Capricorn

The Platypus lives in an aquatic environment, suckles its young like a mammal, lays eggs, and has webbed feet and a bill resembling that of a duck.

Huge truck rigs known as Road Trains, which can reach up to 175 ft (53.5 m) in length, carry freight across the vast distances of the Australian interior. They often have as many as three trailers, weighing more than 100 tons (tonnes) in total.

New Zealand

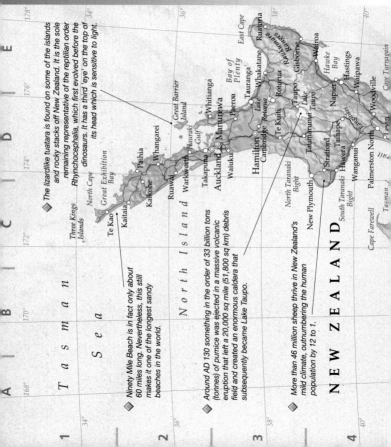

◊ The lizardlike tuatara is found on some of the islands and rocky stacks off New Zealand. It is the sole remaining representative of the reptilian order *Rhynchocephalia*, which first evolved before the dinosaurs. It has a third 'eye' on the top of its head which is sensitive to light.

◊ Ninety Mile Beach is in fact only about 60 miles long. Nevertheless, this still makes it one of the longest sandy beaches in the world.

◊ Around AD 130 something in the order of 33 billion tons (tonnes) of pumice was ejected in a massive volcanic eruption that left a 20,000 sq mile (51,800 sq km) debris field and created an enormous caldera that subsequently became Lake Taupo.

◊ More than 46 million sheep thrive in New Zealand's mild climate, outnumbering the human population by 12 to 1.

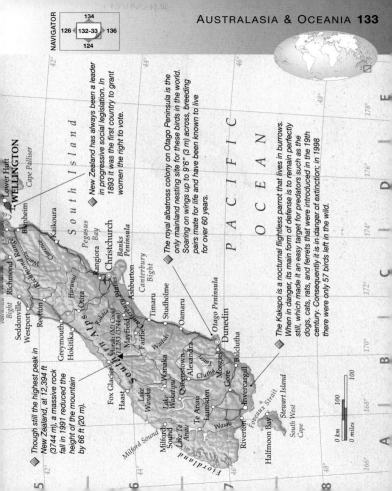

◆ Though still the highest peak in New Zealand, at 12,394 ft (3744 m), a massive rock fall in 1991 reduced the height of the mountain by 66 ft (20 m).

◆ New Zealand has always been a leader in progressive social legislation. In 1893 it was the first country to grant women the right to vote.

◆ The royal albatross colony on Otago Peninsula is the only mainland nesting site for these birds in the world. Soaring on wings up to 9'6" (3 m) across, breeding pairs mate for life and have been known to live for over 60 years.

◆ The Kakapo is a nocturnal flightless parrot that lives in burrows. When in danger, its main form of defense is to remain perfectly still, which made it an easy target for predators such as the dogs, cats, rats, and ferrets that were introduced in the 19th century. Consequently it is in danger of extinction; in 1998 there were only 57 birds left in the wild.

PACIFIC OCEAN

South Island

WELLINGTON
Lower Hutt
Cape Palliser

Blenheim
Richmond
Seddonville
Westport
Reefton
Greymouth
Hokitika
Kaikoura
Pegasus Bay
Christchurch
Rangiora
Banks Peninsula
Pegasus Bay
Ashburton
Canterbury Bight
Timaru
Studholme
Oamaru
Otago Peninsula
Dunedin
Mosgiel
Balclutha
Otira
Aoraki (Mt Cook) 12,333 (3744m)
Mayfield
Fairlie
Fox Glacier
Haast
Wanaka
Lake Wanaka
Lake Wakatipu
Alexandra
Queenstown
Gore
Te Anau
Lake Te Anau
Lumsden
Invercargill
Riverton
Waiau
Milford Sound
Fiordland
Halfmoon Bay
Stewart Island
Foveaux Strait
South West Cape
Waitaki
Clutha
Southern Alps

Tasman Bight
Nelson
Richmond Range
Buller
Grey
Rakaia
Rangitata
Waimakariri
Huranui

0 km   100
0 miles   100

The Pacific Ocean

◆ Challenger Deep in the Mariana Trench is 35,838 ft
(10,923 m), or almost 7 miles (11 km), below the
surface of the Pacific. At this depth water pressures
is around 16,000 lbs/sq inch (1,127 kg/cm sq).

Arctic Circle
Ob' Yenisey
Lena
Bering Strait
Bering Sea
Aleutian Basin
Aleutian Islands
Aleutian Trench
Sea of Okhotsk
Kurile Islands
Kurile Trench
Northwest Pacific Basin
Chinook Trough
Vladivostok
ASIA
Gobi
Yellow River
Yellow Sea
Sea of Japan (East Sea)
Shanghai Osaka Tokyo
Yangtze Nagoya
Hong Kong (Xianggang) Japan
Taiwan Ryukyu Trench Shikoku Basin
Mendocino F
Midway Islands (to US)
Hawaiian Ridge
Mid-Pacific Mountains
Wake Island (to US)
Johnston Atoll (to US)
Tropic of Cancer
Philippine Sea
Northern Mariana Islands (to US)
PACI
Manila
Philippines
Philippine Trench
Mariana Trench
Guam (to US)
36,201ft (11,034m)
Challenger Deep
MICRONESIA
Caroline Islands
Micronesia
MARSHALL ISLANDS
Central Pacific Basin
Kingman Reef (to US)
Baker & Howland Is. (to US)
Jarvis I. (to US)
South China Sea
Celebes Sea
PALAU
Melanesian Basin
Ontong Java Rise
NAURU
KIRIBATI
Equator
Sumatra Borneo
East Indies Celebes
Jakarta Java
Banda Sea
New Guinea
Melanesia
Tokelau (to NZ)
TUVALU
Wallis & Futuna (to France)
SAMOA
American Samoa (to US)
INDIAN
Timor Sea
Arafura Sea
SOLOMON ISLANDS
Coral Sea
VANUATU
FIJI
TONGA
Cook Island (to
Coral Sea Islands (to Australia)
New Caledonia (to France)
Tropic of Capricorn
OCEAN
AUSTRALIA
Great Dividing Range
Great Barrier Reef
Lord Howe Rise
Niue (to NZ)
Great Australian Bight
Murray
Sydney
Kermadec Islands (to NZ)
Norfolk Island (to Australia)
P
South Australian Basin
Tasman Sea
Hobart
Tasmania
North Island
New Zealand Chatham Islands (to NZ)
South Island
Campbell Plateau
0 km 2000
0 miles 2000
International Dateline

◆ Manua Loa on the Big Island of Hawaii rises 33,132 ft
(10,098 m) from the ocean floor to it's peak 13,677 ft
(4169 m) above the surface of the Pacific Ocean, and
contains around 9,700 cubic miles (39,731 cu km) of rock.

Antarctic Circle
ANTARCTICA
Pacific
Antarct

A | A | B | C | D

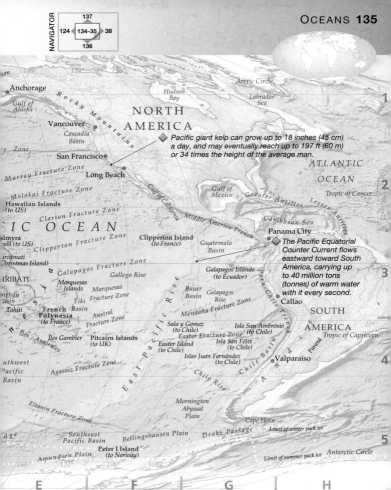

Anchorage
Gulf of Alaska
Rocky Mountains
Vancouver
Cascadia Basin
San Francisco
Long Beach

NORTH AMERICA

Murray Fracture Zone
Molokai Fracture Zone
Hawaiian Islands (to US)
Clarion Fracture Zone
IC OCEAN
almyra toll (to US)
Clipperton Fracture Zone
ristimati (Christmas Island)
Galapagos Fracture Zone
IRIBATI
Marquesas Islands
Marquesas Fracture Zone
Gallego Rise
nthyn asin
Tahiti
French Polynesia (to France)
Tiki
Austral Fracture Zone
les Gambier
Pitcairn Islands (to UK)
Easter Island (to Chile)
Easter Fracture Zone
uthwest Pacific Basin
Agassiz Fracture Zone
East Pacific Rise
Chile Rise
Eltanin Fracture Zone
Southeast Pacific Basin
Peter I Island (to Norway)
Amundsen Plain
dge

Arctic Circle
Hudson Bay
Labrador Sea

Pacific giant kelp can grow up to 18 inches (45 cm) a day, and may eventually reach up to 197 ft (60 m) or 34 times the height of the average man.

ATLANTIC OCEAN
Tropic of Cancer
Gulf of Mexico
Greater Antilles
Lesser Antilles
Middle America Trench
Gulf of California
Caribbean Sea
Panama City
Clipperton Island (to France)
Guatemala Basin

The Pacific Equatorial Counter Current flows eastward toward South America, carrying up to 40 million tons (tonnes) of warm water with it every second.

Galapagos Islands (to Ecuador)
Bauer Basin
Galapagos Rise
Mendaña Fracture Zone
Callao
SOUTH AMERICA
Tropic of Capricorn
Sala y Gomez (to Chile)
Isla San Ambrosio (to Chile)
Isla San Félix (to Chile)
Islas Juan Fernández (to Chile)
Peru-Chile Trench
Andes
Paraná
Valparaiso
Chile Basin
Mornington Abyssal Plain
Cape Horn
Limit of winter pack ice
Drake Passage
Bellingshausen Plain
Limit of summer pack ice
Antarctic Circle

140 120 100 80 60 40

E F G H

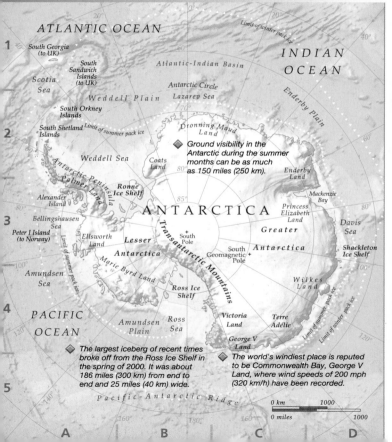

ATLANTIC OCEAN

INDIAN OCEAN

1

South Georgia (to UK)

Scotia Sea

South Sandwich Islands (to UK)

Weddell Plain

Atlantic-Indian Basin

Antarctic Circle
Lazarev Sea

Enderby Plain

2

South Orkney Islands

South Shetland Islands

Limit of summer pack ice

Dronning Maud Land

Weddell Sea

Coats Land

Antarctic Peninsula
Palmer Land

Ronne Ice Shelf

Enderby Land

◆ Ground visibility in the Antarctic during the summer months can be as much as 150 miles (250 km).

Alexander Island

ANTARCTICA

Mackenzie Bay

3

Bellingshausen Sea

Ellsworth Land

Lesser Antarctica

South Pole

Princess Elizabeth Land

Greater Antarctica

Davis Sea

Peter I Island (to Norway)

Transantarctic Mountains

South Geomagnetic Pole

Shackleton Ice Shelf

Amundsen Sea

Marie Byrd Land

Ross Ice Shelf

Wilkes Land

4

PACIFIC OCEAN

Amundsen Plain

Ross Sea

Victoria Land

Terre Adélie

Limit of summer pack ice

◆ The largest iceberg of recent times broke off from the Ross Ice Shelf in the spring of 2000. It was about 186 miles (300 km) from end to end and 25 miles (40 km) wide.

George V Land

◆ The world's windiest place is reputed to be Commonwealth Bay, George V Land, where wind speeds of 200 mph (320 km/h) have been recorded.

5

Pacific-Antarctic Ridge

0 km 1000
0 miles 1000

A B C D

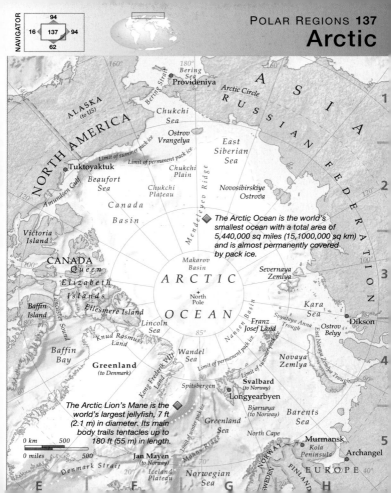

160°   180°   180°
Bering
Sea   • Provideniya   Arctic Circle

ALASKA   Chukchi   A S I A
(to US)   Sea
NORTH AMERICA   R U S S I A N
Ostrov   East
Vrangelya   Siberian
Limit of summer pack ice   Sea   F E D E R A T I O N
• Tuktoyaktuk   Limit of permanent pack ice Chukchi
Plain
Beaufort   Novosibirskiye
Sea   Chukchi   Ostrova
Plateau

Canada
Basin   ◆ The Arctic Ocean is the world's
smallest ocean with a total area of
5,440,000 sq miles (15,1000,000 sq km)
and is almost permanently covered
by pack ice.

Victoria
Island

CANADA   Queen   Makarov   Severnaya
Elizabeth   Basin   Zemlya
Islands
A R C T I C
Baffin   Ellesmere Island   + North   Kara
Island   Pole   Sea
Lincoln   O C E A N   Ostrov • Dikson
Sea   Franz   Belyy
85°   Josef Land
Knud Rasmuss   Nansen Basin   Soyalnaya Anna
Land   Trough
Baffin   Wandel   Novaya
Bay   Greenland   Sea   Limit of permanent pack ice Zemlya
(to Denmark)   80°
Kong Frederik VIII   Limit of summer pack ice
Land   Spitsbergen   • Svalbard
The Arctic Lion's Mane is the   ◆   (to Norway)
world's largest jellyfish, 7 ft   • Longyearbyen
(2.1 m) in diameter. Its main   Bjørnøya
body trails tentacles up to   Greenland   (to Norway)   Barents
180 ft (55 m) in length.   Sea   Sea
North Cape
0 km   500   • Murmansk
Kola   • Archangel
0 miles   500   • Jan Mayen   Peninsula
(to Norway)
Denmark Strait   Norwegian   E U R O P E 40°
Iceland   Sea
Plateau

The

Country
Factfiles

Franz Josef Land
(to Russia)

Svalbard
(to Norway)

Jan Mayen
(to Norway)

Greenland
(Denmark)

NUUK

St Pierre &
Miquelon

Baffin
Bay

Labrador

Gulf of
St Lawrence

Lawrence

Baffin Island

Laurentian Mountains

ARCTIC
OCEAN

North Pole

Queen Elizabeth
Islands

Hudson
Bay

C A N A D A

Lake
Superior

Reindeer Lake

Lake Winnipeg

Great Bear
Lake

Great Slave Lake

Lake Athabasca

Mackenzie

ASIA

C A N A D A

Arctic Circle

ALASKA

Yukon

R o c k y   M o u n t

Snake

PACIFIC
OCEAN

U N I T E D   S T A T E S

ATLANTIC

OCEAN

Sargasso Sea

Bermuda
(UK)

British Virgin
Islands *(UK)*

Virgin Islands *(US)*

Anguilla *(UK)*

ST KITTS
& NEVIS

ANTIGUA &
BARBUDA

Guadeloupe
(France)

Puerto
Rico *(US)*

SANTO
DOMINGO

Turks & Caicos
Islands *(UK)*

DOMINICAN
REPUBLIC

Montserrat *(UK)*

DOMINICA

Martinique *(France)*

ST LUCIA

BARBADOS

WASHINGTON, DC

Lake Ontario

Lake Erie

Ohio

Appalachian Mountains

Nassau

BAHAMAS

HAITI

PORT-AU-PRINCE

KINGSTON

ST VINCENT & THE GRENADINES

GRENADA

Netherlands
Antilles *(Neth.)*

TRINIDAD
& TOBAGO

Lake Michigan

Mississippi

Missouri

HAVANA

C U B A

JAMAICA

Cayman
Islands *(UK)*

Aruba *(Neth.)*

PANAMA CITY

PANAMA

SOUTH

A M E R I C A

Andes

Equator

Colorado

Arkansas

O F   A M E R I C A

Rio Grande

Gulf of Mexico

BELMOPAN

BELIZE

HONDURAS

TEGUCIGALPA

GUATEMALA CITY

GUATEMALA

SAN SALVADOR

EL SALVADOR

MANAGUA

NICARAGUA

COSTA RICA

SAN JOSÉ

MEXICO CITY

M E X I C O

Sierra Madre Occidental

Clipperton Island
(French Polynesia)

Tropic of Cancer

Equator

**COUNTRY WITH HIGHEST
POPULATION DENSITY:**
Barbados 1627 people per sq mile
(628 people per sq km)

LARGEST COUNTRY:
Canada 3,855,171 sq miles
(9,984,670 sq km)

SMALLEST COUNTRY:
St. Kitts & Nevis 101 sq miles
(261 sq km)

POLITICAL FACTFILE

TOTAL AREA:
9,400,000 sq miles
(24,346,000 sq km)

TOTAL NUMBER OF COUNTRIES:
23

TOTAL POPULATION:
511.3 million

LARGEST CITY WITH POPULATION:
Mexico City, Mexico 22.8 million

0 km   1000

0 miles   1000

ATLANTIC
OCEAN

Equator

Caribbean Sea

Isthmus of Panama

BRAZIL

BRASÍLIA

São Francisco
Represa de
Sobradinho

Tocantins

Araguaia

Xingu

Amazon

Amazon Basin

Madeira

Río Negro

Guiana Highlands

GEORGETOWN
PARAMARIBO
CAYENNE
French
Guiana
(France)
SURINAME

GUYANA

CARACAS

VENEZUELA

Orinoco

Meta

Guaviare

BOGOTÁ

COLOMBIA

Magdalena

Cauca

Caquetá

Putumayo

QUITO

ECUADOR

Napo

Marañón

Juruá

Purus

Madre de Dios

Beni

Lake
Titicaca

PERU

Andes

LIMA

LA PAZ

SUCRE

BOLIVIA

PARAGUAY

Equator

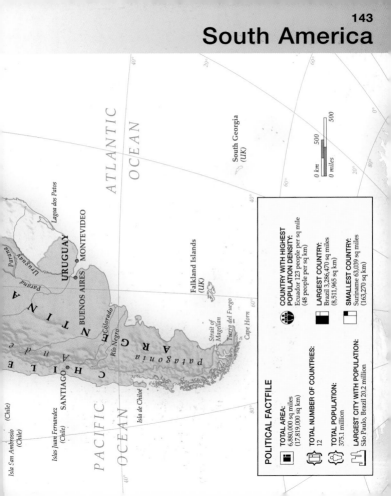

ATLANTIC

OCEAN

South Georgia
(UK)

0 km   500

0 miles   500

PACIFIC

OCEAN

Isla San Ambrosio   (Chile)
(Chile)

Islas Juan Fernández
(Chile)

SANTIAGO

CHILE

Isla de Chiloé

Andes

Patagonia

ARGENTINA

Río Negro

Río Colorado

BUENOS AIRES

URUGUAY

MONTEVIDEO

Lagoa dos Patos

Paraná

Paraguay

Uruguay

Strait of Magellan

Tierra del Fuego

Cape Horn

Falkland Islands
(UK)

POLITICAL FACTFILE

TOTAL AREA:
6,880,000 sq miles
(17,819,000 sq km)

TOTAL NUMBER OF COUNTRIES:
12

TOTAL POPULATION:
375.1 million

LARGEST CITY WITH POPULATION:
São Paulo, Brazil 20.2 million

COUNTRY WITH HIGHEST POPULATION DENSITY:
Ecuador 123 people per sq mile
(48 people per sq km)

LARGEST COUNTRY:
Brazil 3,286,470 sq miles
(8,511,965 sq km)

SMALLEST COUNTRY:
Suriname 63,039 sq miles
(163,270 sq km)

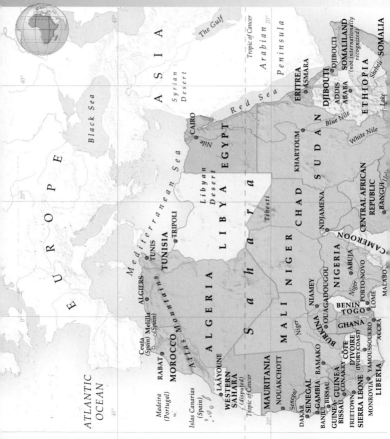

ATLANTIC
OCEAN

EUROPE

Black Sea

Mediterranean Sea

ASIA

The Gulf

Arabian Peninsula

Tropic of Cancer

Syrian Desert

Red Sea

Madeira
(Portugal)

Islas Canarias
(Spain)

Ceuta
(Spain) Melilla
(Spain)

Atlas Mountains

ALGIERS

TUNIS

TUNISIA

TRIPOLI

Libyan Desert

LIBYA

CAIRO

Nile

EGYPT

KHARTOUM

Blue Nile

White Nile

SUDAN

ERITREA

ASMARA

DJIBOUTI

ADDIS
ABABA

SOMALILAND
(not internationally
recognized)

SOMALIA

ETHIOPIA

Lake

Shebeli

RABAT

MOROCCO

Sahara

Tibesti

NIGER

CHAD

NDJAMENA

CENTRAL AFRICAN
REPUBLIC

CAMEROON

LAÂYOUNE

WESTERN
SAHARA
(disputed)

Tropic of Cancer

MAURITANIA

NOUAKCHOTT

ALGERIA

MALI

BAMAKO

Niger

NIAMEY

OUAGADOUGOU

BURKINA

NIGERIA

ABUJA

PORTO-NOVO

BENIN

Niger

MALABO

DAKAR

SENEGAL

Senegal

BANJUL

GAMBIA

GUINEA-
BISSAU

BISSAU

CONAKRY

GUINEA

FREETOWN

SIERRA LEONE

MONROVIA

LIBERIA

YAMOUSSOUKRO

CÔTE
D'IVOIRE
(IVORY COAST)

GHANA

LOMÉ

TOGO

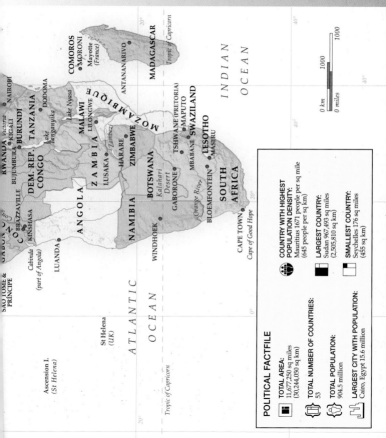

COMOROS
MORONI
Mayotte
(France)

MADAGASCAR

ANTANANARIVO

I N D I A N

O C E A N

NAIROBI
KWANDA Victoria **KIGALI**
BUJUMBURA **BURUNDI**
DODOMA
TANZANIA
Lake Nyasa
Lake Tanganyika
MALAWI
ZAMBIA LILONGWE
Zambezi
LUSAKA **HARARE**
ZIMBABWE
TSHWANE (PRETORIA)
MAPUTO
BOTSWANA MBABANE **SWAZILAND**
Kalahari GABORONE **LESOTHO**
Desert MASERU
NAMIBIA **SOUTH**
Orange River **AFRICA**
WINDHOEK BLOEMFONTEIN
CAPE TOWN
Cape of Good Hope

MOZAMBIQUE

ANGOLA
Cabinda
(part of Angola)
LUANDA

SAO TOME & PRINCIPE
BRAZZAVILLE
KINSHASA
DEM. REP. CONGO
CONGO
GABON

St Helena
(UK)

Ascension I.
(Ascension I.)

A T L A N T I C

O C E A N

Tropic of Capricorn

0 km   1000
0 miles   1000

POLITICAL FACTFILE

TOTAL AREA:
11,677,250 sq miles
(30,244,050 sq km)

TOTAL NUMBER OF COUNTRIES:
53

TOTAL POPULATION:
904.5 million

LARGEST CITY WITH POPULATION:
Cairo, Egypt 15.6 million

COUNTRY WITH HIGHEST POPULATION DENSITY:
Mauritius 1671 people per sq mile
(645 people per sq km)

LARGEST COUNTRY:
Sudan 967,493 sq miles
(2,505,810 sq km)

SMALLEST COUNTRY:
Seychelles 176 sq miles
(455 sq km)

POLITICAL FACTFILE

TOTAL AREA:
4,809,200 sq miles
(12,456,000 sq km)

TOTAL NUMBER OF COUNTRIES:
45

TOTAL POPULATION:
710.8 million

LARGEST CITY WITH POPULATION:
Moscow, European Russia 13.8 million

**COUNTRY WITH HIGHEST
POPULATION DENSITY:**
Monaco 43,212 people per sq mile
(16,620 people per sq km)

LARGEST COUNTRY:
European Russia 1,527,341 sq miles
(3,955,818 sq km)

SMALLEST COUNTRY:
Vatican City, Italy 0.17 sq miles
(0.44 sq km)

REYKJAVÍK **ICELAND**   Arctic Circle

*Norwegia
Sea*

Faeroe Islands
(Denmark)

Shetland Islands

*Outer
Hebrides*   *Orkney Islands*   **OSLO**

*British
Isles*   *North
Sea*

IRELAND   **DENMARK**

DUBLIN **UNITED
KINGDOM**   COPENHAGEN

AMSTERDAM

LONDON   **NETH.**   BERLIN

THE
HAGUE

Channel Is. **BELGIUM**   **GERMANY**
(UK)   BRUSSELS

LUXEMBOURG   PRA

LUXEMBOURG   *Rhine*   **CZECH REPU**

Bay of Biscay   **FRANCE**   LIECH. BRATIS

Loire   VIENN

SWITZERLAND   **AUSTR**

BERN SLOVE

ATLANTIC   **PORTUGAL**   LJUBLJANA

OCEAN   **MONACO**   ZAGRE

Duero   **ANDORRA** **SAN MARINO**   **CROATIA**

LISBON **MADRID**   *Corsica*   SARA
BOS
& H

*Madeira
(Portugal)*   **SPAIN**   **VATICAN CITY** **ITAL**

Guadalquivir   *Balearic Islands*   ROME

Gibraltar   *Sardinia*

*Canary Islands
(Spain)*   Ceuta
(Spain)   *Medeterrane*

Melilla
(Spain)   *Sicily*

Atlas Mountains   **AFRICA**   VALLETTA **MALTA**

NORWAY

FINLAND

Ural Mountains

Ob'

Irtysh

Northern Dvina

Lake Onega

HELSINKI

OCKHOLM

Lake Ladoga

TALLINN

ESTONIA

LATVIA

RIGA

LITHUANIA

ININGRAD
Russ.Fed.)

VILNIUS

MINSK

BELARUS

WARSAW

OLAND

KIEV

UKRAINE

OVAKIA

DAPEST

MOLDOVA

NGARY

CHIŞINĂU

ROMANIA

ELGRADE

BUCHAREST

RBIA

Danube

GORICA

SOFIA

BULGARIA

SKOPJE

ACED.

RANA

TURKEY

BANIA

GREECE

ATHENS

e ā

Crete

Cyprus

R U S S I A N

F E D E R A T I O N

MOSCOW

Volga

Ural

Aral Sea

Don

Dniester

Dnieper

C a u c a s u s

Caspian Sea

Black Sea

A S I A

Baltic Sea

0 km 1000

0 miles 1000

ARCTIC OCEAN

Franz Josef
Land

Severnaya
Zemlya

Kara Sea

Laptev Se

RUSSIAN FEDERATIC

Ob

Irtysh

Yenisey

EUROPE

Black Sea

Lake Baikal

ANKARA

GEORGIA

KAZAKHSTAN

ASTANA

ULAN BATOR

TURKEY

TBILISI

CYPRUS

ARMENIA

Aral Sea

Lake Balkhash

MONGOLIA

NICOSIA

YEREVAN

AZERBAIJAN

UZBEKISTAN

BISHKEK

BEIRUT

SYRIA

BAKU

LEBANON

DAMASCUS

TURKMENISTAN

KYRGYZSTAN

JERUSALEM

AMMAN

ASGABAT

TASHKENT

ISRAEL

JORDAN

Tehrān

DUSHANBE

TAJIKISTAN

C H I N

BAGHDAD

KABUL

IRAQ

IRAN

ISLAMABAD

KUWAIT

AFGHANISTAN

KUWAIT

BAHRAIN

MANAMA

PAKISTAN

NEW

NEPAL

JEDDA

RIYADH

QATAR

DELHI

THIMPHU

BHUTAN

Red Sea

DOHA

U.A.E.

ABU DHABI

KATHMANDU

Indus

Ganges

BANGLADESH

SAUDI
ARABIA

MUSCAT

DHAKA

VIET

MYANMAR

HAN

AFRICA

SANA

OMAN

I N D I A

(BURMA)

PYINMANA

LA

YEMEN

Socotra
(Yemen)

Arabian
Sea

VIENT

RANGOON

THAILA

Bay of
Bengal

BANGKOK

CAMBO

Tropic of Cancer

Laccadive
Islands
(India)

Andaman &
Nicobar Islands
(India)

MALE'

COLOMBO

MALDIVES

SRI
LANKA

MA

KUALA LUMPUR

PUTRAJAYA

SINGAPOR

I

Equator

INDIAN OCEAN

JAK

40°

20°

60°

80°

100°

20°

0°

20°

40°

POLITICAL FACTFILE

TOTAL AREA:
16,838,365 sq miles
(43,608,000 sq km)

TOTAL NUMBER OF COUNTRIES:
49

TOTAL POPULATION:
3933.7 million

LARGEST CITY WITH POPULATION:
Tokyo, Japan 34.2 million

COUNTRY WITH HIGHEST POPULATION DENSITY:
Singapore 18,220 people per sq mile
(7049 people per sq km)

LARGEST COUNTRY:
Asiatic Russia 5,065,394 sq miles
(13,119,382 sq km)

SMALLEST COUNTRY:
Maldives 116 sq miles
(300 sq km)

Aleutian Islands

60°
160°
40°

180°

Sea Of
Okhotsk

Kurile Islands

160°

Tropic of Cancer

20°

180°

160°

140°

**NORTH
KOREA**
PYONGYANG
SEOUL
**SOUTH
KOREA**

JAPAN
TOKYO

Ryukyu Islands

TAIPEI

TAIWAN

PACIFIC

OCEAN

MANILA

PHILIPPINES

**BANDAR
SERI BEGAWAN**
NEI

Equator

0 km   1000

0 miles   1000

ONESIA

AUSTRALASIA
& OCEANIA

Pante Maksar
(E.Timor)

DILI
EAST TIMOR

120°

160°

20°

180°

160°

140°

Australasia & Oceania

Philippine Sea

Wake Island
(to US)

Northern
Mariana
Islands
(US)

Micronesia

HAGÅTÑA
Guam
(US)

**MARSHALL
ISLANDS**

MAJUR

Caroline Islands

PALIKIR

KOROR
Babeldaob

MICRONESIA

PALAU

Melanesia

NAURU

NAURU

BAIR

KIRIBA

**PAPUA NEW
GUINEA**

TUVA

FONGAF

Equator

A S I A

**SOLOMON
ISLANDS**

PORT MORESBY

HONIARA

VANUATU

PORT VILA

Coral Sea
Islands
(Australia)

New Caledonia
(France)

NOUMÉA

Ashmore &
Cartier Islands
(Australia)

*INDIAN
OCEAN*

Great Dividing Range

AUSTRALIA

Lake Eyre North

Darling

Lake Torrens

Lake Gairdner

Norfolk Island
(Australia)

Lord Howe
Island
(Australia)

**NEW
ZEALAND**

Tropic of Capricorn

Murray

CANBERRA

WELLINGTON

*Tasman
Sea*

Tasmania

Auckland Islands
(New Zealand)

Australasia & Oceania

POLITICAL FACTFILE

TOTAL AREA:
3,376,700 sq miles (8,745,750 sq km)

TOTAL NUMBER OF COUNTRIES:
14

TOTAL POPULATION:
32.2 million

LARGEST CITY WITH POPULATION:
Sydney, Australia 4.4 million

COUNTRY WITH HIGHEST POPULATION DENSITY:
Nauru 1611 people per sq mile (621 people per sq km)

LARGEST COUNTRY:
Australia 2,967,893 sq miles (7,686,860 sq km)

SMALLEST COUNTRY:
Nauru 8.1 sq miles (21 sq km)

Johnston Atoll
(US)

aker & Howland Islands
(US)

Jarvis Island
(US)

KIRIBATI

Phoenix Islands

KIRIBATI

PACIFIC

OCEAN

Equator

Tokelau
(NZ)

lis &
na

SAMOA American Samoa
(US)

Cook Islands
(NZ)

Marquesas Islands

Á'UTU APIA

PAGO PAGO

TONGA

Niue
(NZ)

PAPEETE

Society Islands

NUKU' ALOFA

AVARUA

French Polynesia
(France)

Iles Australes

Pitcairn
Islands
(UK)

Tropic of Capricorn

International Dateline

ermadec Islands
(New Zealand)

Chatham Islands
(New Zealand)

0 km   1000

0 miles   1000

Key to factfile maps

FOREWORD

THIS FACTFILE is intended as a guide to a world that is continually changing as political fashions and personalities come and go. Nevertheless, all the material in these factfiles has been researched from the most up-to-date and authoritative sources to give an incisive portrait of the geographical, social, and economic characteristics that make each country unique.

KEY TO MAP SYMBOLS

ELEVATION

4000m / 13,124ft
3000m / 9843ft
2000m / 6562ft
1000m / 3281ft
500m / 1640ft
200m / 656ft
0
Below sea level

BORDERS

—————— Full international

– – – – – Disputed *de facto*

············· Territorial claim

✶✶✶✶✶✶✶ Cease-fire line

—————— State / Province

DRAINAGE FEATURES

—————— River

—————— Seasonal river

·············· Canal

⬭ Lake

⬭ Seasonal lake

SYMBOLS

● Capital city

○ Major town

✈ International airport

▲ Mountain

The asterisk in the Factfile denotes the country's official language(s)

Date of formation denotes the date of political origin or independence; the second date (if any) identifies when its current borders were establishe

The area figure denotes total land area

Afghanistan

Landlocked in southwestern Asia, about 75% of Afghanistan is inaccessible. The strict Islamist regime imposed by the *taliban* was swept aside with the help of the US in 2001.

GEOGRAPHY
Predominantly mountainous. Highest range is the Hindu Kush. Mountains are bordered by fertile plains. Desert plateau in the south.

CLIMATE
Harsh continental. Hot, dry summers. Cold winters with heavy snow, especially in the Hindu Kush.

PEOPLE & SOCIETY
Mujahideen factions fought first against Soviet invaders (from 1979), and then against each other (after 1989), before the *taliban* won control in 1996. Under their strict Islamist regime women were denied all rights and ethnic tensions were exacerbated. The US assisted anti-*taliban* forces in 2001 as part of its "war on terrorism." A new democratic government struggles to maintain control over the war-ravaged country.

THE ECONOMY
Economy has collapsed: infrastructure destroyed. Illicit opium trade is the main earner. Hopes from oil pipelines crossing Afghan territory.

◆ **INSIGHT:** *The UN estimates that it could take 100 years to remove the ten million landmines laid in the country*

FACTFILE

OFFICIAL NAME: Islamic State of Afghanistan
DATE OF FORMATION: 1919
CAPITAL: Kabul
POPULATION: 29.9 million
TOTAL AREA: 250,000 sq. miles (647,500 sq. km)

DENSITY: 119 people per sq. mile
LANGUAGES: Pashtu*, Dari*, Tajik, other
RELIGIONS: Sunni Muslim 84%, Shi'a Muslim 15%, other 1%
ETHNIC MIX: Pashtun 38%, Tajik 25%, Hazara 19%, Uzbek, Turkmen, other 18%
GOVERNMENT: Presidential system
CURRENCY: New afghani = 100 puls

Albania

Lying at the southeastern end of the Adriatic Sea, Albania was the last east European country to liberalize its economy. The regional wars of the 1990s have left a difficult legacy.

GEOGRAPHY
Narrow coastal plain. Interior is mostly hills and mountains. Forest and scrub cover over 40% of the land.

CLIMATE
Mediterranean coastal climate, with warm summers and cool winters. Mountains receive heavy rains or snows in winter.

PEOPLE & SOCIETY
The pace of economic reform remains a major issue, particularly as the country steers toward European integration. Mosques and churches have reopened in what was once the world's only officially atheist state. Greek minority in the south suffers much discrimination.

◆ **INSIGHT:** *The Albanians' name for their country, Shqipërisë, means "Land of the Eagles"*

THE ECONOMY
Oil and gas reserves plus steady growth have potential to offset rudimentary infrastructure and lack of foreign investment.

2000m/6562ft
1000m/3281ft
500m/1640ft
200m/656ft
Sea Level

0   50 km
0   50 miles

FACTFILE
OFFICIAL NAME: Republic of Albania
DATE OF FORMATION: 1912
CAPITAL: Tirana
POPULATION: 3.1 million
TOTAL AREA: 11,100 sq. miles (28,748 sq. km)
DENSITY: 293 people per sq. mile

LANGUAGES: Albanian*, Greek
RELIGIONS: Sunni Muslim 70%, Orthodox Christian 20%, Roman Catholic 10%
ETHNIC MIX: Albanian 93%, Greek 5%, other 2%
GOVERNMENT: Parliamentary system
CURRENCY: Lek = 100 qindarka (qintars)

Algeria

Africa's second-largest country, Algeria won independence from France in 1962. Today, national reconciliation is key to recovery from a bloody conflict launched by Islamic extremists in 1992.

GEOGRAPHY
85% of the country lies within the Sahara Desert. Fertile coastal region with plains and hills rises from the southeast to the Atlas Mountains.

CLIMATE
Coastal areas are warm and temperate, with most rainfall during the mild winters. The south is very hot, with negligible rainfall.

PEOPLE & SOCIETY

Algerians are predominantly Arab, under 30 years of age, and urban. Most indigenous Berbers consider the mountainous Kabylia region in the northeast to be their homeland. They have been granted greater ethnic rights in recent years. The Sahara sustains just 500,000 people, mainly oil workers and Tuareg nomads with goat and camel herds, who move between the irrigated oases.

THE ECONOMY
Oil and gas exports. Political turmoil has led to exodus of skilled foreign labor. Limited agriculture.

INSIGHT: *The world's highest dunes are located in the deserts of east central Algeria*

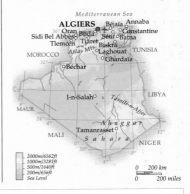

FACTFILE
OFFICIAL NAME: People's Democratic Republic of Algeria
DATE OF FORMATION: 1962
CAPITAL: Algiers
POPULATION: 32.9 million
TOTAL AREA: 919,590 sq. miles (2,381,740 sq. km)

DENSITY: 36 people per sq. mile
LANGUAGES: Arabic*, Tamazight, French
RELIGIONS: Sunni Muslim 99%, Christian and Jewish 1%
ETHNIC MIX: Arab 75%, Berber 24%, European and Jewish 1%
GOVERNMENT: Presidential system
CURRENCY: Algerian dinar = 100 centimes

Andorra

A tiny landlocked principality, Andorra lies high in the eastern Pyrenees between France and Spain. It held its first full elections in 1993. Tourism is the main source of income.

 GEOGRAPHY
High mountains, with six deep, glaciated valleys that drain into the Valira River as it flows into Spain.

 CLIMATE
Cool, wet springs followed by dry, warm summers. Mountain snows linger until March.

 PEOPLE & SOCIETY
Immigration is strictly monitored and restricted by quota to French and Spanish nationals seeking employment in Andorra. Low taxes attract wealthy expatriates. A referendum in 1993 ended 715 years of semifeudal status, but Andorran society remains conservative.

◆ **INSIGHT:** *Andorra's coprincipality status dates from the 13th century. The "princes" are the president of France and the bishop of Urgel in Spain.*

THE ECONOMY
Tourism and duty-free sales dominate the economy. Strict banking secrecy laws and low consumer taxes promote investment and commerce. France and Spain effectively decide economic policy. Dependence on imported food and raw materials.

FRANCE

P y r e n e e s

42°35'   Arinsal   Soldeu
          Ordino   Canillo
                  Encamp   Port
                            d'Envalira
          Escaldes
42°30' **ANDORRA LA VELLA**
        Sant Julià de Lòria   1°40'

                              1°35'
1°25'   1°30'   S P A I N

2000m/6562ft
1000m/3281ft   0   5 km
500m/1640ft   0   5 miles

FACTFILE

OFFICIAL NAME: Principality of Andorra
DATE OF FORMATION: 1278
CAPITAL: Andorra la Vella
POPULATION: 70,549
TOTAL AREA: 181 sq. miles (468 sq. km)
DENSITY: 392 people per sq. mile

LANGUAGES: Spanish, Catalan*, French, Portuguese
RELIGIONS: Roman Catholic 94%, other 6%
ETHNIC MIX: Spanish 46%, Andorran 28%, other 18%, French 8%
GOVERNMENT: Parliamentary system
CURRENCY: Euro = 100 cents

Angola

Located in southwest Africa, Angola suffered almost constant civil war following independence from Portugal in 1975. A 2002 peace deal ended the conflict, but elections are yet to be held.

 GEOGRAPHY
Most of the land is hilly and grass-covered. Desert in the south. Mountains in the center and north.

 CLIMATE
Varies from temperate to tropical. Rainfall decreases north to south. Coast is cooler and dry.

 PEOPLE & SOCIETY
Civil war was fought between UNITA, representing the Ovimbundu, and the ruling Kimbundu-dominated MPLA. Free and fair elections in 1991–1992, after the MPLA had abandoned Marxism, failed to stall the war for long. Hundreds of thousands of people died. A peace deal in 2002 saw UNITA join the government.

◆ **INSIGHT:** *Angola has the greatest number of amputees (caused by landmines) in the world*

THE ECONOMY
Potentially one of Africa's richest countries, but civil war has hampered economic development. Oil and diamonds are exported.

FACTFILE

OFFICIAL NAME: Republic of Angola
DATE OF FORMATION: 1975
CAPITAL: Luanda
POPULATION: 15.9 million
TOTAL AREA: 481,351 sq. miles (1,246,700 sq. km)
DENSITY: 33 people per sq. mile

LANGUAGES: Portuguese*, Umbundu, Kimbundu, Kikongo
RELIGIONS: Roman Catholic 50%, other 30%, Protestant 20%
ETHNIC MIX: Ovimbundu 37%, other 25%, Kimbundu 25%, Bakongo 13%
GOVERNMENT: Presidential system
CURRENCY: Readjusted kwanza = 100 lwei

Antarctica

The circumpolar continent of Antarctica is almost entirely covered by ice, some up to 1.2 miles (2 km) thick. It also contains 90% of the Earth's freshwater reserves.

GEOGRAPHY
The bulk of Antarctica's ice is contained in the Greater Antarctic Ice Sheet – a huge dome that rises steeply from the coast and flattens to a plateau in the interior.

CLIMATE
Powerful winds create a storm belt around the continent, which brings cloud, fog, and blizzards. Winter temperatures can fall to –112°F (–80°C).

PEOPLE & SOCIETY
No indigenous population. Scientists and logistical staff work at the 40 permanent, and as many as 100 temporary, research stations. A few Chilean settler families live on King George Island. Tourism is mostly by cruise ship to the Antarctic Peninsula. Annual tourist numbers had reached 27,000 by 2005.

Territorial Claims:

Chilean claim
Argentinian claim
Brazilian zone of interest
British claim
Norwegian undefined limit

Australian claim

French claim
New Zealand claim

The Antarctic Treaty of 1959 holds all territorial claims in abeyance in the interest of international cooperation

South Orkney Is.
South Shetland Is.
King George I.
Antarctic Peninsula
Weddell Sea
Ronne Ice Shelf
Ellsworth Land
Lesser Antarctica
Amundsen Sea
Ross Ice Shelf
Ross Sea
Balleny Is.

Antarctic Circle

Queen Maud Land

Enderby Land

Greater Antarctica

South Pole

Transantarctic Mts.

Victoria Land

Wilkes Land

South Magnetic Pole

SOUTHERN OCEAN

SOUTHERN OCEAN

SOUTHERN OCEAN

Ice Cap
Permanent Ice

FACTFILE

DATE OF FORMATION: 1961
TOTAL AREA: 5,405,000 sq. miles (14,000,000 sq. km)

INSIGHT: *If the ice sheets of Antarctica were to melt, the world's oceans would rise by as much as 200–210 ft (60–65 m)*

Antigua & Barbuda

A former colony of Spain, France, and the UK, Antigua and Barbuda lies at the outer edge of the Leeward Islands group in the Caribbean, and includes the uninhabited islet of Redonda.

GEOGRAPHY
Mainly low-lying limestone and coral islands with some higher volcanic areas. Antigua's coast is indented with bays and harbors.

CLIMATE
Tropical, moderated by trade winds and sea breezes. Humidity and rainfall are low for the region.

PEOPLE & SOCIETY
Population almost entirely of African origin, with small communities of Europeans and South Asians. Women's status has risen as a result of greater access to education. Wealth disparities are small. The Bird family dominated politics from 1960, but lost power to the UPP at the 2004 election.

◆ INSIGHT: *In 1865, Redonda was "claimed" by an eccentric Englishman as a kingdom for his son*

THE ECONOMY
Tourism is the main source of revenue and the biggest provider of jobs. Financial services and Internet gambling are expanding. High debt.

FACTFILE

OFFICIAL NAME: Antigua and Barbuda

DATE OF FORMATION: 1981

CAPITAL: St. John's

POPULATION: 68,722

TOTAL AREA: 170 sq. miles (442 sq. km)

DENSITY: 404 people per sq. mile

LANGUAGES: English*, English patois

RELIGIONS: Anglican 45%, other Protestant 42%, Roman Catholic 10%, other 2%, Rastafarian 1%

ETHNIC MIX: Black African 95%, other 5%

GOVERNMENT: Parliamentary system

CURRENCY: E. Caribbean $ = 100 cents

Argentina

Argentina occupies most of the southern portion of South America. After 30 years of intermittent military rule, multiparty democracy returned in 1983. The economy collapsed in 2001.

GEOGRAPHY
The Andes form a natural border with Chile in the west. East are the heavily wooded plains (Gran Chaco) and treeless but fertile Pampas plains. Bleak and arid Patagonia in the south.

CLIMATE
The Andes are semiarid in the north and snowy in the south. Pampas have a mild climate with summer rains.

PEOPLE & SOCIETY
People are largely of European descent; over one-third are of Italian origin. Indigenous peoples are now in a minority, living mainly in Andean regions or in the Gran Chaco. The middle classes were worst hit by the economic meltdown of 2001–2002.

INSIGHT: *The Tango originated in the poorer quarters of Buenos Aires at the end of the 19th century*

THE ECONOMY
The 2001 crisis saw the world's largest default on debt. Agricultural exports have led a rapid revival.

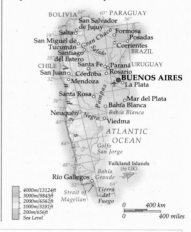

4000m/13124ft	
3000m/9843ft	
2000m/6562ft	
1000m/3281ft	
200m/656ft	
Sea Level	

0   400 km
0   400 miles

FACTFILE
OFFICIAL NAME: Republic of Argentina
DATE OF FORMATION: 1816
CAPITAL: Buenos Aires
POPULATION: 38.7 million
TOTAL AREA: 1,068,296 sq. miles (2,766,890 sq. km)
DENSITY: 37 people per sq. mile

LANGUAGES: Spanish*, Italian, Amerindian languages
RELIGIONS: Roman Catholic 90%, other 6%, Protestant 2%, Jewish 2%
ETHNIC MIX: Indo-European 83%, Mestizo 14%, Jewish 2%, Amerindian 1%
GOVERNMENT: Presidential system
CURRENCY: Argentine peso = 100 centavos

Armenia

The smallest of the former USSR's republics, Armenia lies landlocked in the Lesser Caucasus Mountains. Since 1988, the confrontation with Azerbaijan has dominated national life.

 GEOGRAPHY
Rugged and mountainous, with expanses of semidesert and a large lake in the east: Sevana Lich.

 CLIMATE
Continental climate, with little rainfall in the lowlands. The winters are often bitterly cold.

 PEOPLE & SOCIETY
Christianity is the dominant religion, but minority groups are well integrated. War with Azerbaijan over the enclave of Nagorno Karabakh forced 350,000 Armenians living in Azerbaijan to return home, many to live in poverty. There are close and important ties to the five-million-strong Armenian diaspora.

◆ **INSIGHT:** *In the 4th century, Armenia became the first country to adopt Christianity as its state religion*

THE ECONOMY
Few natural resources. Agriculture accounts for over 25% of GDP. Main products are wine, tobacco, potatoes, and fruit. Well-developed machine-building and manufacturing – includes textiles and bottling of mineral water.

FACTFILE

OFFICIAL NAME: Republic of Armenia
DATE OF FORMATION: 1991
CAPITAL: Yerevan
POPULATION: 3 million
TOTAL AREA: 11,506 sq. miles (29,800 sq. km)
DENSITY: 261 people per sq. mile

LANGUAGES: Armenian*, Azeri, Russian
RELIGIONS: Armenian Apostolic Church (Orthodox) 88%, Armenian Catholic Church 6%, other 6%
ETHNIC MIX: Armenian 98%, Yezidi 1%, other 1%
GOVERNMENT: Presidential system
CURRENCY: Dram = 100 luma

Australia

An island continent in its own right, Australia is the world's sixth-largest country. European settlement began over 200 years ago. Most Australians now live in cities along the coast.

GEOGRAPHY

Located between the Indian and Pacific Oceans, Australia has a variety of landscapes including tropical rainforests, the arid plateaus, ridges, and vast deserts of the "red center," the lowlands and river systems draining into Lake Eyre, rolling tracts of pastoral land, and magnificent beaches around much of the coastline. In the far east are the mountains of the Great Dividing Range. Famous natural features include Uluru (Ayers Rock) and the Great Barrier Reef.

CLIMATE

The west and south are semi-arid with hot summers. The arid interior can reach 120°F (50°C) in the central desert areas. The north is hot throughout the year, and humid during the summer monsoon. East, southeast, and southwest coastal areas are temperate.

PEOPLE & SOCIETY

The first settlers arrived in Australia at least 100,000 years ago. Today, the Aborigines make up around 2% of the population. European colonization began in 1788, and was dominated by British and Irish immigrants, some of whom were convicts. White-only immigration drives brought many Europeans to Australia, but since the 1960s multi-culturalism has been encouraged and most new settlers are Asian; Cantonese is now the third most widely spoken language after English and Italian. Wealth disparities are small, but Aborigines, the exception in an otherwise integrated society, are marginalized: their average life expectancy is around 17 years less than other Australians. Politics is increasingly right-wing and illegal immigration is a major concern. Obesity is a growing problem among adults.

FACTFILE

OFFICIAL NAME: Commonwealth of Australia

DATE OF FORMATION: 1901

CAPITAL: Canberra

POPULATION: 20.2 million

TOTAL AREA: 2,967,893 sq. miles (7,686,850 sq. km)

DENSITY: 7 people per sq. mile

LANGUAGES: English*, Italian, other

RELIGIONS: Various Protestant 38%, other 36%, Roman Catholic 26%

ETHNIC MIX: European 92%, Asian 5%, Aboriginal 2%, other 1%

GOVERNMENT: Parliamentary system

CURRENCY: Australian dollar = 100 cents

Australia

$ THE ECONOMY

Efficient mining and agricultural industries: particular success in viticulture. Large resource base. Tourism growing. Concentration on Asian markets; hit hard by the 1997 financial crisis which tipped the region into recession. Regional competition is intense. Protectionism abandoned to open up Australian markets. Japan remains the most important trading partner, though China's expanding market for minerals has spurred strong economic growth.

◆ INSIGHT: *Sydney has the world's largest suburban area, a conurbation so vast that the city is twice as large as Beijing and six times the size of Rome*

Arafura Sea

Bamaga ○ Cape York

Timor Sea

Darwin ○

P A C I F I C

O C E A N

Arnhem Land

Gulf of Carpentaria

Great Barrier Reef

I N D I A N

O C E A N

Kimberley Plateau

N O R T H E R N

T E R R I T O R Y

Cairns ○

Coral Sea

Port Hedland ○

Great Sandy Desert

Lake Mackay

Townsville ○

Hamersley Range

Lake Disappointment

Gibson Desert

Macdonnell Ranges Alice Springs ○

Mount Isa ○

Mackay ○

Carnarvon ○

Uluru △ (Ayers Rock) (867m)

Simpson Desert

Q U E E N S L A N D

Rockhampton ○

Bundaberg ○

Meekatharra ○

Lake Carnegie

Great Victoria Desert

Lake Eyre

S O U T H

Fraser I.

Gympie ○

Toowoomba ○ Brisbane ○

Geraldton ○

A U S T R A L I A

Ipswich ○ Gold Coast Surfers Paradise

Kalgoorlie ○

Nullarbor Plain

Flinders Ranges

A U S T R A L I A

Darling

Grafton ○

Perth ○ *Darling Range*

Port Augusta ○

Broken Hill ○

N E W S O U T H

Coffs Harbour ○

Fremantle ○ Rockingham ○ Bunbury ○ Cape Leeuwin

Whyalla ○

Port Pirie ○

W A L E S

Esperance ○

Port Lincoln ○

Elizabeth ○

Wagga Wagga ○

Newcastle ○

Albany ○

Adelaide ○

Albury ○

Sydney ○ Wollongong ○

Great Australian Bight

Kangaroo I.

Bendigo ○ Ballarat ○ ○ Geelong

Murray

● CANBERRA

AUSTRALIAN CAPITAL TERRITORY *Australian Alps*

V I C T O R I A Melbourne ○

Tasman Sea

Burnie ○

Bass Strait

T A S M A N I A ○ Launceston

| 1000m/3281ft |
| 500m/1640ft |
| 200m/656ft |
| Sea Level |
| Below Sea Level |

0   400 km

0   400 miles

Hobart ○

South East Cape

Austria

Bordering eight countries in the heart of Europe, Austria was created in 1918 after the collapse of the Habsburg Empire. It joined the EU in 1995 and adopted the euro fully in 2002.

GEOGRAPHY
Mainly mountainous. Alps and foothills cover the west and south. Lowlands in the east are part of the Danube River basin.

CLIMATE
Temperate continental climate. The western Alpine regions have colder winters and more rainfall.

PEOPLE & SOCIETY
Austrian society is homogeneous. Though Austrians speak German, they like to stress their distinctive identity in relation to Germany. Minorities are few; there are some ethnic Croats, Slovenes, and Hungarians, plus refugees from conflict in former Yugoslavia. Though strongly Roman Catholic, Austrian society is less conservative than some southern German *Länder*. Class divisions remain strong.

THE ECONOMY
Large manufacturing base, despite lack of energy resources. The skilled labor force is key to the production of high-tech exports. Euro has boosted investment.

◆ **INSIGHT:** *Many of the world's great composers were Austrian, including Mozart, Haydn, Schubert, and Strauss*

FACTFILE

OFFICIAL NAME: Republic of Austria
DATE OF FORMATION: 1918
CAPITAL: Vienna
POPULATION: 8.2 million
TOTAL AREA: 32,378 sq. miles (83,858 sq. km)
DENSITY: 257 people per sq. mile

LANGUAGES: German*, Croatian, Slovenian, Hungarian
RELIGIONS: Roman Catholic 78%, nonreligious 9%, other 8%, Protestant 5%
ETHNIC MIX: Austrian 93%, Croat, Slovene, and Hungarian 6%, other 1%
GOVERNMENT: Parliamentary system
CURRENCY: Euro = 100 cents

Azerbaijan

 Situated on the western coast of the Caspian Sea, Azerbaijan was the first Soviet republic to declare independence in 1991. Territorial disputes with Armenia have dominated politics since.

GEOGRAPHY

Caucasus Mountains in west, including Naxçivan exclave south of Armenia. Flat, low-lying terrain on the coast of the Caspian Sea.

CLIMATE
Low rainfall. Continental, with bitter winters, inland. Subtropical in coastal regions.

PEOPLE & SOCIETY
Azeris, a Muslim people with ethnic links to Turks, form a large majority. Thousands of Armenians, Russians, and Jews have left since independence. Influx of half a million Azeri refugees fleeing war with Armenia over the disputed enclave of Nagorno Karabakh. Armenians there operate de facto independence. The status of women deteriorated after the fall of communism but they are slowly regaining their position.

THE ECONOMY
Extensive oil and gas reserves have come on stream. Legacy of war still drains state resources. Industry antiquated; infrastructure poor.

INSIGHT: *The fire-worshipping Zoroastrian faith originated in Azerbaijan in the 6th century BCE*

FACTFILE

OFFICIAL NAME: Republic of Azerbaijan
DATE OF FORMATION: 1991
CAPITAL: Baku
POPULATION: 8.4 million
TOTAL AREA: 33,436 sq. miles (86,600 sq. km)
DENSITY: 251 people per sq. mile

LANGUAGES: Azeri*, Russian
RELIGIONS: Shi'a Muslim 68%, Sunni Muslim 26%, Russian Orthodox 3%, Armenian Orthodox 2%, other 1%
ETHNIC MIX: Azeri 91%, other 3%, Lazs 2%, Russian 2%, Armenian 2%
GOVERNMENT: Presidential system
CURRENCY: Manat = 100 gopik

Bahamas

 Located off the Florida coast in the western Atlantic, the Bahamas comprises an archipelago of some 700 islands and 2400 cays, only around 30 of which are inhabited.

GEOGRAPHY

Long, mainly flat coral formations with a few low hills. Some islands have pine forests, lagoons, and mangrove swamps.

CLIMATE

Subtropical. Hot summers and mild winters. Heavy rainfall, especially in summer. Hurricanes can strike in July–December.

PEOPLE & SOCIETY
Over 60% of the population live on New Providence. Tourism employs over 30% of the labor force. The remainder are engaged in traditional fishing and agriculture, or in administration. Haitian and Cuban immigrants form the poorest group in society. More women are now entering the professions. Government priorities are tackling narcotics trafficking and money laundering.

THE ECONOMY

Major tourist destination, especially for US visitors. Financial services: banking and insurance.

◆ **INSIGHT:** *Only a tiny fraction of the country's extensive merchant fleet is owned by Bahamians*

FACTFILE

OFFICIAL NAME: Commonwealth of the Bahamas
DATE OF FORMATION: 1973
CAPITAL: Nassau
POPULATION: 323,000
TOTAL AREA: 5382 sq. miles (13,940 sq. km)

DENSITY: 84 people per sq. mile
LANGUAGES: English*, English Creole, French Creole
RELIGIONS: Baptist 32%, other 29%, Anglican 20%, Roman Catholic 19%
ETHNIC MIX: Black African 85%, other 15%
GOVERNMENT: Parliamentary system
CURRENCY: Bahamian dollar = 100 cents

Bahrain

Bahrain is an archipelago of 49 islands between the Qatar peninsula and the Saudi Arabian mainland. Only three of the islands are inhabited. It was the first Gulf emirate to export oil.

GEOGRAPHY

All islands are low-lying. The largest, Bahrain Island, is mainly sandy plains and salt marshes.

CLIMATE

Summers are hot and humid. Winters are mild. Low rainfall.

PEOPLE & SOCIETY

The key social division is between the Shi'a majority and Sunni minority. Sunnis hold the best jobs in bureaucracy and business while Shi'as tend to do menial work. The al-Khalifa family has ruled since 1783, and only transformed Bahrain into a constitutional monarchy, with limited democracy, in 2002. Bahrain is socially liberal.

INSIGHT: *The 16 Hawar Islands were awarded to Bahrain in 2001 after a lengthy dispute with Qatar*

THE ECONOMY

Main exports are refined petroleum and aluminum products. As oil reserves run out, gas is of increasing importance. Regional offshore banking center. Government debts are high.

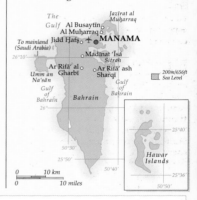

FACTFILE

OFFICIAL NAME: Kingdom of Bahrain
DATE OF FORMATION: 1971
CAPITAL: Manama
POPULATION: 727,000
TOTAL AREA: 239 sq. miles (620 sq. km)
DENSITY: 2663 people per sq. mile

LANGUAGES: Arabic
RELIGIONS: Muslim (mainly Shi'a) 99%, other 1%
ETHNIC MIX: Bahraini 70%, Iranian, Indian, and Pakistani 24%, other Arab 4%, European 2%
GOVERNMENT: Monarchy
CURRENCY: Bahraini dinar = 1000 fils

Bangladesh

Bangladesh lies at the north end of the Bay of Bengal. It seceded from Pakistan in 1971 and, after much political instability, returned to democracy in 1991.

GEOGRAPHY

Mostly flat alluvial plains and deltas of the Brahmaputra and Ganges Rivers. Southeast coasts are fringed with mangrove forests.

CLIMATE

Hot and humid. During the monsoon, water levels can rise 20 ft (6 m) above sea level.

PEOPLE & SOCIETY

Bangladesh often suffers devastating floods, cyclones, and famine. Democracy was restored in 1991 after a period of military rule. Half of the population live in poverty, but living standards are improving. Women are prominent in politics, but their rights are neglected.

INSIGHT: *Torrential monsoon rains flood two-thirds of the country every year*

THE ECONOMY

Agriculture is vulnerable to unpredictable climate. Bangladesh accounts for 90% of world jute fiber exports. Poor infrastructure deters investment. Growing textile industry.

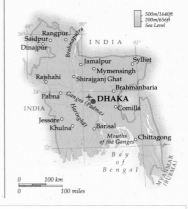

FACTFILE

OFFICIAL NAME: People's Republic of Bangladesh
DATE OF FORMATION: 1971
CAPITAL: Dhaka
POPULATION: 142 million
TOTAL AREA: 55,598 sq. miles (144,000 sq. km)

DENSITY: 2743 people per sq. mile
LANGUAGES: Bengali*, Urdu, Chakma, Marma, Garo, Khasi, Santhali, Tripuri, Mro
RELIGIONS: Muslim (mainly Sunni) 87%, Hindu 12%, other 1%
ETHNIC MIX: Bengali 98%, other 2%
GOVERNMENT: Parliamentary system
CURRENCY: Taka = 100 poisha

Barbados

Barbados is the most easterly of the Caribbean islands. Once solely inhabited by the native Arawak, Barbados was first colonized by British settlers in the 1620s.

GEOGRAPHY
Encircled by coral reefs. Fertile and predominantly flat, with a few gentle hills to the north.

CLIMATE
Moderate tropical climate. Sunnier and drier than its more mountainous neighbors.

PEOPLE & SOCIETY
Some latent tension between white community, which controls politics and much of the economy, and majority black population, but violence is rare. Increasing social mobility has enabled black Barbadians to enter the professions. Despite political stability, and good welfare and education services, pockets of abject poverty remain.

◆ **INSIGHT:** *Barbados retains a strong British influence and is referred to by its neighbors as "Little England"*

THE ECONOMY
Well-developed tourist industry based on climate and accessibility. Financial services and information processing are important new growth sectors. Sugar industry, once the main cash crop, now ailing.

FACTFILE
OFFICIAL NAME: Barbados
DATE OF FORMATION: 1966
CAPITAL: Bridgetown
POPULATION: 270,000
TOTAL AREA: 166 sq. miles (430 sq. km)
DENSITY: 1627 people per sq. mile

LANGUAGES: Bajan (Barbadian English), English*
RELIGIONS: Anglican 40%, other 24%, nonreligious 17%, Pentecostal 8%, Methodist 7%, Roman Catholic 4%
ETHNIC MIX: Black African 92%, other 8%
GOVERNMENT: Parliamentary system
CURRENCY: Barbados dollar = 100 cents

Belarus

Literally "White Russia," Belarus lies landlocked in eastern Europe. It reluctantly became independent of the USSR in 1991. There are few resources other than agriculture.

GEOGRAPHY

Mainly plains and low hills. The Dnieper and Dvina Rivers drain the eastern lowlands. Vast Pripet Marshes in the southwest.

CLIMATE

Extreme continental climate. Winters are long, sub-freezing, but mainly dry; summers are hot.

PEOPLE & SOCIETY

Only 2% of people are non-Slav, so ethnic tension is minimal. Russian culture dominates. Belarus was the slowest ex-Soviet state to implement political reform; President Lukashenka has been labeled as Europe's last dictator. Enthusiasm for a merger with Russia has waned. Wealth is held by a small ex-communist elite. Fallout from 1986 Chernobyl nuclear disaster in Ukraine still seriously affects health and the environment.

THE ECONOMY

Low unemployment but high inflation. Outmoded industry; dependence on Russia for energy and raw materials. Privatization stalled.

◆ **INSIGHT:** *The number of cancer and leukemia cases has soared since the 1986 Chernobyl disaster*

FACTFILE

OFFICIAL NAME: Republic of Belarus
DATE OF FORMATION: 1991
CAPITAL: Minsk
POPULATION: 9.8 million
TOTAL AREA: 80,154 sq. miles (207,600 sq. km)
DENSITY: 122 people per sq. mile

LANGUAGES: Belarussian*, Russian*
RELIGIONS: Orthodox Christian 60%, other (including Muslim, Jewish, and Protestant) 32%, Roman Catholic 8%
ETHNIC MIX: Belarussian 81%, Russian 11%, Polish 4%, Ukrainian 2%, other 2%
GOVERNMENT: Presidential system
CURRENCY: Belarussian rouble = 100 kopeks

Belgium

Belgium lies in northwestern Europe. Its history has been marked by tensions between the majority Dutch-speaking (Flemish) and minority French-speaking (Walloon) communities.

GEOGRAPHY
Low-lying coastal plain covers two-thirds of the country. Land becomes hilly and forested in the southeast (Ardennes) region.

CLIMATE
Maritime climate with Gulf Stream influences. Temperatures are mild, with heavy cloud cover and rain. More rainfall and weather fluctuations at the coast.

PEOPLE & SOCIETY
Since 1970, Flemish regions have become more prosperous than those of the minority Walloons, overturning traditional roles and increasing friction. In order to contain tensions, Belgium began to move toward federalism in 1980. Both groups now have their own governments and have control over most of their own affairs.

THE ECONOMY
Variety of industrial exports, including steel, glassware, cut diamonds, and textiles. Very high levels of public debt. Bureaucracy larger than European average.

◆ **INSIGHT:** *The Ardennes region, in the southeast of the country, is famous for its forests, cuisine, and lakes*

FACTFILE
OFFICIAL NAME: Kingdom of Belgium
DATE OF FORMATION: 1830
CAPITAL: Brussels
POPULATION: 10.4 million
TOTAL AREA: 11,780 sq. miles (30,510 sq. km)
DENSITY: 821 people per sq. mile

LANGUAGES: Dutch*, French*, German*
RELIGIONS: Roman Catholic 88%, other 10%, Muslim 2%
ETHNIC MIX: Fleming 58%, Walloon 33%, other 6%, Italian 2%, Moroccan 1%
GOVERNMENT: Parliamentary system
CURRENCY: Euro = 100 cents

Belize

Belize lies on the eastern shore of the Yucatan Peninsula. Formerly called British Honduras, Belize was the last Central American country to gain its independence, in 1981.

GEOGRAPHY
Almost half the land area is forested. Low mountains in south-east. Flat swampy coastal plains.

CLIMATE
Tropical. Very hot and humid, with May–December rainy season.

PEOPLE & SOCIETY
English-speaking black Creoles are outnumbered by Spanish speakers, including native *mestizos* and immigrants from neighboring states. The Creoles have traditionally dominated society, but high levels of emigration to the US have weakened their influence. Newcomers provide manpower for agriculture. The Afro-Carib *garifuna* have their own language.

◆ **INSIGHT:** *Belize's barrier reef is the second-largest in the world*

THE ECONOMY
Tourism, agriculture and offshore banking. Oil extraction began in 2005. Sugar, textiles, lobsters, and shrimp are exported. Serious hurricane damage is a recurring problem.

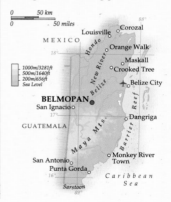

FACTFILE
OFFICIAL NAME: Belize
DATE OF FORMATION: 1981
CAPITAL: Belmopan
POPULATION: 270,000
TOTAL AREA: 8867 sq. miles (22,966 sq. km)
DENSITY: 31 people per sq. mile

LANGUAGES: English Creole, Spanish, English*, Mayan, Garifuna (Carib)
RELIGIONS: Roman Catholic 62%, other 20%, Anglican 12%, Methodist 6%
ETHNIC MIX: Mestizo 49%, Creole 25%, Maya 11%, other 9%, Garifuna 6%
GOVERNMENT: Parliamentary system
CURRENCY: Belizean dollar = 100 cents

Benin

Benin stretches north from the west African coast. In 1990, it became one of the pioneers of African democratization, ending 17 years of one-party Marxist-Leninist rule.

 GEOGRAPHY
Sandy coastal region. Numerous lagoons lie just behind the shoreline. Forested plateaus inland. Mountains in the northwest.

 CLIMATE
Hot and humid in the south. Two rainy seasons. Hot, dusty *harmattan* winds blow during the December–February dry season.

 PEOPLE & SOCIETY
There are 42 different ethnic groups. The southern Fon have tended to dominate politics. Other major groups are the Adja and Yoruba. The northern Fulani follow a nomadic lifestyle. North–south tension is mainly due to the south being more developed. French culture is highly prized in urban areas. Substantial differences in wealth reflect a strongly hierarchical society.

$ THE ECONOMY
Strong agricultural sector: cash crops include cotton, oil palm, and cashew nuts. Large-scale smuggling is a serious problem. France is the main aid donor.

◇ INSIGHT:
Voodoo is thought to have originated in Benin, and was taken to Haiti by slaves

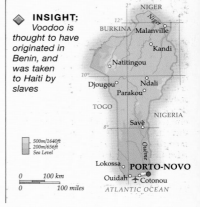

FACTFILE

OFFICIAL NAME: Republic of Benin
DATE OF FORMATION: 1960
CAPITAL: Porto-Novo
POPULATION: 8.4 million
TOTAL AREA: 43,483 sq. miles (112,620 sq. km)
DENSITY: 197 people per sq. mile

LANGUAGES: Fon, Bariba, Yoruba, Adja, Houeda, Somba, French*
RELIGIONS: Voodoo 50%, Muslim 30%, Christian 20%
ETHNIC MIX: Fon 41%, other 21%, Adja 16%, Yoruba 12%, Bariba 10%
GOVERNMENT: Presidential system
CURRENCY: CFA franc = 100 centimes

Bhutan

Perched in the eastern Himalayas between India and China lies the landlocked Kingdom of Bhutan. It is largely closed to the outside world to protect its culture; TV was banned until 1999.

GEOGRAPHY
Low, tropical southern strip rising through fertile central valleys to high Himalayas in the north. Around 70% of the land is forested.

CLIMATE

South is tropical, north is alpine, cold, and harsh. Central valleys warmer in east than west.

PEOPLE & SOCIETY

The king was absolute monarch until 1998, and legislative elections are to be held in 2008. Most people are devoutly Buddhist and originate from Tibet. A quarter are Hindu Nepalese, who settled in the south. Bhutan has 20 languages. In 1988, Dzongkha (a Tibetan dialect native to just 16% of the people) was made the official language. The Nepalese community regard this as "cultural imperialism," causing considerable ethnic tensions.

THE ECONOMY
Reliant on India for trade. Most people farm their own plots of land and herd cattle and yaks. Steep land unsuited for cultivation. Development of cash crops for Asian markets.

INSIGHT: *In 2004 Bhutan became the first country in the world to ban smoking and the sale of tobacco*

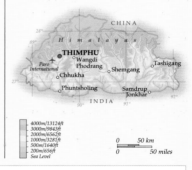

FACTFILE

OFFICIAL NAME: Kingdom of Bhutan
DATE OF FORMATION: 1656
CAPITAL: Thimphu
POPULATION: 2.2 million
TOTAL AREA: 18,147 sq. miles (47,000 sq. km)
DENSITY: 121 people per sq. mile

LANGUAGES: Dzongkha*, Nepali, Assamese
RELIGIONS: Mahayana Buddhist 70%, Hindu 24%, other 6%
ETHNIC MIX: Bhute 50%, other 25%, Nepalese 25%
GOVERNMENT: Monarchy
CURRENCY: Ngultrum = 100 chetrum

Bolivia

Landlocked high in central South America, Bolivia is one of the region's poorest countries. La Paz is the world's highest capital city: 13,385 feet (3631 m) above sea level.

GEOGRAPHY
A high windswept plateau, the *altiplano*, lies between two Andean mountain ranges. Semiarid grasslands to the east; dense tropical forests to the north.

CLIMATE
Altiplano has extreme tropical climate, with night-frost in winter. North and east are hot and humid.

PEOPLE & SOCIETY
The indigenous majority faces widespread discrimination. Wealthy Spanish-descended families have traditionally controlled the economy. Amerindian Evo Morales, president from 2005, has pledged to cut poverty, legalize coca, and redistribute land.

◆ **INSIGHT:** *Between 1825 and 1982 Bolivia averaged more than one armed coup a year*

THE ECONOMY
Gold, silver, zinc, tin, oil and natural gas are extracted. Social issues and nationalization of gas industry have deterred overseas investors. Lack of manufacturing: primary products vulnerable to world price fluctuations.

FACTFILE

OFFICIAL NAME: Republic of Bolivia
DATE OF FORMATION: 1825
CAPITALS: La Paz (administrative); Sucre (judicial)
POPULATION: 9.2 million
TOTAL AREA: 424,162 sq. miles (1,098,580 sq. km)

DENSITY: 22 people per sq. mile
LANGUAGES: Aymara*, Quechua*, Spanish*
RELIGIONS: Roman Catholic 93%, other 7%
ETHNIC MIX: Quechua 37%, Aymara 32%, mixed 13%, European 10%, other 8%
GOVERNMENT: Presidential system
CURRENCY: Boliviano = 100 centavos

Bosnia & Herzegovina

Perched in the highlands of southeast Europe, Bosnia and Herzegovina was the focus of the bitter ethnic conflict which accompanied the dissolution of the former Yugoslav state.

GEOGRAPHY
Hills and mountains, with narrow river valleys. Lowlands in the north. Mainly deciduous forest covers about half of the total area.

CLIMATE
Continental. Hot summers and cold, often snowy winters.

PEOPLE & SOCIETY
Despite sharing the same origin and spoken language, Bosnians have been divided by history between Orthodox Serbs, Roman Catholic Croats, and Muslim Bosniaks. Ethnic cleansing was practiced by all sides in the civil war displacing around 60% of the population. Refugees are still returning.

◆ **INSIGHT:** *The murder of Archduke Ferdinand of Austria in Sarajevo in 1914 triggered the First World War*

THE ECONOMY
Bosnia has the potential to recover its status as a thriving market economy with a strong manufacturing base, but still struggles with the legacy of war. Little investment.

FACTFILE

OFFICIAL NAME: Bosnia and Herzegovina
DATE OF FORMATION: 1992
CAPITAL: Sarajevo
POPULATION: 3.9 million
TOTAL AREA: 19,741 sq. miles (51,129 sq. km)

DENSITY: 198 people per sq. mile
LANGUAGES: Serbo-Croat
RELIGIONS: Muslim 40%, Orthodox Christian 31%, Catholic 15%, other 14%
ETHNIC MIX: Bosniak 44%, Serb 31%, Croat 17%, other 8%
GOVERNMENT: Parliamentary system
CURRENCY: Marka = 100 pfeninga

Botswana

Landlocked in the heart of southern Africa, Botswana boasts the world's largest inland river delta. Diamonds provide potential wealth, but the country is crippled by HIV/AIDS.

GEOGRAPHY

Lies on vast plateau, high above sea level. Hills in the east. Kalahari Desert in center and southwest. Swamps and salt pans elsewhere and in Okavango Basin.

CLIMATE

Dry and prone to drought. Summer wet season, April–October. Winters are warm, with cold nights.

PEOPLE & SOCIETY

Tswana make up 98% of the population. The San bushmen, the first inhabitants, are marginalized. They were ordered in 2002 to abandon their nomadic lifestyle. Botswana had the highest rate of HIV-positive adults in the world (38.8%) in 2001–2002.

◆ **INSIGHT:** *Water, Botswana's most precious resource, is honored in the name of the currency – pula*

THE ECONOMY

Diamonds are the leading export. Deposits of other minerals. Beef is exported to Europe. Tourism aimed at wealthy wildlife enthusiasts. AIDS is devastating the population.

FACTFILE

OFFICIAL NAME: Republic of Botswana
DATE OF FORMATION: 1966
CAPITAL: Gaborone
POPULATION: 1.8 million
TOTAL AREA: 231,803 sq. miles (600,370 sq. km)
DENSITY: 8 people per sq. mile

LANGUAGES: Setswana, English*, Shona, San, Khoikhoi, isiNdebele
RELIGIONS: Traditional beliefs 50%, Christian (mainly Protestant) 30%, other (including Muslim) 20%
ETHNIC MIX: Tswana 98%, other 2%
GOVERNMENT: Presidential system
CURRENCY: Pula = 100 thebe

Brazil

Covering almost half of South America, Brazil is the site of the world's largest and ecologically most important rainforest. The country has immense natural and economic resources.

GEOGRAPHY
Rainforest grows around the massive Amazon River and its delta, covering almost half of Brazil's total land area. Apart from the basin of the River Plate to the south, the rest of the country consists of highlands. The mountainous east is part-forested and part-desert. The coastal plain in the southeast has swampy areas. The Atlantic coastline is 1240 miles (2000 km) long.

CLIMATE
Brazil's share of the Amazon Basin, occupying half the country, has a model tropical equatorial climate. Temperatures are high with almost no seasonal variation. The Brazilian plateau has far greater ranges of temperature and rainfall. The east is very dry and suffers from frequent droughts. The south has hot summers and cool winters.

PEOPLE & SOCIETY
Diverse population includes Amerindians, blacks, European immigrants, and people of mixed race. Amerindians suffer prejudice from most other peoples in Brazil. Shanty towns in the cities attract poor migrants from the northeast. Urban crime, violent land disputes, and unchecked development in Amazonia tarnish Brazil's image as a modern nation. Catholicism and the family unit remain strong.

THE ECONOMY
Dominant regional economy. Huge potential for growth based on abundant natural resources. Brazil is a leading exporter of coffee, sugar, and orange juice. Social tension threatens stability. Debts are high.

Equator

COLOMBE

PERU

FACTFILE
OFFICIAL NAME: Federative Rep. of Brazil
DATE OF FORMATION: 1822
CAPITAL: Brasília
POPULATION: 186 million
TOTAL AREA: 3,286,470 sq. miles (8,511,965 sq. km)
DENSITY: 57 people per sq. mile

LANGUAGES: Portuguese*, German, Italian, Spanish, Polish, Japanese, other
RELIGIONS: Roman Catholic 74%, Protestant 15%, atheist 7%, other 4%
ETHNIC MIX: White 54%, mixed race 38%, Black 6 %, other 2%
GOVERNMENT: Presidential system
CURRENCY: Real = 100 centavos

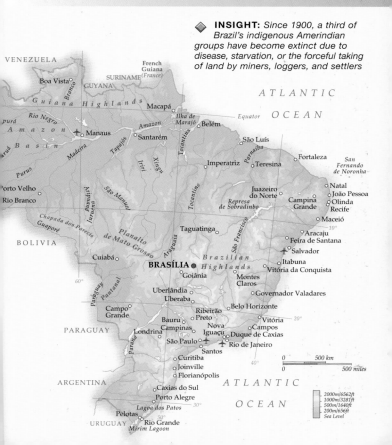

INSIGHT: *Since 1900, a third of Brazil's indigenous Amerindian groups have become extinct due to disease, starvation, or the forceful taking of land by miners, loggers, and settlers*

VENEZUELA

French Guiana *(France)*

SURINAME

Boa Vista

GUYANA

Guiana Highlands

Macapá

ATLANTIC

OCEAN

Rio Negro

Ilha de Marajó

Equator

purá

Amazon

Belém

Amazon Basin

Manaus

Santarém

São Luís

Madeira

Tapajós

Iriri

Xingu

Parnaíba

Fortaleza

San Fernando de Noronha

Purus

Imperatriz

Teresina

Porto Velho

Rio Branco

Juazeiro do Norte

Natal

João Pessoa

Olinda

Recife

Tocantins

Represa de Sobradinho

Campina Grande

Maceió

Chapada dos Parecis

Guaporé

Jurumena

São Manuel

Araguaia

Tocantins

Planalto de Mato Grosso

Taguatinga

São Francisco

Aracaju

Feira de Santana

–10°

BOLIVIA

Cuiabá

Brazilian Highlands

Salvador

Itabuna

Vitória da Conquista

Pantanal

BRASÍLIA

Goiânia

Montes Claros

Paraguay

60°

Uberlândia

Uberaba

Campo Grande

Ribeirão Preto

Belo Horizonte

Governador Valadares

Vitória

PARAGUAY

Paraná

Bauru

Campinas

Londrina

São Paulo

Nova Iguaçu

Duque de Caxias

Campos

20°

Rio de Janeiro

Santos

0   500 km

Curitiba

0   500 miles

Joinville

40°

Florianópolis

ATLANTIC

ARGENTINA

Caxias do Sul

Porto Alegre

OCEAN

Lagoa dos Patos

30°

2000m/6562ft

1000m/3281ft

500m/1640ft

200m/656ft

Sea Level

Pelotas

50°

URUGUAY

Rio Grande

Mirim Lagoon

Brunei

Lying on the northern coast of the island of Borneo, Brunei is surrounded and divided in two by the Malaysian state of Sarawak. It has been independent since 1984.

GEOGRAPHY
Mostly dense lowland rainforest and mangrove swamps, with some mountains in the southeast.

CLIMATE
Tropical. Six-month rainy season with very high humidity.

PEOPLE & SOCIETY
Malays benefit from positive discrimination. Many in the Chinese community are stateless. Since a failed rebellion in 1962, Brunei has been ruled by decree of the sultan. In 1990, "Malay Muslim Monarchy" was introduced, promoting Islamic values as state ideology. Women, less restricted than in some Muslim states, are obliged to wear headscarves but not the veil.

◆ INSIGHT: *The sultan spent US$450 million building the world's largest palace at Bandar Seri Begawan*

THE ECONOMY
Oil and natural gas reserves have brought one of the world's highest standards of living. Massive overseas investments. Major consumer of high-tech hi-fi, video equipment, and Western designer clothes.

FACTFILE
OFFICIAL NAME: Sultanate of Brunei
DATE OF FORMATION: 1984
CAPITAL: Bandar Seri Begawan
POPULATION: 374,000
TOTAL AREA: 2228 sq. miles (5770 sq. km)
DENSITY: 184 people per sq. mile

LANGUAGES: Malay*, English, Chinese
RELIGIONS: Muslim (mainly Sunni) 66%, Buddhist 14%, other 10%, Christian 10%
ETHNIC MIX: Malay 67%, Chinese 16%, other 11%, indigenous 6%
GOVERNMENT: Monarchy
CURRENCY: Brunei dollar = 100 cents

Bulgaria

Located in southeastern Europe, Bulgaria was under communist rule from 1947 to 1989. Since then, the country has made gradual progress with political and economic reform.

GEOGRAPHY
Mountains run east–west across center and along southern border. Danube plain in north, Thracian plain in southeast. Black Sea to the east.

CLIMATE
Warm summers and snowy winters, especially in mountains. East winds bring seasonal extremes.

PEOPLE & SOCIETY
The communists tried forcibly to suppress cultural identities, leading to a large exodus of Bulgarian Turks in 1989. Recent privatization programs have left many Turks landless and prompted further emigration. Roma suffer discrimination at all levels of society. Women have equal rights in theory, but society remains patriarchal. Organized crime, human trafficking, and corruption needed curbing as a precondition of EU accession in 2007.

THE ECONOMY
Good agricultural production, including grapes, for well-developed wine industry, and tobacco. Expertise in software development. Industry and infrastructure are outdated.

◆ **INSIGHT:** *Archaeologists have found evidence of wine-making in Bulgaria dating back over 5000 years*

FACTFILE
OFFICIAL NAME: Republic of Bulgaria
DATE OF FORMATION: 1908
CAPITAL: Sofia
POPULATION: 7.7 million
TOTAL AREA: 42,822 sq. miles
(110,910 sq. km)
DENSITY: 180 people per sq. mile

LANGUAGES: Bulgarian*, Turkish, Romani
RELIGIONS: Orthodox Christian 83%, Muslim 12%, other 4%, Catholic 1%
ETHNIC MIX: Bulgarian 84%, Turkish 9%, Roma 5%, other 2%
GOVERNMENT: Parliamentary system
CURRENCY: Lev = 100 stotinki

Burkina

 Known as Upper Volta until 1984, the west African state of Burkina has been ruled by military dictators for most of its postindependence history. It is now a multiparty state.

GEOGRAPHY

The Sahara covers the north of the country. The south is largely savanna. The three main rivers are the Black, White, and Red Voltas.

CLIMATE

Tropical. Dry, cool weather November–February. Erratic rain March–April, mostly in southeast.

PEOPLE & SOCIETY

No single ethnic group is dominant, but the Mossi, from around Ouagadougou, have always played an important part in government. The people from the west are much more ethnically mixed. Extreme poverty has led to a strong sense of egalitarianism. Most women are still denied access to education, though their absence from public life belies their real power and social influence.

THE ECONOMY

Cotton is the major cash crop, but the soil quality is poor and worsening as the Sahara Desert encroaches.

INSIGHT: *Droughts and poor soils mean that many Burkinabes seek work southward in Ghana and Côte d'Ivoire*

FACTFILE

OFFICIAL NAME: Burkina Faso
DATE OF FORMATION: 1960
CAPITAL: Ouagadougou
POPULATION: 13.2 million
TOTAL AREA: 105,869 sq. miles
(274,200 sq. km)
DENSITY: 125 people per sq. mile

LANGUAGES: Mossi, Fulani, French*, Tuareg, Dyula, Songhai
RELIGIONS: Muslim 55%, Traditional beliefs 35%, Roman Catholic 9%, other Christian 1%
ETHNIC MIX: Other 52%, Mossi 48%
GOVERNMENT: Presidential system
CURRENCY: CFA franc = 100 centimes

Burundi

Small, densely populated and landlocked, Burundi lies just south of the equator, on the Nile–Congo watershed in central Africa. Ethnic tensions are the main factor in politics.

GEOGRAPHY

Hilly with high plateaus in center and savanna in the east. Great Rift Valley on western side.

CLIMATE

Temperate, with high humidity. Heavy and frequent rainfall, mostly October–May. Highlands have frost.

PEOPLE & SOCIETY

Most people are subsistence farmers. Burundi has been riven by ethnic conflict between majority Hutu and the Tutsi, who controlled the army – with repeated large-scale massacres. Hundreds of thousands of people have been killed since 1993. A power-sharing deal is now in place. Twa pygmies were not involved in the conflict.

◆ **INSIGHT:** *Burundi's fertility rate is one of the highest in Africa. On average, women have seven children*

THE ECONOMY

Overwhelmingly agricultural economy. Small quantities of gold and tungsten. Potential of oil in Lake Tanganyika. Little prospect of lasting stability.

FACTFILE

OFFICIAL NAME: Republic of Burundi
DATE OF FORMATION: 1962
CAPITAL: Bujumbura
POPULATION: 7.5 million
TOTAL AREA: 10,745 sq. miles (27,830 sq. km)
DENSITY: 757 people per sq. mile

LANGUAGES: Kirundi*, French*, Kiswahili
RELIGIONS: Christian (mainly Roman Catholic) 60%, traditional beliefs 39%, Muslim 1%
ETHNIC MIX: Hutu 85%, Tutsi 14%, Twa 1%
GOVERNMENT: Presidential system
CURRENCY: Burundi franc = 100 centimes

Cambodia

Located on the Indochinese peninsula in southeast Asia, Cambodia has emerged from two decades of civil war and invasion from Vietnam. Rice is the principal crop.

GEOGRAPHY

Mostly low-lying basin. Tônlé Sap (Great Lake) drains into the Mekong River. Forested mountains and plateau east of the Mekong.

CLIMATE

Tropical. High temperatures throughout the year. Heavy rainfall during May–October monsoon.

PEOPLE & SOCIETY

Under Pol Pot's Marxist Khmer Rouge regime, between 1975 and 1979, over one million Cambodians died. Effects of revolution and civil war are still felt and are reflected in the high rates of orphans, widows, and land-mine victims. A fragile stability has lasted since elections in 1993. The Khmer Rouge discontinued its armed struggle after the death of Pol Pot in 1998. King Norodom Sihanouk, a key figure in politics, abdicated in 2004.

THE ECONOMY

Economy is still recovering from civil war. Modest trade in rubber and timber, and self-sufficiency in rice. Reliant on imports and aid. Small tax base limits the scope of reforms.

◆ **INSIGHT:** *Cambodia has many impressive temples, dating from when the country was the center of the Khmer empire*

FACTFILE

OFFICIAL NAME: Kingdom of Cambodia
DATE OF FORMATION: 1953
CAPITAL: Phnom Penh
POPULATION: 14.1 million
TOTAL AREA: 69,900 sq. miles (181,040 sq. km)
DENSITY: 207 people per sq. mile

LANGUAGES: Khmer*, French, Chinese, Vietnamese, Cham
RELIGIONS: Buddhist 93%, Muslim 6%, Christian 1%
ETHNIC MIX: Khmer 90%, other 5%, Vietnamese 4%, Chinese 1%
GOVERNMENT: Parliamentary system
CURRENCY: Riel = 100 sen

Cameroon

Situated in the corner of the Gulf of Guinea, Cameroon was effectively a one-party state for 30 years. Multiparty elections were held in 1992, returning the former ruling party to power.

GEOGRAPHY

Over half the land is forested: equatorial rainforest in north, evergreen forest and wooded savanna in south. Mountains in the west.

CLIMATE

South is equatorial, with plentiful rainfall, declining inland. Far north is beset by drought.

PEOPLE & SOCIETY

Around 230 ethnic groups; no single group is dominant. The Bamileke is the largest, though it has never held political power. North–south tensions are diminished by the ethnic diversity. There is more rivalry between majority French- and minority English-speakers.

◆ **INSIGHT:** *Cameroon's name derives from the Portuguese word* camarões – *after the shrimp fished by the early European explorers*

THE ECONOMY

Oil reserves. Very diversified agricultural economy – timber, cocoa, bananas, coffee. Fuel smuggling from Nigeria undermines refinery profits. Corruption is widespread.

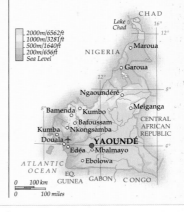

2000m/6562ft
1000m/3281ft
500m/1640ft
200m/656ft
Sea Level

CHAD
Lake
Chad
NIGERIA
Maroua
Garoua
Ngaoundéré
Bamenda • Kumbo
Bafoussam
Kumba • Nkongsamba
Douala •
Edéa • Mbalmayo
Ebolowa
ATLANTIC
OCEAN
EQ.
GUINEA
YAOUNDÉ
Meiganga
CENTRAL
AFRICAN
REPUBLIC
GABON
CONGO

0   100 km
0   100 miles

FACTFILE

OFFICIAL NAME: Republic of Cameroon
DATE OF FORMATION: 1960
CAPITAL: Yaoundé
POPULATION: 16.3 million
TOTAL AREA: 183,567 sq. miles
(475,400 sq. km)
DENSITY: 91 people per sq. mile

LANGUAGES: Bamileke, Fang, Fulani, French*, English*
RELIGIONS: Catholic 35%, traditional beliefs 25%, Muslim 22%, Protestant 18%
ETHNIC MIX: Highlanders 31%, other 39%, equatorial Bantu 19%, Kirdi 11%
GOVERNMENT: Presidential system
CURRENCY: CFA franc = 100 centimes

Canada

Canada extends from its long border with the US to the Arctic Ocean. The relationship of French-speaking Québec with the rest of the country has become a less contentious issue.

GEOGRAPHY

The world's second-largest country, stretching north to Cape Colombia on Ellesmere Island, south to Lake Erie, and across five time zones from the Pacific seaboard to Newfoundland. Arctic tundra and islands in the far north give way southward to forests, interspersed with lakes and rivers, and then the vast Canadian Shield, which covers over half the area of Canada. Rocky Mountains in west, beyond which are the Coast Mountains, islands, and fjords. Fertile lowlands in the east.

CLIMATE

Ranges from polar and subpolar in the north, to continental in the south. Winters in the interior are colder and longer than on the coast, with temperatures well below freezing and deep snow; summers are hotter. Pacific coast has the mildest winters.

PEOPLE & SOCIETY

Two-thirds of the population live in the Great Lakes–St. Lawrence lowlands, fostering some shared cultural values with the neighboring US. Important differences, however, include wider welfare provision and Commonwealth membership. The Québécois wish to preserve their culture and language from further Anglicization, and demand to be recognized as a "distinct society." The government welcomes ethnic diversity among immigrants, promoting a policy which encourages each group to maintain its own culture. Land claims made by the indigenous peoples are being redressed. Nunavut, an Inuit-governed territory which covers nearly a quarter of Canada's land area, was created from a portion of the Northwest Territories in 1999. Women are well represented at most levels of business and government.

FACTFILE

OFFICIAL NAME: Canada
DATE OF FORMATION: 1867
CAPITAL: Ottawa
POPULATION: 32.3 million
TOTAL AREA: 3,851,788 sq. miles (9,976,140 sq. km)
DENSITY: 9 people per sq. mile

LANGUAGES: English*, French*, other
RELIGIONS: Roman Catholic 44%, Protestant 29%, other 27%
ETHNIC ORIGIN: British, French and other European 27m, Asian 3m, Amerindian, Métis, and Inuit 1.3m
GOVERNMENT: Parliamentary system
CURRENCY: Canadian dollar = 100 cents

Canada

$ THE ECONOMY

Wide-ranging resources, providing exports, cheap energy, and raw materials for manufacturing, underpin a high standard of living, with smaller wealth disparities than in the US. Prices for primary exports fluctuate, but the high oil price has enabled the development of Alberta's vast oil fields. Manufactured exports have flourished under growing global competition, especially since Canada joined NAFTA. Unemployment has fallen steadily over the last decade from a high of around 10%. Economic growth quickly rebounded from the effect of the 2001 slowdown in the US.

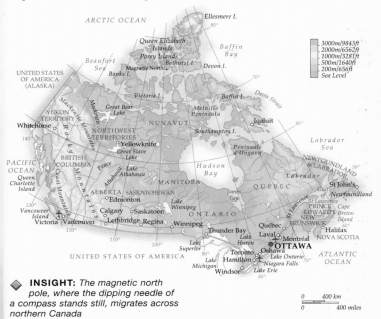

	3000m/9843ft
	2000m/6562ft
	1000m/3281ft
	500m/1640ft
	200m/656ft
	Sea Level

INSIGHT: *The magnetic north pole, where the dipping needle of a compass stands still, migrates across northern Canada*

0   400 km
0   400 miles

Cape Verde

 Off the west coast of Africa, in the Atlantic Ocean, lies the group of islands that make up Cape Verde, a Portuguese colony until it gained independence in 1975.

 GEOGRAPHY
Ten main islands and eight smaller islets, all of volcanic origin. Mostly mountainous, with steep cliffs and rocky headlands.

CLIMATE
Warm, and very dry. Subject to droughts that can sometimes last for years at a time.

 PEOPLE & SOCIETY
Most people are of mixed Portuguese–African origin; the rest are largely African, descended from slaves or more recent immigrants. Creolization of the culture negates ethnic tensions. Half of the population live on Santiago. Over 600,000 Cape Verdeans now live abroad.

◆ **INSIGHT:** *Poor soils and lack of surface water mean that Cape Verde is dependent on food aid*

THE ECONOMY
Most people are subsistence farmers. Clothing is the main export. Only minerals produced are salt, and volcanic rock for cement.

FACTFILE
OFFICIAL NAME: Republic of Cape Verde
DATE OF FORMATION: 1975
CAPITAL: Praia
POPULATION: 507,000
TOTAL AREA: 1557 sq. miles
(4033 sq. km)
DENSITY: 326 people per sq. mile

LANGUAGES: Creole, Portuguese*
RELIGIONS: Roman Catholic 97%, other 2%, Protestant 1%
ETHNIC MIX: Mestiço 60%, African 30%, other 10%
GOVERNMENT: Mixed presidential–parliamentary system
CURRENCY: C.V. escudo = 100 centavos

Central African Republic

The Central African Republic (CAR) is a landlocked country lying between the basins of the Chad and Congo Rivers. The country is prone to coups; the last was in 2003.

GEOGRAPHY

Comprises a low plateau, covered by scrub or savanna. Equatorial rainforests in the south. The Ubangi River forms the border with the Democratic Republic of the Congo.

CLIMATE

The south is equatorial; the north is hot and dry. Rain occurs all year round, with heaviest falls between July and October.

PEOPLE & SOCIETY

The Baya and Banda are the largest ethnic groups, but the lingua franca is Sango, a trading creole spoken by the minorities in the south who have traditionally provided most political leaders. Women have considerable power. Ethnic diversity helps limit disputes. Less than 2% of the population live in the arid north.

THE ECONOMY

Dominated by subsistence farming. Exports include gold, diamonds, cotton, and timber. Self-sufficient in food. Instability and poor infrastructure hinder progress.

INSIGHT: *"Emperor" Bokassa's eccentric rule from 1965 to 1979 was followed by military dictatorship until democracy was restored in 1993*

1000m/3281ft
500m/1640ft
200m/656ft
Sea Level

FACTFILE

OFFICIAL NAME: Central African Republic
DATE OF FORMATION: 1960
CAPITAL: Bangui
POPULATION: 4 million
TOTAL AREA: 240,534 sq. miles (622,984 sq. km)
DENSITY: 17 people per sq. mile

LANGUAGES: Sango, Banda, Gbaya, French*
RELIGIONS: Traditional beliefs 60%, Christian 35%, Muslim 5%
ETHNIC MIX: Baya 34%, Banda 27%, Mandjia 21%, Sara 10%, other 8%
GOVERNMENT: Presidential system
CURRENCY: CFA franc = 100 centimes

Chad

Landlocked in north central Africa, Chad has had a turbulent history since independence from France in 1960. Intermittent periods of civil war followed a military coup in 1975.

 GEOGRAPHY
Mostly plateaus sloping west-ward to Lake Chad. Northern third is Sahara. Tibesti Mountains in north rise to 10,826 ft (3300 m).

 CLIMATE
Three distinct zones: desert in north, semiarid region in center, and tropics in south.

 PEOPLE & SOCIETY
Half the population live in the southern fifth of Chad. Northern third has only 100,000 people, mainly Muslim Toubou nomads. Democracy was restored in 1996 by ex-coup leader Idriss Déby. Four years of political strife between northern Muslims and southern Christians ended in 2003, but rebellion has since erupted in the east.

 INSIGHT: *Lake Chad is slowly drying up – it is now estimated to be just 10% of the size it was in 1970*

THE ECONOMY
The discovery of oil, and the opening of a pipeline to the coast via Cameroon, are transforming Chad's economy, though the new wealth is unlikely to reach most people.

3000m/9843ft	
2000m/6562ft	
1000m/3281ft	
500m/1640ft	
200m/656ft	
Sea Level	

0   200 km
0   200 miles

FACTFILE

OFFICIAL NAME: Republic of Chad
DATE OF FORMATION: 1960
CAPITAL: N'Djamena
POPULATION: 9.7 million
TOTAL AREA: 495,752 sq. miles
(1,284,000 sq. km)
DENSITY: 20 people per sq. mile

LANGUAGES: French*, Sara, Arabic*, Maba
RELIGIONS: Muslim 55%, traditional beliefs 35%, Christian 10%
ETHNIC MIX: Other 30%, Sara 28%, Mayo-Kebbi 12%, Arab 12%, Ouaddai 9%, Kanem-Bornou 9%
GOVERNMENT: Presidential system
CURRENCY: CFA franc = 100 centimes

Chile

Chile extends in a ribbon down the west coast of South America. It returned to elected civilian rule in 1989 after a referendum had rejected military dictator General Pinochet.

GEOGRAPHY
Fertile valleys in the center between the coast and the Andes. Atacama Desert in north. Deep sea channels, lakes, and fjords in south.

CLIMATE
Arid in the north. Hot, dry summers and mild winters in the center. Higher Andean peaks have glaciers and year-round snow. Very wet and stormy in the south.

PEOPLE & SOCIETY
Most people are of mixed Spanish–Amerindian descent, and are highly urbanized; a third of the population live in Santiago, many in large slums. There are three main indigenous groups, including the Rapa Nui of Easter Island. General Pinochet's dictatorship was brutally repressive, but the business and middle classes prospered.

THE ECONOMY
World's biggest copper producer. Growth in foreign investment due to political stability. Exports include wine, fishmeal, fruits, and salmon.

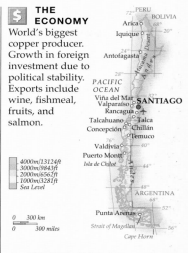

PERU
BOLIVIA
72°
Arica
68°
Iquique
20°
24°
Antofagasta
28°
PACIFIC OCEAN
Viña del Mar
32°
Valparaíso
SANTIAGO
Rancagua
Talcahuano
Talca
Concepción
Chillán
Temuco
76°
Valdivia
40°
Puerto Montt
Isla de Chiloé
44°
ARGENTINA
68°
48°
52°
Punta Arenas
Strait of Magellan
56°
Cape Horn

4000m/13124ft
3000m/9843ft
2000m/6562ft
1000m/3281ft
Sea Level

0   300 km
0   300 miles

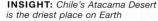

◆ **INSIGHT:** *Chile's Atacama Desert is the driest place on Earth*

FACTFILE

OFFICIAL NAME: Republic of Chile
DATE OF FORMATION: 1818
CAPITAL: Santiago
POPULATION: 16.3 million
TOTAL AREA: 292,258 sq. miles (756,950 sq. km)
DENSITY: 56 people per sq. mile

LANGUAGES: Spanish*, Amerindian languages
RELIGIONS: Roman Catholic 80%, other and nonreligious 20%
ETHNIC MIX: Mixed and European 90%, other Amerindian 9%, Mapuche 1%
GOVERNMENT: Presidential system
CURRENCY: Chilean peso = 100 centavos

China

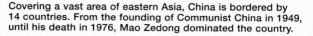

Covering a vast area of eastern Asia, China is bordered by 14 countries. From the founding of Communist China in 1949, until his death in 1976, Mao Zedong dominated the country.

GEOGRAPHY

A land of huge physical diversity, China has a long Pacific coastline to the east. Two-thirds of the country is uplands. The southwestern mountains include Tibet, the world's highest plateau; in the northwest, the Tien Shan Mountains separate the arid Tarim and Dzungarian basins. The rolling hills and plains of the low-lying east are home to two-thirds of the population.

CLIMATE

China is divided into two main climatic regions. The north and west are semiarid or arid, with extreme temperature variations. The south and east are warmer and more humid, with year-round rainfall. Winter temperatures vary with latitude, but are warmest on the subtropical southeast coast. Summer temperatures are more uniform, rising above 70°F (21°C).

PEOPLE & SOCIETY

Most people are Han Chinese. The rest of the population belong to one of 55 minority nationalities, or recognized ethnic groups. Many of these groups have a disproportionate political significance as they live in strategic border areas. A policy of resettling Han Chinese in remote regions is deeply resented and has led to uprisings in Xinjiang and Tibet. The government has relaxed the one-child family policy for minorities after some small groups were brought close to extinction; Han Chinese still face controls. Chinese society is patriarchal in practice, and generations tend to live together. However, economic change is breaking down the social controls of the Mao era. Divorce and unemployment are rising; materialism has replaced the puritanism of the past. A resurgence of religious belief has occurred in recent years.

FACTFILE

OFFICIAL NAME: People's Rep. of China
DATE OF FORMATION: 960
CAPITAL: Beijing
POPULATION: 1.32 billion
TOTAL AREA: 3,705,386 sq. miles (9,596,960 sq. km)
DENSITY: 365 people per sq. mile

LANGUAGES: Mandarin*, other
RELIGIONS: Nonreligious 59%, traditional beliefs 20%, other 13%, Buddhist 6%, Muslim 2%
ETHNIC MIX: Han 92%, other 4%, Hui 1%, Miao 1%, Manchu 1%, Zhuang 1%
GOVERNMENT: One-party state
CURRENCY: Yuan = 10 jiao = 100 fen

THE ECONOMY

China has shifted from a centrally planned to a market-oriented economy; liberalization has gone furthest in the south where the emerging business class is based. The Tenth Five-Year Plan (2001–2005) emphasized rapid development, while the Eleventh Plan aims to address widening wealth disparities. The government now runs a record deficit of almost $40 billion. A substantial growth in imports followed a deal with the EU and the normalization of US trade relations, while a boost in exports has aided GDP growth of over 9% since 2003, placing China among the world's top five economies.

INSIGHT: *China has the world's oldest continuous civilization. Its recorded history began 4000 years ago, with the Shang dynasty*

4000m/13124ft	
3000m/9843ft	
2000m/6562ft	
1000m/3281ft	
500m/1640ft	
200m/656ft	
Sea Level	

0   400 km

0   400 miles

Colombia

Lying in northwest South America, Colombia has coastlines on both the Caribbean and the Pacific. It is primarily noted for its coffee, emeralds, gold, and narcotics trafficking.

 GEOGRAPHY
The densely forested and almost uninhabited east is separated from the western coastal plains by the Andes, which divide into three ranges (*cordilleras*) with intervening valleys.

 CLIMATE
Coastal plains are hot and wet. The highlands are much cooler. The equatorial east has two wet seasons.

PEOPLE & SOCIETY
Most Colombians are of mixed blood. Blacks and Amerindians have the least political representation. The four-decade-long civil conflict has displaced millions of people, and left over 50,000 dead. The war is now entwined with the narcotics trade. Violent crime is common.

◆ **INSIGHT:** *Over 50% of the world's cocaine is produced in Colombia*

THE ECONOMY
Healthy and diversified export sector – includes coffee and coal. Considerable growth potential, but drugs-related violence and corruption deter foreign investors.

 FACTFILE

OFFICIAL NAME: Republic of Colombia
DATE OF FORMATION: 1819
CAPITAL: Bogotá
POPULATION: 45.6 million
TOTAL AREA: 439,733 sq. miles
(1,138,910 sq. km)
DENSITY: 114 people per sq. mile

LANGUAGES: Spanish*, Amerindian languages, English Creole
RELIGIONS: Catholic 95%, other 5%
ETHNIC MIX: Mestizo 58%, White 20%, European–African 14%, Black African 4%, Black Amerindian 3%, other 1%
GOVERNMENT: Presidential system
CURRENCY: Peso = 100 centavos

Comoros

Off the east African coast, between Mozambique and Madagascar, lies the archipelago republic of the Comoros, comprising three main islands and a number of smaller islets.

 GEOGRAPHY
Main islands are of volcanic origin and are heavily forested. The remainder are coral atolls.

 CLIMATE
Hot and humid all year round, especially on the coasts. November to May is hottest and wettest period.

 PEOPLE & SOCIETY
The Comoros has absorbed a diversity of people over the years, including Africans, Arabs, Polynesians, and Persians. There have also been Portuguese, Dutch, French, and Indian immigrants. Ethnic discord is rare, but regional tensions between islands are marked. The country is politically unstable and there have been frequent coups over the last decade. A fragile new federal system has been in place since 2002. Wealth is concentrated among a political and business elite.

THE ECONOMY
One of the world's poorest countries. Subsistence-level farming. Vanilla and cloves are main cash crops. Lack of basic infrastructure.

INSIGHT: *The Comoros is the world's largest producer of ylang-ylang – an extract from tree blossom used in manufacturing perfumes*

FACTFILE

OFFICIAL NAME: Union of the Comoros
DATE OF FORMATION: 1975
CAPITAL: Moroni
POPULATION: 798,000
TOTAL AREA: 838 sq. miles (2170 sq. km)
DENSITY: 927 people per sq. mile

LANGUAGES: Arabic*, Comoran*, French*
RELIGIONS: Muslim (mainly Sunni) 98%, other 1%, Roman Catholic 1%
ETHNIC MIX: Comoran 97%, other 3%
GOVERNMENT: Presidential system
CURRENCY: Comoros franc = 100 centimes

Congo

Astride the equator in west central Africa, this former French colony emerged from 20 years of Marxist-Leninist rule in 1990. Democracy was soon overshadowed by years of violence.

GEOGRAPHY

Mostly forest- or savanna-covered plateaus, drained by the Ubangi and Congo River systems. Narrow coastal plain is lined with sand dunes and lagoons.

CLIMATE

Hot, tropical. Temperatures rarely fall below 86°F (30°C). Two wet and two dry seasons. Rainfall is heaviest south of the equator.

PEOPLE & SOCIETY

One of the most tribally conscious and heavily urbanized countries in Africa, with most people living in the Brazzaville–Pointe-Noire region. Main tensions are between the Bakongo in the north and the Mbochi in the south. Relative peace was secured in 1999, and "ninja" rebels in the Pool region, around Brazzaville, signed a peace deal in 2003.

THE ECONOMY

Oil provides over 80% of export revenue. Timber supplies. Substantial industrial base around Brazzaville and Pointe-Noire. Large foreign debt.

INSIGHT: *In 1970, Congo became the first African country to declare itself a communist state*

FACTFILE

OFFICIAL NAME: Republic of the Congo
DATE OF FORMATION: 1960
CAPITAL: Brazzaville
POPULATION: 4 million
TOTAL AREA: 132,046 sq. miles (342,000 sq. km)
DENSITY: 30 people per sq. mile

LANGUAGES: Kongo, Teke, Lingala, French*
RELIGIONS: Traditional 50%, Catholic 25%, Protestant 23%, Muslim 2%
ETHNIC MIX: Bakongo 51%, Teke 17%, other 16%, Mbochi 11%, Mbédé 5%
GOVERNMENT: Presidential system
CURRENCY: CFA franc = 100 centimes

Congo, (DRC)

Lying in east-central Africa, the Democratic Republic of the Congo (DRC) is one of Africa's largest countries, and the scene of one of its worst regional wars.

 GEOGRAPHY
Rainforested basin of Congo River occupies 60% of the land area. High mountain ranges and lakes stretch down the eastern border.

 CLIMATE
Tropical and humid. Distinct wet and dry seasons south of the equator. The north is mainly wet.

 PEOPLE & SOCIETY
There are over 12 main ethnic groups and around 190 smaller ones. The indigenous forest pygmies are now a marginalized group, victimized during the war. Civil war from 1996 drew neighboring countries into a long and bloody conflict. Peace was achieved in 2003 but tensions remain.

◆ **INSIGHT:** *The DRC's rainforests comprise 6% of the world's, and 50% of Africa's, remaining woodlands*

$ **THE ECONOMY**
Rich resource base: diamonds provide half of export earnings. 80% of debt was canceled in 2003. War, corruption, and mismanagement have seen economy collapse. Food aid is needed to ease humanitarian crisis.

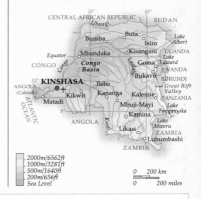

FACTFILE

OFFICIAL NAME: Democratic Republic of the Congo
DATE OF FORMATION: 1960
CAPITAL: Kinshasa
POPULATION: 57.5 million
TOTAL AREA: 905,563 sq. miles (2,345,410 sq. km)

DENSITY: 66 people per sq. mile
LANGUAGES: Kiswahili, Tshiluba, French*
RELIGIONS: Christian 70%, Kimbanguist 10%, traditional beliefs 10%, Muslim 10%,
ETHNIC MIX: Other 55%, Bantu and Hamitic 45%
GOVERNMENT: Transitional regime
CURRENCY: Congolese franc = 100 centimes

Costa Rica

Costa Rica is the most stable country in Central America. Its neutrality in foreign affairs is long-standing, but it has strong ties with the US. The national army was abolished in 1949.

GEOGRAPHY
Coastal plains of swamp and savanna rise to a fertile central plateau, which leads to a mountain range with active volcanic peaks.

CLIMATE
Hot and humid in coastal regions. Temperate central uplands. High annual rainfall.

PEOPLE & SOCIETY
Most people are *mestizo*, of partly Spanish origin. There is a black, English-speaking minority and around 35,000 indigenous Amerindians. Plantation-owners are the wealthiest group, while a fifth of people live in poverty. Nonetheless, living standards are high for the region.

◆ **INSIGHT:** *Costa Rica's constitution is the only one in the world to forbid a national army*

THE ECONOMY
Bananas, beef, and coffee are the leading exports but are all vulnerable to fluctuating world prices. Tourism is booming and also fuels construction industry. The country's stability has attracted multinationals. History of high inflation.

FACTFILE
OFFICIAL NAME: Republic of Costa Rica
DATE OF FORMATION: 1838
CAPITAL: San José
POPULATION: 4.3 million
TOTAL AREA: 19,730 sq. miles (51,100 sq. km)
DENSITY: 218 people per sq. mile

LANGUAGES: Spanish*, English Creole, Bribri, Cabecar
RELIGIONS: Roman Catholic 76%, other (including Protestant) 24%
ETHNIC MIX: Mestizo and European 96%, Black 2%, Chinese 1%, Amerindian 1%
GOVERNMENT: Presidential system
CURRENCY: Colón = 100 céntimos

Côte d'Ivoire (Ivory Coast)

One of the larger nations along the coast of west Africa, Côte d'Ivoire is the world's biggest cocoa producer. An image of stability was rocked by civil war in 2002–2005.

GEOGRAPHY

Sandy coastal strip backed by a largely rainforested interior, and a savanna plateau in the north.

CLIMATE

High temperatures all year round. South has two wet seasons; north has one, with lower rainfall.

PEOPLE & SOCIETY

There are more than 60 tribes, the key ones being the two main Akan groups: Baoulé in the center and Agni in the east, Senufo in the north, and Dan-Yacouba in the west. Christians in the south harbor resentment against non-Ivorian Muslims in the north. Conflict from 2002 forced hundreds of thousands of migrant workers to flee.

◆ **INSIGHT:** *The Basilica of Our Lady of the Peace in Yamoussoukro is the largest church in the world*

THE ECONOMY

Main crops are cocoa and coffee. Expanding oil and gas industries. Instability threatens investment. Lack of professional training.

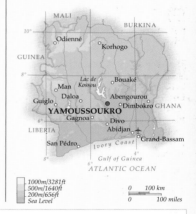

1000m/3281ft
500m/1640ft
200m/656ft
Sea Level

0   100 km
0   100 miles

FACTFILE

OFFICIAL NAME: Republic of Côte d'Ivoire
DATE OF FORMATION: 1960
CAPITAL: Yamoussoukro
POPULATION: 18.2 million
TOTAL AREA: 124,502 sq. miles (322,460 sq. km)

DENSITY: 148 people per sq. mile
LANGUAGES: Akan, French*, Kru, Voltaic
RELIGIONS: Muslim 38%, Christian 31%, traditional beliefs 25%, other 6%
ETHNIC MIX: Akan 42%, Voltaïque 18%, Mandé du Nord 17%, Krou 11%, other 12%
GOVERNMENT: Presidential system
CURRENCY: CFA franc = 100 centimes

Croatia

Though it was controlled by Hungary from medieval times and was a part of the Yugoslav state for much of the 20th century, Croatia has a very strong national identity.

GEOGRAPHY
Rocky, mountainous Adriatic coastline is dotted with islands. Interior is a mixture of wooded mountains and broad valleys.

CLIMATE
The interior has a temperate continental climate. Mediterranean climate along the Adriatic coast.

PEOPLE & SOCIETY
Croats are ethnically similar to Bosniaks and Serbs. They are distinguished by their Roman Catholic faith and their use of the Latin alphabet. War greatly altered Croatia's ethnic makeup. Serbs now constitute just 5% of the population. Minority rights are a key issue in the quest for EU membership.

◆ **INSIGHT:** *Croatia only regained control of Serb-occupied Eastern Slavonia, around Vukovar, in 1998*

THE ECONOMY
The war cost the economy an estimated $50 billion. There has been steady growth since, and tourism is thriving on the Dalmatian coast, but unemployment is persistently high.

FACTFILE

OFFICIAL NAME: Republic of Croatia
DATE OF FORMATION: 1991
CAPITAL: Zagreb
POPULATION: 4.6 million
TOTAL AREA: 21,831 sq. miles (56,542 sq. km)
DENSITY: 211 people per sq. mile

LANGUAGES: Croatian
RELIGIONS: Roman Catholic 88%, other 7%, Orthodox Christian 4%, Muslim 1%
ETHNIC MIX: Croat 90%, other 5%, Serb 5%
GOVERNMENT: Parliamentary system
CURRENCY: Kuna = 100 lipa

Cuba

A former Spanish colony, Cuba is the largest island in the Caribbean and the only communist country in the Americas. It has been led by Fidel Castro since 1959.

GEOGRAPHY

Mostly fertile plains and basins. Three mountainous areas. Forests of pine and mahogany cover one-quarter of the country.

CLIMATE

Subtropical. Hot all year round, and very hot in summer. Heaviest rainfall in the mountains. Hurricanes can strike in the fall.

PEOPLE & SOCIETY

Castro's regime has reduced formerly extreme wealth disparities, given education a high priority, and established an efficient health service. Political dissent, however, is not tolerated. A dramatic fall in living standards since the late 1980s has led thousands of Cubans to flee to the US, to seek asylum. About 70% of Cubans are of Spanish descent, and ethnic tension is minimal.

THE ECONOMY

The 30-year-old US trade embargo continues. The sugar industry has collapsed and has been replaced as Cuba's main industry by tourism. The free use of the US dollar, legal tender from 1993 to 2004, boosted investment and created a "dollarized" elite.

INSIGHT: *Most modern cars in Cuba are imported, along with computers, in exchange for sugar in a special trading deal with Japan*

FACTFILE

OFFICIAL NAME: Republic of Cuba
DATE OF FORMATION: 1902
CAPITAL: Havana
POPULATION: 11.3 million
TOTAL AREA: 42,803 sq. miles (110,860 sq. km)
DENSITY: 264 people per sq. mile

LANGUAGES: Spanish
RELIGIONS: Nonreligious 49%, Roman Catholic 40%, atheist 6%, other 4%, Protestant 1%
ETHNIC MIX: White 66%, European–African 22%, Black 12%
GOVERNMENT: One-party state
CURRENCY: Cuban peso = 100 centavos

Cyprus

Cyprus lies south of Turkey in the eastern Mediterranean. Since 1974, it has been partitioned between the Turkish-occupied north and the Greek-Cypriot south.

 GEOGRAPHY
Mountains in the center-west give way to a fertile plain in the east, flanked by hills to the northeast.

 CLIMATE
Mediterranean. Summers are hot and dry. Winters are mild, with snow in the mountains.

 PEOPLE & SOCIETY
The Greek majority practice Orthodox Christianity. Since the 16th century, a minority community of Turkish Muslims has lived in the north of the island. In 1974 Turkish troops occupied the north, which was proclaimed the Turkish Republic of Northern Cyprus, but is recognized only by Turkey. Over 100,000 mainland Turks have settled there since. UN-led mediation failed to reunite the island ahead of EU accession in 2004, so the south alone became a member.

THE ECONOMY
Tourism is booming in the south where wages are more than double levels in the north. Shipping and light manufacturing. The north's isolation has hindered foreign investment.

INSIGHT: *The Green Line, which separates north from south, was opened for the first time in 2003*

FACTFILE

OFFICIAL NAME: Republic of Cyprus
DATE OF FORMATION: 1960
CAPITAL: Nicosia
POPULATION: 835,000
TOTAL AREA: 3571 sq. miles (9250 sq. km)
DENSITY: 234 people per sq. mile

LANGUAGES: Greek*, Turkish*
RELIGIONS: Orthodox Christian 78%, Muslim 18%, other 4%
ETHNIC MIX: Greek 81%, Turkish 11%, other 8%
GOVERNMENT: Presidential systems
CURRENCY: Cyprus pound = 100 cents (Turkish lira in TRNC = 100 kurus)

Czech Republic

Once part of Czechoslovakia in central Europe, the Czech Republic became independent in 1993, after peacefully dissolving its federal union with Slovakia.

GEOGRAPHY
Landlocked in central Europe. Bohemia, the western territory, is a plateau surrounded by mountains. Moravia, in the east, is characterized by hills and lowlands.

CLIMATE
Cool, sometimes cold winters and warm summer months, which bring most of the annual rainfall.

PEOPLE & SOCIETY
Secular and urban society, with high divorce rates. Czechs make up the vast majority of the population, while the next largest group are Moravians. The 300,000 Slovaks left after partition are now permitted dual citizenship. Ethnic tensions are few, but there is widespread hostility toward the Roma minority. A new commercial elite is emerging alongside postcommunist entrepreneurs.

THE ECONOMY
Traditional heavy industries (machinery, iron, car-making) have been successfully privatized. Large tourism revenues. Skilled labor force. Plans to join euro in 2010.

INSIGHT: *Charles University in Prague was founded in the 13th century.*

FACTFILE

OFFICIAL NAME: Czech Republic
DATE OF FORMATION: 1993
CAPITAL: Prague
POPULATION: 10.2 million
TOTAL AREA: 30,450 sq. miles (78,866 sq. km)
DENSITY: 335 people per sq. mile

LANGUAGES: Czech*, Slovak, Hungarian
RELIGIONS: Roman Catholic 39%, atheist 38%, other 18%, Protestant 3%, Hussite 2%
ETHNIC MIX: Czech 90%, other 4%, Moravian 4%, Slovak 2%
GOVERNMENT: Parliamentary system
CURRENCY: Czech koruna = 100 haleru

Denmark

 Denmark occupies the Jutland peninsula and over 400 islands in southern Scandinavia. Greenland and the Faeroe Islands are self-governing associated territories.

GEOGRAPHY
Fertile farmland covers two-thirds of the terrain, which is among the flattest in the world. About 100 islands are inhabited.

CLIMATE
Damp, temperate climate with mild summers and cold, wet winters. Rainfall is moderate.

PEOPLE & SOCIETY
Society is homogeneous. There are growing ethnic tensions with the small immigrant population. Almost all women now work and Denmark is a world leader in childcare provision. Marriage is becoming less common and most babies are born to cohabiting parents. Income distribution is the most even in the West.

◆ **INSIGHT:** *Denmark is Europe's oldest kingdom – the monarchy dates back to the 10th century*

THE ECONOMY
Gas and oil reserves. Skilled workforce key to high-tech industrial success. Pigmeat and dairy products are exported. Opted not to join the euro, though its currency is pegged.

FACTFILE
OFFICIAL NAME: Kingdom of Denmark
DATE OF FORMATION: 950
CAPITAL: Copenhagen
POPULATION: 5.4 million
TOTAL AREA: 16,639 sq. miles (43,094 sq. km)
DENSITY: 330 people per sq. mile

LANGUAGES: Danish
RELIGIONS: Evangelical Lutheran 89%, other 10%, Roman Catholic 1%
ETHNIC MIX: Danish 96%, other (including Scandinavian and Turkish) 3%, Faeroese and Inuit 1%
GOVERNMENT: Parliamentary system
CURRENCY: Danish krone = 100 øre

Djibouti

A city-state with a desert hinterland, Djibouti lies in northeast Africa at the entrance to the Red Sea. Once known as the French Territory of the Afars and Issas, independence came in 1977.

GEOGRAPHY
Mainly low-lying desert and semidesert, with a volcanic mountain range in the north.

CLIMATE
Almost no rain, though the monsoon is very humid. The 109°F (45°C) heat of summer is unbearable.

PEOPLE & SOCIETY
The main ethnic groups are the Issas in the south, and the nomadic Afars in the north. Tensions between them developed into a guerrilla war in 1991–1994. Smaller tribal groups make up the rest of the population, and the rural peoples are mostly nomadic. Wealth is concentrated in Djibouti city. France exerts considerable influence in Djibouti, supporting it financially and maintaining a naval base and a military garrison.

THE ECONOMY
Djibouti's major assets are its ports in a key Red Sea location.

◆ **INSIGHT:** *Chewing the leaves of the mildly narcotic qat shrub is an age-old social ritual in Djibouti*

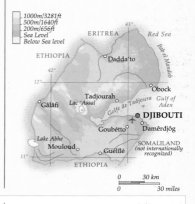

FACTFILE
OFFICIAL NAME: Republic of Djibouti
DATE OF FORMATION: 1977
CAPITAL: Djibouti
POPULATION: 793,000
TOTAL AREA: 8494 sq. miles (22,000 sq. km)
DENSITY: 89 people per sq. mile

LANGUAGES: Somali, Afar, French*, Arabic*
RELIGIONS: Muslim (mainly Sunni) 94%, Christian 6%
ETHNIC MIX: Issa 60%, Afar 35%, other 5%
GOVERNMENT: Presidential system
CURRENCY: Djibouti franc = 100 centimes

Dominica

Dominica is renowned as the Caribbean island that resisted European colonization until the 18th century. It achieved independence from the UK in 1978.

GEOGRAPHY
Mountainous and densely forested. Volcanic activity has given the land very fertile soils, hot springs, geysers, and black sand beaches.

CLIMATE
Tropical, cooled by constant trade winds. Heavy annual rainfall. Tropical depressions and hurricanes are likely June–November.

PEOPLE & SOCIETY
The majority of Dominicans are descendants of African slaves brought over to work on banana plantations. The Carib Territory on the northeast of the island is home to the only surviving indigenous community in the Caribbean. Wealth disparities are not as marked as elsewhere in the region, but the alleviation of poverty has become a major plank of government policy.

THE ECONOMY
Bananas and tourism are the economic mainstays, though preferential access for Dominican bananas to the EU has now gone.

INSIGHT: *Dominica is known as "Nature Island" due to its spectacular flora and fauna*

FACTFILE

OFFICIAL NAME: Commonwealth of Dominica
DATE OF FORMATION: 1978
CAPITAL: Roseau
POPULATION: 69,029
TOTAL AREA: 291 sq. miles (754 sq. km)

DENSITY: 238 people per sq. mile
LANGUAGES: French Creole, English*
RELIGIONS: Roman Catholic 77%, Protestant 15%, other 8%
ETHNIC MIX: Black 87%, mixed 9%, Carib 3%, other 1%
GOVERNMENT: Parliamentary system
CURRENCY: East Caribbean $ = 100 cents

Dominican Republic

The Dominican Republic occupies the eastern two-thirds of the island of Hispaniola in the Caribbean. Spanish-speaking, it seeks closer ties to the anglophone West Indies.

GEOGRAPHY

Highlands and rainforested mountains – including highest peak in Caribbean, Pico Duarte – interspersed with fertile valleys. Extensive coastal plain in the east.

CLIMATE

Hot and humid close to sea level, cooler at altitude. Heavy rainfall, especially in the northeast.

PEOPLE & SOCIETY

White landowners – especially those descended from the original Spanish settlers – form the wealthy elite. Mixed-race (mulatto) majority control commerce and form the bulk of the professional middle classes. White and mixed-race women are entering the professions. Great disparities of wealth exist; the black and Haitian-immigrant population occupy the bottom of the social ladder.

THE ECONOMY

Mining – mainly of nickel and gold – and sugar are major sectors. Hidden economy based on trans-shipment of narcotics to the US. Recent growth in tourism.

INSIGHT: *Santo Domingo is the oldest city in the Americas. It was founded in 1496 by the brother of Christopher Columbus*

FACTFILE

OFFICIAL NAME: Dominican Republic
DATE OF FORMATION: 1865
CAPITAL: Santo Domingo
POPULATION: 8.9 million
TOTAL AREA: 18,679 sq. miles (48,380 sq. km)
DENSITY: 476 people per sq. mile

LANGUAGES: Spanish*, French Creole
RELIGIONS: Roman Catholic 92%, other and nonreligious 8%
ETHNIC MIX: Mixed 75%, White 15%, Black 10%
GOVERNMENT: Presidential system
CURRENCY: Dominican Republic peso = 100 centavos

East Timor

East Timor occupies the once Portuguese-owned eastern half of the island of Timor. Invaded by Indonesia in 1975, it became independent in 2002 following a long struggle.

GEOGRAPHY
A narrow coastal plain gives way to forested highlands. Timor's mountain backbone rises to 9715 ft (2963 m).

CLIMATE
Tropical. Heavy rain in wet season (December–March), then dry and hot, particularly in the north.

PEOPLE & SOCIETY
The population is almost entirely Roman Catholic. The Timorese are a mix of Malay and Papuan peoples, and many indigenous Papuan tribes survive. There is an urban Chinese minority, and ethnic Indonesian settlers became numerous after annexation in 1975. Preindependence violence in 1999 was politically rather than ethnically motivated. Women do not have access to the professions and levels of domestic violence are notably high. Living standards are low.

THE ECONOMY
Agreement with Australia on the division of oil revenue from the Timor Sea. Coffee is the key export. Violence in 1999 damaged infrastructure. Riots in 2006 undermined stability, further deterring foreign investment.

◆ **INSIGHT:** *Once dependent on sandalwood, the economy could be transformed by oil under the Timor Sea*

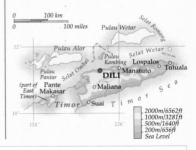

FACTFILE
OFFICIAL NAME: Democratic Republic of Timor Leste
DATE OF FORMATION: 2002
CAPITAL: Dili
POPULATION: 947,000
TOTAL AREA: 5756 sq. miles (14,874 sq. km)

DENSITY: 168 people per sq. mile
LANGUAGES: Tetum*, Bahasa Indonesia, Portuguese*
RELIGIONS: Catholic 95%, other 5%
ETHNIC MIX: Malay/Papuan groups c.85%, Indonesian c.13%, Chinese 2%
GOVERNMENT: Parliamentary system
CURRENCY: US dollar = 100 cents

Ecuador

Once part of the Inca heartland, Ecuador sits high on South America's western coast. Its territory includes the fascinating Galápagos Islands, 610 miles (970 km) to the west.

GEOGRAPHY

Broad coastal plain, inter-Andean central highlands, dense jungle in upper Amazon basin.

CLIMATE

The climate is hot and moist on the coast, cool in the Andes, and hot equatorial in the Amazon basin.

PEOPLE & SOCIETY

Over half of the population is of Amerindian–Spanish extraction (*mestizo*). Black communities exist on the coast. The strong and largely unified Amerindian movement is at the forefront of social protests. One-fifth of the population lives in extreme poverty, unable to afford basic levels of food.

◆ **INSIGHT:** *Darwin's study on the Galápagos Islands in 1856 played a major part in his theory of evolution*

THE ECONOMY

The world's biggest banana exporter, and a net oil exporter. Fishing industry. US dollar offers stability, but less control. Poor infrastructure and land productivity.

| 0 | | 100 km |
| 0 | | 100 miles |

PACIFIC OCEAN

COLOMBIA

Esmeraldas
Ibarra
San Miguel
Equator
Santo Domingo de los Colorados
QUITO
Napo
Manta
Portoviejo
Ambato
Riobamba
Milagro
Guayaquil
Gulf of Guayaquil
Cuenca
Machala
Loja

PERU

76°
80°
4°

4000m/13124ft
3000m/9843ft
2000m/6562ft
1000m/3281ft
500m/1640ft
200m/656ft
Sea Level

FACTFILE

OFFICIAL NAME: Republic of Ecuador
DATE OF FORMATION: 1830
CAPITAL: Quito
POPULATION: 13.2 million
TOTAL AREA: 109,483 sq. miles (283,560 sq. km)
DENSITY: 123 people per sq. mile

LANGUAGES: Spanish*, Quechua, other Amerindian languages
RELIGIONS: Roman Catholic 93%, Protestant, Jewish, and other 7%
ETHNIC MIX: Mestizo 55%, Amerindian 25%, White 10%, Black 10%
GOVERNMENT: Presidential system
CURRENCY: US dollar = 100 cents

Egypt

Occupying the northeast corner of Africa, Egypt is divided by the highly fertile Nile Valley. Its essentially pro-Western, military-backed regime is being challenged by Islamic fundamentalists.

GEOGRAPHY
Fertile Nile Valley separates arid Libyan Desert from smaller semiarid eastern desert. Sinai peninsula has mountains in south.

CLIMATE
Summers are very hot, but winters are cooler. Rainfall is negligible, except on the coast.

PEOPLE & SOCIETY
There is a long tradition of ethnic and religious tolerance, though the rise of Islamism has sparked clashes between Muslims and Copts (Coptic Christianity is one of the Church's earliest branches). Women play a full part in education and the economy, though this is threatened by Islamism. The rapidly growing population is a serious problem. Poverty is rife around Cairo, Africa's largest city.

THE ECONOMY
Oil and gas are main sources of revenue. Tolls from the Suez Canal. Successful tourist industry. High birth-rate and rural poverty main problems.

INSIGHT: *Egypt has been a major tourist destination since the 1880s*

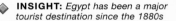

FACTFILE

OFFICIAL NAME: Arab Republic of Egypt

DATE OF FORMATION: 1936

CAPITAL: Cairo

POPULATION: 74 million

TOTAL AREA: 386,660 sq. miles (1,001,450 sq. km)

DENSITY: 193 people per sq. mile

LANGUAGES: Arabic*, French, English, Berber

RELIGIONS: Muslim (mainly Sunni) 94%, Coptic Christian and other 6%

ETHNIC MIX: Egyptian 99%, other (Nubian, Armenian, Greek, Berber) 1%

GOVERNMENT: Presidential system

CURRENCY: Egyptian pound = 100 piastres

El Salvador

El Salvador is Central America's smallest and most densely populated country. Already struggling to recover from a civil war in the 1980s, it was badly struck by earthquakes in 2001.

GEOGRAPHY

El Salvador is a narrow coastal belt backed by two mountain ranges. There is a central plateau. Located within a seismic zone, there are more than 20 volcanic peaks.

CLIMATE

Tropical coastal belt is very hot, with seasonal rains. Cooler, temperate climate in highlands.

PEOPLE & SOCIETY

Population is largely *mestizo*; ethnic tensions are few. The 1981–1991 civil war was fought between the US-backed right-wing government and left-wing FMLN guerrillas, over gross economic disparities, which still exist despite some reform. During the war 75,000 people died, many of whom were unarmed civilians, and human rights abuses were widespread. The FMLN is now a major political party.

THE ECONOMY
Overdependence on coffee, main export crop. Series of powerful earthquakes in early 2001 devastated infrastructure and deepened the country's reliance on aid. There are no significant resources.

◆ **INSIGHT:** *Independent since 1841, El Salvador is named after Jesus Christ, "the savior" of Christians*

GUATEMALA · Metapán
Santa · Chalatenango
Chalchuapa · Ana · Lempa
Ahuachapán · Embalse · Sensuntepeque
Sonsonate · Cerrón Grande · Cojutepeque
SAN · San Vicente · San Francisco
SALVADOR · San Miguel
Zacatecoluca · Usulután · La Unión
· Jiquilisco
HONDURAS
PACIFIC OCEAN

2000m/6562ft
1000m/3281ft
500m/1640ft
200m/656ft
Sea Level

0   25 km
0   25 miles

FACTFILE

OFFICIAL NAME: Republic of El Salvador
DATE OF FORMATION: 1841
CAPITAL: San Salvador
POPULATION: 6.9 million
TOTAL AREA: 8124 sq. miles (21,040 sq. km)
DENSITY: 862 people per sq. mile

LANGUAGES: Spanish
RELIGIONS: Roman Catholic 80%, Evangelical 18%, other 2%
ETHNIC MIX: Mestizo 94%, Amerindian 5%, White 1%
GOVERNMENT: Presidential system
CURRENCIES: Salvadorean colón = 100 centavos; US dollar = 100 cents

Equatorial Guinea

Comprising the mainland territory of Río Muni and five islands on the west coast of central Africa, Equatorial Guinea lies, as its name suggests, just north of the equator.

GEOGRAPHY
The islands are mountainous and volcanic. The mainland is lower, with mangrove swamps along the coast.

CLIMATE
Bioko is extremely wet and humid. The mainland is only marginally drier and cooler.

PEOPLE & SOCIETY
Equatorial Guinea is the only Spanish-speaking country in Africa. Río Muni is sparsely populated and most people there are Fang, an ethnic group also found in Cameroon and northern Gabon. Bioko is populated mostly by Bubi and a minority of Creoles known as Fernandinos. Tensions between the two territories have been reignited by the discovery of oil off Bioko. Wealth is concentrated in the ruling clan, oil revenue has made little impact on most people as yet.

THE ECONOMY
Oil and gas reserves have come on stream; the government has promised to reinvest the new funds in development. Timber and coffee.

INSIGHT: *In 2003, state radio declared President Obiang Nguema to be "like God in Heaven"*

2000m/6562ft
1000m/3281ft
500m/1640ft
200m/656ft
Sea Level

MALABO

3°30'N
Isla
da
Bioco
Bight of Biafra 9°

ATLANTIC
OCEAN

CAMEROON

Gulf
of
Guinea   Bata   Niefang   Micomeseng 2°

Mbini   Mongomo
                              R í o   Uolo
Cabo   Etembue   M u n i
San   Cogo   Nsoc
Juan
Isla de   GABON
Corisco
10°

0   40 km
0   40 miles

FACTFILE

OFFICIAL NAME: Republic of Equatorial Guinea

DATE OF FORMATION: 1968

CAPITAL: Malabo

POPULATION: 504,000

TOTAL AREA: 10,830 sq. miles (28,051 sq. km)

DENSITY: 47 people per sq. mile

LANGUAGES: Spanish*, Fang, Bubi, French*

RELIGIONS: Roman Catholic 90%, other 10%

ETHNIC MIX: Fang 85%, other 11%, Bubi 4%

GOVERNMENT: Presidential system

CURRENCY: CFA franc = 100 centimes

Eritrea

Lying along the southwest shore of the Red Sea, Eritrea won a long war for independence from Ethiopia in 1993. The two neighbors fought a bitter border war in 1998–2000.

GEOGRAPHY
Mostly consists of rugged mountains, bush, and the Danakil Desert, which falls below sea level.

CLIMATE
Warm in the mountains; desert areas are hot. Droughts from July onward are common.

PEOPLE & SOCIETY
Tigrinya-speakers, mainly Orthodox Christians, are the most numerous of nine main ethnic groups. A strong sense of nationhood has been forged by war. Women played a vital role in combat. Over 80% of people are subsistence farmers. Multiparty elections, expected since 1997, have been persistently postponed.

◆ **INSIGHT:** *Eritrea is the only country to secede successfully in postcolonial Africa*

THE ECONOMY
Legacy of disruption and destruction from wars. Susceptible to drought and famine. Most of the population live at subsistence level. Potential for mining of gold, copper, silver, and zinc. Possible foreign earnings from oil exports.

```
        0      100 km
        0      100 miles
```

SUDAN   Kerora   Red Sea
                              Dahlak
                              Archipelago
         Keren   Massawa
Akurdet   Barentu   ★ ASMARA
   Teseney   ✛ Adi Ugri
                                    Suwa
         ETHIOPIA   Red Sea
                          Danakil
                                      Aseb
                              DJIBOUTI

```
  2000m/6562ft
  1000m/3281ft
  500m/1640ft
  200m/656ft
  Sea Level
  Below Sea Level
```

FACTFILE
OFFICIAL NAME: State of Eritrea
DATE OF FORMATION: 1993
CAPITAL: Asmara
POPULATION: 4.4 million
TOTAL AREA: 46,842 sq. miles (121,320 sq. km)
DENSITY: 97 people per sq. mile

LANGUAGES: Tigrinya*, English*, Tigre, Afar, Arabic*, Bilen, Kunama, other
RELIGIONS: Christian 45%, Muslim 45%, other 10%
ETHNIC MIX: Tigray 50%, Tigray and Kunama 40%, Afar 4%, other 6%
GOVERNMENT: Transitional regime
CURRENCY: Nakfa = 100 cents

Estonia

Traditionally the most Western-oriented of the Baltic states, Estonia is the smallest and most developed of the three. However, the standard of living is well below the EU average.

GEOGRAPHY
Estonia's terrain is flat, boggy, and partly forested, with over 1500 islands. Lake Peipus forms much of the eastern border with Russia.

CLIMATE
Maritime, with some continental extremes. Harsh winters, with cool summers and damp springs.

PEOPLE & SOCIETY
Estonians are related ethnically and linguistically to the Finns. Friction between ethnic Estonians and the large Russian minority led to a reassertion of Estonian culture and language. Outright discrimination against the Russian language was only ended in 2000. Estonians are predominantly Lutheran. Families are small and divorce rates are high. Market reforms have increased prosperity; a few people have become very rich.

THE ECONOMY
Stable currency pegged to the euro. Good productivity. Timber and oil shale are the most important of few natural resources. Estonia is dependent on imported energy.

INSIGHT: *Estonia is a popular tourist destination for Finns, who come for the water and winter sports, architectural heritage, and nature tours*

FACTFILE
OFFICIAL NAME: Republic of Estonia
DATE OF FORMATION: 1991
CAPITAL: Tallinn
POPULATION: 1.3 million
TOTAL AREA: 17,462 sq. miles (45,226 sq. km)
DENSITY: 75 people per sq. mile

LANGUAGES: Estonian*, Russian
RELIGIONS: Evangelical Lutheran 56%, Russian Orthodox 25%, other 19%
ETHNIC MIX: Estonian 68%, Russian 26%, other 4%, Ukrainian 2%
GOVERNMENT: Parliamentary system
CURRENCY: Kroon = 100 senti

Ethiopia

Located in northeast Africa, the former empire of Ethiopia was a Marxist regime in 1974–1991. Now a free-market democracy, it has suffered a series of economic, civil, and natural crises.

GEOGRAPHY
Great Rift Valley divides mountainous northwest region from desert lowlands in northeast and southeast. Ethiopian Plateau is drained mainly by the Blue Nile.

CLIMATE
Moderate with summer rains. Highlands are warm, with night frost and snowfalls on the mountains.

PEOPLE & SOCIETY
76 Ethiopian nationalities speak 286 languages. Oromo (or Gallas) are the largest group. Ethnic representation is a major political issue. Orthodox Christianity has a very ancient history in Ethiopia. Former emperor Haile Selassie inspired Rastafarianism.

◆ **INSIGHT:** *King Solomon and the Queen of Sheba are said to have founded the Kingdom of Abyssinia (Ethiopia) c.1000 BCE*

THE ECONOMY
Ethiopia is overwhelmingly dependent on agriculture. War-damaged infrastructure and periodic serious droughts and famines undermine growth. There is a heavy reliance on food aid.

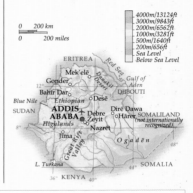

4000m/13124ft	
3000m/9843ft	
2000m/6562ft	
1000m/3281ft	
500m/1640ft	
200m/656ft	
Sea Level	
Below Sea Level	

0   200 km
0   200 miles

ERITREA
Red Sea
Mek'elē
Gonder
Gulf of
Aden
Bahir Dar
Danakil Desert
DJIBOUTI
Blue Nile
Ethiopian
Desē
SUDAN
ADDIS ABABA
Diré Dawa
Härer
SOMALILAND
(not internationally recognized)
Debre Zeyit
Highlands
Nazrēt
Ogaden
Jima
Great Rift Valley
L. Turkana
SOMALIA
KENYA

FACTFILE

OFFICIAL NAME: Federal Democratic Republic of Ethiopia
DATE OF FORMATION: 1896
CAPITAL: Addis Ababa
POPULATION: 77.4 million
TOTAL AREA: 435,184 sq. miles (1,127,127 sq. km)

DENSITY: 181 people per sq. mile
LANGUAGES: Amharic*, Tigrinya, other
RELIGIONS: Orthodox Christian 40%, Muslim 40%, traditional 15%, other 5%
ETHNIC MIX: Oromo 32%, Amhara 30%, other 26%, Tigraway 6%, Somali 6%
GOVERNMENT: Parliamentary system
CURRENCY: Ethiopian birr = 100 cents

A volcanic archipelago in the southern Pacific Ocean, comprising two large islands and 880 islets. Severe tensions exist between native Fijians and the substantial Indian minority.

GEOGRAPHY
Main islands are mountainous, fringed by coral reefs. Remainder are limestone and coral formations.

CLIMATE
Tropical. High temperatures all year round. Cyclones are a hazard.

PEOPLE & SOCIETY
The British introduced workers from India in the late 19th century, and by 1946 their descendants outnumbered the indigenous Fijian population. Ethnic-Fijian nationalism is strong and the first ethnic Indian-dominated government was overthrown in 2000; serious tensions persist. Many Indo-Fijians have left the country. Women are lobbying for more rights.

◆ **INSIGHT:** *Both Fijians and Indians practice fire-walking; Indians walk on hot embers, Fijians on heated stones*

THE ECONOMY
Well-diversified economy based on sugar production, gold mining, timber, and commercial fishing. Tourists are returning after a drop in numbers prompted by instability.

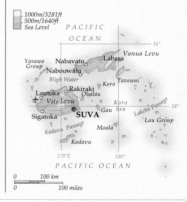

1000m/3281ft
500m/1640ft
Sea Level

PACIFIC OCEAN

16°

Yasawa Group
Nabavatu
Labasa
Vanua Levu
Nabouwalu
Bligh Water
Koro
Taveuni
Lautoka
Rakiraki
Ovalau
Viti Levu
Koro
Sea
Lakeba Passage
18°
Sigatoka
SUVA
Gau
Lau Group
Kadavu Passage
Moala
Kadavu
178°E
180°
PACIFIC OCEAN

0   100 km
0   100 miles

FACTFILE
OFFICIAL NAME: Republic of the Fiji Islands
DATE OF FORMATION: 1970
CAPITAL: Suva
POPULATION: 848,000
TOTAL AREA: 7054 sq. miles (18,270 sq. km)
DENSITY: 120 people per sq. mile

LANGUAGES: Fijian, English*, Hindi, Urdu, Tamil, Telugu
RELIGIONS: Hindu 38%, Methodist 37%, Catholic 9%, Muslim 8%, other 8%
ETHNIC MIX: Melanesian (Fijian) 51%, Indian 44%, other 5%
GOVERNMENT: Parliamentary system
CURRENCY: Fiji dollar = 100 cents

Finland

Finland's language and national identity have been influenced by both its Scandinavian and Russian neighbors. Once closely associated with the USSR, Finland is now a member of the EU.

GEOGRAPHY

South and center are flat, with low hills and many lakes. Uplands and low mountains in the north. 60% of the land area is forested.

CLIMATE

Long, harsh winters with frequent snowfalls. Short, warmer summers. Rainfall is low, and decreases northward.

PEOPLE & SOCIETY

One in four of the population live in the Greater Helsinki region. The Swedish minority live mainly in the Åland Islands in the southwest. The Sami (Lapps) lead a seminomadic existence inside the Arctic Circle. Women make up 48% of the labor force, continuing a long tradition of equality between the sexes. Families tend to be close-knit, though marriage is becoming less common.

THE ECONOMY

Strong engineering and electronics sectors. World leader in pulp and paper production.

◆ **INSIGHT:** *Finland has Europe's largest inland waterway system*

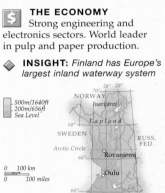

FACTFILE

OFFICIAL NAME: Republic of Finland
DATE OF FORMATION: 1917
CAPITAL: Helsinki
POPULATION: 5.2 million
TOTAL AREA: 130,127 sq. miles (337,030 sq. km)
DENSITY: 44 people per sq. mile

LANGUAGES: Finnish*, Swedish*, Sami
RELIGIONS: Evangelical Lutheran 89%, other 9%, Orthodox Christian 1%, Roman Catholic 1%
ETHNIC MIX: Finnish 93%, other (including Sami) 7%
GOVERNMENT: Parliamentary system
CURRENCY: Euro = 100 cents

France

Stretching across western Europe, from the English Channel (la Manche) to the Mediterranean Sea, France was Europe's first modern republic, and is still a leading industrial power.

GEOGRAPHY
Broad plain covers northern half of the country. Tall mountain ranges in the east and southwest, with a mountainous plateau in the center.

CLIMATE
Three main climates: temperate and damp northwest; continental east; and Mediterranean south.

PEOPLE & SOCIETY
Strong French national identity coexists with pronounced regional differences, including local languages. Immigration laws have been tightened since the 1970s, but ethnic minorities growing up in city suburbs feel increasingly alienated. New rules aim to bring more women into politics.

◆ **INSIGHT:** *France is the most popular tourist destination in the world, with over 76 million visitors a year*

THE ECONOMY
Chemicals, electronics, heavy engineering, and aircraft typify a strong and diversified export sector. World leader in cosmetics, perfumes, and quality wines.

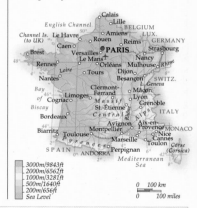

3000m/9843ft	
2000m/6562ft	
1000m/3281ft	
500m/1640ft	
200m/656ft	
Sea Level	

0   100 km
0   100 miles

📖 FACTFILE

OFFICIAL NAME: French Republic
DATE OF FORMATION: 987
CAPITAL: Paris
POPULATION: 60.5 million
TOTAL AREA: 211,208 sq. miles (547,030 sq. km)
DENSITY: 285 people per sq. mile

LANGUAGES: French*, Provençal, other
RELIGIONS: Catholic 88%, Muslim 8%, Protestant 2%, Jewish 1%, Buddhist 1%
ETHNIC MIX: French 90%, North African 6%, German 2%, Breton 1%, other 1%
GOVERNMENT: Mixed presidential–parliamentary system
CURRENCY: Euro = 100 cents

Gabon

Gabon is a former French colony straddling the equator on Africa's west coast. Independent since 1960, it returned to multiparty politics in 1990, after 22 years of one-party rule.

GEOGRAPHY

Low plateaus and mountains lie beyond the coastal strip. Two-thirds of the land is covered by rainforest.

CLIMATE

Hot and tropical, with little distinction between seasons. Cold Benguela current cools the coast.

PEOPLE & SOCIETY

Some 40 different languages are spoken. The Fang, who live mainly in the north, are the largest ethnic group, but have yet to gain control of the government. Oil wealth has led to the growth of an affluent middle class. Menial jobs are done by immigrant workers. Education follows the French system. With over 80% of people living in towns, Gabon is one of Africa's most urbanized countries. The government is encouraging population growth.

THE ECONOMY

Oil is the main source of revenue. Tropical hardwoods are being exploited. Cocoa beans, coffee, and rice are grown for export.

INSIGHT: *Libreville was founded as a settlement for freed French slaves in 1849*

FACTFILE

OFFICIAL NAME: Gabonese Republic
DATE OF FORMATION: 1960
CAPITAL: Libreville
POPULATION: 1.4 million
TOTAL AREA: 103,346 sq. miles (267,667 sq. km)
DENSITY: 14 people per sq. mile

LANGUAGES: Fang, French*, Punu, other
RELIGIONS: Christian (predominantly Roman Catholic) 55%, traditional beliefs 40%, other 4%, Muslim 1%
ETHNIC MIX: Fang 26%, Shira-punu 24%, other 24%, foreign 15%, Nzabi-duma 11%
GOVERNMENT: Presidential system
CURRENCY: CFA franc = 100 centimes

Gambia

Gambia is a narrow state on the west coast of Africa, almost entirely surrounded by Senegal. It was renowned for its stability until its government was overthrown in a coup in 1994.

GEOGRAPHY
Located on the narrow strip of land bordering the Gambia River. Long, sandy beaches are backed by mangrove swamps along the river. Savanna and tropical forests higher up.

CLIMATE
Subtropical, with wet, humid months July–October, and warm, dry season November–May.

PEOPLE & SOCIETY
Little tension between various ethnic groups. The largest group, the Mandinka, has traditionally held power. Islam is a strong social influence, though there is no official state religion. A small expatriate community from the UK lives on the coast. Each year seasonal migrants come from neighboring states to farm groundnuts. Women are very active as traders.

THE ECONOMY
Around 80% of the labor force is involved in agriculture. Groundnuts are the principal crop. Fish stocks are declining. "Eco-tourism" is promoted, though most visitors come for the beaches. Smuggling problems. Banjul is one of west Africa's finest deepwater ports.

◆ **INSIGHT:** *Overfishing in the waters off the Gambia and Senegal, mainly by foreign vessels, is a growing problem*

FACTFILE

OFFICIAL NAME: Republic of the Gambia
DATE OF FORMATION: 1965
CAPITAL: Banjul
POPULATION: 1.5 million
TOTAL AREA: 4363 sq. miles (11,300 sq. km)
DENSITY: 389 people per sq. mile

LANGUAGES: Mandinka, Fulani, Wolof, Jola, Soninke, English*
RELIGIONS: Sunni Muslim 90%, Christian 9%, traditional beliefs 1%
ETHNIC MIX: Mandinka 40%, Fulani 19%, Wolof 15%, Jola 11%, Serahuli 9%, other 6%
GOVERNMENT: Presidential system
CURRENCY: Dalasi = 100 butut

Georgia

Located on the eastern shore of the Black Sea, Georgia has been torn by civil war and ethnic disputes since achieving independence from the Soviet Union in 1991.

 GEOGRAPHY
Kura Valley lies between Caucasus Mountains in the north and Lesser Caucasus range in south. Lowlands along the Black Sea coast.

 CLIMATE
Subtropical along the coast, changing to continental extremes at high altitudes. Rainfall is moderate.

 PEOPLE & SOCIETY
Paternalistic society, with strong family, cultural, and literary traditions. Georgia was converted to Christianity in 326 CE. Civil conflict and wars against Abkhaz and Osset separatists in the early 1990s displaced over 300,000 people. Abkhazia and South Ossetia now effectively operate as separate states. A small, wealthy elite is found in Tbilisi while the ethnic Armenians of the south are among the poorest people in society.

$ THE ECONOMY
Georgia is a gateway to the West for Azeri oil. It has a long-established and booming wine industry, exporting mostly to Russia. Political instability deters investment.

◆ **INSIGHT:** *Western Georgia was the land of the legendary Golden Fleece of Greek mythology*

FACTFILE

OFFICIAL NAME: Georgia
DATE OF FORMATION: 1991
CAPITAL: Tbilisi
POPULATION: 4.5 million
TOTAL AREA: 26,911 sq. miles (69,700 sq. km)
DENSITY: 167 people per sq. mile

LANGUAGES: Georgian*, Russian, other
RELIGIONS: Georgian Orthodox 65%, Muslim 11%, Russian Orthodox 10%, Armenian Orthodox 8%, other 6%
ETHNIC MIX: Georgian 84%, Armenian 6%, Azeri 6%, Russian 2%, other 2%
GOVERNMENT: Presidential system
CURRENCY: Lari = 100 tetri

Germany

Europe's strongest industrial power and its most populous nation, Germany was divided after military defeat in 1945 into a democratic west and a communist east, but reunified in 1990.

GEOGRAPHY
Central European coastal plains in the north, rising to rolling hills of central region and Alps in far south.

CLIMATE
Damp, temperate in northern and central regions. Continental extremes in mountainous south.

PEOPLE & SOCIETY
Regionalism is strong. The north is mainly Protestant while the south is staunchly Roman Catholic. Social and economic differences still exist between east and west. Turks are the largest single ethnic minority; many came as guest workers in the 1950s–1970s. Immigration rules now favor skilled workers. Feminism is strong.

◆ INSIGHT: *Germany's rivers and canals carry as much freight as its busy highways*

THE ECONOMY
Massive exports of electronics, heavy engineering, chemicals, and cars. Growth restored after 2001 global slowdown, but unemployment high.

2000m/6562ft
1000m/3281ft
500m/1640ft
200m/656ft
Sea Level

0   100 km
0   100 miles

FACTFILE
OFFICIAL NAME: Federal Republic of Germany
DATE OF FORMATION: 1871
CAPITAL: Berlin
POPULATION: 82.7 million
TOTAL AREA: 137,846 sq. miles (357,021 sq. km)

DENSITY: 613 people per sq. mile
LANGUAGES: German*, Turkish
RELIGIONS: Protestant 34%, Roman Catholic 33%, other 30%, Muslim 3%
ETHNIC MIX: German 92%, other 3%, other European 3%, Turkish 2%
GOVERNMENT: Parliamentary system
CURRENCY: Euro = 100 cents

Ghana

The heartland of the ancient Ashanti kingdom, Ghana in west Africa was once known as the Gold Coast. It has experienced intermittent periods of military rule since independence in 1957.

GEOGRAPHY
Mostly low-lying. The west is covered by rainforest. One of the world's largest artificial lakes – Lake Volta – was created by damming the White Volta River.

CLIMATE
Tropical. There are two wet seasons in the south, but the north is drier, and has just one.

PEOPLE & SOCIETY
Around 75 cultural-linguistic groups. The largest is the Akan, who include the Ashanti and Fanti peoples. Over 100 languages and dialects are spoken. Southern peoples are richer and more urban than those of the north. There are few tribal tensions. Family ties are strong. The election of John Kufuor in 2000 marked Ghana's first peaceful handover of power since independence.

THE ECONOMY
Produces 17% of the world's cocoa. Gold-mining is also important. Hardwood trees such as maple and sapele. Hydropower is exported.

INSIGHT: *Ghana was the first colony in west Africa to gain independence*

FACTFILE
OFFICIAL NAME: Republic of Ghana
DATE OF FORMATION: 1957
CAPITAL: Accra
POPULATION: 22.1 million
TOTAL AREA: 92,100 sq. miles (238,540 sq. km)
DENSITY: 249 people per sq. mile

LANGUAGES: Twi, Fanti, Ewe, Ga, Adangbe, Gurma, Dagomba, English*
RELIGIONS: Christian 69%, Muslim 16%, traditional beliefs 9%, other 6%
ETHNIC MIX: Akan 49%, Mole-Dagbani 17%, Ewe 13%, other 13%, Ga 8%
GOVERNMENT: Presidential system
CURRENCY: Cedi = 100 pesewas

Greece

The Balkan state of Greece is bounded on three sides by the Mediterranean, Aegean, and Ionian Seas. It has a strong seafaring tradition, with some of the world's richest shipowners.

GEOGRAPHY

Mountainous peninsula and over 2000 islands. Large plain along the mainland's Aegean coast.

CLIMATE

Mainly Mediterranean with dry, hot summers. Alpine climate in northern mountain areas.

PEOPLE & SOCIETY

Postwar industrial development altered the dominance of agriculture and seafaring. The rural exodus to industrial cities has been stemmed but a third of the population now live in Athens. Age-old culture and Greek Orthodox Church balance social mobility. Civil marriage and divorce only became legal in 1982.

◆ **INSIGHT:** *Classical sights have made tourism one of the most important industries in Greece*

THE ECONOMY
One of Europe's leading tourist destinations. The world's largest beneficially owned shipping fleets. Large black economy. Public debt and unemployment remain high.

FACTFILE
OFFICIAL NAME: Hellenic Republic
DATE OF FORMATION: 1829
CAPITAL: Athens
POPULATION: 11.1 million
TOTAL AREA: 50,942 sq. miles (131,940 sq. km)
DENSITY: 220 people per sq. mile

LANGUAGES: Greek*, Turkish, Macedonian, Albanian
RELIGIONS: Orthodox Christian 98%, Muslim 1%, other 1%
ETHNIC MIX: Greek 98%, other 2%
GOVERNMENT: Parliamentary system
CURRENCY: Euro = 100 cents

Grenada

The southernmost of the Windward Islands, Grenada became a focus of world attention in 1983 when the US and Caribbean allies mounted an invasion to sever links with Castro's Cuba.

 GEOGRAPHY
Volcanic in origin, with densely forested central mountains. Its territory also includes the islands of Carriacou and Petite Martinique.

 CLIMATE
Tropical, tempered by trade winds. Hurricanes are a hazard in the July–November wet season.

 PEOPLE & SOCIETY
Grenadians are mainly of African origin; their traditions remain strong, especially on Carriacou. Inter-ethnic marriage has reduced tensions between the groups. Extended families, often headed by women, are the norm. Wealth disparities are not marked, but levels of poverty are growing.

 INSIGHT: *Known as "the spice island of the Caribbean," it is the world's second-largest nutmeg producer*

THE ECONOMY
Severe damage from Hurricane Ivan in 2004; nutmeg production still to recover. Mace, cocoa, saffron, and cloves are also exported. Smuggling is a serious problem.

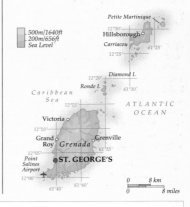

FACTFILE

OFFICIAL NAME: Grenada
DATE OF FORMATION: 1974
CAPITAL: St. George's
POPULATION: 89,502
TOTAL AREA: 131 sq. miles (340 sq. km)
DENSITY: 683 people per sq. mile

LANGUAGES: English*, English Creole
RELIGIONS: Roman Catholic 68%, Anglican 17%, other 15%
ETHNIC MIX: Black African 82%, Mulatto 13%, East Indian 3%, other 2%
GOVERNMENT: Parliamentary system
CURRENCY: East Caribbean $ = 100 cents

Guatemala

The largest and most populous nation on the Central American isthmus, Guatemala returned to civilian rule in 1986 after 32 years of violent and repressive military rule.

GEOGRAPHY
Narrow Pacific coastal plain. Central highlands with volcanoes. Short coast on the Caribbean Sea. Tropical rainforests in the north.

CLIMATE

Tropical: hot and humid in coastal regions and north. More temperate in central highlands.

PEOPLE & SOCIETY

Amerindians, concentrated in the highlands, form a majority. Power, wealth, and land are controlled by a *ladino* elite. Roman Catholicism is predominant, mixed with traditional Amerindian spiritual beliefs. Over 30% of the population live below the UN's poverty line of $2 a day.

◆ **INSIGHT:** *Guatemala, which means "land of trees," was the center of the ancient Mayan civilization*

THE ECONOMY
Agriculture is the key sector. Coffee, sugar, bananas, and shrimp are top exports. Wealth inequalities inhibit domestic market.

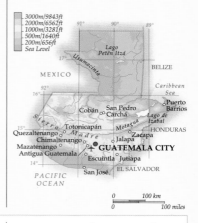

FACTFILE
OFFICIAL NAME: Republic of Guatemala
DATE OF FORMATION: 1838
CAPITAL: Guatemala City
POPULATION: 12.6 million
TOTAL AREA: 42,042 sq. miles (108,890 sq. km)
DENSITY: 301 people per sq. mile

LANGUAGES: Quiché, Mam, Cakchiquel, Kekchí, Spanish*
RELIGIONS: Roman Catholic 65%, Protestant 33%, other 2%
ETHNIC MIX: Amerindian 60%, Mestizo 30%, other 10%
GOVERNMENT: Presidential system
CURRENCY: Quetzal = 100 centavos

Guinea

Facing the Atlantic Ocean, on the west coast of Africa, Guinea became the first French colony in Africa to gain independence, in 1958. The country was under military rule from 1984 to 1995.

GEOGRAPHY
Coastal plains and mangrove swamps in west rise to forested or savanna highlands in the south. Semidesert in the north.

CLIMATE
Tropical, with a wet season April–October. Conakry is especially rainy. Hot, dry *harmattan* wind blows from Sahara during dry season.

PEOPLE & SOCIETY
Peul and Malinke make up most of the population, but rivalries between them have allowed coastal peoples such as the Soussou to come to dominate politics. Daily life revolves around the extended family. Women acquired influence under Marxist party rule between 1958 and 1984, but the Muslim revival since then has reversed the trend. Private enterprise has created a business class.

THE ECONOMY
Over 80% of people are farmers. Cash crops include bananas and palm oil. Substantial gold, diamond, and especially bauxite reserves.

INSIGHT: *The colors of Guinea's flag represent the three words of the country's motto: work (red), justice (yellow), and solidarity (green)*

1000m/3281ft
500m/1640ft
200m/656ft
Sea Level

0   100 km
0   100 miles

FACTFILE
OFFICIAL NAME: Republic of Guinea
DATE OF FORMATION: 1958
CAPITAL: Conakry
POPULATION: 9.4 million
TOTAL AREA: 94,925 sq. miles (245,857 sq. km)
DENSITY: 99 people per sq. mile

LANGUAGES: Pulaar, Malinke, Soussou, French*
RELIGIONS: Muslim 65%, traditional beliefs 33%, Christian 2%
ETHNIC MIX: Peul 39%, Malinke 23%, other 21%, Soussou 11%, Kissi 6%
GOVERNMENT: Presidential system
CURRENCY: Guinea franc = 100 centimes

Guinea-Bissau

Known as Portuguese Guinea while a colony, Guinea-Bissau is situated on Africa's west coast. Since 1994, multiparty democracy has been interrupted by coups and rebellions.

GEOGRAPHY
Low-lying, apart from savanna highlands in northeast. Rainforests and swamps are found along coastal areas.

CLIMATE
Tropical, with wet season May–November and dry season December–April. Hot, dry *harmattan* desert wind blows during dry season.

PEOPLE & SOCIETY
The largest ethnic group is the Balante, who live in the south. Though only around 1% of the population, the mixed Portuguese–African *mestiços* dominate the top ranks of government and bureaucracy. Most people live and work on small family farms, grouped in self-contained villages. The bulk of the urban population live in the capital, Bissau, where they face economic hardship and increasing political instability.

THE ECONOMY
Mostly subsistence farming – maize, sweet potatoes, cassava. Lack of sufficiency in rice staple. Main cash crops are cashew nuts and cotton. Offshore oil as yet untapped. Fisheries and timber potential.

◆ **INSIGHT:** *In 1974, Guinea-Bissau became the first Portuguese colony to gain independence*

FACTFILE
OFFICIAL NAME: Rep. of Guinea-Bissau
DATE OF FORMATION: 1974
CAPITAL: Bissau
POPULATION: 1.6 million
TOTAL AREA: 13,946 sq. miles (36,120 sq. km)
DENSITY: 147 people per sq. mile

LANGUAGES: Portuguese Creole, Balante, Fulani, Malinke, Portuguese*
RELIGIONS: Indigenous beliefs 52%, Muslim 40%, Christian 8%
ETHNIC MIX: Balante 30%, other 24%, Fulani 20%, Mandyako 14%, Mandinka 12%,
GOVERNMENT: Presidential system
CURRENCY: CFA franc = 100 centimes

Guyana

On the northeast coast of the continent, Guyana is South America's only English-speaking country. Independent since 1966, it has close ties with the anglophone Caribbean.

 GEOGRAPHY
Mainly artificial coast, reclaimed by dikes and dams from swamps and tidal marshes. Forests cover 85% of the interior, rising to savanna uplands and mountains.

 CLIMATE
Tropical. Coast cooled by sea breezes. Lowlands are hot, wet, and humid. Highlands are a little cooler.

 PEOPLE & SOCIETY
Guyana is a complex multiracial society. Tension exists between the Afro-Guyanese, descended from slaves, and the Indo-Guyanese, descendants of laborers brought over after slavery was abolished. Politics is highly polarized around this split and often spills over into violence on the streets. Amerindian subsistence farmers are the poorest people in society and have little representation.

THE ECONOMY
Diverse exports: bauxite, gold, timber, sugar, rice, and diamonds. High unemployment and rising crime.

INSIGHT: *Guyana means "land of many waters," reflecting its dense network of rivers*

FACTFILE

OFFICIAL NAME: Cooperative Republic of Guyana
DATE OF FORMATION: 1966
CAPITAL: Georgetown
POPULATION: 751,000
TOTAL AREA: 83,000 sq. miles (214,970 sq. km)

DENSITY: 10 people per sq. mile
LANGUAGES: Creole, Hindi, English*
RELIGIONS: Christian 57%, Hindu 33%, Muslim 9%, other 1%
ETHNIC MIX: East Indian 43%, Black African 30%, other 18%, Amerindian 9%
GOVERNMENT: Presidential system
CURRENCY: Guyanese dollar = 100 cents

Haiti

Formerly a French colony, Haiti shares the Caribbean island of Hispaniola with the Dominican Republic. At independence in 1804, it became the world's first black republic.

GEOGRAPHY
Predominantly mountainous, with forests and fertile plains.

CLIMATE
Tropical, with rain throughout the year. Humid in coastal areas, much cooler in the mountains.

PEOPLE & SOCIETY
Most Haitians are of African descent. A few have European roots, primarily French. The rigid class structure maintains vast disparities of wealth. The majority of the population live in extreme poverty; Haiti is one of the poorest countries in the Americas. A combination of political oppression and a collapsing economy has led thousands to seek asylum in the US or the Dominican Republic. As well as being Christians, many Haitians practice Voodoo, which was recognized as an official religion in 2003.

THE ECONOMY
Few natural resources. Transshipment of narcotics to the US provides a large source of income to smugglers. 70% unemployment.

INSIGHT: *A slave rebellion headed by Toussaint Louverture in 1791 led to Haiti's independence*

FACTFILE

OFFICIAL NAME: Republic of Haiti
DATE OF FORMATION: 1804
CAPITAL: Port-au-Prince
POPULATION: 8.5 million
TOTAL AREA: 10,714 sq. miles (27,750 sq. km)
DENSITY: 799 people per sq. mile

LANGUAGES: French Creole*, French*
RELIGIONS: Roman Catholic 80%, Protestant 16%, other 3%, nonreligious 1%; Voodoo is widely practiced
ETHNIC MIX: Black African 95%, Mulatto and European 5%
GOVERNMENT: Presidential system
CURRENCY: Gourde = 100 centimes

Honduras

Straddling the Central American isthmus, Honduras returned to democratic civilian rule in 1984, after a period of military government. Hurricane Mitch devastated the country in 1998.

GEOGRAPHY

Narrow plains along both coasts, with a mountainous interior, cut by river valleys. Tropical forests, swamps, and lagoons in the east.

CLIMATE

Tropical coastal lowlands are hot and humid, with May–October rains. Interior is cooler and drier.

PEOPLE & SOCIETY

The majority of the population is *mestizo* (mixed race). An English-speaking *garífuna* (black) community and Miskito Amerindians struggle to preserve their rights to land along the remote Caribbean coast. Women's status remains low. Hurricane Mitch killed 5600 people in 1998 and impoverished 85% of the population. Wealth inequalities are large and poverty is at the root of social tension. Violent crime is a major issue.

THE ECONOMY

Coffee, bananas, and shellfish are the main exports; low world prices have hit revenues. Honduras qualified for debt relief from 2005. Corruption and high underemployment.

◆ **INSIGHT:** *The Honduran currency is named after a Lenca Indian chief who was the main leader of resistance to the Spanish conquest in the 16th century*

FACTFILE

OFFICIAL NAME: Republic of Honduras
DATE OF FORMATION: 1838
CAPITAL: Tegucigalpa
POPULATION: 7.2 million
TOTAL AREA: 43,278 sq. miles (112,090 sq. km)
DENSITY: 167 people per sq. mile

LANGUAGES: Spanish*, Garífuna, English Creole
RELIGIONS: Roman Catholic 97%, Protestant 3%
ETHNIC MIX: Mestizo 90%, Black African 5%, Amerindian 4%, White 1%
GOVERNMENT: Presidential system
CURRENCY: Lempira = 100 centavos

Hungary

Landlocked in central Europe, Hungary was once the heart of the powerful Habsburg Empire. It lost two-thirds of its historical territory for supporting Germany in World War I.

GEOGRAPHY
Landlocked. Fertile plains in east and northwest; west and north are hilly. The Danube River cuts through the country and the capital.

CLIMATE
Continental, with wet springs, late but very hot summers, and cold, cloudy winters. The transition between seasons tends to be sudden.

PEOPLE & SOCIETY
Hungary's population shrank in the 1990s. Mostly ethnic Hungarian (Magyar), there are small minorities of Germans, Jews, and neighboring peoples. Roma face particular discrimination. The government is greatly concerned about the fate of ethnic Hungarians in Romania, Serbia, and Slovakia. Living standards are high, though working hours are longer than in Western Europe.

THE ECONOMY
High industrial production. Open access for foreign investors. Return of export-led growth, notably high-tech goods and wine. Budget deficit must be cut to join eurozone.

◆ INSIGHT: *The Hungarian language is Asian in origin and is most closely related to Finnish*

FACTFILE

OFFICIAL NAME: Republic of Hungary
DATE OF FORMATION: 1918
CAPITAL: Budapest
POPULATION: 10.1 million
TOTAL AREA: 35,919 sq. miles (93,030 sq. km)
DENSITY: 283 people per sq. mile

LANGUAGES: Hungarian*
RELIGIONS: Catholic 52%, Calvinist 16%, other 15%, nonreligious 14%, Lutheran 3%
ETHNIC MIX: Magyar 94%, other 5%, Roma 1%
GOVERNMENT: Parliamentary system
CURRENCY: Forint = 100 fillér

Iceland

Europe's westernmost country, Iceland has a strategic location in the north Atlantic, straddling the Mid-Atlantic Ridge. Its spectacular landscape is largely uninhabited.

GEOGRAPHY
Grassy coastal lowlands, with fjords in the north. Central plateau of cold lava desert, geothermal springs, and glaciers. Around 200 volcanoes, with numerous geysers and solfataras.

CLIMATE
Its location in the middle of the Gulf Stream moderates the climate. Mild winters and brief, cool summers.

PEOPLE & SOCIETY
Prosperous and homogeneous, Icelandic society includes only a few thousand foreign residents. There is high social mobility, free health care, and low-cost heating (geothermal and hydropower). Longevity rates are among the highest in the world. Strong emphasis on education and literacy. The Icelandic language has changed little in 700 years, in part due to the country's isolation.

THE ECONOMY
The high-tech fishing industry dominates export earnings. Tourism is growing. Geothermal and hydro-electric energy are abundant.

◆ **INSIGHT:** *The word geyser is taken from Geysir (the "gusher") in southwest Iceland*

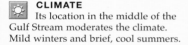

	1000m/3281ft
	500m/1640ft
	200m/656ft
	Sea Level
	Ice Cap

0   50 km
0   50 miles

FACTFILE
OFFICIAL NAME: Republic of Iceland
DATE OF FORMATION: 1944
CAPITAL: Reykjavík
POPULATION: 295,000
TOTAL AREA: 39,768 sq. miles (103,000 sq. km)
DENSITY: 8 people per sq. mile

LANGUAGES: Icelandic*
RELIGIONS: Evangelical Lutheran 93%, nonreligious 6%, other (mostly Christian) 1%
ETHNIC MIX: Icelandic 94%, other 5%, Danish 1%
GOVERNMENT: Parliamentary system
CURRENCY: Icelandic króna = 100 aurar

India

India is the world's second most populous country. The birth-rate has recently been falling, but even at its current level India's population will probably overtake China's by 2030.

GEOGRAPHY

Separated from northern Asia by the Himalaya mountain range, India forms a subcontinent. As well as the Himalayas, there are two other main geographical regions, the Indo-Gangetic plain, which lies between the foothills of the Himalayas and the Vindhya Mountains, and the central-southern Deccan plateau. The Ghats are smaller mountain ranges located on the east and west coasts.

CLIMATE

Varies greatly according to latitude, altitude, and season. Most of India has three seasons: hot, wet, and cool. In summer, temperatures in the north can reach 104°F (40°C). The monsoon breaks in June and peters out in September to October. In the cool season, the weather is mainly dry. The climate in the warmer south is less variable than in the north.

PEOPLE & SOCIETY

Cultural and religious pressures encourage large families. Nationwide awareness campaigns aim to promote the idea of smaller families. India's planners consider the rise in the population the most significant brake on development. Despite a major birth control program, the decrease in population growth has been marginal. Rural deprivation encourages urban growth. Almost 80% of people survive on less than $2 a day. The majority of Indians are Hindu. Various attempts to reform the Hindu caste system, which determines social standing and even marriage, have met with violent opposition. Severe tensions exist between Hindus and the Muslim minority, especially in Kashmir and Gujarat. Smaller ethnic groups exist in the northeast, and many struggle for greater autonomy. Over five million people are living with HIV/AIDS.

FACTFILE

OFFICIAL NAME: Republic of India
DATE OF FORMATION: 1947
CAPITAL: New Delhi
POPULATION: 1.1 billion
TOTAL AREA: 1,269,338 sq. miles
(3,287,590 sq. km)
DENSITY: 961 people per sq. mile

LANGUAGES: Hindi*, English*, Urdu, Bengali, Marathi, Telugu, Tamil, other
RELIGIONS: Hindu 83%, Muslim 11%, Christian 2%, Sikh 2%, other 2%
ETHNIC MIX: Indo-Aryan 72%, Dravidian 25%, Mongoloid and other 3%
GOVERNMENT: Parliamentary system
CURRENCY: Indian rupee = 100 paise

$ THE ECONOMY

India has the fastest-growing economy in Asia after China. Protectionism has given way to free-market economics. The success of "Bollywood" films and high-tech industries contrast with massive levels of poverty.

◆ **INSIGHT:** India's national animal, the tiger, was worshipped as early as 4000 years ago by the Mohenjo-Daro civilization

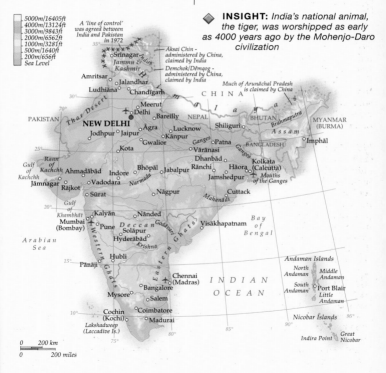

5000m/16405ft
4000m/13124ft
3000m/9843ft
2000m/6562ft
1000m/3281ft
500m/1640ft
200m/656ft
Sea Level

A 'line of control' was agreed between India and Pakistan in 1972

35°

Aksai Chin - administered by China, claimed by India

Demchok/Dêmqog - administered by China, claimed by India

Srinagar
Jammu & Kashmir
Amritsar
Jalandhar
Ludhiāna Chandigarh

30°
70°

Much of Arunāchal Pradesh is claimed by China

CHINA

Thar Desert

Meerut
Delhi
NEW DELHI
Jodhpur Jaipur Āgra
Bareilly Lucknow
Kānpur

Shiliguri

NEPAL

BHUTAN

Brahmaputra

MYANMAR (BURMA)

25°

Kota

Gwalior
Vārānasi
Ganges Patna

Assam

Imphāl

BANGLADESH

Dhanbād
Ranchī

Kolkata (Calcutta)

Gulf of Kachchh

Rann of Kachchh

Ahmadābād Indore
Jāmnagar
Rājkot Vadodara
Sūrat

Bhōpāl Jabalpur
Narmada

Nāgpur

Jamshedpur Hāora
Mouths of the Ganges

Cuttack

Mahanadi

20°

Gulf of Khambhāt

Mumbai (Bombay)
Kalyān Nānded
Pune
Deccan
Solāpur
Hyderābād

Godavari

Visākhapatnam

B a y
o f
B e n g a l

Arabian Sea

Western Ghats

Hubli
Pānaji

Krishna

Eastern Ghats

15°

Chennai (Madras)

Andaman Islands
North Andaman
Middle Andaman
South Andaman
Port Blair
Little Andaman

Bangalore
Mysore Salem

Coimbatore

I N D I A N
O C E A N

95°

10°

Cochin (Kochi)
Lakshadweep (Laccadive Is.)

Madurai

Nicobar Islands

90°

Indira Point

Great Nicobar

PAKISTAN

0   200 km
0   200 miles

75° 80° 85°

Indonesia

Formerly known as the Dutch East Indies, Indonesia is the world's largest archipelago. Its 18,108 islands stretch 3000 miles (5000 km) eastward from the Indian Ocean to the Pacific.

GEOGRAPHY

Indonesia is highly mountainous with numerous tropical swamps. The land is covered with dense rainforest, especially on New Guinea, where it remains largely unexplored. There are more than 200 volcanoes in the region, many of which are still active. The land masses of Java, Bali, Sumatra, Lombok, and Borneo were once joined together by dry land, which has since been submerged by rising sea levels. Some of the islands are large enough to have formed coastal lowlands.

CLIMATE

The climate of Indonesia is predominantly tropical monsoon. Variations relate mainly to differences in latitude and altitude; hilly areas are cooler overall. Rain falls throughout the year, often in thunderstorms, but there is a relatively dry season from June to September.

THE ECONOMY

Varied resources, especially energy. Cheap and plentiful labor pool. Bureaucracy and corruption damages investor confidence. Large foreign debt has been rescheduled. Piracy is a serious problem.

FACTFILE

OFFICIAL NAME: Republic of Indonesia
DATE OF FORMATION: 1949
CAPITAL: Jakarta
POPULATION: 223 million
TOTAL AREA: 741,096 sq. miles (1,919,440 sq. km)
DENSITY: 321 people per sq. mile

LANGUAGES: Javanese, Sundanese, Madurese, Bahasa Indonesia*, Dutch
RELIGIONS: Sunni Muslim 87%, Christian 9%, Hindu 2%, other 2%
ETHNIC MIX: Javanese 42%, other 31%, Sundanese 15%, coastal Malays 12%
GOVERNMENT: Presidential system
CURRENCY: Rupiah = 100 sen

Indonesia

PEOPLE & SOCIETY

The basic Melanesian–Malay ethnic division disguises a diverse society. Bahasa Indonesia, the national language, coexists with at least 250 other spoken languages or dialects. Attempts by the Javanese political elite to suppress local cultures have been vigorously opposed, especially by the Aceh of northern Sumatra, and the Papuans. Religious and interethnic hostility is increasing. There have been clashes between Christians and Muslims in many areas, and discrimination against ethnic Chinese has encouraged vicious attacks on their businesses. Gender equality is enshrined in law, and women are active in public life. The *tsunami* (tidal wave) in 2004 devastated northern Sumatra; around 128,000 people were killed with 37,000 more missing.

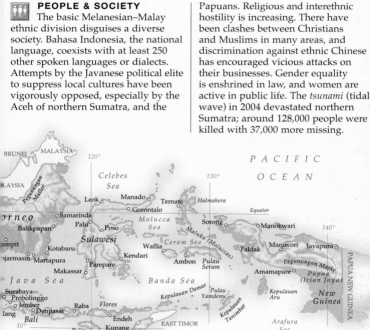

◆ **INSIGHT:** *Indonesia has a very youthful population; almost 30% of its people are under 15 years of age*

Iran

Since the 1979 Islamic fundamentalist revolution led by
Ayatollah Khomeini, the Middle Eastern country of Iran
has become the world's largest theocracy.

GEOGRAPHY
High desert plateau with large
salt pans in the east. West and north are
mountainous. Coastal land bordering
Caspian Sea is rainy and forested.

CLIMATE
Desert climate. Hot summers,
and bitterly cold winters. Area around
the Caspian Sea is more temperate.

PEOPLE & SOCIETY
Many ethnic groups, including
Persians, Azaris (ethnically related to
Azeris), and Kurds. Militant Shi'a
Islamism has dominated since the
1979 revolution. The mullahs' belief
that adherence to religious values is
more important than economic welfare
has resulted in declining living
standards. Female emancipation
has also been reversed. Liberal
attitudes, particularly prevalent
among students, have led to clashes.

THE ECONOMY
One of the world's biggest oil
producers. Government restricts
contact with the West, blocking
acquisition of vital technology.
High unemployment and inflation.

◆ **INSIGHT:** *More than a hundred
offenses carry the death penalty*

FACTFILE
OFFICIAL NAME: Islamic Republic of Iran
DATE OF FORMATION: 1502
CAPITAL: Tehrān
POPULATION: 69.5 million
TOTAL AREA: 636,293 sq. miles
(1,648,000 sq. km)
DENSITY: 110 people per sq. mile

LANGUAGES: Farsi*, Azeri, Luri, Gilaki,
Mazanderani, Kurdish, Turkmen, Arabic
RELIGIONS: Shi'a Muslim 93%, Sunni
Muslim 6%, other 1%
ETHNIC MIX: Persian 50%, Azari 24%,
other 10%, Kurd 8%, Lur and Bakhtiari 8%
GOVERNMENT: Islamic theocracy
CURRENCY: Iranian rial = 100 dinars

Iraq

Oil-rich Iraq is situated in the central Middle East. The last 50 years have been dominated by periods of war and civil conflict. A US-led Coalition ousted Saddam Hussein in April 2003.

GEOGRAPHY

Mainly desert. The Tigris and Euphrates Rivers water fertile regions and create the southern marshland. Mountains along northeast border.

CLIMATE

Southern deserts have hot, dry summers and mild winters. North has dry summers, but winters can be harsh in the mountains. Rainfall is low.

PEOPLE & SOCIETY

Carved out of remnants of the Ottoman Empire, Iraq is home to three distinct ethnic groups, as well as smaller minorities. The Arab Muslims are divided between Shi'a and Sunni. The northern Kurds were persecuted by the regime of Saddam Hussein. Since his removal, religious tensions have fuelled an insurgency bordering on all-out civil war. After years of war and sanctions, poverty is widespread.

THE ECONOMY
The country's infrastructure has been destroyed. If stability can be achieved, hopes of recovery rest on massive oil reserves and aid.

INSIGHT: *As Mesopotamia, Iraq was the site where the Sumerians established the world's first civilization*

FACTFILE

OFFICIAL NAME: Republic of Iraq
DATE OF FORMATION: 1932
CAPITAL: Baghdad
POPULATION: 28.8 million
TOTAL AREA: 168,753 sq. miles (437,072 sq. km)
DENSITY: 171 people per sq. mile

LANGUAGES: Arabic*, Kurdish, Turkic languages, Armenian, Assyrian
RELIGIONS: Shi'a Muslim 60%, Sunni Muslim 35%, other 5%
ETHNIC MIX: Arab 80%, Kurdish 15%, Turkmen 3%, other 2%
GOVERNMENT: Parliamentary system
CURRENCY: New Iraqi dinar = 1000 fils

Ireland

Lying in the Atlantic Ocean, off the west coast of Britain, the Irish republic occupies about 85% of the island of Ireland, with the remainder (Northern Ireland) being part of the UK.

GEOGRAPHY
Low mountain ranges along an irregular coastline surround an inland plain punctuated by lakes, undulating hills, and peat bogs.

CLIMATE
The Gulf Stream accounts for the mild and wet climate. Snow is rare, except in the mountains.

PEOPLE & SOCIETY
Though homogeneous in ethnicity and Roman Catholic religion, the population show signs of change. The younger Irish question teachings on birth control, divorce, and abortion. Traditionally an emigrant nation, there is now net immigration. Living standards have improved greatly. The Good Friday peace agreement over Northern Ireland was reached in 1998, though a definitive peace remains elusive.

THE ECONOMY
Historically high, unemployment in Ireland is now one of the lowest rates in Europe. The workforce is highly educated. Efficient agriculture and food-processing industries.

◆ **INSIGHT:** *About 40% of Irish people speak Irish Gaelic*

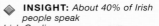

FACTFILE

OFFICIAL NAME: Ireland
DATE OF FORMATION: 1922
CAPITAL: Dublin
POPULATION: 4.1 million
TOTAL AREA: 27,135 sq. miles (70,280 sq. km)
DENSITY: 154 people per sq. mile

LANGUAGES: English*, Irish Gaelic*
RELIGIONS: Roman Catholic 88%, other and nonreligious 9%, Anglican 3%
ETHNIC MIX: Irish 99%, other 1%
GOVERNMENT: Parliamentary system
CURRENCY: Euro = 100 cents

Israel

Created as a new state in 1948, Israel lies in the eastern Mediterranean. The Palestinian population launched the latest *intifada* (armed struggle) against Israeli occupation in 2000.

GEOGRAPHY
Coastal plain. Desert in the south. In the east lie the Great Rift Valley and the Dead Sea – the lowest point on the Earth's land surface.

CLIMATE
Summers are hot and dry. Wet season, March–November, is mild.

PEOPLE & SOCIETY
Large numbers of Jews settled in Palestine before Israel was founded in 1948. After World War II, there was a massive increase in immigration. Sephardi Jews from the Middle East and Mediterranean are now in the majority, but Ashkenazi Jews from central Europe still dominate business and politics. Palestinians in Gaza and Jericho gained limited autonomy in 1994 but their desire, backed by most of the world, for a separate state has led to years of fierce violence.

THE ECONOMY
The benefits of a modern infrastructure and educated labor force are overshadowed by conflict.

◆ **INSIGHT:** *All Jews worldwide have the right to Israeli citizenship*

FACTFILE

OFFICIAL NAME: State of Israel
DATE OF FORMATION: 1948
CAPITAL: Jerusalem (unrecognized by UN)
POPULATION: 6.7 million
TOTAL AREA: 8019 sq. miles (20,770 sq. km)
DENSITY: 854 people per sq. mile

LANGUAGES: Hebrew*, Arabic*, Yiddish, German, Russian, Polish, other
RELIGIONS: Jewish 76%, Muslim (mainly Sunni) 16%, other 6%, Christian 2%
ETHNIC MIX: Jewish 76%, other (mostly Arab) 24%
GOVERNMENT: Parliamentary system
CURRENCY: Shekel = 100 agorot

Italy

The Italian peninsula was home to the Roman Empire, one of the greatest ancient civilizations. The south has two famous volcanoes, Vesuvius and Etna.

 GEOGRAPHY

The Appennino form the backbone of a rugged peninsula, extending from the Alps into the Mediterranean Sea. Alluvial plain in the north.

CLIMATE

Mediterranean in the south. Seasonal extremes in the mountains and on the northern alluvial plain.

 PEOPLE & SOCIETY

Ethnically homogeneous, but with a gulf between the prosperous, industrial north and the poorer, agricultural south. Strong regional identities persist, especially on the islands of Sicily and Sardinia. Allegiance to the family survives the lessened influence of the Church.

◆ **INSIGHT:** *Italy was a collection of dukedoms, monarchies, and city-states before unification in the 1860s*

$ THE ECONOMY

World leader in industrial and product design, as well as textiles. Strong tourism and agriculture sectors. Large public sector debt.

3000m/9843ft
2000m/6562ft
1000m/3281ft
500m/1640ft
200m/656ft
Sea Level

SWITZERLAND
AUSTRIA
Lago di Como
Alps
Bolzano
SLOVENIA
Torino
Milano
Verona
Trieste
FRANCE
Piacenza
Parma
Venezia
Golfo di Venezia
Genova
Bologna
Rimini
San Remo
Pisa
Livorno
Firenze
Ancona
SAN MARINO
Adriatic Sea
Perugia
ROME
VATICAN CITY
Bari
Lecce
Sassari
Napoli
Taranto
Alghero
Salerno
Sardegna (Sardinia)
Cosenza
Ionian Sea
Cagliari
Tyrrhenian Sea
Messina
Reggio di Calabria
Mediterranean Sea
Palermo
Catania
Sicilia (Sicily)
Siracusa

0   100 km
0   100 miles

📖 FACTFILE

OFFICIAL NAME: Italian Republic
DATE OF FORMATION: 1861
CAPITAL: Rome
POPULATION: 58.1 million
TOTAL AREA: 116,305 sq. miles (301,230 sq. km)
DENSITY: 512 people per sq. mile

LANGUAGES: Italian*, German, French, Rhaeto-Romanic, Sardinian
RELIGIONS: Roman Catholic 85%, other and nonreligious 13%, Muslim 2%
ETHNIC MIX: Italian 94%, other 4%, Sardinian 2%
GOVERNMENT: Parliamentary system
CURRENCY: Euro = 100 cents

Jamaica

First colonized by the Spanish and then by the English, the Caribbean island of Jamaica achieved independence in 1962. It remains an influential force in Caribbean politics.

GEOGRAPHY

Mainly mountainous, with lush tropical vegetation. Inaccessible limestone area in the northwest. Low, irregular coastal plains are broken by hills and plateaus.

CLIMATE

Tropical. Hot and humid at sea level, with temperate mountain areas. Hurricanes are likely June–November.

PEOPLE & SOCIETY

Social tensions result from vast disparities in wealth, rather than race. Economic and political life is dominated by a few wealthy, long-established families. Many women hold senior positions in public life. Armed crime, much of it narcotics-related, is a problem. Large areas of Kingston, which have their own *patois*, are ruled by violent gangs. Jamaican music styles are influential worldwide.

THE ECONOMY

Major producer of bauxite (aluminum ore). Tourism well developed. Light industry and data processing for US companies. Sugar, bananas, coffee, and rum are exported.

INSIGHT: *Jamaica's Rastafarians look to the late emperor of Ethiopia, Haile Selassie, as their spiritual leader, and Africa as their spiritual home*

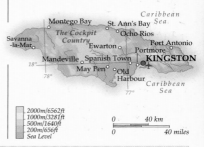

FACTFILE

OFFICIAL NAME: Jamaica
DATE OF FORMATION: 1962
CAPITAL: Kingston
POPULATION: 2.7 million
TOTAL AREA: 4243 sq. miles (10,990 sq. km)
DENSITY: 646 people per sq. mile

LANGUAGES: English Creole, English*
RELIGIONS: Protestant 55%, other and nonreligious 45%
ETHNIC MIX: Black African 92%, Mulatto 6%, European and Chinese 1%, East Indian 1%
GOVERNMENT: Parliamentary system
CURRENCY: Jamaican dollar = 100 cents

Japan

Japan is located off the east Asian coast and comprises four principal islands and over 3000 smaller ones. A powerful economy, it has an emperor as ceremonial head of state.

GEOGRAPHY

The terrain is predominantly mountainous, with fertile coastal plains; over two-thirds is woodland. There is no single continuous mountain range; the mountains divide into many small land blocks separated by lowlands and dissected by numerous river valleys. The islands lie on the Pacific "Ring of Fire," and earthquakes and volcanic eruptions are frequent. The Pacific coast is vulnerable to *tsunamis* – tidal waves triggered by submarine earthquakes.

CLIMATE

Generally temperate–oceanic. Spring is warm and sunny, while summer is hot and humid, with high rainfall. In western Hokkaido and northwest Honshu, winters are very cold, with heavy snowfall. Freak storms and damaging floods in recent years have raised concern over global climate changes.

PEOPLE & SOCIETY

One of the most racially homogeneous societies in the world. Its sense of order is reflected in the phenomenon of the lifetime employer. People define themselves by the company they work for, not the job they do. Employers organize social activities and even encourage and approve marriages. Women traditionally run the home; though, some are beginning to take up long-term careers. Social form remains very important. Respect for elders and social and business superiors is strongly ingrained. There is little tradition of generation rebellion, but the youth market is powerful and current fashions focus on teenagers. The education system is highly pressurized. Nongraduates have difficulty reaching management-level jobs, so competition for university places is intense.

FACTFILE

OFFICIAL NAME: Japan
DATE OF FORMATION: 1590
CAPITAL: Tokyo
POPULATION: 128 million
TOTAL AREA: 145,882 sq. miles (377,835 sq. km)
DENSITY: 881 people per sq. mile

LANGUAGES: Japanese*, Korean, Chinese
RELIGIONS: Shinto and Buddhist 76%, Buddhist 16%, other (including Christian) 8%
ETHNIC MIX: Japanese 99%, other (mainly Korean) 1%
GOVERNMENT: Parliamentary system
CURRENCY: Yen = 100 sen

Japan

THE ECONOMY

The world's most competitive producer of high-tech electronic goods and cars. Talent for developing ideas from abroad. Once-revolutionary management and production methods. Global spread of business, especially to EU and US. Commitment to long-term research and development. Trade surplus is a source of international tension. Period of zero inflation ended in 2006. Desperately needed reform of financial sector has been slow, obstructed by traditional economic power brokers.

INSIGHT: *The Japanese are among the world's most avid newspaper readers, with daily sales exceeding 70 million copies*

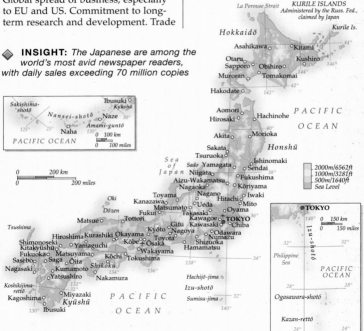

Jordan

The Kingdom of Jordan lies east of Israel, and borders the Palestinian West Bank. Its relations with its Arab neighbors are troubled by its relatively close ties to the US.

GEOGRAPHY
Mostly desert plateaus, with occasional salt pans. Lowest parts lie along the eastern shores of the Dead Sea and the Jordan River.

CLIMATE
Hot, dry summers. Cool, wet winters. Areas below sea level very hot in summer, and warm in winter.

PEOPLE & SOCIETY
A predominantly Muslim country with a strong national identity, Jordan's population has Bedouin roots. There is a Christian minority while half of the population are Palestinians who emigrated from Israeli-occupied territory. Jordan ceded its claim to the West Bank to the aspiring Palestinian state in 1988. The monarchy's power base lies among the rural tribes, which also provide the backbone of the military.

THE ECONOMY
Main exports are phosphates, chemicals, and fertilizers. Tourism hit by regional instability and terrorism.

◆ **INSIGHT:** *The Nabataean ruins of the ancient city of Petra attract thousands of tourists every year*

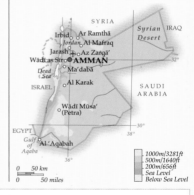

FACTFILE

OFFICIAL NAME: Hashemite Kingdom of Jordan
DATE OF FORMATION: 1946
CAPITAL: Amman
POPULATION: 5.6 million
TOTAL AREA: 35,637 sq. miles (92,300 sq. km)

DENSITY: 163 people per sq. mile
LANGUAGES: Arabic
RELIGIONS: Muslim (mainly Sunni) 92%, other (mostly Christian) 8%
ETHNIC MIX: Arab 98%, Circassian 1%, Armenian 1%
GOVERNMENT: Monarchy
CURRENCY: Jordanian dinar = 1000 fils

Kazakhstan

Mineral-rich Kazakhstan was the last of the former Soviet republics to declare independence. Foreign investment in the oil and gas sector are strengthening its regional power.

GEOGRAPHY

Mainly steppe. Volga delta and Caspian Sea in the west. Central plateau. Inhospitable Altai Mountains in the east. Semidesert in the south.

CLIMATE

Dry continental. Temperature variations between desert south and northern steppes are large. Winters are mildest near the Caspian Sea.

PEOPLE & SOCIETY

Kazakhstan's ethnic diversity arose mainly from forced settlements there during Soviet times. The proportion of ethnic Russians has dropped considerably since independence. Many emigrated, while ethnic Kazakhs arrived from neighboring states. Very few Kazakhs maintain a nomadic lifestyle, but Islam and loyalty to traditional clans remain strong.

THE ECONOMY

Vast mineral resources: gas, oil, bismuth, and cadmium. Increasing foreign investment. The sale of farm land has only been allowed since 2003. Large disparities of wealth.

INSIGHT: *The Soviet-built Baykonyr space center is still an important launch site for international missions*

FACTFILE

OFFICIAL NAME: Republic of Kazakhstan
DATE OF FORMATION: 1991
CAPITAL: Astana
POPULATION: 14.8 million
TOTAL AREA: 1,049,150 sq. miles (2,717,300 sq. km)
DENSITY: 14 people per sq. mile

LANGUAGES: Kazakh*, Russian, Ukrainian, Tatar, Uzbek, Uighur, other
RELIGIONS: Muslim (mainly Sunni) 47%, Orthodox Christian 44%, other 9%
ETHNIC MIX: Kazakh 57%, Russian 27%, other 10%, Ukrainian 3%, Uzbek 3%
GOVERNMENT: Presidential system
CURRENCY: Tenge = 100 tiyn

Kenya

Kenya straddles the equator on Africa's east coast. After nearly 40 years in power the KANU party was soundly defeated in elections in 2002. Corruption is a serious issue.

GEOGRAPHY

A central plateau is divided by the Great Rift Valley. North of the equator is mainly semidesert. To the east lies a fertile coastal belt.

CLIMATE

The coast and the Great Rift Valley are hot and humid. The plateau interior is temperate. The northeastern desert is hot and dry. Rain usually falls April–May and October–November.

PEOPLE & SOCIETY

70 ethnic groups share about 40 languages. Strong clan and family links in rural areas are being weakened by urban migration. Poverty, severe drought, and years of high population growth exacerbate ethnic tensions.

 INSIGHT: *Kenya has more than 50 game reserves, national parks, and marine reservations*

THE ECONOMY

Tourism is the leading foreign exchange earner. Tea and coffee are grown as cash crops. There is a large and diversified manufacturing sector.

	5000m/16405ft	
	4000m/13124ft	
	3000m/9843ft	
	2000m/6562ft	
	1000m/3281ft	
	500m/1640ft	
	200m/656ft	
	Sea Level	

0   100 km
0   100 miles

FACTFILE

OFFICIAL NAME: Republic of Kenya
DATE OF FORMATION: 1963
CAPITAL: Nairobi
POPULATION: 34.3 million
TOTAL AREA: 224,961 sq. miles (582,650 sq. km)
DENSITY: 157 people per sq. mile

LANGUAGES: Kiswahili*, English*, Kikuyu, Luo, Kalenjin, Kamba
RELIGIONS: Christian 60%, traditional beliefs 25%, other 9%, Muslim 6%
ETHNIC MIX: Other 41%, Kikuyu 21%, Luhya 14%, Luo 13%, Kalenjin 11%
GOVERNMENT: Presidential system
CURRENCY: Kenya shilling = 100 cents

Kiribati

Part of the British colony of the Gilbert and Ellice Islands in the mid-Pacific, the Gilberts adopted the name Kiribati (pronounced "Keer-ee-bus") at independence in 1979.

GEOGRAPHY

Kiribati consists of three groups of tiny, very low-lying coral atolls scattered across 1,930,000 sq. miles (5 million sq. km) of ocean. Most of the 33 atolls have central lagoons.

CLIMATE

Central islands have a maritime equatorial climate. Those to north and south are tropical, with constant high temperatures. There is little rainfall.

PEOPLE & SOCIETY

Officially I-Kiribati, many local people still refer to themselves as Gilbertese. Almost all are Micronesian, apart from the inhabitants of the island of Banaba, who employed anthropologists to establish their racial distinction. Most people are poor subsistence farmers and many travel abroad to work. The islands are effectively ruled by traditional chiefs.

THE ECONOMY

Since Banaba's phosphate deposits were exhausted in 1980, coconuts, copra, and fish have become the main exports. Foreign aid is vital to compensate for the country's isolation and the lack of resources.

INSIGHT: *In 1981, the UK paid A$10 million to Banabans for the destruction of their island by mining*

FACTFILE

OFFICIAL NAME: Republic of Kiribati
DATE OF FORMATION: 1979
CAPITAL: Bairiki (Tarawa Atoll)
POPULATION: 103,092
TOTAL AREA: 277 sq. miles
(717 sq. km)
DENSITY: 376 people per sq. mile

LANGUAGES: English*, Kiribati
RELIGIONS: Roman Catholic 53%, Kiribati Protestant Church 39%, other 8%
ETHNIC MIX: Micronesian 99%, other 1%
GOVERNMENT: Nonparty system
CURRENCY: Australian dollar = 100 cents

North Korea

Separated from the democratic South by the world's most heavily defended border, the Stalinist North Korean state has been isolated from the outside world since its creation in 1948.

GEOGRAPHY

Mostly mountainous, with fertile plains in the southwest.

CLIMATE

Continental. Warm summers and cold winters, especially in the north, where snow is common.

PEOPLE & SOCIETY

Life is heavily regulated; divorce is nonexistent, extramarital sex is highly frowned upon, and religion, including Korea's own Chondogyo, is strictly regulated. Women are expected to work and to run the home. Children are looked after in state-run crèches. The Korean Worker's Party is the sole political party. The political elite leads a privileged lifestyle. Its grip on power relies on its international isolation.

◆ **INSIGHT:** Only the political elite are allowed phones and private cars

THE ECONOMY

Other than minerals, there are few economic strengths. Vital aid streams were lost with the global collapse of communism after 1989. Decades of economic mismanagement have caused chronic food shortages.

FACTFILE

OFFICIAL NAME: Democratic People's Republic of Korea
DATE OF FORMATION: 1948
CAPITAL: Pyongyang
POPULATION: 22.5 million
TOTAL AREA: 46,540 sq. miles (120,540 sq. km)

DENSITY: 484 people per sq. mile
LANGUAGES: Korean*, Chinese
RELIGIONS: Government-controlled religions include Chondogyo, Buddhism, and Christianity
ETHNIC MIX: Korean 100%
GOVERNMENT: One-party state
CURRENCY: N. Korean won = 100 chon

South Korea

South Korea occupies the southern half of the Korean peninsula Under US sponsorship, it was separated from the communist North in 1948, and is now a successful capitalist economy.

GEOGRAPHY
Over 80% is mountainous and two-thirds is forested. The flattest and most populous parts lie along the west coast and in the extreme south.

CLIMATE
There are four distinct seasons. Winters are dry, and bitterly cold. Summers are hot and humid.

PEOPLE & SOCIETY
Inhabited for the last 2000 years by a single ethnic group. The nuclear family is replacing traditional extended households. Since the 1953 armistice, North and South Korea have remained technically at war. Reunification is still the ultimate goal. Talks spurred new links in 2000, but progress has since stalled amid mutual suspicion.

◆ **INSIGHT:** *Half of all Koreans are named Kim, Lee, Park, or Choi*

THE ECONOMY
World's biggest shipbuilder. High demand in China for Korean goods, especially cars. There is very strong competition from Japan.

1000m/3281ft
500m/1640ft
200m/656ft
Sea Level

NORTH KOREA

128°

East Sea

126°

SEOUL
Inch'ŏn ● Sŏngnam
Suwŏn

38°
Kangnŭng
Tonghae

Yellow Sea

● Taejŏn

36°

Kunsan
Taegu
Ulsan

Kwangju ● Masan ● Pusan
Mokp'o ● Yŏsu

Korea Strait

Cheju Strait 34°
Cheju ● Cheju-do

0   50 km
0   50 miles

FACTFILE

OFFICIAL NAME: Republic of Korea
DATE OF FORMATION: 1948
CAPITAL: Seoul
POPULATION: 47.8 million
TOTAL AREA: 38,023 sq. miles (98,480 sq. km)
DENSITY: 1254 people per sq. mile

LANGUAGES: Korean*, Chinese
RELIGIONS: Mahayana Buddhist 47%, Protestant 38%, Roman Catholic 11%, Confucianist 3%, other 1%
ETHNIC MIX: Korean 100%
GOVERNMENT: Presidential system
CURRENCY: South Korean won = 100 chon

Kuwait

Kuwait lies at the northwest extreme of the Gulf, dwarfed by its neighbors Iraq, Iran, and Saudi Arabia. It was a British protectorate until 1961, when full independence was granted.

GEOGRAPHY
Terrain is low-lying desert. The lowest land is in the north. Cultivation is only possible along the coast.

CLIMATE
Summers are very hot and dry. Winters are cooler, with some rain and occasional frost at night.

PEOPLE & SOCIETY
An oil-rich monarchy, ruled by the al-Sabah family. Oil wealth has attracted workers from India, Pakistan, and other Arab states, and immigrants outnumber native Kuwaitis. Though it is a very conservative Sunni Muslim society, women are relatively free. Nonetheless, a decree to give women the vote was blocked for six years by Islamic traditionalists in parliament. Kuwait was invaded by Iraq in 1990 and was used as the launchpad for the 2003 invasion of its northern neighbor.

THE ECONOMY
Oil and gas production dominates the economy. Skilled labor, raw materials, and food are imported. Strategic vulnerability has deterred significant foreign investment.

◆ INSIGHT: *During the 1991 Gulf War, 800 of Kuwait's 950 oil wells were deliberately set on fire*

FACTFILE

OFFICIAL NAME: State of Kuwait
DATE OF FORMATION: 1961
CAPITAL: Kuwait City
POPULATION: 2.7 million
TOTAL AREA: 6880 sq. miles (17,820 sq. km)
DENSITY: 392 people per sq. mile

LANGUAGES: Arabic*, English
RELIGIONS: Sunni Muslim 45%, Shi'a Muslim 40%, Christian, Hindu, and other 15%
ETHNIC MIX: Kuwaiti 45%, other Arab 35%, South Asian 9%, other 11%
GOVERNMENT: Monarchy
CURRENCY: Kuwaiti dinar = 1000 fils

Kyrgyzstan

A small and very mountainous landlocked state in central Asia, Kyrgyzstan is one of the least urbanized of the ex-Soviet republics, and was slow to develop its own cultural nationalism.

GEOGRAPHY

The mountainous spurs of the Tien Shan range contain glaciers, alpine meadows, forests, and narrow valleys. Semidesert in the west.

CLIMATE

Varies from permanent snow and cold deserts at high altitudes, to hot deserts in low regions.

PEOPLE & SOCIETY

Ethnic Kyrgyz have only been in the majority since the late 1980s – due to a high birthrate and the emigration of ethnic Russians. Wary of losing skills vital to the economy, the government has attempted to deter Russians from leaving; concessions include making Russian an official language. There are tensions between Kyrgyz and Uzbeks. The trend in politics is toward greater Islamization, and the rural population is growing.

THE ECONOMY

The economy remains under state control. Agriculture employs half of the labor force. Mining of gold, other metals, and small quantities of coal, oil, and gas. There is great potential for hydroelectric power.

◆ **INSIGHT:** *Kyrgyz folklore is based around the 1000-year-old poem,* Manas, *which takes a week to recite*

FACTFILE

OFFICIAL NAME: Kyrgyz Republic
DATE OF FORMATION: 1991
CAPITAL: Bishkek
POPULATION: 5.3 million
TOTAL AREA: 76,641 sq. miles (198,500 sq. km)
DENSITY: 69 people per sq. mile

LANGUAGES: Kyrgyz*, Russian*, other
RELIGIONS: Muslim (mainly Sunni) 70%, Orthodox Christian 30%
ETHNIC MIX: Kyrgyz 65%, Uzbek 14%, Russian 13%, other 6%, Dungan 1%, Ukrainian 1%
GOVERNMENT: Presidential system
CURRENCY: Som = 100 tiyin

Laos

A former French colony, independent in 1953, Laos lies landlocked in southeast Asia. Heavily bombed during the Vietnam War, it has been under communist rule since 1975.

 GEOGRAPHY
Largely forested mountains, broadening in the north to a plateau. Lowlands along the Mekong valley.

 CLIMATE
Monsoon rains September–May. The rest of the year is hot and dry.

 PEOPLE & SOCIETY
There are over 60 ethnic groups. Lowland Laotians (Lao Loum) live along the Mekong River and are rice farmers. Upland and highland Laotians (Lao Theung and Lao Soung) traditionally employ environmentally damaging slash-and-burn farming, and grow illegal cash crops (notably opium). Government efforts to reform these practices are resisted.

◆ **INSIGHT:** *Three small Laotian kingdoms were unified under French control in 1899*

THE ECONOMY
Laos is one of the world's least developed nations. Coffee, timber, and garments are the main exports. Levels of foreign investment are rising, especially in expanding mining sector.

| 2000m/6562ft |
| 1000m/3281ft |
| 500m/1640ft |
| 200m/656ft |
| Sea Level |

FACTFILE

OFFICIAL NAME: Lao People's Democratic Republic
DATE OF FORMATION: 1953
CAPITAL: Vientiane
POPULATION: 5.9 million
TOTAL AREA: 91,428 sq. miles (236,800 sq. km)

DENSITY: 66 people per sq. mile
LANGUAGES: Lao*, Mon-Khmer, other
RELIGIONS: Buddhist 85%, other (including animist) 15%
ETHNIC MIX: Lao Loum 66%, Lao Theung 30%, Lao Soung 2%, other 2%
GOVERNMENT: One-party state
CURRENCY: New kip = 100 at

Latvia

Latvia lies on the east coast of the Baltic Sea, between Estonia and Lithuania. Like its Baltic neighbors, it became independent from Moscow in 1991. It retains a large Russian population.

GEOGRAPHY

A flat coastal plain which is deeply indented by the Gulf of Riga. Poor drainage creates many bogs and swamps in the forested interior.

CLIMATE

Temperate, with warm summers and cold winters. There is steady rainfall throughout the year.

PEOPLE & SOCIETY

Latvians make up just over half of the population and are mostly Lutheran. They have been officially favored by the state since 1991 over the largely Orthodox Christian Russian minority. Latvian was declared the only official language in 2000 and has been used exclusively in schools since 2004. This discrimination has strained relations with neighboring Russia. Women enjoy full equality. The divorce rate is high.

THE ECONOMY

The thriving services sector now accounts for over 70% of GDP: tourism is growing. Manufacturing industry remains buoyant. Germany has replaced Russia as the main trading partner as Latvia turns increasingly to the West.

INSIGHT: *Ethnic Latvians form a minority of the population in Riga*

FACTFILE

OFFICIAL NAME: Republic of Latvia
DATE OF FORMATION: 1991
CAPITAL: Riga
POPULATION: 2.3 million
TOTAL AREA: 24,938 sq. miles (64,589 sq. km)
DENSITY: 92 people per sq. mile

LANGUAGES: Latvian*, Russian
RELIGIONS: Lutheran 55%, Catholic 24%, other 12%, Orthodox Christian 9%
ETHNIC MIX: Latvian 59%, Russian 29%, Belarussian 4%, Ukrainian 3%, Polish 3%, other 2%
GOVERNMENT: Parliamentary system
CURRENCY: Lats = 100 santimi

Lebanon

Once a vibrant cultural hotspot, Lebanon suffered badly from years of civil war and occupation until a 1989 peace deal. Reconstruction was reversed by Israeli bombardment in 2006.

GEOGRAPHY
Behind a narrow Mediterranean coastal plain, two parallel mountain ranges run the length of the country, separated by the fertile Beqaa Valley.

CLIMATE

Winters are mild and summers are hot, with high coastal humidity. Snow falls on high ground in winter.

PEOPLE & SOCIETY

Politics has long been dominated by divisions between Sunni and Shi'a Muslims and the traditional ruling group of Maronite Christians. A power-sharing deal ended 14 years of civil war in 1989, but left Syria as the main power broker until it was forced to withdraw in 2005. Israel attacked from the south in 2006 in a bid to crush Iranian-backed Hezbollah militants. A huge economic gulf exists between the poor and a small, immensely rich elite.

THE ECONOMY
Much infrastructure destroyed in 2006. Instability undermines Beirut's role as regional financial center. Wine and fruit production.

INSIGHT: *The Cedar of Lebanon has been the nation's symbol for more than 2000 years*

FACTFILE

OFFICIAL NAME: Republic of Lebanon
DATE OF FORMATION: 1941
CAPITAL: Beirut
POPULATION: 3.6 million
TOTAL AREA: 4015 sq. miles (10,400 sq. km)
DENSITY: 911 people per sq. mile

LANGUAGES: Arabic*, French, Armenian, Assyrian
RELIGIONS: Muslim 70%, Christian 30%
ETHNIC MIX: Arab 94%, Armenian 4%, other 2%
GOVERNMENT: Parliamentary system
CURRENCY: Lebanese pound = 100 piastres

Lesotho

The landlocked Kingdom of Lesotho is entirely surrounded by – and economically dependent on – South Africa, which even sent in troops to restore calm after rioting in 1998.

 GEOGRAPHY
A high mountainous plateau, cut by valleys and ravines. The Maluti range runs through the center. The Drakensberg range lies to the east.

CLIMATE
Temperate. Summers are hot with torrential rain storms. Snow is frequent in the mountains in winter.

 PEOPLE & SOCIETY
The overwhelming majority of people are Sotho, though there are some South Asians, Europeans, and Chinese. A strong sense of national identity has tended to minimize ethnic tensions. Many men work as migrant laborers in South Africa, leaving women to run households.

◆ **INSIGHT:** *Lesotho has one of the highest literacy rates in Africa – and one of the highest rates of HIV/AIDS*

$ THE ECONOMY
Few natural resources; dependent on South Africa. Subsistence farming is the main activity. Water and energy are being exported from the new Highlands Water Scheme.

3000m/9843ft
2000m/6562ft
1000m/3281ft

0   50 km
0   50 miles

📖 FACTFILE

OFFICIAL NAME: Kingdom of Lesotho
DATE OF FORMATION: 1966
CAPITAL: Maseru
POPULATION: 1.8 million
TOTAL AREA: 11,720 sq. miles (30,355 sq. km)
DENSITY: 154 people per sq. mile

LANGUAGES: English*, Sesotho*, isiZulu
RELIGIONS: Christian 90%, traditional beliefs 10%
ETHNIC MIX: Sotho 97%, European and Asian 3%
GOVERNMENT: Parliamentary system
CURRENCY: Loti = 100 lisente

Liberia

Liberia, Africa's oldest republic, faces the Atlantic Ocean.
A tentative peace deal in 2003 ended more than a decade of
brutal civil war, but gang violence and looting are widespread.

 GEOGRAPHY
A coastline of beaches and
mangrove swamps rises to forested
plateaus and highlands inland.

 CLIMATE
High temperatures. There is only
one wet season, from May to October,
except in the extreme southeast.

 PEOPLE & SOCIETY
The key social distinction used
to be between Americo-Liberians –
descendants of freed slaves – and the
indigenous tribal peoples. However,
political assimilation and intermarriage
have eased tensions. Intertribal tension
is now a much more serious problem,
fueling the civil war which ravaged
the country from 1990 to 2003.

◆ **INSIGHT:** *Liberia is named after
the people liberated from slavery
who arrived from the US in the 1800s*

THE ECONOMY
Civil war caused the collapse
of the economy – there is very little
commercial activity. Only 1% of the
land is suitable for cultivation. There
are an estimated one billion tonnes
of iron ore reserves at Mount Nimba.

FACTFILE

OFFICIAL NAME: Republic of Liberia
DATE OF FORMATION: 1847
CAPITAL: Monrovia
POPULATION: 3.3 million
TOTAL AREA: 43,000 sq. miles
(111,370 sq. km)
DENSITY: 89 people per sq. mile

LANGUAGES: Kpelle, Vai, Bassa, Kru,
Grebo, Kissi, Gola, Loma, English*
RELIGIONS: Christian 68%, traditional
beliefs 18%, Muslim 14%
ETHNIC MIX: Indigenous tribes (16 main
groups) 95%, Americo-Liberians 5%
GOVERNMENT: Presidential system
CURRENCY: Liberian dollar = 100 cents

Libya

Situated on the Mediterranean coast of north Africa, Libya is a military dictatorship. Years of political marginalization by the West for its terrorist links have now ended.

GEOGRAPHY

Apart from the coastal strip and a mountain range in the south, Libya is desert or semidesert. Natural oases provide the agricultural land.

CLIMATE

Hot and arid. The coastal area has a temperate climate, with mild, wet winters and hot, dry summers.

PEOPLE & SOCIETY

Most Libyans are of Arab and Berber origin. A revolution in 1969 brought Colonel Gaddafi to power. He represents independence, Islamic faith, belief in communal lifestyle, and hatred of the urban rich. Revolution wiped out private enterprise and the middle classes. Jews and European settlers were banished. Since then, Libya has changed from being largely a nation of nomads and livestock herders to almost 90% city dwellers.

THE ECONOMY

Oil is key export. Dates, olives, peaches, and grapes grown in oases. Sanctions ended after Libya offered compensation for terrorist bombings.

◆ **INSIGHT:** *90% of Libya is still desert, despite grand irrigation schemes*

2000m/6562ft	
1000m/3281ft	
500m/1640ft	
200m/656ft	
Sea Level	
Below Sea Level	

0   200 km
0   200 miles

📖 FACTFILE

OFFICIAL NAME: Great Socialist People's Libyan Arab Jamahariyah
DATE OF FORMATION: 1951
CAPITAL: Tripoli
POPULATION: 5.9 million
TOTAL AREA: 679,358 sq. miles (1,759,540 sq. km)

DENSITY: 9 people per sq. mile
LANGUAGES: Arabic*, Tuareg
RELIGIONS: Muslim (mainly Sunni) 97%, other 3%
ETHNIC MIX: Arab and Berber 95%, other 5%
GOVERNMENT: One-party state
CURRENCY: Libyan dinar = 1000 dirhams

Liechtenstein

Perched in the Alps between Switzerland and Austria, the small state of Liechtenstein became an independent principality of the Holy Roman Empire in 1719. It has close links with Switzerland.

GEOGRAPHY

The upper Rhine Valley covers the western third of the country. The mountains and narrow valleys of the eastern Alps make up the remainder.

CLIMATE

Warm, dry summers. Winters are cold, with heavy snow in the mountains from December to March.

PEOPLE & SOCIETY

The country's role as a financial center accounts for its many foreign residents (a third of the population), of whom almost a third are Swiss. A high standard of living results in few social or ethnic tensions. There is a close alliance with Switzerland, which handles its foreign relations and defense policies.

◆ INSIGHT: *Women in Liechtenstein only received the vote in 1984*

THE ECONOMY

Banking secrecy and low taxes help to attract foreign investment. A well-diversified export market includes dental products, furniture, chemicals, and precision instruments.

FACTFILE

OFFICIAL NAME: Principality of Liechtenstein

DATE OF FORMATION: 1719

CAPITAL: Vaduz

POPULATION: 33,717

TOTAL AREA: 62 sq. miles (160 sq. km)

DENSITY: 544 people per sq. mile

LANGUAGES: German*, Alemannish dialect, Italian

RELIGIONS: Catholic 81%, other 19%

ETHNIC MIX: Liechtensteiner 66%, other 18%, Swiss 10%, Austrian 6%

GOVERNMENT: Parliamentary system

CURRENCY: Swiss franc = 100 centimes

Lithuania

Lying on the eastern coast of the Baltic Sea, Lithuania is the largest and most powerful of the Baltic states. It was the first Soviet republic to declare independence from Moscow in 1991.

GEOGRAPHY

Mostly flat with moors, bogs, and an intensively farmed central lowland. Numerous lakes and forested sandy ridges in the east.

CLIMATE

Coastal location moderates continental extremes. Cold winters, cool summers, and steady rainfall.

PEOPLE & SOCIETY

Homogeneous population, with Lithuanians forming a large majority. Strong Roman Catholic tradition and historic links with Poland. There are better relations among ethnic groups than in other Baltic states and inter-ethnic marriages are fairly common. However, ethnic Russians and Poles see a threat from "Lithuanianization." Only 4000 Jews, known as Litvaks, remain in Lithuania. A large income gap has grown since independence.

THE ECONOMY

A wide range of high-tech and heavy industries includes textiles, engineering, shipbuilding, and food processing. Litas pegged to the euro.

◆ **INSIGHT:** *The "amber coasts" of the Baltic states, particularly Lithuania, produce most of the world's amber – fossilized resin*

FACTFILE

OFFICIAL NAME: Republic of Lithuania
DATE OF FORMATION: 1991
CAPITAL: Vilnius
POPULATION: 3.4 million
TOTAL AREA: 25,174 sq. miles (65,200 sq. km)
DENSITY: 135 people per sq. mile

LANGUAGES: Lithuanian*, Russian
RELIGIONS: Roman Catholic 83%, other 12%, Protestant 5%
ETHNIC MIX: Lithuanian 83%, Polish 7%, Russian 6%, other 3%, Belarussian 1%
GOVERNMENT: Parliamentary system
CURRENCY: Litas = 100 centu

Luxembourg

Making up part of the plateau of the Ardennes in western Europe, Luxembourg is one of Europe's richest states. A tax haven and banking center, it is also home to key EU institutions.

GEOGRAPHY
Dense Ardennes forests in the north, with a low, open plateau to the south. Undulating terrain throughout.

CLIMATE
The climate is moist, with warm summers and mild winters. Snow is common only in the Ardennes.

PEOPLE & SOCIETY
Ethnic tensions are rare, despite a large proportion of foreigners (over a third of residents). Integration has been straightforward; most are fellow western Europeans and Catholics, mainly from Italy and Portugal. Low unemployment and high salaries promote stability. Divorce is rising and marriage is becoming less common.

◆ **INSIGHT:** *Luxembourg's capital is home to around 2000 investment funds and over 160 banks*

THE ECONOMY
Traditional industries such as steelmaking have given way in recent years to a thriving banking and service sector. Its banking and secrecy laws attract foreign companies.

500m/1640ft
200m/656ft
Sea Level

Clervaux

GERMANY

Ettelbrück

Echternach

Mersch

BELGIUM

Moselle

● LUXEMBOURG

Pétange

Differdange
Esch-sur-Alzette
Dudelange

FRANCE

0   10 km
0   10 miles

📖 FACTFILE
OFFICIAL NAME: Grand Duchy of Luxembourg
DATE OF FORMATION: 1867
CAPITAL: Luxembourg-Ville
POPULATION: 465,000
TOTAL AREA: 998 sq. miles (2586 sq. km)
DENSITY: 466 people per sq. mile

LANGUAGES: Luxembourgish*, German*, French*
RELIGIONS: Roman Catholic 97%, Jewish, Greek Orthodox, and Protestant 3%
ETHNIC MIX: Luxembourger 62%, foreign residents 38%
GOVERNMENT: Parliamentary system
CURRENCY: Euro = 100 cents

Macedonia

Landlocked in the southern Balkans, Macedonia was troubled by the sanctions placed on its northern trading partners in the mid-1990s, and by violent conflict with ethnic Albanians in 2001.

GEOGRAPHY

Mainly mountainous or hilly, with deep river basins in the center. Plains in the northeast and southwest.

CLIMATE

Continental climate with wet springs and dry autumns. Heavy snowfalls in northern mountains.

PEOPLE & SOCIETY

Slav Macedonians comprise two-thirds of the population; they are mostly Orthodox Christians, with some Muslims. Officially 25% of the population are Muslim Albanians, though they claim to account for a third. Albanian militants fought a bitter war against the government in 2001. A peace deal promised greater equality. The Greek government is still wary that Macedonia may try to absorb historic "Macedonian" lands in northern Greece.

THE ECONOMY

Regional instability deterred foreign investment, but the country has now been granted EU candidate status. High levels of unemployment and large gray economy.

◆ **INSIGHT:** *Ohrid is the deepest lake in Europe at 964 ft (294 m)*

FACTFILE

OFFICIAL NAME: Republic of Macedonia
DATE OF FORMATION: 1991
CAPITAL: Skopje
POPULATION: 2 million
TOTAL AREA: 9781 sq. miles (25,333 sq. km)
DENSITY: 201 people per sq. mile

LANGUAGES: Macedonian*, Albanian*
RELIGIONS: Orthodox Christian 59%, Muslim 26%, other 11%, Catholic 4%
ETHNIC MIX: Macedonian 64%, Albanian 25%, other 5%, Turkish 4%, Serb 2%
GOVERNMENT: Mixed presidential–parliamentary system
CURRENCY: Macedonian denar = 100 deni

Madagascar

Lying off the east African coast in the Indian Ocean, the former French colony of Madagascar is the world's fourth-largest island. An electoral dispute spilled over into civil conflict in 2002.

GEOGRAPHY
More than two-thirds of the country forms a savanna-covered plateau, which drops sharply to a narrow coastal belt in the east.

CLIMATE
Tropical and often hit by cyclones. Monsoons affect the east coast. The southwest is much drier.

PEOPLE & SOCIETY
People are Malay-Indonesian in origin, intermixed with later migrants from the African mainland. The main ethnic division is between the Merina of the central plateau and the poorer *côtier* (coastal) peoples. The Merina were the country's historic rulers, and remain the social elite.

◆ **INSIGHT:** *80% of Madagascar's plants and many of its animal species are found nowhere else*

THE ECONOMY
The majority of people are farmers. Vanilla, cloves, and coffee are the most important cash crops. Prawns are a valuable export.

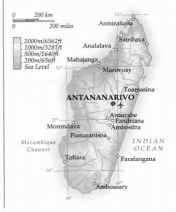

FACTFILE
OFFICIAL NAME: Republic of Madagascar
DATE OF FORMATION: 1960
CAPITAL: Antananarivo
POPULATION: 18.6 million
TOTAL AREA: 226,656 sq. miles (587,040 sq. km)
DENSITY: 83 people per sq. mile

LANGUAGES: Malagasy*, French*
RELIGIONS: Traditional beliefs 52%, Christian 41%, Muslim 7%
ETHNIC MIX: Other Malay 46%, Merina 26%, Betsimisaraka 15%, Betsileo 12%, other 1%
GOVERNMENT: Presidential system
CURRENCY: Ariary = 5 iraimbilanja

Malawi

A former colony of the UK, Malawi lies landlocked in southeast Africa, following the Great Rift Valley. Its name means "the land where the sun is reflected in the water like fire."

GEOGRAPHY
Lake Nyasa takes up one-fifth of the landscape. Highlands lie west of the lake. Much of the land is covered by forests and savanna.

CLIMATE
Mainly subtropical. The south is hot and humid. Highlands are cooler.

PEOPLE & SOCIETY
Ethnicity has not been exploited for political ends in Malawi as has been the case in neighboring states. Most Malawians share a common Bantu origin. The election in 1994 of a member of the Muslim minority as president signaled the failure of previous attempts to enforce Protestant dominance.

◆ **INSIGHT:** *Lake Nyasa is 353 miles (568 km) in length and contains at least 500 species of fish*

THE ECONOMY
Tobacco accounts for just under half of export earnings. Tea and sugar production. Drought is a serious problem.

0   100 km
0   100 miles

Karonga
TANZANIA
Mzuzu
Euthini
ZAMBIA
Chisumulti Likoma (to Malawi)
MOZAMBIQUE
Lake Nyasa
LILONGWE
Salima
Dedza
Mangochi
MOZAMBIQUE
Zomba
Blantyre
Nsanje

2000m/6562ft
1000m/3281ft
500m/1640ft
200m/656ft
Sea Level

FACTFILE
OFFICIAL NAME: Republic of Malawi
DATE OF FORMATION: 1964
CAPITAL: Lilongwe
POPULATION: 12.9 million
TOTAL AREA: 45,745 sq. miles (118,480 sq. km)
DENSITY: 355 people per sq. mile

LANGUAGES: Chewa, Lomwe, Yao, Ngoni, English*
RELIGIONS: Protestant 55%, Muslim 20%, Catholic 20%, traditional beliefs 5%
ETHNIC MIX: Bantu 99%, other 1%
GOVERNMENT: Presidential system
CURRENCY: Malawi kwacha = 100 tambala

Malaysia

Comprising the three territories of Peninsular Malaysia, Sarawak, and Sabah, Malaysia stretches 1240 miles (2000 km) from the Malay peninsula to eastern Borneo.

GEOGRAPHY
Almost three-quarters of the land is tropical rainforest or swamp forest. A central mountain chain, the Banjaran Titiwangsa, divides Peninsular Malaysia, separating a narrow eastern coastal belt from fertile western plains and sheltered beaches and bays. The territories of Sarawak and Sabah share the island of Borneo with Indonesia, and surround Brunei. They are characterized by swampy coastal plains rising to mountains along the southern border.

CLIMATE
Warm equatorial. Rainfall is heavy throughout the year, but with distinct rainy seasons from March to May and from September to November. Coastal areas are subject to the alternating southwest and northeast monsoon winds.

INSIGHT: *Malaysia is southeast Asia's major tourist destination, with over 15 million visitors a year. Most come for the beaches and highlands of Malaya, or the ancient rainforests of Borneo*

THAILAND
Kangar
Kota Bharu
George Town
Malay
Kuala Terengganu
Taiping
Tasik Kenyir
Dungun
Ipoh
Kuala Lipis
Chukai
Peninsula
Kuantan
KUALA LUMPUR
Petaling Jaya
PUTRAJAYA
Klang
Seremban
Mersing
Segamat
Keluang
Johor Baharu
SINGAPORE
Strait of Malacca
INDONESIA

2000m/6562ft
1000m/3281ft
500m/1640ft
200m/656ft
Sea Level

FACTFILE
OFFICIAL NAME: Federation of Malaysia
DATE OF FORMATION: 1963
CAPITALS: Kuala Lumpur and Putrajaya
POPULATION: 25.3 million
TOTAL AREA: 127,316 sq. miles (329,750 sq. km)
DENSITY: 199 people per sq. mile

LANGUAGES: Bahasa Malaysia*, Malay, Chinese, Tamil, English
RELIGIONS: Muslim 53%, Buddhist 19%, Chinese faiths 12%, other 9%, Christian 7%
ETHNIC MIX: Malay 50%, Chinese 25%, indigenous tribes 11%, other 14%
GOVERNMENT: Parliamentary system
CURRENCY: Ringgit = 100 sen

Malaysia

PEOPLE & SOCIETY

The key distinction in Malaysian society is between the indigenous Malays, termed the "Bumiputras" (literally, sons of the soil), and the Chinese. The Malays form the larger group, accounting for half of the population. However, the smaller Chinese population has traditionally controlled most economic activity. Malays have been favored in the education system and job market since the 1970s, in order to address this imbalance. There are estimated to be more than one million Indonesian and Filipino immigrants, attracted by labor shortages; a recent amnesty saw 300,000 illegal immigrants return home. Gender discrimination was only outlawed in 2001. In an attempt to promote Islamic tradition, Muslim women are encouraged to wear veils.

THE ECONOMY

Rapid growth since late 1980s, largely state-directed and underpinned by a push for foreign investment and privatization of state assets. Asian financial crisis of 1997–1998 forced Malaysia to adopt economic austerity measures, and revise plans for industrialization. Successful car and electronics industries – the *Proton* car is regarded as a national success, while the new capital Putrajaya is being promoted as a high-tech center. Tourism is a major earner. Heavy industries such as steel. Leading producer of palm oil, pepper, tin, and tropical hardwoods. High level of debt. Shortage of skilled labor.

Maldives

The Maldives is an archipelago of 1190 small coral islands, or atolls, set in the Indian Ocean, southwest of Sri Lanka. The word atoll comes from the Dhivehi word "atolu."

GEOGRAPHY
Consists of low-lying islands and coral atolls. The larger ones are covered in lush, tropical vegetation.

CLIMATE
Tropical. Rain falls throughout the year, but is heaviest June–November, during the monsoon. Violent storms occasionally hit the northern islands.

PEOPLE & SOCIETY
Maldivians, who are all Sunni Muslim, are descended from Sinhalese, Dravidian, Arab, and black ancestors. About 25% of the population live on Male'. Tourism has grown on separate resort islands away from residents. Politics has been controlled by a small group of influential families, with Maumoon Abdul Gayoom as president since 1978. However, a new, young elite has pushed for political reform: political parties were legalized in 2005.

THE ECONOMY
Too dependent on the fluctuating tourist industry, which is the economic mainstay. Fish, especially tuna, are the leading exports.

INSIGHT:
The islands, which all lie below 4 ft (1.2 m), are threatened by rising sea levels, brought about by global warming and climatic changes

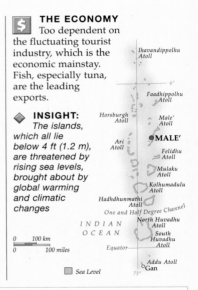

Ihavandippolhu Atoll

Faadhippolhu Atoll

Horsburgh Atoll

Male' Atoll

Ari Atoll

●MALE'

Felidhu Atoll

Mulaku Atoll

Kolhumadulu Atoll

Hadhdhunmathi Atoll

One and Half Degree Channel

North Huvadhu Atoll

INDIAN OCEAN

South Huvadhu Atoll

Equator

Addu Atoll
°Gan

0   100 km
0   100 miles

6°

73°

☐ Sea Level

FACTFILE
OFFICIAL NAME: Republic of Maldives
DATE OF FORMATION: 1965
CAPITAL: Male'
POPULATION: 329,000
TOTAL AREA: 116 sq. miles (300 sq. km)

DENSITY: 2836 people per sq. mile
LANGUAGES: Dhivehi* (Maldivian), Sinhala, Tamil, Arabic
RELIGIONS: Sunni Muslim 100%
ETHNIC MIX: All Maldivians are of Arab–Sinhalese–Malay descent
GOVERNMENT: Nonparty system
CURRENCY: Rufiyaa = 100 laari

Mali

A former French colony, Mali is landlocked in the heart of west Africa. The 1991 coup ended the 23-year dictatorship of Moussa Traoré and ushered in multiparty elections from 1992.

GEOGRAPHY
The northern half of the country lies in the Sahara. The inland delta of the Niger River flows through a grassy savanna region in the south.

CLIMATE
In the south, intensely hot, dry weather precedes the westerly rains. The north is almost rainless.

PEOPLE & SOCIETY
Most people live in southern savanna region. The Bambara tribe are culturally and politically dominant. A few nomadic Fulani and Tuareg herders travel the northern plains. There is tension between the peoples of the south and Tuareg in the north. Malian women have little status.

◆ **INSIGHT:** *Tombouctou (Timbuktu) was the center of the 14th-century Malinke trading empire*

THE ECONOMY
Less than 2% of land can be cultivated. Most people are farmers, herders, or river fishermen. Cotton is major crop. Vulnerable to drought. Gold deposits are now being mined.

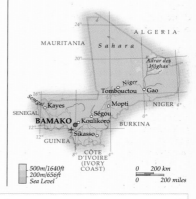

FACTFILE

OFFICIAL NAME: Republic of Mali

DATE OF FORMATION: 1960

CAPITAL: Bamako

POPULATION: 13.5 million

TOTAL AREA: 478,764 sq. miles (1,240,000 sq. km)

DENSITY: 29 people per sq. mile

LANGUAGES: Bambara, Fulani, Senufo, Soninke, French*

RELIGIONS: Muslim 80%, traditional beliefs 18%, Christian 1%, other 1%

ETHNIC MIX: Bambara 32%, other 33%, Fulani 14%, Senufu 12%, Soninka 9%

GOVERNMENT: Presidential system

CURRENCY: CFA franc = 100 centimes

Malta

The Maltese archipelago lies midway between Europe and Africa. Controlled throughout its history by successive colonial powers, it gained independence from the UK in 1964.

 GEOGRAPHY
The main island of Malta has low hills and a ragged coastline with numerous harbors, bays, sandy beaches, and rocky coves. The island of Gozo is more densely vegetated.

CLIMATE
Mediterranean climate. There are many hours of sunshine all year round, with very little rainfall.

 PEOPLE & SOCIETY
Over the centuries, the Maltese have been subject to Arab, Sicilian, Spanish, French, and British influences. Today, the population is socially conservative and devoutly Roman Catholic – on a percentage basis more so than virtually any other nation. Only 30% of the female labor force have jobs. Divorce is illegal. Since joining the EU, Malta has become a target for illegal migration from Africa.

 THE ECONOMY
Tourism is the chief source of income. Developing offshore banking and foreign high-tech industry. Hopes to join eurozone in 2008. Almost all requirements have to be imported.

◆ **INSIGHT:** *The Maltese language has Phoenician origins but features Arabic etymology and intonation*

FACTFILE

OFFICIAL NAME: Republic of Malta
DATE OF FORMATION: 1964
CAPITAL: Valletta
POPULATION: 402,000
TOTAL AREA: 122 sq. miles (316 sq. km)
DENSITY: 3242 people per sq. mile

LANGUAGES: Maltese*, English*
RELIGIONS: Roman Catholic 98%, other and nonreligious 2%
ETHNIC MIX: Maltese 96%, other 4%
GOVERNMENT: Parliamentary system
CURRENCY: Maltese lira = 100 cents

Marshall Islands

Under US rule as part of the UN Trust Territory of the Pacific Islands until independence in 1986, the Marshall Islands comprises a group of 34 widely scattered atolls.

GEOGRAPHY

Narrow coral rings with sandy beaches enclosing lagoons. Those in the south have thicker vegetation. Kwajalein is the world's largest atoll.

CLIMATE

Tropical oceanic, cooled year round by northeast trade winds.

PEOPLE & SOCIETY

Majuro, the capital city and commercial center, is home to almost half the population. Tensions are high due to poor living conditions. Life on the outlying islands is still traditional, based around subsistence agriculture and fishing. Marshallese society is matrilineal: titles are chiefly handed down from the mother's side.

◆ **INSIGHT:** *In 1954, Bikini Atoll was the site for the testing of the largest US H-bomb – the 18–22 megaton Bravo*

THE ECONOMY

Almost totally dependent on US aid and the rent paid by the US for its missile base on Kwajalein Atoll. Revenue from Japan for the use of Marshallese waters for tuna fishing. Copra and coconut oil are the only significant agricultural exports.

FACTFILE

OFFICIAL NAME: Republic of the Marshall Islands
DATE OF FORMATION: 1986
CAPITAL: Majuro
POPULATION: 59,071
TOTAL AREA: 70 sq. miles (181 sq. km)
DENSITY: 844 people per sq. mile

LANGUAGES: Marshallese*, English*, Japanese, German
RELIGIONS: Protestant 90%, Roman Catholic 8%, other 2%
ETHNIC MIX: Micronesian 97%, other 3%
GOVERNMENT: Presidential system
CURRENCY: US dollar = 100 cents

Mauritania

Two-thirds of Mauritania's territory is desert – the only productive land is that drained by the Senegal River. The country has taken a strongly Arab direction since 1964.

 GEOGRAPHY
The Sahara, barren except for some scattered oases, covers the north. Savanna lands lie to the south.

CLIMATE
The climate is generally hot and dry, aggravated by the dusty *harmattan* wind. Summer rain in the south, virtually none in the north.

PEOPLE & SOCIETY
The majority Maures control political life. There is a sizable black minority. Ethnic tension centers on the oppression of blacks by Maures. Tens of thousands of blacks are estimated to be in illegal slavery. Family solidarity among nomadic peoples is particularly strong.

◆ **INSIGHT:** *Slavery officially became illegal in Mauritania in 1980, but de facto slavery still persists*

THE ECONOMY
Agriculture and herding. Iron and copper mining. World's largest gypsum deposits. Some of the best fishing grounds in west Africa.

500m/1640ft
200m/656ft
Sea Level

ALGERIA
WESTERN SAHARA
Zouérat
Nouâdhibou
Atâr
Sahara
MALI
ATLANTIC OCEAN
Tidjikja
NOUAKCHOTT
Rosso
Kaédi
Kiffa
Néma
Senegal
SENEGAL
MALI

0   200 km
0   200 miles

FACTFILE

OFFICIAL NAME: Islamic Republic of Mauritania
DATE OF FORMATION: 1960
CAPITAL: Nouakchott
POPULATION: 3.1 million
TOTAL AREA: 397,953 sq. miles (1,030,700 sq. km)

DENSITY: 8 people per sq. mile
LANGUAGES: Hassaniyah Arabic*, Wolof, French
RELIGIONS: Sunni Muslim 100%
ETHNIC MIX: Maure 81%, Wolof 7%, Tukolor 5%, other 4%, Soninka 3%
GOVERNMENT: Transitional regime
CURRENCY: Ouguiya = 5 khoums

Mauritius

The islands that make up Mauritius lie in the Indian Ocean east of Madagascar. They have enjoyed considerable economic success following recent industrial diversification and expansion.

GEOGRAPHY

The volcanic main island of Mauritius is ringed by coral reefs, and rises from the coast to a fertile central plateau. The outer islands – Rodriguez, the Agalega Islands, and the Cargados Carajos Shoals – lie some 300 miles (500 km) to the north.

CLIMATE

Warm and humid. Tropical storms are frequent December–March, the hottest and wettest months.

PEOPLE & SOCIETY

Most people are descendants of laborers brought over from India in the 19th century. A small minority of French descent form the wealthiest group. The Creole community complains of discrimination. Criminal offenses are usually traffic-related; the outer islands are virtually free from crime altogether.

THE ECONOMY

Clothing manufacture, tourism, and sugar are main sources of income. Loss of preferential trade terms for sugar exports. Offshore financial center. Most food has to be imported.

INSIGHT: *The islands lie on the Mascarene Archipelago – once a land bridge between Asia and Africa*

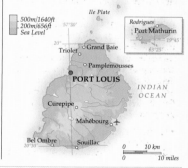

FACTFILE

OFFICIAL NAME: Republic of Mauritius
DATE OF FORMATION: 1968
CAPITAL: Port Louis
POPULATION: 1.2 million
TOTAL AREA: 718 sq. miles (1860 sq. km)
DENSITY: 1671 people per sq. mile

LANGUAGES: French Creole, Hindi, Urdu, Tamil, Chinese, English*, French
RELIGIONS: Hindu 52%, Catholic 26%, Muslim 17%, other 3%, Protestant 2%
ETHNIC MIX: Indo-Mauritian 68%, Creole 27%, other 5%
GOVERNMENT: Parliamentary system
CURRENCY: Mauritian rupee = 100 cents

Mexico

Mexico stretches from the US border southward into the ancient Aztec and Mayan heartlands. Independence from Spain came in 1836. One in four Mexicans lives in the sprawling capital.

GEOGRAPHY

Coastal plains along the Pacific and Atlantic seaboards rise to a high arid central plateau. To the east and west are the Sierra Madre mountain ranges. Limestone lowlands form the projecting Yucatan peninsula.

CLIMATE
The plateau and high mountains are warm for much of the year. Pacific coast is tropical: storms occur mostly March–December. Northwest is dry.

PEOPLE & SOCIETY

Most Mexicans are *mestizos* of mixed Spanish and Amerindian descent. Rural Amerindians are largely segregated from Hispanic society and most live in poverty, though their culture is promoted by the state. Zapatista movement backs indigenous rights. Few women in male-dominated politics and business.

THE ECONOMY
$
One of the world's largest oil producers. Remittances from abroad are second foreign exchange earner. Exotic fruits and vegetables are cash crops. The North American Free Trade Agreement (1994) boosted exports, but exposes farmers to subsidized US competition. Huge wealth disparities.

INSIGHT: *More people cross the US–Mexican border each year – illegally or legally – than any other border in the world*

UNITED STATES OF AMERICA

	3000m/9843ft
	2000m/6562ft
	1000m/3281ft
	500m/1640ft
	200m/656ft
	Sea Level

Tijuana
Ciudad Juárez
Chihuahua
Monterrey
San Luis Potosí
León
Guadalajara
MEXICO CITY
Puebla
Mérida
Acapulco

Gulf of California (Baja California)
Océano Pacífico
Río Grande
Sierra Madre Occidental
Sierra Madre Oriental
Gulf of Mexico
Yucatán Peninsula
PACIFIC OCEAN
Sierra Madre del Sur
BEL.
GUAT.

0   500 km
0   500 miles

FACTFILE

OFFICIAL NAME: United Mexican States
DATE OF FORMATION: 1836
CAPITAL: Mexico City
POPULATION: 107 million
TOTAL AREA: 761,602 sq. miles (1,972,550 sq. km)
DENSITY: 145 people per sq. mile

LANGUAGES: Spanish*, Nahuatl, Mayan, Zapotec, Mixtec, Otomi, Totonac, other
RELIGIONS: Roman Catholic 88%, other 7%, Protestant 5%
ETHNIC MIX: Mestizo 60%, Amerindian 30%, European 9%, other 1%
GOVERNMENT: Presidential system
CURRENCY: Mexican peso = 100 centavos

Micronesia

The Federated States of Micronesia (FSM), situated in the western Pacific, comprise 607 islands and atolls grouped into four main island states: Pohnpei, Kosrae, Chuuk, and Yap.

GEOGRAPHY

Mixture of high volcanic islands with forested interiors, and low-lying coral atolls. Some of the islands have coastal mangrove swamps.

CLIMATE

Tropical, with high humidity. There is very heavy rainfall outside the January–March dry season.

INSIGHT: *Chuuk's lagoon contains the sunken wrecks of over 100 Japanese ships and 270 planes from World War II*

PEOPLE & SOCIETY

Micronesians are physically, culturally, and linguistically diverse. Melanesians live on Yap and Polynesians in Pohnpei. Most islanders live without electricity or running water. Society is traditionally matrilineal.

THE ECONOMY

Dependent on US aid. Tourism, fishing, betel nuts, and copra are economic mainstays. Fishing licenses are a key source of foreign revenue.

Philippine Sea — 10°

Yap Namonuito Hall Is. Murilo Pohnpei Is.

Sorol Lamotrek Chuuk Is. Oroluk

Ngulu Olimarao Weno Nama **PALIKIR**

Woleai Pulusuk Pohnpei

Caroline Islands

200m/656ft
Sea Level

Mortlock
Islands — 5°

140° 145° 150° Satawan 160° Kosrae

0   200 km
0   200 miles

Nukuoro

155°

PACIFIC OCEAN

FACTFILE

OFFICIAL NAME: Federated States of Micronesia

DATE OF FORMATION: 1986

CAPITAL: Palikir (Pohnpei Island)

POPULATION: 108,105

TOTAL AREA: 271 sq. miles (702 sq. km)

DENSITY: 399 people per sq. mile

LANGUAGES: Trukese, Pohnpeian, Mortlockese, Kosraean, English*

RELIGIONS: Roman Catholic 50%, Protestant 48%, other 2%

ETHNIC MIX: Chuukese 49%, Pohnpeian 24%, other 19%, Kosraean 6%, Asian 2%

GOVERNMENT: Nonparty system

CURRENCY: US dollar = 100 cents

Moldova

The smallest and most densely populated of the former Soviet republics, Moldova has strong ethnic, linguistic, and cultural links with Romania to the west.

 GEOGRAPHY
The steppes and hilly plains are drained by Dniester and Prut Rivers.

CLIMATE
Warm summers and relatively mild winters. Moderate rainfall is evenly spread throughout the year.

PEOPLE & SOCIETY
A shared heritage with Romania defines national identity, though in 1994 Moldovans voted against possible reunification with Romania. Most of the population is engaged in intensive agriculture. Transdniestria is a breakaway state along the east bank of the Dniester, home to a largely ethnic Slav population. The Gagauz, in the south, have accepted autonomy.

INSIGHT: *Vast underground wine vaults contain entire "streets" of bottles built into rock quarries*

THE ECONOMY
Poorest country in Europe. Well-developed agricultural sector: wine, tobacco, cotton, food processing. Light manufacturing. Chronic instability deters investors.

FACTFILE

OFFICIAL NAME: Republic of Moldova
DATE OF FORMATION: 1991
CAPITAL: Chisinau
POPULATION: 4.2 million
TOTAL AREA: 13,067 sq. miles (33,843 sq. km)
DENSITY: 323 people per sq. mile

LANGUAGES: Moldovan*, Ukrainian, Russian
RELIGIONS: Orthodox Christian 98%, Jewish 2%
ETHNIC MIX: Moldovan 64%, Ukrainian 14%, Russian 13%, Gagauz 4%, other 5%
GOVERNMENT: Parliamentary system
CURRENCY: Moldovan leu = 100 bani

Monaco

Monaco is a tiny enclave on the Côte d'Azur. Its destiny changed radically when the casino was opened in 1863. Today, it promotes its image as an upmarket, glamorous destination.

GEOGRAPHY
A rocky promontory overlooking a narrow coastal strip that has been enlarged through land reclamation.

CLIMATE
Mediterranean. Summers are hot and dry; days with 12 hours of sunshine are not uncommon. Winters are mild and sunny.

PEOPLE & SOCIETY
Less than 20% of residents are Monégasques. Around a third are French, the rest Italian, American, British, Belgian, and many others. Nationals enjoy considerable privileges, including housing subsidies to protect them from Monaco's high property prices, and the right of first refusal before a job can be offered to a foreigner. Women have equal status but only acquired the vote in 1962.

THE ECONOMY
Tourism and gambling are the mainstays. Banking secrecy laws and tax-haven conditions are attractive to foreign investment. Monaco is almost totally dependent on imports due to its lack of natural resources.

INSIGHT: *High-profile social and sporting events attract large crowds each spring, including the Rose Ball, Tennis Open, and Grand Prix*

FACTFILE

OFFICIAL NAME: Principality of Monaco
DATE OF FORMATION: 1861
CAPITAL: Monaco-Ville
POPULATION: 32,409
TOTAL AREA: 0.75 sq. miles (1.95 sq. km)
DENSITY: 43,212 people per sq. mile

LANGUAGES: French*, Italian, Monégasque, English
RELIGIONS: Roman Catholic 89%, Protestant 6%, other 5%
ETHNIC MIX: French 32%, other 29%, Italian 20%, Monégasque 19%
GOVERNMENT: Monarchy
CURRENCY: Euro = 100 cents

Mongolia

Landlocked between Russia and China, Mongolia is a vast and isolated country with a large nomadic population. Over two-thirds of the country is part of the vast Gobi Desert.

 GEOGRAPHY
A mountainous steppe plateau in the north, with lakes in the north and west. The desert region of the Gobi dominates the south.

 CLIMATE
Continental. Mild summers and long, dry, very cold winters, with heavy snowfall. Temperatures can drop as low as –22°F (–30°C).

 PEOPLE & SOCIETY
Mongolia was unified by Genghis Khan in 1206 and was later absorbed into Manchu China. A majority of ethnic Mongolians live over the border in Inner Mongolia. Tibetan Buddhism dominates. The traditional, nomadic way of life has been eroded as urban migration continues, spurred by recent ferocious winters, known as *zud*, which have devastated the rural economy.

$ THE ECONOMY
Rich deposits of oil, coal, copper, uranium, and other minerals remain largely untapped. Democracy, from 1990, has brought a shift toward a market economy, but also rising poverty. State involvement in mining is an issue. Agriculture employs 40% of the workforce, mainly animal herding.

◆ **INSIGHT:** *Horseracing, wrestling, and archery are the national sports*

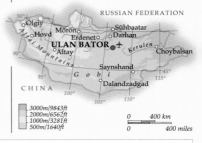

RUSSIAN FEDERATION

Olgiy • Hovd • Mörön • Erdenet • Sühbaatar • Darhan
ULAN BATOR •
Altay • Kerulen • Choybalsan
Saynshand
G o b i
CHINA • Dalandzadgad

3000m/9843ft
2000m/6562ft
1000m/3281ft
500m/1640ft

0 — 400 km
0 — 400 miles

📖 FACTFILE

OFFICIAL NAME: Mongolia
DATE OF FORMATION: 1924
CAPITAL: Ulan Bator
POPULATION: 2.6 million
TOTAL AREA: 604,247 sq. miles (1,565,000 sq. km)
DENSITY: 4 people per sq. mile

LANGUAGES: Khalkha Mongolian*, other
RELIGIONS: Tibetan Buddhist 96%, Muslim 4%
ETHNIC MIX: Khalkh 82%, other 9%, Kazakh 4%, Dorvod 3%, Bayad 2%
GOVERNMENT: Mixed presidential–parliamentary system
CURRENCY: Tugrik (tögrög) = 100 möngö

Montenegro

Perched on the Adriatic coast, the tiny republic of Montenegro became a separate state in 2006, after 88 years of federation with its neighbors in various forms of the state of Yugoslavia.

GEOGRAPHY
A narrow coastal strip on the Adriatic. Fertile lowland plains around Lake Skadar. Mountainous interior with deep canyons.

CLIMATE
The lowlands have hot, dry summers and mild winters. Heavy snow in winter in the mountains.

PEOPLE & SOCIETY
Most Montenegrins are Orthodox Christians. They speak a language closely related to Serbian, using the same Cyrillic script. Muslim Albanians, who make up 80% of the population of the southern Ulcinj region, supported independence and are now asking for autonomy.

◆ **INSIGHT:** *Dark forests once cloaked Montenegro's mountains; its name means "Black Mountain"*

THE ECONOMY
Sanctions aimed at Serbia also hurt Montenegro before it seceded. Economy dominated by black market; cigarette smuggling is rife. Tourism now expanding along Adriatic. Return of international aid and investment. Hopes for eventual EU accession.

FACTFILE

OFFICIAL NAME: Republic of Montenegro
DATE OF FORMATION: 2006
CAPITAL: Podgorica
POPULATION: 620,145
TOTAL AREA: 5332 sq. miles (13,812 sq. km)
DENSITY: 116 people per sq. mile

LANGUAGES: Montenegrin*, Serbian, Albanian
RELIGIONS: Orthodox Christian 74%, Muslim 18%, Catholic 4%, other 4%
ETHNIC MIX: Montenegrin 43%, Serb 32%, other 12%, Bosniak 8%, Albanian 5%
GOVERNMENT: Parliamentary system
CURRENCY: Euro = 100 cents

Morocco

Morocco is a former French colony in northwest Africa. Since 1975 it has occupied the territory of Western Sahara, the future of which is yet to be determined by UN-supervised referendum.

GEOGRAPHY

Fertile coastal plain is interrupted in the east by the Rif Mountains. Atlas Mountain ranges to the south. Beyond lies the outer fringe of the Sahara.

CLIMATE

Ranges from temperate and warm in the north, to semiarid in the south. Cooler in the mountains.

PEOPLE & SOCIETY

Around 30% of the population are descendants of original Berber inhabitants of north Africa, and live mainly in mountain villages. The Arab majority inhabits the lowlands. Morocco is unusual among Arab states in granting Jews religious freedom and civil rights. The government is pressured by Islamic traditionalists who fear the loss of Arab identity. The king is spiritual leader and head of state.

THE ECONOMY

A leading world exporter of phosphates. Tourism and agriculture have great potential. Production of cannabis complicates closer EU links.

◆ **INSIGHT:** *Karueein University in Fès, founded in 859 CE, is the world's oldest existing educational institution*

FACTFILE

OFFICIAL NAME: Kingdom of Morocco
DATE OF FORMATION: 1956
CAPITAL: Rabat
POPULATION: 31.5 million
TOTAL AREA: 172,316 sq. miles (446,300 sq. km)
DENSITY: 183 people per sq. mile

LANGUAGES: Arabic*, Tamazight (Berber), French, Spanish
RELIGIONS: Muslim (mainly Sunni) 99%, other (mostly Christian) 1%
ETHNIC MIX: Arab 70%, Berber 29%, European 1%
GOVERNMENT: Monarchy
CURRENCY: Dirham = 100 centimes

Mozambique

Mozambique lies on the southeast African coast. It was torn apart by a savage and devastating civil war between the Marxist government and a rebel faction between 1977 and 1992.

GEOGRAPHY
Largely a savanna-covered plateau. The coast is fringed by coral reefs and lagoons. The Zambezi River bisects the country.

CLIMATE
Tropical. Temperatures are hottest on the coast. Extremes of rainfall: drought and flood.

PEOPLE & SOCIETY
Tensions exist between north and south, rather than ethnic groups. Life is centered on the extended family. Polygamy is fairly common. The country is struggling with the legacy of a war which killed over one million people, and the effects of terrible flooding in 2000 and 2001. Half of the population live in abject poverty.

◆ **INSIGHT:** *Maputo's busy port serves Zimbabwe and South Africa*

THE ECONOMY
Mozambique is almost entirely dependent on foreign aid. Mineral resources have yet to be fully exploited.

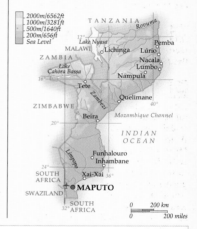

FACTFILE

OFFICIAL NAME: Rep. of Mozambique
DATE OF FORMATION: 1975
CAPITAL: Maputo
POPULATION: 19.8 million
TOTAL AREA: 309,494 sq. miles (801,590 sq. km)
DENSITY: 65 people per sq. mile

LANGUAGES: Makua, Xitsonga, Sena, Lomwe, Portuguese*
RELIGIONS: Traditional beliefs 56%, Christian 30%, Muslim 14%
ETHNIC MIX: Makua Lomwe 47%, Tsonga 23%, Malawi 12%, Shona 11% other 7%
GOVERNMENT: Presidential system
CURRENCY: Metical = 100 centavos

Myanmar (Burma)

Forming the eastern shores of the Bay of Bengal and the Andaman Sea in southeast Asia, Myanmar suffers from extensive political repression and ethnic conflict.

GEOGRAPHY
The fertile Irrawaddy basin lies at the center. Mountains to the west, Shan plateau to the east. Tropical rainforest covers much of the land.

CLIMATE
Tropical. Hot summers, with high humidity, and warm winters.

PEOPLE & SOCIETY
The military, in power since 1962, rules Myanmar with little regard to human rights. Opposition is not tolerated. The National League for Democracy won elections in 1990, but was kept from power. Its leader, Aung San Suu Kyi, is frequently detained. Minority groups maintain low-level guerrilla activity against the state.

◆ **INSIGHT:** *Myanmar is the one of the world's biggest teak exporters, though reserves are diminishing rapidly*

THE ECONOMY
Aid suspensions and sanctions. The ruling junta has encouraged foreign investment. Prices are soaring on the black market. Illicit opium production. Teak, rice, and gems exported.

FACTFILE

OFFICIAL NAME: Union of Myanmar
DATE OF FORMATION: 1948
CAPITAL: Rangoon (Yangon)/Pyinmana
POPULATION: 50.5 million
TOTAL AREA: 261,969 sq. miles (678,500 sq. km)
DENSITY: 199 people per sq. mile

LANGUAGES: Burmese*, Shan, Karen, Rakhine, Chin, Yangbye, Kachin, Mon
RELIGIONS: Buddhist 87%, Christian 6%, Muslim 4%, other 2%, Hindu 1%
ETHNIC MIX: Burman 68%, other 13%, Shan 9%, Karen 6%, Rakhine 4%
GOVERNMENT: Military-based regime
CURRENCY: Kyat = 100 pyas

Namibia

Located in southwestern Africa, Namibia gained independence from South Africa in 1990, after 24 years of armed struggle. It regained the territory of Walvis Bay in 1994.

GEOGRAPHY
The Namib Desert stretches along the coastal strip. Inland, a ridge of mountains rises to 8000 ft (2500 m). The Kalahari Desert lies in the east.

CLIMATE
Almost rainless. The coast is usually shrouded in thick fog, unless the hot, dry *berg* wind is blowing.

PEOPLE & SOCIETY
The largest ethnic group, the Ovambo, live mainly in the north. Whites, including a large German community, are centered around Windhoek. Whites still control the economy. The minority San and Khoi bushmen are among the oldest human communities in the world. Toleration of homosexuality is slowly increasing.

◆ **INSIGHT:** *The Namib is the Earth's oldest, and one of its driest, deserts*

THE ECONOMY
Varied mineral resources, including uranium and diamonds. Rich offshore fishing grounds. High unemployment, and a growing AIDS epidemic.

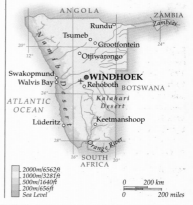

2000m/6562ft
1000m/3281ft
500m/1640ft
200m/656ft
Sea Level

0   200 km
0   200 miles

FACTFILE
OFFICIAL NAME: Republic of Namibia
DATE OF FORMATION: 1990
CAPITAL: Windhoek
POPULATION: 2 million
TOTAL AREA: 318,694 sq. miles (825,418 sq. km)
DENSITY: 6 people per sq. mile

LANGUAGES: Ovambo, Kavango, English*, Bergdama, German, Afrikaans
RELIGIONS: Christian 90%, traditional beliefs 10%
ETHNIC MIX: Ovambo 50%, other tribes 25%, Kavango 9%, Damara 8%, Herero 8%
GOVERNMENT: Presidential system
CURRENCY: Namibian dollar = 100 cents

Nauru

Nauru lies in the Pacific, northeast of Australia. Phosphate deposits made its citizens among the wealthiest in the world, but economic mismanagement has left it facing ruin.

 GEOGRAPHY

A single low-lying coral atoll, with a fertile coastal belt. Coral cliffs encircle an elevated interior plateau.

 CLIMATE

Equatorial, moderated by sea breezes. Occasional long droughts.

 PEOPLE & SOCIETY

Native Nauruans are of mixed Micronesian and Polynesian origin. Most live in simple, traditional houses and spend their money on luxury cars and consumer goods. Welfare and education are free. A diet of imported processed foods has caused widespread obesity and diabetes. Mining was left to an imported labor force, mainly from Kiribati, who live in enclaves of male-only barracks and have few rights. Many of the young attend boarding schools in Australia and New Zealand.

 THE ECONOMY

Phosphate revenues all but dried up by 2003. No other resources. State trust fund invested badly overseas. Offshore banking facilities were closed after international pressure.

◆ **INSIGHT:** *Phosphate mining has left 80% of the island uninhabitable*

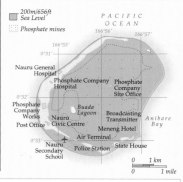

FACTFILE

OFFICIAL NAME: Republic of Nauru
DATE OF FORMATION: 1968
CAPITAL: None
POPULATION: 13,048
TOTAL AREA: 8.1 sq. miles (21 sq. km)
DENSITY: 1611 people per sq. mile

LANGUAGES: Nauruan*, Kiribati, Chinese, Tuvaluan, English
RELIGIONS: Nauruan Congregational Church 60%, Catholic 35%, other 5%
ETHNIC MIX: Nauruan 62%, other Pacific islanders 27%, Asian 8%, European 3%
GOVERNMENT: Parliamentary system
CURRENCY: Australian $ = 100 cents

Nepal

Nepal, lying between India and China on the southern shoulder of the Himalayas, is one of the world's poorest countries. Its agricultural economy is heavily dependent on the monsoon.

GEOGRAPHY
Mainly mountainous. The area includes some of the highest mountains in the world, such as Everest. Flat, fertile river plains form the south.

CLIMATE
Warm monsoon season from July to October. The rest of the year is dry, sunny, and mild. Winter temperatures in the Himalayas average 14°F (–10°C).

PEOPLE & SOCIETY
There are few tensions between the diverse ethnic groups. Sherpa women, like other Buddhists, face fewer social restrictions than Hindus. A Maoist insurgency, seeking a socialist republic, began in 1999 and threw the country into a state of virtual civil war. In 2002, the king sacked the government; opposition protests forced the return of democracy in 2006, with the king reduced to a figurehead.

THE ECONOMY
Agriculture employs over 90% of people. Crops include rice, maize, and millet. Tourism has been affected by instability and Maoist insurgency. There is potential for hydropower.

INSIGHT: *Southern Nepal was the birthplace of Buddha (Prince Siddhartha Gautama) in 563 BCE*

Dadeldhurā
Jumlā
CHINA
Baglung
Pokharā
Mt. Everest 29,035ft (8850m) (Sagarmatha)
KATHMANDU
Lalitpur
Bhaktapur
INDIA
Janakpur
Ilām
Birātnagar

4000m/13124ft
3000m/9843ft
2000m/6562ft
1000m/3281ft
500m/1640ft
200m/656ft
Sea Level

0   100 km
0   100 miles

FACTFILE

OFFICIAL NAME: Kingdom of Nepal
DATE OF FORMATION: 1769
CAPITAL: Kathmandu
POPULATION: 27.1 million
TOTAL AREA: 54,363 sq. miles (140,800 sq. km)
DENSITY: 513 people per sq. mile

LANGUAGES: Nepali*, Maithili, Bhojpuri
RELIGIONS: Hindu 90%, Buddhist 5%, Muslim 3%, other 2%
ETHNIC MIX: Other 52%, Chhetri 16%, Hill Brahman 13%, Tharu 7%, Magar 7%, Tamang 5%
GOVERNMENT: Parliamentary system
CURRENCY: Nepalese rupee = 100 paisa

Netherlands

Astride the delta of five major rivers in northwest Europe, the Netherlands was one of the world's first confederative republics. The main port, Rotterdam, is also the world's largest.

 GEOGRAPHY
Mainly flat, with 27% of the land below sea level and protected by dunes, dikes, and canals. There are a few low hills in the south and east.

 CLIMATE
Mild, rainy winters and cool summers. Gales from the North Sea are common in fall and winter.

 PEOPLE & SOCIETY
The Dutch have a long history of welcoming immigrants from former colonies and refugees seeking asylum. However, lack of integration is now raising fears about the failing asylum system, immigrant crime, and militant Islam. Population density is high and mostly urban. The state does not try to impose a particular morality on its citizens. Laws concerning sexuality, narcotics-taking, and euthanasia, are among the world's most liberal.

THE ECONOMY
Diverse industrial sector exports metals, machinery, electronics, and chemicals. High-profile multinationals. The social welfare system is costly.

INSIGHT: *In 2002 the Netherlands became the first country in the world to legalize euthanasia*

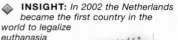

FACTFILE

OFFICIAL NAME: Kingdom of the Netherlands
DATE OF FORMATION: 1648
CAPITALS: Amsterdam and The Hague
POPULATION: 16.3 million
TOTAL AREA: 16,033 sq. miles (41,526 sq. km)

DENSITY: 1245 people per sq. mile
LANGUAGES: Dutch*, Frisian
RELIGIONS: Roman Catholic 36%, other 34%, Protestant 27%, Muslim 3%
ETHNIC MIX: Dutch 82%, other 12%, Surinamese, Turkish, and Moroccan 6%
GOVERNMENT: Parliamentary system
CURRENCY: Euro = 100 cents

New Zealand

Lying in the South Pacific, 990 miles (1600 km) southeast of Australia, New Zealand comprises North and South Island, separated by the Cook Strait, and many smaller islands.

GEOGRAPHY
North Island contains hot springs and geysers, and the bulk of the population. South Island is mostly mountainous, with eastern lowlands.

CLIMATE
Generally temperate and damp. The far north is almost subtropical, whereas southern winters are cold.

PEOPLE & SOCIETY
Maoris were the first settlers, 1200 years ago. Today's majority European population is descended mainly from British migrants who settled after 1840. Maoris' living and education standards are generally lower than average. The government is continuing to negotiate the settlement of Maori land claims.

◆ **INSIGHT:** *New Zealand women were the first to get the vote (1893)*

THE ECONOMY
Modern agricultural sector; one of the world's five biggest exporters of dairy products. Manufacturing and tourism industries growing. Very high debt.

2000m/6562ft
1000m/3281ft
500m/1640ft
200m/656ft
Sea Level

North Island

36°

Auckland
Manurewa
Hamilton Tauranga
Rotorua
New Taupo
Plymouth
Napier
Hastings
Palmerston
North
Blenheim Lower Hutt
WELLINGTON

Tasman Sea

40°

176°

South Island

Cook Strait

Christchurch

Southern Alps

Timaru
44° 172°

PACIFIC
OCEAN

Dunedin

Invercargill
Stewart Island
168°

0   200 km
0   200 miles

FACTFILE
OFFICIAL NAME: New Zealand
DATE OF FORMATION: 1947
CAPITAL: Wellington
POPULATION: 4 million
TOTAL AREA: 103,737 sq. miles (268,680 sq. km)
DENSITY: 39 people per sq. mile

LANGUAGES: English*, Maori*
RELIGIONS: Anglican 24%, other 22%, Presbyterian 18%, nonreligious 16%, Roman Catholic 15%, Methodist 5%
ETHNIC MIX: European 75%, Maori 15%, other 7%, Samoan 3%
GOVERNMENT: Parliamentary system
CURRENCY: New Zealand $ = 100 cents

Nicaragua

Nicaragua lies at the heart of Central America. The Sandinista revolution of 1978 led to 11 years of civil war between the left-wing Sandinistas and the right-wing US-backed, Contras.

GEOGRAPHY
Extensive forested plains in the east. Central mountain region with many active volcanoes. The Pacific coastlands are dominated by lakes.

CLIMATE
Tropical. The lowlands are hot all year round. The mountains are cooler. Prone to occasional hurricanes.

PEOPLE & SOCIETY
Most of the population is mixed race, and there is a large white elite. The Caribbean regions are home to communities of Miskito Amerindians and blacks, who gained autonomy in 1987. The revolution improved the status of women, but these gains have been undone by rampant poverty.

◆ **INSIGHT:** *Lake Nicaragua is the only freshwater lake in the world to contain ocean animals*

THE ECONOMY
Coffee, meat, and gold are the main exports; affected by world price fluctuations. Corruption. A heavy debt burden, though substantial debt relief has recently been approved.

1000m/3281ft
500m/1640ft
200m/656ft
Sea Level

Coco
HONDURAS
14°
Ocotal
Estelí   Jinotega
Matagalpa
Chinandega   Telica   Matiguas
Corinto
León   MANAGUA
Nagarote   Juigalpa
12°   Granada
San Rafael del Sur   Nandaime   Bluefields
Diriamba   Rivas   Lago de
Jinotepe   Nicaragua
(Lake Nicaragua)
86°
COSTA RICA   San Juan
84°

Caribbean
Sea

Mosquito Coast

0   100 km
0   100 miles

📖 FACTFILE

OFFICIAL NAME: Republic of Nicaragua
DATE OF FORMATION: 1838
CAPITAL: Managua
POPULATION: 5.5 million
TOTAL AREA: 49,998 sq. miles (129,494 sq. km)
DENSITY: 120 people per sq. mile

LANGUAGES: Spanish*, English Creole, Miskito
RELIGIONS: Roman Catholic 80%, Protestant Evangelical 17%, other 3%
ETHNIC MIX: Mestizo 69%, White 14%, Black 8%, Amerindian 5%, Zambo 4%
GOVERNMENT: Presidential system
CURRENCY: Córdoba oro = 100 centavos

Niger

Landlocked in the west of Africa, Niger is linked to the sea by the Niger River. It was ruled by one-party or military regimes until 1992, when a multiparty constitution was introduced.

GEOGRAPHY

The north and northeast regions are part of the Sahara. The Aïr Mountains in the center rise high above the desert. Savanna lies to the south.

CLIMATE

High temperatures persist for most of the year at around 95°F (35°C). The north is virtually rainless.

PEOPLE & SOCIETY

Considerable tensions exist between Tuareg nomads in the north and groups in the south. Tuareg have felt alienated from mainstream politics. A five-year rebellion by northern Tuareg ended in 1995 with a peace agreement. A sense of community and egalitarianism among the southern peoples helps to combat economic difficulties. Niger is largely Islamic. Women have limited rights, and restricted access to education.

THE ECONOMY

Niger has vast uranium deposits. Frequent droughts and the southwest expansion of the Sahara are problems.

INSIGHT: *Niger's name is derived from the Tuareg word n'eghirren, which means "flowing water"*

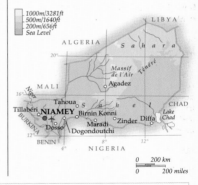

1000m/3281ft
500m/1640ft
200m/656ft
Sea Level

FACTFILE

OFFICIAL NAME: Republic of Niger
DATE OF FORMATION: 1960
CAPITAL: Niamey
POPULATION: 14 million
TOTAL AREA: 489,188 sq. miles (1,267,000 sq. km)
DENSITY: 29 people per sq. mile

LANGUAGES: Hausa, French*, other
RELIGIONS: Muslim 85%, traditional beliefs 14%, other 1%
ETHNIC MIX: Hausa 55%, Djerma and Songhai 21%, Peul 9%, Tuareg 9%, other 6%
GOVERNMENT: Presidential system
CURRENCY: CFA franc = 100 centimes

Nigeria

Lying in west Africa, Nigeria (a former UK colony) is now a federation of 36 states and the capital, Abuja. Dominated by military governments since 1966, democracy returned in 1999.

GEOGRAPHY
Coastal area of beaches, swamps, and lagoons gives way to rainforest, and then to savanna on the high plateaus. Semidesert to the north.

CLIMATE
The south is hot, rainy and humid for most of the year. The arid north has one very humid wet season. The Jos Plateau and highlands are cooler.

PEOPLE & SOCIETY
Some 250 ethnic groups: the largest are the Hausa, Yoruba, Ibo, and Fulani. Tensions between groups threaten national unity, and fierce intercommunal violence is common. The northern states have introduced *sharia* (Islamic law) for their majority Muslim populations. In the south, women are allowed economic independence; in the north they are restricted by conservative Islam.

THE ECONOMY
Nigeria has been overdependent on oil, its principal export, since the 1970s. Corruption is a serious issue.

INSIGHT: *Nigeria is Africa's most populous state – one in every seven Africans is Nigerian*

1000m/3281ft
500m/1640ft
200m/656ft
Sea Level

FACTFILE
OFFICIAL NAME: Federal Republic of Nigeria
DATE OF FORMATION: 1960
CAPITAL: Abuja
POPULATION: 132 million
TOTAL AREA: 356,667 sq. miles (923,768 sq. km)

DENSITY: 374 people per sq. mile
LANGUAGES: Hausa, English*, Yoruba, Ibo
RELIGIONS: Muslim 50%, Christian 40%, traditional beliefs 10%
ETHNIC MIX: Hausa 21%, Yoruba 21%, Ibo 18%, Fulani 11%, other 29%
GOVERNMENT: Presidential system
CURRENCY: Naira = 100 kobo

Norway

The Kingdom of Norway traces the rugged western coast of Scandinavia. Settlements are largely restricted to southern and coastal areas. Vast oil and gas revenues bring prosperity.

GEOGRAPHY

The western coast is indented with numerous fjords and features tens of thousands of islands. Mountains and plateaus cover most of the country.

CLIMATE

Mild coastal climate. Inland, weather is more extreme, with warm summers and cold, snowy winters.

PEOPLE & SOCIETY

Fairly homogeneous, with some recent refugees from the Bosnian conflict. There is a strong family tradition despite the high divorce rate. Fair-minded consensus promotes female equality, boosted by the generous child-care provision. Wealth is more evenly distributed than in most developed countries.

◆ **INSIGHT:** *Near Narvik, mainland Norway is only 4 miles (7 km) wide*

THE ECONOMY

Major European producer and exporter of oil and gas. Metal, engineering, and chemical industries.

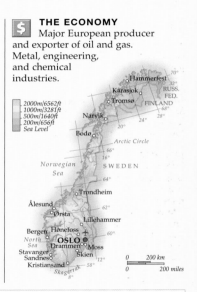

2000m/6562ft
1000m/3281ft
500m/1640ft
200m/656ft
Sea Level

Hammerfest
Karasjok
Tromsø
RUSS. FED.
FINLAND
Narvik
Bodø
Arctic Circle
Norwegian Sea
SWEDEN
Trondheim
Ålesund
Ørsta
Lillehammer
Bergen
Hønefoss
OSLO
North Sea
Drammen
Moss
Stavanger
Sandnes
Skien
Kristiansand
Skagerrak

0   200 km
0   200 miles

FACTFILE

OFFICIAL NAME: Kingdom of Norway
DATE OF FORMATION: 1905
CAPITAL: Oslo
POPULATION: 4.6 million
TOTAL AREA: 125,181 sq. miles (324,220 sq. km)
DENSITY: 39 people per sq. mile

LANGUAGES: Norwegian* (Bokmål and Nynorsk), Sami
RELIGIONS: Evangelical Lutheran 89%, other 10%, Roman Catholic 1%
ETHNIC MIX: Norwegian 93%, other 6%, Sami 1%
GOVERNMENT: Parliamentary system
CURRENCY: Norwegian krone = 100 øre

Oman

Situated on the eastern coast of the Arabian Peninsula, Oman occupies a strategic position at the entrance to the Persian Gulf. It is the least developed Gulf state, despite modest oil exports.

 GEOGRAPHY
Mostly gravelly desert, with mountains in the north and south. Some narrow fertile coastal strips.

 CLIMATE
Blistering heat in the west. Summer temperatures often climb above 113°F (45°C). Southern uplands receive rains June–September.

PEOPLE & SOCIETY
Urban drift has seen most Omanis move to northern towns. The majority are Ibadi Muslims who follow an appointed leader, the imam. Ibadism is not opposed to freedom for women, and a few women hold positions of authority. Baluchi from Pakistan are the largest group of foreign workers.

◆ **INSIGHT:** *Until the late 1980s, Oman was closed to all but business or official visitors*

THE ECONOMY
Oil and gas account for most export revenue. Other exports include fish, animals, dates, and tomatoes. Foreigners work in all sectors.

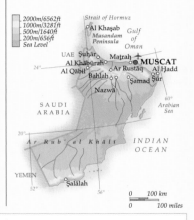

2000m/6562ft
1000m/3281ft
500m/1640ft
200m/656ft
Sea Level

Strait of Hormuz
Al Khaşab
Musandam Peninsula
Gulf of Oman
UAE Şuḩār
Al Khābūrah Maṭraḥ
24° Al Qābil Ar Rustāq MUSCAT
Bahlah Al Hadd
Nazwā Samad Şūr
SAUDI ARABIA
60° Arabian Sea
20° A r   R u b '   a l   K h ā l ī INDIAN OCEAN
YEMEN Şalālah
52° 56°

0   100 km
0   100 miles

FACTFILE

OFFICIAL NAME: Sultanate of Oman
DATE OF FORMATION: 1951
CAPITAL: Muscat
POPULATION: 2.6 million
TOTAL AREA: 82,031 sq. miles (212,460 sq. km)
DENSITY: 32 people per sq. mile

LANGUAGES: Arabic*, Baluchi, other
RELIGIONS: Ibadi Muslim 75%, other Muslim and Hindu 25%
ETHNIC MIX: Arab 88%, Baluchi 4%, Persian 3%, Indian and Pakistani 3%, African 2%
GOVERNMENT: Monarchy
CURRENCY: Omani rial = 1000 baisa

Pakistan

Once a part of British India, Pakistan was created in 1947 in response to demands for an independent, largely Muslim state. Bangladesh (former East Pakistan) gained independence in 1971.

GEOGRAPHY

The floodplain of the Indus River dominates east and south. Hindu Kush mountains in the north. The west is semidesert plateau and mountains.

CLIMATE

Temperatures can soar to 122°F (50°C) in south and west, and fall to –4°F (–20°C) in the Hindu Kush.

PEOPLE & SOCIETY

Punjabis dominate government and the army. There are many tensions with minority groups, exacerbated by the vast gap between rich and poor. Strong family ties permeate all aspects of politics and business. Relations with India are very tense over the issue of Kashmir.

◆ INSIGHT: *In 1988, Pakistan elected the first female prime minister in the Muslim world*

THE ECONOMY

Leading producer of cotton and rice, but unpredictable weather conditions often affect the crop. Oil and gas reserves. Aid for earthquake reconstruction and "war on terror."

5000m/16405ft
4000m/13124ft
3000m/9843ft
2000m/6562ft
1000m/3281ft
500m/1640ft
200m/656ft
Sea Level

CHINA

Hindu Kush

Karakoram Range

ISLĀMĀBĀD
Khyber Pass
Peshāwar
Rāwalpindi
Sargodha
Faisalābād
Quetta
Multān
Bahāwalpur
Sukkur
Hyderābād
Karāchi

Sialkot
Gujrānwāla
Lahore
Punjab

AFGHANISTAN

Baluchistan

Sindh

Thar Desert

INDIA

IRAN

Arabian Sea

Indus

0   200 km
0   200 miles

FACTFILE

OFFICIAL NAME: Islamic Rep. of Pakistan
DATE OF FORMATION: 1947
CAPITAL: Islamabad
POPULATION: 158 million
TOTAL AREA: 310,401 sq. miles (803,940 sq. km)
DENSITY: 531 people per sq. mile

LANGUAGES: Punjabi, Sindhi, Pashtu, Urdu*, Baluchi, Brahui
RELIGIONS: Sunni Muslim 77%, Shi'a Muslim 20%, Hindu 2%, Christian 1%
ETHNIC MIX: Punjabi 50%, Pathan 15%, Sindhi 14%, other 14%, Mohajir 7%
GOVERNMENT: Presidential system
CURRENCY: Pakistani rupee = 100 paisa

Palau

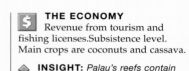

The 300-island Palau archipelago (known locally as Belau) lies in the western Pacific Ocean. It achieved independence in 1994, and is gradually reducing its aid dependence.

GEOGRAPHY

Terrain varies from thickly forested mountains to limestone and coral reefs. Babeldaob, the largest island, is volcanic, with many rivers and waterfalls.

CLIMATE

Hot and wet. Little variation in daily and seasonal temperatures. February–April is the dry season.

PEOPLE & SOCIETY

Native Palauans are a mix of the original southeast Asian migrants and Pacific settlers. A modern influx from Asia has led to tension. 70% of the population live on the island-city of Koror, prompting the construction of a new capital on Babeldaob. Native culture is preserved on outer islands despite strong influence from the US and Japan. Modekngei is a blend of Christianity and local beliefs.

THE ECONOMY
Revenue from tourism and fishing licenses. Subsistence level. Main crops are coconuts and cassava.

INSIGHT: *Palau's reefs contain 1500 species of fish and 700 types of coral*

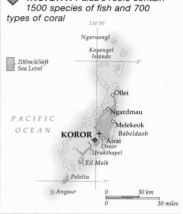

134°30'

Ngaruangl

Kayangel Islands

8°

■ 200m/656ft Sea Level

Ollei

Ngardmau

PACIFIC

Melekeok

OCEAN

Babeldaob

KOROR

Airai
Oreor
Urudthapel

Eil Malk

7°

Peleliu

Angaur

0   30 km

0   30 miles

FACTFILE

OFFICIAL NAME: Republic of Palau
DATE OF FORMATION: 1994
CAPITAL: Koror
POPULATION: 20,303
TOTAL AREA: 177 sq. miles (458 sq. km)
DENSITY: 104 people per sq. mile

LANGUAGES: Palauan*, English*, Japanese, Angaur, Tobi, Sonsorolese
RELIGIONS: Christian 66%, Modekngei 34%
ETHNIC MIX: Palauan 74%, Filipino 16%, other 6%, Chinese and other Asian 4%
GOVERNMENT: Nonparty system
CURRENCY: US dollar = 100 cents

Panama

Panama is the southernmost country in Central America. The colossal Panama Canal (which was under US-control until 2000) links the Pacific and Atlantic Oceans.

GEOGRAPHY
Lowlands along both coasts, with savanna-covered plains and rolling hills. Mountainous interior. Swamps and rainforests in the east.

CLIMATE
Hot and humid, with heavy rainfall in the May–December wet season. Cooler at high altitudes.

PEOPLE & SOCIETY
A multiethnic society, dominated by people of Spanish origin. Amerindians live in remote areas. The Panama Canal and former US military bases (the last of which closed in 1999) have given society a cosmopolitan outlook, but Catholicism and the extended family remain strong. Crime is high; money-laundering, narcotics trafficking, and corruption are rife.

THE ECONOMY
Colón Free Trade Zone: second-largest in the world. Income from the canal. Earnings from merchant ships sailing under Panamanian flag. Banana and fish exports.

◆ **INSIGHT:** *The Panama Canal shortens the sea route between the east coast of the US and Japan by 3000 miles (4800 km)*

FACTFILE

OFFICIAL NAME: Republic of Panama
DATE OF FORMATION: 1903
CAPITAL: Panama City
POPULATION: 3.2 million
TOTAL AREA: 30,193 sq. miles (78,200 sq. km)
DENSITY: 109 people per sq. mile

LANGUAGES: English Creole, Spanish*, Amerindian and Chibchan languages
RELIGIONS: Roman Catholic 86%, other 8%, Protestant 6%
ETHNIC MIX: Mestizo 60%, White 14%, Black 12%, Amerindian 8%, other 6%
GOVERNMENT: Presidential system
CURRENCY: Balboa = 100 centésimos

Papua New Guinea

A former Australian colony, Papua New Guinea (PNG) occupies the eastern section of the island of New Guinea and several other island groups. Much of the country is isolated.

GEOGRAPHY

Mountainous and forested mainland, with broad, swampy river valleys. 40 active volcanoes in the north. Around 600 outer islands.

CLIMATE

Hot and humid in lowlands, cooling toward highlands, where snow can fall on highest peaks.

PEOPLE & SOCIETY

Around 750 language groups and even more tribes. The main social distinction is between lowlanders, who have frequent contact with the outside world, and the very isolated, but increasingly threatened, highlanders. Great tensions exist between highland tribes, and vendettas can often last several generations. The island of Bougainville has been granted autonomy and an eventual referendum on independence.

THE ECONOMY

Minerals: significant quantities of gold, copper, oil, and natural gas. High government spending almost led to national bankruptcy in 2002.

INSIGHT: *PNG is home to the only known poisonous birds; contact with the feathers of some species of pitohui produce skin blisters*

FACTFILE

OFFICIAL NAME: Independent State of Papua New Guinea
DATE OF FORMATION: 1975
CAPITAL: Port Moresby
POPULATION: 5.9 million
TOTAL AREA: 178,703 sq. miles (462,840 sq. km)

DENSITY: 34 people per sq. mile
LANGUAGES: Pidgin English, Papuan, English*, Motu, c.750 native languages
RELIGIONS: Protestant 60%, Roman Catholic 37%, other 3%
ETHNIC MIX: Melanesian and mixed 100%
GOVERNMENT: Parliamentary system
CURRENCY: Kina = 100 toea

Paraguay

Landlocked in central South America, and once a Spanish colony, Paraguay's postindependence history has included periods of military rule. Free elections were held in 1993.

GEOGRAPHY
The Paraguay River divides hilly and forested east from a flat alluvial plain with marsh and semidesert scrub land in the west.

CLIMATE
Subtropical. The Gran Chaco is generally hotter and drier. All areas experience floods and droughts.

PEOPLE & SOCIETY
Population mainly of mixed Spanish and native Guaraní origin. Most people are bilingual, though in rural areas Guaraní is more widely heard. Cattle-ranchers populate the Chaco, along with communities of the German-origin Mennonite Church. The army is politically active.

◆ **INSIGHT:** *The War of the Triple Alliance (1864–1870) killed almost 90% of Paraguay's male population*

THE ECONOMY
Agriculture: soybeans are the main export. Massive hydroelectric dams allow Paraguay to export electricity. Political instability deters foreign investment. Large informal economy. Corruption and smuggling.

FACTFILE
OFFICIAL NAME: Republic of Paraguay
DATE OF FORMATION: 1811
CAPITAL: Asunción
POPULATION: 6.2 million
TOTAL AREA: 157,046 sq. miles (406,750 sq. km)
DENSITY: 40 people per sq. mile

LANGUAGES: Guaraní, Spanish*, German
RELIGIONS: Roman Catholic 96%, Protestant (including Mennonite) 4%
ETHNIC MIX: Mestizo 91%, other 7%, Amerindian 2%
GOVERNMENT: Presidential system
CURRENCY: Guaraní = 100 céntimos

Peru

Once the heart of the Inca empire, before the Spanish conquest in the 16th century, Peru lies on the Pacific coast of South America, just south of the equator.

 GEOGRAPHY
Coastal plain rises to Andes mountains. Uplands, dissected by fertile valleys, lie east of the Andes. Tropical forest in extreme east.

 CLIMATE
Coast is mainly arid. Middle slopes of the Andes are temperate; higher peaks are snow-covered. East is hot, humid, and very wet.

 PEOPLE & SOCIETY
Though populated mainly by Amerindians or mixed-race *mestizos*, society is dominated by a small group of Spanish descendants. Amerindians, and the small black community, suffer discrimination in towns, but access to information and political power are growing, with the first Amerindian president in 2001–2006. Clashes with left-wing militants killed almost 70,000 people between 1980 and 2000.

$ THE ECONOMY
Abundant mineral resources: notably copper and gold. Rich Pacific fish stocks. Leading coca producer.

 INSIGHT: *Lake Titicaca is the world's highest navigable lake*

FACTFILE

OFFICIAL NAME: Republic of Peru
DATE OF FORMATION: 1824
CAPITAL: Lima
POPULATION: 28 million
TOTAL AREA: 496,223 sq. miles (1,285,200 sq. km)
DENSITY: 57 people per sq. mile

LANGUAGES: Spanish*, Quechua*, Aymara
RELIGIONS: Roman Catholic 95%, other 5%
ETHNIC MIX: Amerindian 50%, Mestizo 40%, White 7%, other 3%
GOVERNMENT: Presidential system
CURRENCY: New sol = 100 céntimos

Philippines

Lying in the western Pacific Ocean, the Philippines is the world's second-largest archipelago. It comprises 7107 islands, of which 4600 are named and 1000 inhabited.

GEOGRAPHY
Larger islands are forested and mountainous. Over 20 active volcanoes. Frequent earthquakes.

CLIMATE
Tropical. Warm and humid all year round. Typhoons occur in the rainy season: June–October.

PEOPLE & SOCIETY
Over 100 ethnic groups; most are of Malay origin and Roman Catholic. The Church is a dominant cultural force; it opposes family-planning programs, despite the high population growth rate. The Chinese minority has been established for 400 years. Women play a prominent part in society. San Carlos University was founded in 1595 by the Spanish.

◆ **INSIGHT:** *Mass "People Power" demonstrations have brought down two presidents, in 1986 and 2001*

THE ECONOMY
Agricultural productivity is rising; coconuts, sugar, bananas, and pineapples are exported. Corruption and poor infrastructure limit growth.

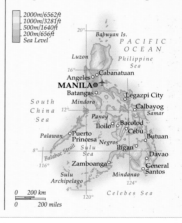

FACTFILE

OFFICIAL NAME: Rep. of the Philippines
DATE OF FORMATION: 1946
CAPITAL: Manila
POPULATION: 83.1 million
TOTAL AREA: 115,830 sq. miles (300,000 sq. km)
DENSITY: 722 people per sq. mile

LANGUAGES: Filipino*, Tagalog, Cebuano, Hiligaynon, other including English*
RELIGIONS: Roman Catholic 83%, Protestant 9%, Muslim 5%, other 3%
ETHNIC MIX: Tagalog 28%, Cebuano 13%, Ilocano 9%, Hiligaynon 8%, other 42%
GOVERNMENT: Presidential system
CURRENCY: Philippine peso = 100 centavos

Poland

Located in the heart of Europe, Poland has undergone massive social, economic, and political change since the collapse of communism in 1989, culminating with EU membership in 2004.

GEOGRAPHY
Lowlands, part of the North European Plain, cover most of the country. The Tatra mountains run along the southern border.

CLIMATE
Rainfall peaks during the hot summers. Cold winters with snow, especially in mountains.

PEOPLE & SOCIETY
Ethnic homogeneity masks a number of tensions. Secular liberals criticize the semiofficial status of the Roman Catholic Church, and emerging wealth disparities are resented by those unaffected by free-market reforms. The German minority in the west is growing more assertive.

◆ **INSIGHT:** *Poland was the second country in Europe to have a written constitution*

THE ECONOMY
Foreign investment reflects the country's large potential market. Rapid privatization is now slowing. High unemployment. Heavy industries dominate, though services growing.

1000m/3281ft
500m/1640ft
200m/656ft
Sea Level

0   100 km
0   100 miles

FACTFILE
OFFICIAL NAME: Republic of Poland
DATE OF FORMATION: 1918
CAPITAL: Warsaw
POPULATION: 38.5 million
TOTAL AREA: 120,728 sq. miles (312,685 sq. km)
DENSITY: 328 people per sq. mile

LANGUAGES: Polish
RELIGIONS: Roman Catholic 93%, other and nonreligious 5%, Orthodox Christian 2%
ETHNIC MIX: Polish 97%, other 2%, Silesian 1%
GOVERNMENT: Parliamentary system
CURRENCY: Zloty = 100 groszy

Portugal

Portugal, with its long Atlantic coast, lies on the western side of the Iberian Peninsula, which it shares with Spain. It is the most westerly country on the European mainland.

GEOGRAPHY
The Tagus River bisects the country roughly east to west, dividing mountainous north from lower and more undulating south.

CLIMATE
North is cool and moist. South is warmer with dry, mild winters.

PEOPLE & SOCIETY
A homogeneous and stable society, which is losing some of its conservative traditions. History of immigration from former colonies, and recently from eastern Europe. Urban areas and the south are more socially liberal. The north is more responsive to traditional Roman Catholic values. Family ties remain important.

◆ **INSIGHT:** *Portugal is the world's leading producer of cork, which comes from the bark of the cork oak*

THE ECONOMY
Agricultural economy declining: vegetables, fruits, and wine. Clothing and car exports. Strong banking and tourism sectors. High budget deficit.

FACTFILE
OFFICIAL NAME: Republic of Portugal
DATE OF FORMATION: 1139
CAPITAL: Lisbon
POPULATION: 10.5 million
TOTAL AREA: 35,672 sq. miles
(92,391 sq. km)
DENSITY: 296 people per sq. mile

LANGUAGES: Portuguese
RELIGIONS: Roman Catholic 97%, other 2%, Protestant 1%
ETHNIC MIX: Portuguese 98%, African and other 2%
GOVERNMENT: Parliamentary system
CURRENCY: Euro = 100 cents

Qatar

Projecting north from the Arabian Peninsula into the Gulf, Qatar was a founder member of OPEC. Its plentiful reserves of oil and gas make it one of the wealthiest states in the region.

GEOGRAPHY
Flat, semiarid desert with dunes and salt pans. Vegetation is limited to small patches of scrub.

CLIMATE
Hot and humid. Temperatures in summer can soar to over 104°F (40°C). Rainfall is rare.

PEOPLE & SOCIETY
Only one in five residents are native-born; the rest are guest workers from the Indian subcontinent, Iran, and north Africa. Qataris were once nomadic Bedouins, but since the advent of oil wealth around 90% now live in Doha and its suburbs. As a result, the north is dotted with abandoned villages. Women enjoy relative freedom; most wear the veil.

◆ INSIGHT: *There are twice as many men as women in Qatar*

THE ECONOMY
Steady supply of crude oil and huge gas reserves, plus related industries. Economy is heavily dependent on foreign workforce. All raw materials and most foods, except vegetables, are imported.

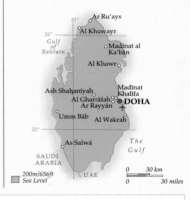

Ar Ru'ays
51°
Al Khuwayr
26°
Gulf of Bahrain
Madīnat al Ka'bān
Al Khawr
Ash Shahānīyah
Madīnat Khalīfa
Al Gharrāfah
Ar Rayyān ● **DOHA**
Umm Bāb
Al Wakrah
25°
As Salwā
The Gulf
SAUDI ARABIA
200m/656ft Sea Level
UAE
0   30 km
0   30 miles

FACTFILE

OFFICIAL NAME: State of Qatar
DATE OF FORMATION: 1971
CAPITAL: Doha
POPULATION: 813,000
TOTAL AREA: 4416 sq. miles (11,437 sq. km)
DENSITY: 191 people per sq. mile

LANGUAGES: Arabic
RELIGIONS: Muslim (mainly Sunni) 95%, other 5%
ETHNIC MIX: Arab 40%, Indian 18%, Pakistani 18%, other 14%, Iranian 10%
GOVERNMENT: Monarchy
CURRENCY: Qatar riyal = 100 dirhams

Romania

Once dominated by Poles, Hungarians, and Ottomans, Romania has been slowly converting to a free-market economy since the overthrow of its communist regime in 1989.

GEOGRAPHY
Carpathian Mountains encircle the Transylvanian plateau. Wide plains to the south and east. Danube River forms southern border.

CLIMATE
Continental. Summers are hot and humid, winters are cold and snowy. Very heavy spring rains.

PEOPLE & SOCIETY
Romanians are ethnically distinct from their Slav and Hungarian (Magyar) neighbors. Hungarians are the largest minority and are based in Transylvania. They are protected by the influence of Hungary, unlike the Roma, who suffer from discrimination. The overall population is shrinking.

◆ **INSIGHT:** *In 2001, Romania became the last country in Europe to lift its ban on homosexuality*

THE ECONOMY
Pollution-spreading, outdated heavy industries and unmechanized agricultural sector. Exports of textiles and metals have led recovery from 1990s recession. EU membership in 2007. Privatization continues.

2000m/6562ft
1000m/3281ft
500m/1640ft
200m/656ft
Sea Level

0   100 km
0   100 miles

FACTFILE

OFFICIAL NAME: Romania
DATE OF FORMATION: 1878
CAPITAL: Bucharest
POPULATION: 21.7 million
TOTAL AREA: 91,699 sq. miles (237,500 sq. km)
DENSITY: 244 people per sq. mile

LANGUAGES: Romanian*, Hungarian
RELIGIONS: Romanian Orthodox 87%, Roman Catholic 5%, Protestant 4%, other 2%, Greek Orthodox 1%, Uniate 1%
ETHNIC MIX: Romanian 89%, Magyar 7%, Roma 2%, other 2%
GOVERNMENT: Presidential system
CURRENCY: Romanian leu

Russian Federation

The Russian Federation was the core of the old Soviet Union, which broke up in 1991. Russia is still the world's largest state. Its diversity is a source of both strength and problems.

GEOGRAPHY

The Ural Mountains divide the European steppes and forests from the tundra and forests of Siberia. South-central deserts and mountains.

CLIMATE

Continental in European Russia. Elsewhere climate ranges from sub-arctic to Mediterranean and hot desert.

PEOPLE & SOCIETY

Ethnic Russians make up around 80% of the population, but there are many minorities; 57 "nationalities" have territorial status, while a further 95 lack their own region. Most ethnic republics are concentrated in European Russia. There are a growing number of Muslims in Russia. The ongoing war with Chechnya highlights the potential for ethnic crisis. Wealth disparities, rising crime, and black-market activities have accompanied reforms.

◆ **INSIGHT:** *The Trans-Siberian Railroad, which runs 5800 miles (9335 km) from Moscow to Vladivostok, is the longest in the world, passing through seven time zones*

FACTFILE

OFFICIAL NAME: Russian Federation
DATE OF FORMATION: 1480
CAPITAL: Moscow
POPULATION: 143 million
TOTAL AREA: 6,592,735 sq. miles (17,075,200 sq. km)
DENSITY: 22 people per sq. mile

LANGUAGES: Russian*, Tatar, Ukrainian, Chavash, other national languages
RELIGIONS: Orthodox Christian 75%, Muslim 14%, other 11%
ETHNIC MIX: Russian 80%, other 13%, Tatar 4%, Ukrainian 2%, Chavash 1%
GOVERNMENT: Presidential system
CURRENCY: Russian rouble = 100 kopeks

Russian Federation

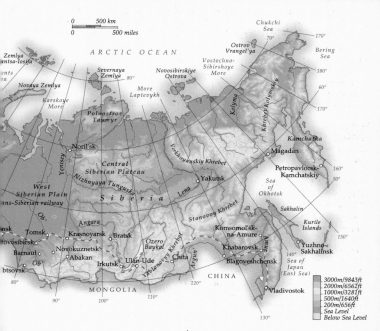

ARCTIC OCEAN

Zemlya
antsa-Iosifa
ents

Novaya Zemlya

Severnaya
Zemlya

Novosibirskiye
Ostrova

Ostrov
Vrangel'ya

Vostochno-
Sibirshoye
More

Bering
Sea

*Karskoye
More*

More
Laptevykh

Poluostrov
Taymyr

Kolyma

Khrebet Kolymskiy

Kamchatka

Noril'sk

*Central
Siberian Plateau*

Verkhoyánskiy Khrebet

Magadan

Petropavlovsk-
Kamchatskiy

Yeniséy

Nizhnyaya Tunguska

S i b e r i a

Yakutsk

Lena

Sea
of
Okhotsk

*West
Siberian Plain*
rans-Siberian railway

Angara

*Ozero
Baykal*

Stanovoy Khrebet

Sakhalin

Kurile
Islands

ansk

Tomsk

Krasnoyarsk

Bratsk

Komsomol'sk-
na-Amure

ovosibirsk

Ob'

Novokuznetsk

Abakan

Irkutsk

Ulan-Ude

Chita

Yablonovyy Khrebet

Argun

Khabarovsk

Amur

Yuzhno-
Sakhalinsk

Barnaul

Ob'

Blagoveshchensk

Sea
of
Japan
(East Sea)

btsovsk

MONGOLIA

CHINA

Vladivostok

	3000m/9843ft
	2000m/6562ft
	1000m/3281ft
	500m/1640ft
	200m/656ft
	Sea Level
	Below Sea Level

$ THE ECONOMY

Lingering inefficiencies since transition to market economy sap Russia's obvious strengths: huge natural resources, in particular oil and gas, precious metals, timber, and hydrocarbons, which account for 80% of export earnings. High oil prices are driving economic growth and have allowed Russia to repay its Soviet-era debt. Important engineering, military, and scientific base. Tax evasion and corruption are widespread. Organized crime syndicates own huge areas of the economy, and the black market accounts for 40% of trade.

Rwanda

Rwanda lies just south of the equator in east central Africa, far from the nearest sea port. Since independence from France in 1962, ethnic tensions have dominated politics.

GEOGRAPHY

A series of plateaus descend from the ridge of volcanic peaks in the west to the Akagera River on the eastern border. The Great Rift Valley also passes through this region.

CLIMATE

Tropical, though tempered by the altitude. Two wet seasons are separated by a dry season, from June to August. Heaviest rain in the west.

PEOPLE & SOCIETY

For over 500 years the cattle-owning Tutsi minority were politically dominant over the land-owning Hutu. In 1959, violent revolt led to a reversal of the roles. Ethnic tensions are fierce; in the most recent violence, in 1994, over 800,000 people, mostly Tutsi, were massacred in an act of state-backed genocide; trials are ongoing. Rwandans live a subsistence existence.

THE ECONOMY

Rwanda has few resources, but if it could achieve lasting stability, it could become a key producer of coffee and tea. The potential from possible oil and gas reserves is offset by the high cost of transportation.

INSIGHT: *Rwanda is the most densely populated country in mainland Africa*

FACTFILE

OFFICIAL NAME: Republic of Rwanda
DATE OF FORMATION: 1962
CAPITAL: Kigali
POPULATION: 9 million
TOTAL AREA: 10,169 sq. miles
(26,338 sq. km)
DENSITY: 934 people per sq. mile

LANGUAGES: Kinyarwanda*, French*, Kiswahili, English*
RELIGIONS: Catholic 56%, traditional beliefs 25%, Muslim 10%, Protestant 9%
ETHNIC MIX: Hutu 90%, Tutsi 9%, other (including Twa) 1%
GOVERNMENT: Presidential system
CURRENCY: Rwanda franc = 100 centimes

St. Kitts & Nevis

A popular Caribbean tourist destination, St. Kitts and Nevis lies in the northern part of the Leeward Island chain. Nevis is the less developed of the two islands.

GEOGRAPHY
Volcanic in origin, with forested, mountainous interiors. Nevis has hot and cold springs.

CLIMATE
Tropical, tempered by trade winds. Little seasonal variation in temperature. Moderate rainfall.

PEOPLE & SOCIETY
The majority of the population are descended from former African slaves. There are small numbers of Europeans, South Asians, and a community of Lebanese. Levels of emigration are high, and overseas remittances are an important source of national income. The government has pledged to retrain sugar workers. Native professionals and civil servants have largely replaced the former expatriate elite. The secessionist movement on Nevis remains an issue.

THE ECONOMY
Successful and still expanding tourist industry is vulnerable to downturns in US market. Once-key sugar industry closed down in 2005.

INSIGHT: *Nevis has been renowned as a spa since the 18th century, and is known as the "Queen of the Caribbean"*

FACTFILE

OFFICIAL NAME: Federation of Saint Christopher and Nevis
DATE OF FORMATION: 1983
CAPITAL: Basseterre
POPULATION: 38,958
TOTAL AREA: 101 sq. miles (261 sq. km)
DENSITY: 280 people per sq. mile

LANGUAGES: English*, English Creole
RELIGIONS: Anglican 33%, Methodist 29%, other 22%, Moravian 9%, Roman Catholic 7%
ETHNIC MIX: Black 95%, mixed 3%, White 1%, other and Amerindian 1%
GOVERNMENT: Parliamentary system
CURRENCY: East Caribbean $ = 100 cents

St. Lucia

St. Lucia is one of the most beautiful of the Caribbean Windward Islands. Ruled by France and the UK at different times in its past, the island retains the character of both.

GEOGRAPHY
Volcanic and mountainous, with some broad fertile valleys. The Pitons, ancient lava cones, rise from the sea on the forested west coast.

CLIMATE
Tropical, moderated by trade winds. May–October wet season brings daily warm showers. Rainfall is highest in the mountains.

PEOPLE & SOCIETY
Population is a tension-free mixture of descendants of Africans, Caribs, and Europeans. Family life and the Roman Catholic Church are important to most St. Lucians. In rural areas women often head the households, and run much of the farming. Plantation and hotel owners are the richest group. There is growing local resistance to overdevelopment of the island for tourism.

THE ECONOMY
Mainly agricultural, with some light industry. Bananas are biggest export. Successful tourist industry, but most resorts are foreign-owned.

INSIGHT: *St. Lucia has two Nobel laureates, the most per capita in the world*

FACTFILE
OFFICIAL NAME: Saint Lucia
DATE OF FORMATION: 1979
CAPITAL: Castries
POPULATION: 166,312
TOTAL AREA: 239 sq. miles (620 sq. km)
DENSITY: 705 people per sq. mile

LANGUAGES: English*, French Creole
RELIGIONS: Roman Catholic 90%, other 10%
ETHNIC MIX: Black 83%, Mulatto (mixed race) 13%, Asian 3%, White 1%
GOVERNMENT: Parliamentary system
CURRENCY: East Caribbean $ = 100 cents

St. Vincent & the Grenadines

The islands of St. Vincent and the Grenadines form part of the Windward group in the Caribbean. St. Vincent is mostly volcanic, while the Grenadines are flat, mainly bare, coral reefs.

GEOGRAPHY
St. Vincent is mountainous and forested, with one of two active volcanoes in the Caribbean, La Soufrière. The Grenadines are 32 islands and cays fringed by beaches.

CLIMATE
Tropical, with constant trade winds. Hurricanes are likely during July–November wet season.

PEOPLE & SOCIETY
Population is racially diverse; intermarriage has reduced tensions. Society is informal and relaxed, but family life is strongly influenced by the Church. Locals fear that their traditional lifestyle is being threatened by the expanding tourist industry.

◆ INSIGHT: *The islands' precolonial inhabitants, the Carib, named them "Harioun" – home of the blessed*

THE ECONOMY
Dependent on agriculture and tourism. Bananas are the main cash crop. Tourism, targeted at the jet-set and cruise-ship markets, is concentrated on the Grenadines.

FACTFILE

OFFICIAL NAME: Saint Vincent and the Grenadines
DATE OF FORMATION: 1979
CAPITAL: Kingstown
POPULATION: 117,534
TOTAL AREA: 150 sq. miles (389 sq. km)

DENSITY: 897 people per sq. mile
LANGUAGES: English*, English Creole
RELIGIONS: Anglican 47%, Methodist 28%, Roman Catholic 13%, other 12%
ETHNIC MIX: Black 77%, Mulatto (mixed race) 16%, other 3%, Carib 3%, Asian 1%
GOVERNMENT: Parliamentary system
CURRENCY: East Caribbean $ = 100 cents

Samoa

The southern Pacific islands of Samoa gained independence from New Zealand in 1962. Four of the nine volcanic islands are inhabited – Apolima, Manono, Savai'i, and Upolu.

GEOGRAPHY
Comprises two large islands and seven smaller ones. The two largest islands have rainforested, mountainous interiors surrounded by coastal lowlands and coral reefs.

CLIMATE
Tropical, with high humidity. Cooler May–November. Hurricane season December–March.

PEOPLE & SOCIETY
Ethnic Samoans are the world's second-largest Polynesian group, after the Maoris. Their way of life is communal and formalized. Extended family groups own 80% of the land. Each family has an elected chief, who looks after its political and social interests. Large-scale migration to the US and New Zealand reflects the country's lack of jobs and the attractions of a Western lifestyle.

THE ECONOMY
Exports fish. Agricultural products include coconut cream, copra, and taro. Growth of the service sector: tourism and offshore banking. Dependent on aid and expatriate remittances. Rainforests are increasingly exploited for timber.

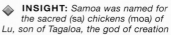

INSIGHT: *Samoa was named for the sacred (sa) chickens (moa) of Lu, son of Tagaloa, the god of creation*

FACTFILE

OFFICIAL NAME: Independent State of Samoa
DATE OF FORMATION: 1962
CAPITAL: Apia
POPULATION: 185,000
TOTAL AREA: 1104 sq. miles (2860 sq. km)

DENSITY: 169 people per sq. mile
LANGUAGES: Samoan*, English*
RELIGIONS: Christian 99%, other 1%
ETHNIC MIX: Polynesian 90%, Euronesian (mixed European and Polynesian) 9%, other 1%
GOVERNMENT: Parliamentary system
CURRENCY: Tala = 100 sene

San Marino

Perched on the slopes of Monte Titano in the Italian Appennino, San Marino has maintained its independence since the 4th century CE, but Italy effectively controls most of its affairs.

GEOGRAPHY
Distinctive limestone outcrop of Monte Titano dominates wooded hills and pastures near Italy's Adriatic coast.

CLIMATE
High altitude and sea breezes moderate a Mediterranean climate. Hot summers and cool, wet winters.

PEOPLE & SOCIETY
Territory is divided into nine "castles," or districts. Tightly knit society, with 16 centuries of tradition. Strict immigration rules require 30-year residence before applying for citizenship. Living standards are similar to those in northern Italy. About 20,000 Sammarinesi live abroad, most in Italy.

◈ **INSIGHT:** *Sales of postage stamps and coins contribute around 10% of the national income*

THE ECONOMY
Tourism provides over half of total government income. Lower tax rates than in Italy. Wine, cheese, olive oil, textiles, cement, ceramics, and building stone are exported. Italian infrastructure is a boon.

500m/1640ft
200m/656ft
Sea Level

44°

Dogana
Serravalle
Fiorina
Cailungo
Gualdicciolo
Borgo
Maggiore ● SAN MARINO
ITALY
Monte Titano △
739m
Faetano
ITALY
Murata
Chiesanuova
Montegiardino

Appennino

12°30'

0   4 km
0   4 miles

FACTFILE

OFFICIAL NAME: Republic of San Marino
DATE OF FORMATION: 1631
CAPITAL: San Marino
POPULATION: 28,880
TOTAL AREA: 23.6 sq. miles (61 sq. km)

DENSITY: 1203 people per sq. mile
LANGUAGES: Italian
RELIGIONS: Roman Catholic 93%, other and nonreligious 7%
ETHNIC MIX: Sammarinese 88%, Italian 10%, other 2%
GOVERNMENT: Parliamentary system
CURRENCY: Euro = 100 cents

São Tomé & Príncipe

A former Portuguese colony São Tomé and Príncipe lies off the west coast of Africa, comprising two main islands and the surrounding islets. Elections in 1991 ended 15 years of Marxism.

GEOGRAPHY
Islands scattered across the equator. São Tomé and Príncipe are heavily forested and mountainous.

CLIMATE
Hot and humid, but cooled by the Benguela Current. Plentiful rainfall.

PEOPLE & SOCIETY
Population is mostly black, though Portuguese culture pre-dominates. Blacks run the political parties. Society is well integrated and free of racial prejudice. Príncipe assumed autonomous status in 1995. There is a growing business class. Extended family offers main form of social security. One of Africa's highest aid-to-population ratios.

◆ **INSIGHT:** *The population is entirely of immigrant descent: the islands were uninhabited when colonized in 1470*

THE ECONOMY
Cocoa provides 90% of export earnings. Coconuts, pepper, and coffee are also farmed. Offshore oil may come onstream in 2007.

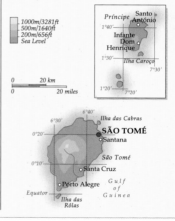

1000m/3281ft
500m/1640ft
200m/656ft
Sea Level

FACTFILE

OFFICIAL NAME: Democratic Republic of São Tomé and Príncipe
DATE OF FORMATION: 1975
CAPITAL: São Tomé
POPULATION: 187,410
TOTAL AREA: 386 sq. miles (1001 sq. km)
DENSITY: 505 people per sq. mile

LANGUAGES: Portuguese Creole, Portuguese*
RELIGIONS: Roman Catholic 84%, other 16%
ETHNIC MIX: Black 90%, Portuguese and Creole 10%
GOVERNMENT: Presidential system
CURRENCY: Dobra = 100 céntimos

Saudi Arabia

Occupying most of the Arabian Peninsula, Saudi Arabia covers an area the size of western Europe. It is the world's largest oil producer and has a major petrochemicals industry.

 GEOGRAPHY
Mostly desert or semidesert plateau. Mountain ranges in the west run parallel to the Red Sea and drop steeply to a coastal plain.

CLIMATE
In summer, temperatures often soar above 118°F (48°C), but in winter they may fall below freezing. Rainfall is rare.

 PEOPLE & SOCIETY
Most Saudis are Sunni Muslims who follow the strictly orthodox Wahhabi interpretation of Islam and embrace *sharia* (Islamic law) in their daily lives. Women are obliged to wear the veil, cannot hold driving licenses, and have no role in public life. The al-Sa'ud family have been absolutist rulers since 1932. With the support of the religious establishment, they control all political life.

THE ECONOMY
Vast oil and gas reserves. Other minerals: iron, gypsum, and limestone. Most people work in services sector.

INSIGHT: *Over two million Muslims a year make the haj (pilgrimage) to the holy city of Mecca. Only practicing Muslims are allowed inside the city*

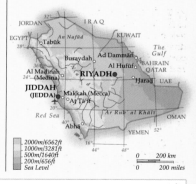

 FACTFILE

OFFICIAL NAME: Kingdom of Saudi Arabia
DATE OF FORMATION: 1932
CAPITALS: Riyadh and Jiddah
POPULATION: 24.6 million
TOTAL AREA: 756,981 sq. miles (1,960,582 sq. km)

DENSITY: 30 people per sq. mile
LANGUAGES: Arabic
RELIGIONS: Sunni Muslim 85%, Shi'a Muslim 15%
ETHNIC MIX: Arab 90%, Afro-Asian 10%
GOVERNMENT: Monarchy
CURRENCY: Saudi riyal = 100 halalat

Senegal

Senegal's capital, Dakar, stands on the westernmost cape of Africa. After independence from France, Senegal became a single-party state. Multiparty elections were first held in 1981.

 GEOGRAPHY
Arid semidesert in the north. The south is mainly savanna bushland. Plains in the southeast.

CLIMATE
Tropical, with humid rainy conditions June–October, and a drier season December–May. The coast is cooled by northern trade winds.

 PEOPLE & SOCIETY
Interethnic marriage has reduced ethnic tensions. Groups can be identified regionally. Dakar is a Wolof area, the Senegal River is dominated by the Toucouleur, and the Malinke mostly live in the east. The Diola (Jola) in Casamance have felt politically excluded, prompting a long-running secessionist struggle; a cease-fire has held since 2004. A large diaspora has raised global awareness of Senegalese culture and music.

THE ECONOMY
Good infrastructure, particularly the key port at Dakar. Development of tourism. Diminishing fish stocks. Potential for oil off Casamance.

INSIGHT: *Senegal's name derives from the Zenega Berbers who invaded in the 1300s, bringing Islam with them*

FACTFILE

OFFICIAL NAME: Republic of Senegal
DATE OF FORMATION: 1960
CAPITAL: Dakar
POPULATION: 11.7 million
TOTAL AREA: 75,749 sq. miles (196,190 sq. km)
DENSITY: 157 people per sq. mile

LANGUAGES: Wolof, Serer, Pulaar, Diola, Mandinka, Malinke, Soninke, French*
RELIGIONS: Sunni Muslim 90%, traditional beliefs 5%, Christian 5%
ETHNIC MIX: Wolof 43%, Serer 15%, other 14%, Peul 14%, Toucouleur 9%, Diola 5%
GOVERNMENT: Presidential system
CURRENCY: CFA franc = 100 centimes

Serbia

The central and eastern rump of what was once Yugoslavia, Serbia was a pariah state until Slobodan Milosevic was ousted in 2000. Montenegro finally broke away from it in 2006.

GEOGRAPHY

Landlocked since secession of Montenegro. Fertile Danube plain in the north, rolling uplands in the center and southeast. Mountains in southwest.

CLIMATE

Continental in north, with wet springs and warm summers. Colder winters with heavy snow in south.

PEOPLE & SOCIETY

Serbs are Orthodox Christian, and their language uses the Cyrillic script. Muslim ethnic Albanians form a majority in Kosovo province, run by the UN since NATO intervened to end Serb oppression in 1999. Albanian nationalists are pushing for Kosovan independence. The Catholic Magyars (Hungarians) live mainly in Vojvodina.

◆ **INSIGHT:** *The medieval Serbian empire reached into northern Greece*

THE ECONOMY

Recovering from sanctions and 1999 NATO bombing. Strong industrial base. Foreign investment growing.

FACTFILE

OFFICIAL NAME: Republic of Serbia
DATE OF FORMATION: 2006
CAPITAL: Belgrade
POPULATION: 9.7 million
TOTAL AREA: 34,116 sq. miles
(88,361 sq. km)
DENSITY: 266 people per sq. mile

LANGUAGES: Serbo-Croat*, Albanian, Hungarian (Magyar)
RELIGIONS: Orthodox Christian 70%, Muslim 18%, other 7%, Catholic 5%
ETHNIC MIX: Serb 66%, Albanian 19%, other 9%, Magyar 4%, Bosniak 2%
GOVERNMENT: Parliamentary system
CURRENCY: Dinar = 100 para

Seychelles

The Seychelles comprises 115 islands in the Indian Ocean.
Formerly a UK colony, multiparty elections were held in
1993 after 14 years as a one-party state.

GEOGRAPHY
Mostly low-lying coral atolls,
but 40, including the largest, Mahé,
are mountainous and are the only
granitic midocean islands in the world.

CLIMATE
Tropical oceanic climate. Hot and
humid. Rainy season December–May.

PEOPLE & SOCIETY
The islands were uninhabited
when French settlers arrived in the
18th century. Today, the population
is homogeneous – a result of intermarriage between ethnic groups.
Almost 90% of people live on Mahé.
Living standards are among Africa's
highest. Poverty is rare and the
welfare system caters for all.

◆ **INSIGHT:** *The Seychelles' unique
species include the giant tortoise and
the world's largest seed, the coco-de-mer*

THE ECONOMY
Tourism is the main source
of income, based on the appeal
of beaches and exotic plants and
animals. Tuna is fished and canned
for export. There are virtually no
mineral resources. All domestic
requirements are imported.

FACTFILE
OFFICIAL NAME: Republic of Seychelles
DATE OF FORMATION: 1976
CAPITAL: Victoria
POPULATION: 81,188
TOTAL AREA: 176 sq. miles
(455 sq. km)
DENSITY: 781 people per sq. mile

LANGUAGES: Creole*, English*, French*
RELIGIONS: Roman Catholic 90%,
Anglican 8%, other (including
Muslim) 2%
ETHNIC MIX: Creole 89%, Indian 5%,
other 4%, Chinese 2%
GOVERNMENT: Presidential system
CURRENCY: Seychelles rupee = 100 cents

Sierra Leone

The west African state of Sierra Leone achieved independence from the UK in 1961. Today, it is still trying to recover from a devastating civil war, and is one of the world's poorest nations.

GEOGRAPHY
Flat plain, running the length of the coast, stretches inland for 83 miles (133 km). Beyond, forests rise to highlands near neighboring Guinea in the northeast.

CLIMATE
Hot tropical weather, with very high rainfall and humidity. The dusty, northeastern *harmattan* wind blows November–April.

PEOPLE & SOCIETY
Mende and Temne are the major ethnic groups. Freetown's citizens are largely descended from slaves freed from Britain and the US, resulting in a strongly Anglicized Creole culture in the capital. The countryside is less developed. A brutal civil war broke out in 1991 and was not properly resolved until a 2001 peace agreement. Two million people were displaced.

THE ECONOMY
Diamonds are the key resource, though smuggling is rife. Cocoa and coffee are exported, though most people live by subsistence farming or are dependent on aid.

INSIGHT: *The British philanthropist Granville Sharp set up a settlement for freed slaves in Freetown in 1787*

1000m/3281ft
500m/1640ft
200m/656ft
Sea Level

GUINEA
Kabala
Makeni
Lunsar
Koidu
FREETOWN
Boajibu
Bo
Kenema
Sherbro I.
Zimmi
LIBERIA
ATLANTIC OCEAN

0   50 km
0   50 miles

FACTFILE
OFFICIAL NAME: Republic of Sierra Leone
DATE OF FORMATION: 1961
CAPITAL: Freetown
POPULATION: 5.5 million
TOTAL AREA: 27,698 sq. miles (71,740 sq. km)
DENSITY: 199 people per sq. mile

LANGUAGES: Mende, Temne, Krio, English*
RELIGIONS: Muslim 30%, traditional beliefs 30%, other 30%, Christian 10%
ETHNIC MIX: Mende 35%, Temne 32%, other 21%, Limba 8%, Kuranko 4%
GOVERNMENT: Presidential system
CURRENCY: Leone = 100 cents

Singapore

Linked to the southernmost tip of the Malay peninsula by a causeway, Singapore was established as a trading settlement in 1819. It is one of Asia's most important commercial centers.

GEOGRAPHY
Little remains of the original vegetation on Singapore Island. The other 54 much smaller islands are little more than swampy jungle.

CLIMATE
Equatorial. Hot and humid, with heavy rainfall all year round.

PEOPLE & SOCIETY
Dominated by the Chinese, who make up three-quarters of the community. The old English-speaking Straits Chinese and newer Mandarin-speakers are now well integrated. Malays are generally the poorest group. There is a significant foreign workforce. Society is highly regulated and government campaigns to improve public behavior are frequent. Crime is limited and punishment can be severe.

$ THE ECONOMY
Massive accumulated wealth is derived from success as an entrepôt and as a center of high-tech industries; Major producer of disk drives. Leads research in new biotechnologies. All food, energy, and water imported.

◆ **INSIGHT:** *Chewing gum was banned outright from 1992 to 2004*

📋 FACTFILE

OFFICIAL NAME: Republic of Singapore
DATE OF FORMATION: 1965
CAPITAL: Singapore
POPULATION: 4.3 million
TOTAL AREA: 250 sq. miles (648 sq. km)
DENSITY: 18,220 people per sq. mile

LANGUAGES: Mandarin*, Malay*, Tamil*, English*
RELIGIONS: Buddhist 55%, Taoist 22%, Muslim 16%, Hindu, Christian, Sikh 7%
ETHNIC MIX: Chinese 77%, Malay 14%, Indian 8%, other 1%
GOVERNMENT: Parliamentary system
CURRENCY: Singapore dollar = 100 cents

Slovakia

Landlocked in central Europe, Slovakia became an independent state in 1993. It is the less developed half of the former Czechoslovakia, with high levels of international debt.

GEOGRAPHY

The Tatra Mountains stretch along the northern border with Poland. Southern lowlands include the fertile Danube plain.

CLIMATE

Continental. Moderately warm summers and steady rainfall. Cold winters with heavy snowfalls.

PEOPLE & SOCIETY

Slovaks are the largest and most dominant group. The largest minority, the Magyars, seek protection of their language and culture, and are backed by Hungary. Magyar parties exist in the political mainstream, and on occasion form part of the ruling coalition. Ethnic Czechs have dual citizenship. Roma are unrepresented and face significant discrimination. The rural eastern regions are least developed.

THE ECONOMY

Emphasis on heavy industry, especially cars. Strong growth in recent years. High unemployment. EU membership from 2004. Koruna linked to euro. Ongoing privatization plans.

INSIGHT: *Bratislava was known as Pozsony when it served as the capital of Hungary from 1526 to 1784*

FACTFILE

OFFICIAL NAME: Slovak Republic
DATE OF FORMATION: 1993
CAPITAL: Bratislava
POPULATION: 5.4 million
TOTAL AREA: 18,859 sq. miles
(48,845 sq. km)
DENSITY: 285 people per sq. mile

LANGUAGES: Slovak*, Hungarian (Magyar), Czech
RELIGIONS: Roman Catholic 60%, other 22%, Atheist 10%, Protestant 8%
ETHNIC MIX: Slovak 86%, Magyar 10%, Roma 2%, Czech 1%, other 1%
GOVERNMENT: Parliamentary system
CURRENCY: Slovak koruna = 100 halierov

Slovenia

The northernmost of the former Yugoslav republics, Slovenia has close links with western Europe. Transition to independence in 1991 avoided the violence of the breakup of Yugoslavia.

GEOGRAPHY
Alpine terrain with hills and mountains. Forests cover almost half the country's area. There is a short coastline on the Adriatic Sea.

CLIMATE
Mediterranean climate on the small coastal strip. The alpine interior has continental extremes.

PEOPLE & SOCIETY
Slovenia's long historical association with western Europe, accounts for its "Alpine," rather than "Balkan," outlook, despite close similarities to other former Yugoslavs. The lack of sizable Serb or Croat minorities made for a relatively peaceful secession from Yugoslavia. There are small communities of Italians and Magyars (Hungarians) in the southwest and east respectively.

THE ECONOMY
Competitive manufacturing industry and healthy exports. First new EU member to join eurozone (in 2007). Inflation being reduced.

INSIGHT: *Slovenia has the highest standard of living of any former Soviet bloc country*

FACTFILE

OFFICIAL NAME: Republic of Slovenia
DATE OF FORMATION: 1991
CAPITAL: Ljubljana
POPULATION: 2 million
TOTAL AREA: 7820 sq. miles (20,253 sq. km)
DENSITY: 256 people per sq. mile

LANGUAGES: Slovene*, Serbo-Croat
RELIGIONS: Roman Catholic 96%, other 3%, Muslim 1%
ETHNIC MIX: Slovene 83%, other 12%, Serb 2%, Croat 2%, Bosniak 1%
GOVERNMENT: Parliamentary system
CURRENCY: Tolar = 100 stotinov

Solomon Islands

The Solomons archipelago comprises several hundred coral reef islands scattered in the southwestern Pacific. Most of the population live on the six largest islands.

GEOGRAPHY

The six largest islands are volcanic, mountainous, and thickly forested. Flat coastal plains provide the only cultivable land.

CLIMATE

Northern islands are hot and humid all year round; further south a cool season develops. November–April wet season brings cyclones.

PEOPLE & SOCIETY

Almost all Solomon Islanders are Melanesian. Tensions are regional; Guadalcanal natives (Isatabu) fought against immigrant Malaitan workers in the 1998–2000 conflict, displacing thousands and ruining the economy. In 2003 Australian-led peacekeepers arrived to restore the rule of law. Outlying islands have pressed for autonomy. Animist beliefs exist alongside Christianity.

THE ECONOMY

Main products are agricultural, though there are significant deposits of gold, copper, and bauxite. Civil conflict bankrupted the government, closed the main gold mine, and severed trade links.

INSIGHT: *The battle for Japanese-held Guadalcanal was the first major US offensive in the Pacific War during World War II*

FACTFILE

OFFICIAL NAME: Solomon Islands
DATE OF FORMATION: 1978
CAPITAL: Honiara
POPULATION: 478,000
TOTAL AREA: 10,985 sq. miles (28,450 sq. km)
DENSITY: 44 people per sq. mile

LANGUAGES: English*, Pidgin English, Melanesian Pidgin
RELIGIONS: Anglican 34%, Catholic 19%, other Protestant 38%, other 9%
ETHNIC MIX: Melanesian 94%, Polynesian 4%, other 2%
GOVERNMENT: Parliamentary system
CURRENCY: Solomon Is $ = 100 cents

Somalia

A semiarid state occupying the Horn of Africa, Somalia was formed from the Italian and British colonies of Somaliland in 1960. The country descended into anarchy from 1991.

 GEOGRAPHY
Highlands in the north, flatter scrub-covered land to the south. Coastal areas are more fertile.

 CLIMATE
Very dry, except for the north coast, which is hot and humid. The interior has among the world's highest average annual temperatures.

 PEOPLE & SOCIETY
The clan system forms the basis of all commercial, political, and social life. Most people are ethnic Somali. The minority Bantu are traditionally seen as socially inferior. The government collapsed in 1991, since when Somalia has lacked a strong central authority. Somaliland has declared independence while Puntland claims autonomy. Islamists now control Mogadishu and are challenging the power of the latest weak transitional government.

$ THE ECONOMY
Ongoing war. Every commodity, except arms, is in short supply. Piracy and banditry. Few natural strengths. Prone to drought. For the relatively stable Somaliland, trade is hampered by lack of international recognition.

◆ **INSIGHT:** *Until 1973 Somali was an unwritten language*

FACTFILE

OFFICIAL NAME: Somalia
DATE OF FORMATION: 1960
CAPITAL: Mogadishu
POPULATION: 8.2 million
TOTAL AREA: 246,199 sq. miles (637,657 sq. km)
DENSITY: 34 people per sq. mile

LANGUAGES: Somali*, Arabic*, English, Italian
RELIGIONS: Sunni Muslim 98%, Christian 2%
ETHNIC MIX: Somali 85%, other 15%
GOVERNMENT: Transitional regime
CURRENCY: Somali shilin = 100 senti

South Africa

South Africa is the southernmost nation on the African continent. After 80 years of white minority rule, the country held its first multiracial, multiparty elections in 1994.

GEOGRAPHY

Much of the interior is grassy *veld*. Desert in the west and far north. Mountains east, south, and west.

CLIMATE

Warm, temperate, and dry. Cape Town has a Mediterranean climate. Semiarid in the west.

PEOPLE & SOCIETY

The majority black population now dominates politically, but the minority white community still controls the economy. A small black middle class is growing, but unemployment among blacks is over 30%. Wealth disparities are widening. Over five million suffer from AIDS and the fight against it is hampered by social attitudes.

◆ **INSIGHT:** *Over the last century, South Africa has produced over half of the world's gold.*

THE ECONOMY

Africa's largest and most developed economy. Rich in mineral resources, particularly metals. Tourism largest foreign exchange earner. Wealth gap and AIDS epidemic worsening.

FACTFILE

OFFICIAL NAME: Republic of South Africa
DATE OF FORMATION: 1934
CAPITAL: Pretoria; Cape Town; Bloemfontein
POPULATION: 47.4 million
TOTAL AREA: 471,008 sq. miles
(1,219,912 sq. km)
DENSITY: 101 people per sq. mile

LANGUAGES: English*, isiZulu*, isiXhosa*, 8 other languages* (including Afrikaans)
RELIGIONS: Christian 68%, animist and traditional beliefs 29%, other 3%
ETHNIC MIX: Black 79%, White 10%, Colored 9%, Asian 2%
GOVERNMENT: Presidential system
CURRENCY: Rand = 100 cents

Spain

Lodged between Europe, Africa, the North Atlantic, and the Mediterranean, Spain has occupied a pivotal global position since unification under Ferdinand and Isabella in 1492.

GEOGRAPHY
Mountain ranges in the north, center, and south, with a huge central plateau. Mediterranean lowlands. Verdant valleys in the northwest.

CLIMATE
Maritime in north. Hotter and drier in south. The central plateau has an extreme climate.

PEOPLE & SOCIETY
A vigorous ethnic regionalism, long suppressed under Franco's regime, now flourishes. There are now 17 autonomous regions. People remain churchgoing, though Roman Catholic teachings on social issues are often flouted. Spanish women are increasingly emancipated, with strong political representation.

◆ **INSIGHT:** *Over 3000 festivals and feasts take place each year in Spain*

THE ECONOMY
One of the fastest-growing economies in the West with a well-qualified workforce. There are few natural resources. Spain has one of the world's largest fishing fleets. Proximity to Africa makes it a target for illegal immigrants.

FACTFILE

OFFICIAL NAME: Kingdom of Spain
DATE OF FORMATION: 1492
CAPITAL: Madrid
POPULATION: 43.1 million
TOTAL AREA: 194,896 sq. miles (504,782 sq. km)
DENSITY: 224 people per sq. mile

LANGUAGES: Spanish*, Catalan*, Galician*, Basque*
RELIGIONS: Roman Catholic 96%, other 4%
ETHNIC MIX: Spanish 72%, Catalan 17%, Galician 6%, other 3%, Basque 2%
GOVERNMENT: Parliamentary system
CURRENCY: Euro = 100 cents

Sri Lanka

The teardrop-shaped island of Sri Lanka is separated from India by the Palk Strait. Civil war between the government and ethnic Tamil rebels – the Tamil Tigers – broke out in 1983.

GEOGRAPHY

The main island is dominated by rugged central highlands. Fertile northern plains are dissected by rivers. Much of the land is tropical jungle.

CLIMATE

Tropical, with breezes on the coast and cooler air in highlands. Northeast is driest and hottest.

PEOPLE & SOCIETY

The Sinhalese are mostly Buddhist, while Tamils are mostly Hindu. Tamils were the minority group favored by the British colonists. Majority-Sinhalese power since independence in 1948 fueled tensions, erupting into civil war in 1983. A peace deal was secured in 2002, with autonomy for the Tamil north and east, but in 2006 fighting escalated once again. Moors are the Muslim descendants of Arab traders.

THE ECONOMY

World's largest tea exporter. Civil war drained government funds. Insecurity continues to deter investors and tourists. Tsunami damage in 2004.

INSIGHT: *Sri Lanka elected the world's first woman prime minister in 1960*

FACTFILE

OFFICIAL NAME: Democratic Socialist Republic of Sri Lanka
DATE OF FORMATION: 1948
CAPITAL: Colombo
POPULATION: 20.7 million
TOTAL AREA: 25,332 sq. miles (65,610 sq. km)

DENSITY: 828 people per sq. mile
LANGUAGES: Sinhala*, Tamil*, English
RELIGIONS: Buddhist 69%, Hindu 15%, Muslim 8%, Christian 8%
ETHNIC MIX: Sinhalese 82%, Tamil 9%, Moor 8%, other 1%
GOVERNMENT: Parliamentary system
CURRENCY: Sri Lanka rupee = 100 cents

Sudan

The largest country in Africa, Sudan has undergone two civil wars between Arab north and black African south, while Darfur in the west now faces a terrible humanitarian crisis.

GEOGRAPHY

Lies within the upper Nile basin. Mostly arid plains, with marshes in the south. Highlands border the Red Sea in the northeast.

CLIMATE

North is hot, arid desert with constant dry winds. Rainy season ranging from two months in the center to eight in the south.

PEOPLE & SOCIETY

Two million people are nomads. Many ethnic and linguistic groups. Key social division is between Arabized Muslims in north, and mostly black African, largely Christian or animist peoples in the south. Attempts to impose Arab and Islamic values were the root cause of the 1983–2005 civil war. Ethnic violence by Arab militias in Darfur since 2004 has killed 300,000 people. Women's rights are restricted.

THE ECONOMY

Oil exports. Sesame is the major crop. Violence and drought hamper farming. Millions of people displaced.

INSIGHT: *Sudan's Sudd is the world's largest swamp*

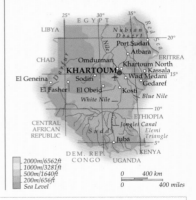

FACTFILE

OFFICIAL NAME: Republic of the Sudan
DATE OF FORMATION: 1956
CAPITAL: Khartoum
POPULATION: 36.2 million
TOTAL AREA: 967,493 sq. miles (2,505,810 sq. km)
DENSITY: 37 people per sq. mile

LANGUAGES: Arabic*, African languages
RELIGIONS: Muslim 70%, Traditional beliefs 20%, Christian 9%, Other 1%
ETHNIC MIX: Black 59% (of which Beja and Dinka 7%), Arab 40%, other 1%
GOVERNMENT: Presidential system
CURRENCY: Sudanese pound or dinar = 100 piastres

Suriname

Suriname is a former Dutch colony on the north coast of South America. Democracy was restored in 1991, after almost 11 years of military rule. The Netherlands is still the main supplier of aid.

 GEOGRAPHY
Mostly covered by tropical rainforest. Coastal plain rises to central plateaus and the Guiana Highlands.

 CLIMATE
Tropical. Hot and humid, but cooled by trade winds. High rainfall, especially in the interior.

 PEOPLE & SOCIETY
Independence provoked mass emigration: over 300,000 Surinamese live in the Netherlands. Of those left, over 90% live near the coast, the rest in scattered rainforest communities. Indigenous Amerindians only number a few thousand. *Bosnegers* – descended from runaway African slaves – fought the Creole-dominated government in the 1980s. Many South Asians and Javanese work in farming. Since return to civilian rule, each group has had a political party representing its interests.

 THE ECONOMY
Aluminum and bauxite are the leading exports. Rice and fruit are main cash crops, though Suriname is a net importer of food.

◆ **INSIGHT:** *Suriname was ceded to Holland by the English, in exchange for what is now New York state, in 1667*

| 1000m/3281ft |
| 500m/1640ft |
| 200m/656ft |
| Sea Level |

0   200 km
0   200 miles

📕 FACTFILE

OFFICIAL NAME: Republic of Suriname
DATE OF FORMATION: 1975
CAPITAL: Paramaribo
POPULATION: 499,000
TOTAL AREA: 63,039 sq. miles (163,270 sq. km)
DENSITY: 8 people per sq. mile

LANGUAGES: Sranan (creole), Dutch*, Javanese, Sarnami, Hindi, other
RELIGIONS: Christian 48%, Hindu 27%, Muslim 20%, traditional beliefs 5%
ETHNIC MIX: Creole 34%, South Asian 34%, Javanese 18%, Black 9%, other 5%
GOVERNMENT: Parliamentary system
CURRENCY: Surinamese $ = 100 cents

Swaziland

The tiny southern African kingdom of Swaziland is economically dependent on South Africa. The strong hereditary monarchy is being challenged by demands for a multiparty government.

GEOGRAPHY
Mainly high plateaus and mountains. Rolling grasslands and low scrub plains to the east. Pine forests on western border.

CLIMATE
Temperatures rise and rainfall declines as the land descends eastward, from high to low grassy *veld*.

PEOPLE & SOCIETY
One of Africa's most conservative states, though there is pressure from urban-based modernizers. Political system promotes Swazi tradition and is dominated by powerful monarchy. Women face discrimination. Swaziland has world's highest HIV infection rate: chastity is promoted to combat spread.

◆ **INSIGHT:** *Polygamy is practiced in Swaziland – when King Sobhuza died in 1982, he left 100 widows*

THE ECONOMY
Sugarcane is the main cash crop. Wood pulp and coal are also exported. Loss of workforce to AIDS, and high cost of health care.

FACTFILE

OFFICIAL NAME: Kingdom of Swaziland
DATE OF FORMATION: 1968
CAPITAL: Mbabane
POPULATION: 1 million
TOTAL AREA: 6704 sq. miles (17,363 sq. km)
DENSITY: 151 people per sq. mile

LANGUAGES: English*, siSwati*, isiZulu, Xitsonga
RELIGIONS: Christian 60%, traditional beliefs 40%
ETHNIC MIX: Swazi 97%, other 3%
GOVERNMENT: Monarchy
CURRENCY: Lilangeni = 100 cents

Sweden

The largest Scandinavian country in both population and area, Sweden has one of the world's most extensive welfare systems, and is among the leading proponents of equal rights for women.

GEOGRAPHY
Heavily forested, with many lakes. Northern plateau extends beyond the Arctic Circle. Southern lowlands are widely cultivated.

CLIMATE
Southern coasts warmed by Gulf Stream. Northern areas have more extreme continental climate.

PEOPLE & SOCIETY
The nuclear family forms the basis of society. Birth rates are rising, but marriages are declining and cohabitation is now common. The comprehensive welfare system was cut back during recession in the 1990s, but remains generous. Women are well represented at all levels. A 20,000-strong minority of Sámi lives in the far north. Most industries and the bulk of the population are based in and around the southern cities.

THE ECONOMY
Companies of global importance, including Volvo, Saab, SFK, Ericsson. Highly developed infra-structure. Up-to-date technology. Skilled labor force.

INSIGHT: *Sweden has maintained a position of armed neutrality since 1815*

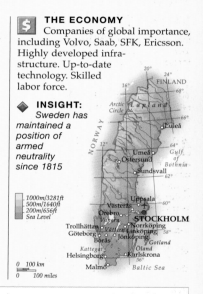

FACTFILE

OFFICIAL NAME: Kingdom of Sweden
DATE OF FORMATION: 1523
CAPITAL: Stockholm
POPULATION: 9 million
TOTAL AREA: 173,731 sq. miles (449,964 sq. km)
DENSITY: 57 people per sq. mile

LANGUAGES: Swedish*, Finnish, Sámi
RELIGIONS: Evangelical Lutheran 82%, other 13%, Roman Catholic 2%, Muslim 2%, Orthodox Christian 1%
ETHNIC MIX: Swedish 88%, recent immigrant 10%, Finnish and Sámi 2%
GOVERNMENT: Parliamentary system
CURRENCY: Swedish krona = 100 öre

Switzerland

One of the world's most prosperous countries, Switzerland lies at the center of Europe. It has managed to retain its neutral status through every major European conflict since 1815.

GEOGRAPHY

Mostly mountainous, with river valleys. The Alps cover 60% of its area; the Jura in the west cover 10%. Lowlands lie along the east–west axis.

CLIMATE

Most rain falls in the warm summer months. Winters are snowy, but milder and foggy away from the mountains. Avalanches are a problem.

PEOPLE & SOCIETY

Switzerland is composed of distinct German-Swiss, French-Swiss, and Italian-Swiss linguistic groups. Germans are in the majority and there is a 36,000-strong Romansch minority in the east. The country is divided into 26 autonomous cantons (states), each with control over housing and economic policy. Society is conservative; marriage is common but the divorce rate is above the EU average.

THE ECONOMY

Diversified economy relies on services – the banking sector manages one-third of the world's offshore private wealth – and specialized industries (engineering, watches, etc).

◆ **INSIGHT:** *Famed for its neutrality, Switzerland only became a member of the UN in 2002*

| 3000m/9843ft |
| 2000m/6562ft |
| 1000m/3281ft |
| 500m/1640ft |
| 200m/656ft |

0   50 km
0   50 miles

📖 FACTFILE

OFFICIAL NAME: Swiss Confederation
DATE OF FORMATION: 1291
CAPITAL: Bern
POPULATION: 7.3 million
TOTAL AREA: 15,942 sq. miles (41,290 sq. km)
DENSITY: 475 people per sq. mile

LANGUAGES: German*, Swiss-German, French*, Italian*, Romansch
RELIGIONS: Roman Catholic 42%, Protestant 35%, other 19%, Muslim 4%
ETHNIC MIX: German 64%, French 20%, other 9%, Italian 6%, Romansch 1%
GOVERNMENT: Parliamentary system
CURRENCY: Franc = 100 rappen/centimes

Syria

Stretching from the eastern Mediterranean to the Tigris River, Syria's borders are regarded as an artificial creation of French colonial rule by many Syrians. Foreign affairs are turbulent.

GEOGRAPHY

A coastal plain is backed by a low range of hills. The Euphrates River cuts through a vast interior desert plateau.

CLIMATE

Mediterranean coastal climate. Inland areas are arid. In winter, snow is common on the mountains.

PEOPLE & SOCIETY

Most Syrians live within 60 miles (100 km) of the coast, where the largest cities are sited. 90% are Muslim, including the politically dominant Alawis. In the north and west are groups of Kurds, Armenians, and Turkic-speaking peoples. Some 435,000 Palestinian refugees live in Syrian camps. There is a growing gulf between rich and poor. Human rights are an issue, but women's rights are among the best in the Arab world.

THE ECONOMY

Crude oil, but exports declining. High defense spending. Agriculture is thriving: crops include cotton, fruit, wheat, and olives. Large public sector.

INSIGHT: *Syria is an ancient land; there are at least 3500 as yet unexcavated archaeological sites*

2000m/6562ft
1000m/3281ft
500m/1640ft
200m/656ft
Sea Level

FACTFILE

OFFICIAL NAME: Syrian Arab Republic
DATE OF FORMATION: 1941
CAPITAL: Damascus
POPULATION: 19 million
TOTAL AREA: 71,498 sq. miles (184,180 sq. km)
DENSITY: 267 people per sq. mile

LANGUAGES: Arabic*, French, Kurdish, Armenian, Circassian, other
RELIGIONS: Sunni Muslim 74%, other Muslim 16%, Christian 10%
ETHNIC MIX: Arab 89%, Kurd 6%, other 3%, Armenian, Turkmen, Circassian 2%
GOVERNMENT: One-party state
CURRENCY: Syrian pound = 100 piastres

Taiwan

The island republic of Taiwan (formerly Formosa) lies 80 miles (130 km) off the southeast coast of mainland China. China still considers it to be a renegade province.

GEOGRAPHY

Mountain region covers two-thirds of the island. Highly fertile lowlands and coastal plains.

CLIMATE

Tropical monsoon. Hot and humid. Typhoons July–September. Snow falls in mountains in winter.

PEOPLE & SOCIETY

Most Taiwanese are Han Chinese, descendants of the 1644 migration of the Ming dynasty from the mainland. The modern republic was created in 1949, when the nationalist Kuomintang was expelled from the mainland following communist victory in the civil war. 100,000 emigrés established themselves as a ruling class. Initial resentment has subsided as a new, Taiwanese generation has taken over the reins of power. The aboriginal minority suffers discrimination.

THE ECONOMY
Successful economy based on small, adaptable manufacturing companies. Goods include televisions, mobile phones, and computer chips.

◆ **INSIGHT:** *Taiwan lost its seat at the UN to Beijing in 1971: both claim to represent "China"*

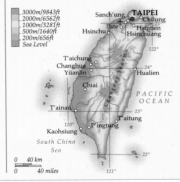

FACTFILE

OFFICIAL NAME: Republic of China (ROC)

DATE OF FORMATION: 1949

CAPITAL: Taipei

POPULATION: 22.9 million

TOTAL AREA: 13,892 sq. miles (35,980 sq. km)

DENSITY: 1838 people per sq. mile

LANGUAGES: Amoy Chinese, Mandarin Chinese*, Hakka Chinese

RELIGIONS: Buddhist, Confucianist, and Taoist 93%, Christian 5%, other 2%

ETHNIC MIX: Indigenous Chinese 84%, mainland Chinese 14%, aboriginal 2%

GOVERNMENT: Presidential system

CURRENCY: Taiwan dollar = 100 cents

Tajikistan

Tajikistan lies landlocked on the western slopes of the Pamirs in central Asia. The Tajik language and traditions are similar to those of Iran, rather than to those of Turkic Uzbekistan.

GEOGRAPHY

Mainly mountainous: the bare slopes of the Pamir ranges cover most of the country. Small but fertile Fergana Valley in northwest.

CLIMATE

Continental extremes in the valleys. Bitterly cold winters in the mountains. Rainfall is low.

PEOPLE & SOCIETY

Unlike the other former Soviet "-stans," Tajikistan is dominated by a people of Persian (Iranian) rather than Turkic origin. The main ethnic conflict is with the Turkic Uzbek minority. Russians are discriminated against and most have left since independence. Civil war in the 1990s, between communists and Islamists, degraded the standard of living. Islamist militants are still active.

THE ECONOMY

Declining cotton revenue. Key resources are uranium and fast-flowing rivers which could provide hydroelectric power exports. Needs reforms to attract foreign investment.

◆ **INSIGHT:** *Carpet-making, an ancient tradition learned from Persia, is still a major source of revenue*

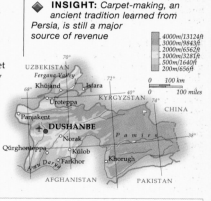

FACTFILE

OFFICIAL NAME: Republic of Tajikistan
DATE OF FORMATION: 1991
CAPITAL: Dushanbe
POPULATION: 6.5 million
TOTAL AREA: 55,251 sq. miles (143,100 sq. km)

DENSITY: 118 people per sq. mile
LANGUAGES: Tajik*, Uzbek, Russian
RELIGIONS: Sunni Muslim 80%, other 15%, Shi'a Muslim 5%
ETHNIC MIX: Tajik 80%, Uzbek 15%, other 3%, Kyrgyz 1%, Russian 1%
GOVERNMENT: Presidential system
CURRENCY: Somoni = 100 diram

Tanzania

The east African state of Tanzania was formed in 1964 by the union of Tanganyika and the Zanzibar islands. A third of its area is game reserve or national park.

GEOGRAPHY
The mainland is mostly a high plateau lying to the east of the Great Rift Valley. Forested coastal plain. Highlands in the north and south.

CLIMATE
Tropical on the coast and Zanzibar. Semiarid on central plateau, semitemperate in the highlands. March–May rains.

PEOPLE & SOCIETY
99% of people belong to one of 120 small ethnic Bantu groups. Arabs, Asians, and Europeans make up the remaining population. Use of Kiswahili as the lingua franca has eliminated ethnic rivalries. The majority of Tanzanians are subsistence farmers.

◆ **INSIGHT:** *At 19,340 ft (5895 m), Kilimanjaro in northeast Tanzania is Africa's highest mountain*

THE ECONOMY
Heavily reliant on agriculture, including forestry and cattle. Cashew nuts, cotton, coffee, and cloves are cash crops. Tourism growing. Gold and diamonds are mined. Boom in nontraditional exports.

FACTFILE
OFFICIAL NAME: United Republic of Tanzania
DATE OF FORMATION: 1964
CAPITAL: Dodoma
POPULATION: 38.3 million
TOTAL AREA: 364,898 sq. miles (945,087 sq. km)

DENSITY: 112 people per sq. mile
LANGUAGES: Kiswahili*, English*, other
RELIGIONS: Muslim 33%, Christian 33%, traditional beliefs 30%, other 4%
ETHNIC MIX: Native African (over 120 tribes) 99%, European, Asian, Arab 1%
GOVERNMENT: Presidential system
CURRENCY: Tanzanian shilling = 100 cents

Thailand

Thailand lies at the heart of mainland southeast Asia. Continuing rapid industrialization has resulted in massive congestion in the capital and a serious depletion of natural resources.

GEOGRAPHY

One-third of the country is occupied by a low plateau, drained by tributaries of the Mekong River. Central plain is the most fertile area.

CLIMATE

Tropical. Hot, humid March–May; monsoon rains May–October; cooler season November–March.

PEOPLE & SOCIETY

Buddhism is a national binding force. The north and northeast are home to about 600,000 hill tribes-people, with their own languages. The Chinese minority is the most assimilated in the region. Islamist Malay rebels in the undeveloped far south are fighting for secession.

◆ **INSIGHT:** *Thailand, meaning "land of the free," is the only SE Asian nation never to have been colonized*

THE ECONOMY

Successful manufacturing. Gas reserves. Tsunami damage affected growth. Leading world exporter of rice and rubber. Sex tourism harms image.

FACTFILE

OFFICIAL NAME: Kingdom of Thailand
DATE OF FORMATION: 1238
CAPITAL: Bangkok
POPULATION: 64.2 million
TOTAL AREA: 198,455 sq. miles (514,000 sq. km)
DENSITY: 325 people per sq. mile

LANGUAGES: Thai*, Chinese, Malay, Khmer, Mon, Karen, Miao
RELIGIONS: Buddhist 95%, Muslim 4%, other (including Christian) 1%
ETHNIC MIX: Thai 83%, Chinese 12%, Malay 3%, Khmer and other 2%
GOVERNMENT: Military regime
CURRENCY: Baht = 100 satang

Togo

Togo lies sandwiched between Ghana and Benin in west Africa. General Eyadema ruled from 1967 until his death in 2005. The port of Lomé is an important entrepôt for west African trade.

GEOGRAPHY
Central forested region bounded by savanna lands to the north and south. Mountain range stretches southwest to northeast.

CLIMATE
Coast hot and humid; drier inland. Rainy season March–July, with heaviest falls in the west.

PEOPLE & SOCIETY
Harsh resentment between Ewe in the south and Kabye in the north. Kabye control military, but the north is undeveloped compared with the south. Extended family is important. Tribalism and nepotism are key factors in everyday life. Some ethnic groups, such as the Mina, have matriarchal societies.

◆ **INSIGHT:** *The "Nana Benz," the market-women of Lomé, control Togo's retail trade*

THE ECONOMY
Most people are farmers. Self-sufficient in basic foodstuffs. Main export crops are cotton, coffee, and cocoa. Togo's phosphate deposits have world's highest mineral content, though cadmium-rich phosphates are facing bans from importers.

FACTFILE
OFFICIAL NAME: Republic of Togo
DATE OF FORMATION: 1960
CAPITAL: Lomé
POPULATION: 6.1 million
TOTAL AREA: 21,924 sq. miles (56,785 sq. km)
DENSITY: 290 people per sq. mile

LANGUAGES: Ewe, Kabye, Gurma, French*
RELIGIONS: Traditional beliefs 50%, Christian 35%, Muslim 15%
ETHNIC MIX: Ewe 46%, other African 41%, Kabye 12%, European 1%
GOVERNMENT: Presidential system
CURRENCY: CFA franc = 100 centimes

Tonga

Tonga is an archipelago of 170 islands in the South Pacific. Only 45 of these islands are inhabited. Politics is effectively controlled by the king, though calls for democracy are growing.

 GEOGRAPHY
Easterly islands are generally low and fertile. Those in the west are higher and volcanic in origin.

CLIMATE
Tropical oceanic. Temperatures range between 68°F (20°C) and 86°F (30°C) all year round. Heavy rainfall, especially February–March.

PEOPLE & SOCIETY
Tonga is the last remaining Polynesian monarchy. All land belongs to the crown, but is administered by nobles who allot it to the common people. Respect for traditional values is high, though younger, Westernized Tongans are starting to question some attitudes. The first elected commoner became prime minister in 2006.

◆ **INSIGHT:** *Unique in the Pacific, it was never brought under foreign rule*

THE ECONOMY
Cash crops are coconuts, vanilla, and squashes. Cassava, citrus fruits, yams, and breadfruit also cultivated. Tourism is increasingly important.

 FACTFILE

OFFICIAL NAME: Kingdom of Tonga
DATE OF FORMATION: 1970
CAPITAL: Nuku'alofa
POPULATION: 112,422
TOTAL AREA: 289 sq. miles (748 sq. km)
DENSITY: 404 people per sq. mile

LANGUAGES: English*, Tongan*
RELIGIONS: Free Wesleyan 41%, other 29%, Roman Catholic 16%, Church of Jesus Christ of Latter-Day Saints 14%
ETHNIC MIX: Tongan 98%, other 2%
GOVERNMENT: Monarchy
CURRENCY: Pa'anga (Tongan dollar) = 100 seniti

Trinidad & Tobago

 The two islands of the former UK colony of Trinidad and Tobago are the most southerly of the Caribbean Windward Islands, lying just 9 miles (15 km) off the coast of Venezuela.

 GEOGRAPHY
Both islands are hilly and wooded. Trinidad has a rugged mountain range in the north, and swamps on its east and west coasts.

CLIMATE
Tropical, with July–December wet season. Escapes the region's hurricanes, which pass to the north.

 PEOPLE & SOCIETY
Trinidad's East Indian community is the largest in the Caribbean and holds on to its Muslim and Hindu heritage. There are rising ethnic tensions with the predominantly Christian blacks; political parties are divided along race lines. Blacks form the majority on Tobago.

INSIGHT: *Trinidad and Tobago is the birthplace of steel bands and Calypso music*

$ THE ECONOMY
Oil and gas exports. Associated industries: world's second-largest producer of methanol. Economic growth. Tourism is particularly strong on wildlife-rich Tobago.

 FACTFILE

OFFICIAL NAME: Republic of Trinidad and Tobago
DATE OF FORMATION: 1962
CAPITAL: Port-of-Spain
POPULATION: 1.3 million
TOTAL AREA: 1980 sq. miles (5128 sq. km)
DENSITY: 656 people per sq. mile

LANGUAGES: English Creole, English*, Hindi, French, Spanish
RELIGIONS: Catholic 32%, Hindu 24%, Protestant 28%, other 9%, Muslim 7%
ETHNIC MIX: East Indian 40%, Black 40%, mixed 18%, White, Chinese 1%, other 1%
GOVERNMENT: Parliamentary system
CURRENCY: Trin. & Tob. dollar = 100 cents

AFRICA **339**
Tunisia

 Tunisia has traditionally been one of the more liberal Arab states, moving toward a multiparty democracy, but its government is now facing a challenge from Islamic fundamentalists.

GEOGRAPHY
Mountains in the north are surrounded by plains. Vast, low-lying salt pans in the center. To the south lies the Sahara Desert.

CLIMATE

Summer temperatures are high. The north is often wet and windy in winter. Far south is arid.

PEOPLE & SOCIETY

The population is almost entirely of Arab-Berber descent, with Jewish and Christian minorities. Many still live in extended family groups, in which three or four generations are represented. Women have better rights than in most other Arab countries and make up almost 30% of the total workforce. Politics, however, remains a male preserve. A low birth-rate is a result of a long-standing family planning policy.

THE ECONOMY
Well-diversified, despite limited resources. Oil and gas exports. Expanding manufacturing. Tourism. European investment.

INSIGHT: *Tunisia was the center of trading empires from the 9th century BCE*

FACTFILE
OFFICIAL NAME: Republic of Tunisia
DATE OF FORMATION: 1956
CAPITAL: Tunis
POPULATION: 10.1 million
TOTAL AREA: 63,169 sq. miles (163,610 sq. km)
DENSITY: 168 people per sq. mile

LANGUAGES: Arabic*, French
RELIGIONS: Muslim (mainly Sunni) 98%, Christian 1%, Jewish 1%
ETHNIC MIX: Arab and Berber 98%, Jewish 1%, European 1%
GOVERNMENT: Presidential system
CURRENCY: Tunisian dinar = 1000 millimes

Turkey

Lying partly in the region of eastern Thrace in Europe, but mostly in Asia, Turkey's position gives it significant influence in the Mediterranean, the Black Sea, and the Middle East.

GEOGRAPHY

Asian Turkey (Anatolia) is dominated by two mountain ranges, separated by a high, semidesert plateau. Coastal regions are fertile.

CLIMATE

Coast has a Mediterranean climate. Interior has cold, snowy winters and hot, dry summers.

PEOPLE & SOCIETY

The Turks are racially diverse. Many are refugees or descendants of refugees, often from the Balkans. However, the sense of national identity is strong. Turkey has close links with other Turkic states. Kurds, the largest minority, are based in the southeast; a violent campaign for greater autonomy has raged since 1984, with intermittent cease-fires. Tensions remain high.

THE ECONOMY

Liberalized economy, boosted by self-sufficient agriculture and strong textiles, tourism, and manufacturing sectors. Pipelines carry oil to Europe.

INSIGHT: *Turkey had two of the seven wonders of the ancient world: the tomb of King Mausolus at Halicarnassus (now Bodrum), and the temple of Artemis at Ephesus*

FACTFILE

OFFICIAL NAME: Republic of Turkey
DATE OF FORMATION: 1923
CAPITAL: Ankara
POPULATION: 73.2 million
TOTAL AREA: 301,382 sq. miles (780,580 sq. km)
DENSITY: 246 people per sq. mile

LANGUAGES: Turkish*, Kurdish, Arabic, Circassian, Armenian, Greek, other
RELIGIONS: Muslim (mainly Sunni) 99%, other 1%
ETHNIC MIX: Turkish 70%, Kurdish 20%, other 8%, Arab 2%
GOVERNMENT: Parliamentary system
CURRENCY: New Turkish lira = 100 kurus

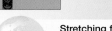

Turkmenistan

Stretching from the Caspian Sea into the deserts of central Asia, Turkmenistan adjusted better than most former Soviet states to independence, but has since been run as a dictatorship.

GEOGRAPHY
Low Karakumy Desert covers 80% of the country. Mountains on southern border with Iran. Fertile Amu Darya Valley in north.

CLIMATE
Arid desert climate with extreme summer heat, but sub-freezing winter temperatures.

PEOPLE & SOCIETY
Before Russia annexed the area in 1884, the Turkmen were a largely nomadic tribal people. Today, the tribal unit remains strong, with population clustered around desert oases. Relations with Uzbek and Russian minorities have become tense in recent years due to the "Turkmenization" of government, education, and religion. Political uncertainty followed the sudden death of President Niyazov in December 2006.

THE ECONOMY
Cotton and gas are the main resources. Over-intensive farming of cotton has damaged the environment. Opening up to private investment.

◆ **INSIGHT:** *President Niyazov created an elaborate personality cult, styling himself as Turkmenbashi – father of all Turkmen*

FACTFILE

OFFICIAL NAME: Turkmenistan
DATE OF FORMATION: 1991
CAPITAL: Aşgabat
POPULATION: 4.8 million
TOTAL AREA: 188,455 sq. miles (488,100 sq. km)
DENSITY: 25 people per sq. mile

LANGUAGES: Turkmen*, Uzbek, Russian, Kazakh, Tatar, other
RELIGIONS: Sunni Muslim 87%, Orthodox Christian 11%, other 2%
ETHNIC MIX: Turkmen 77%, Uzbek 9%, Russian 7%, other 5%, Kazakh 2%
GOVERNMENT: One-party state
CURRENCY: Manat = 100 tenge

Tuvalu

One of the world's smallest, most isolated states, Tuvalu lies in the central Pacific. The nine islands were linked to the Gilbert Islands (Kiribati) as a UK colony until independence.

 ## GEOGRAPHY
A series of coral atolls, none more than 15 ft (4.6 m) above sea level. Poor soils restrict vegetation to bush, coconut palms, and breadfruit trees.

 ## CLIMATE
Hot all year round. Heavy annual rainfall. Hurricane season brings many violent storms.

PEOPLE & SOCIETY
People are mostly Polynesian. Around half the population live on Funafuti, where government jobs are based. Life is communal and traditional. Most people live by subsistence farming, digging pits out of the coral to grow crops. Fresh water is precious due to frequent droughts.

◆ **INSIGHT:** *Tuvaluans have a reputation as excellent sailors, many work overseas on merchant ships*

THE ECONOMY
World's smallest sovereign economy. Fishing licenses sold mostly to foreign boats. Exports are few: copra, stamps, and clothes. Income from trust fund and the lease of .tv Internet suffix.

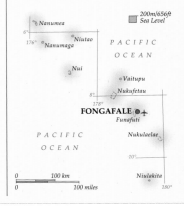

FACTFILE

OFFICIAL NAME: Tuvalu
DATE OF FORMATION: 1978
CAPITAL: Fongafale, on Funafuti Atoll
POPULATION: 11,636
TOTAL AREA: 10 sq. miles (26 sq. km)
DENSITY: 1164 people per sq. mile

LANGUAGES: Tuvaluan, Kiribati, English*
RELIGIONS: Church of Tuvalu 97%, Baha'i 1%, Seventh-day Adventist 1%, other 1%
ETHNIC MIX: Polynesian 92%, other 6%, Kiribati 2%
GOVERNMENT: Nonparty system
CURRENCY: Australian dollar and Tuvaluan dollar = 100 cents each

Uganda

Landlocked in east Africa, Uganda has a history of ethnic strife. Under President Museveni, steps have been taken to restore peace and to rebuild the economy and democracy.

GEOGRAPHY
Predominantly a large plateau with the Ruwenzori mountain range and the Great Rift Valley in the west. Lake Victoria lies to the southeast. Vegetation is of savanna type.

CLIMATE
Altitude and the influence of the lakes modify the equatorial climate. Rain falls throughout the year; spring is the wettest period.

PEOPLE & SOCIETY
The predominantly rural population comprises some 13 main ethnic groups. President Museveni has worked hard to break down traditional ethnic animosities, but a noticeable north–south divide persists, with economic development focused in the south. Two decades of conflict against rebels in the north has killed thousands and left 80% of northerners as refugees.

THE ECONOMY
Coffee, tobacco, tea, and cotton. Oil exploration. Hydroelectric power is to be developed to reduce oil imports. Great potential from the country's underused mines.

 INSIGHT: *Lake Victoria is the world's third-largest lake*

3000m/9843ft
2000m/6562ft
1000m/3281ft
500m/1640ft

SUDAN

KENYA

Arua
Gulu
Albert Nile

DEM. REP. CONGO

Lake Albert
Lake Kyoga
Ruwenzori
Kabarole
Victoria Nile
Iganga
Mbale
Tororo

Kasese
Mubende
Jinja
KAMPALA
Entebbe

Lake Edward
Masaka
Sese Is.
Equator

Rukungirio
Mbarara
Lake Victoria

Kabale
TANZANIA

RWANDA

32°

0   100 km
0   100 miles

FACTFILE
OFFICIAL NAME: Republic of Uganda
DATE OF FORMATION: 1962
CAPITAL: Kampala
POPULATION: 28.8 million
TOTAL AREA: 91,135 sq. miles (236,040 sq. km)
DENSITY: 374 people per sq. mile

LANGUAGES: Luganda, Nkole, Chiga, Lango, Acholi, Teso, Lugbara, English*
RELIGIONS: Catholic 38%, Protestant 33%, trad. beliefs 13%, Muslim 8%, other 8%
ETHNIC MIX: Baganda 17%, Banyakole 10%, Basoga 9%, Iteso 7%, other 57%
GOVERNMENT: Presidential system
CURRENCY: New Ug. shilling = 100 cents

Ukraine

The former "breadbasket of the Soviet Union," Ukraine lies on the northern coast of the Black Sea. Politics is divided between pro-Russian sentiments and assertive nationalism.

GEOGRAPHY
Mainly fertile steppes and forests. Carpathian Mountains in west, Crimean chain in south. Pripet Marshes in northwest.

CLIMATE
Mainly continental climate, with distinct seasons. Southern Crimea has Mediterranean climate.

PEOPLE & SOCIETY
Over 90% of people in the west are Ukrainian, but in cities in the east and south, and in Crimea, Russians form a majority. The government is wary of Crimean separatism. Tatars have been returning there since the Soviet Union's collapse and now comprise around 13% of the local population. Over five million people in Ukraine, Russia, and Belarus live in areas 'contaminated' by the 1986 Chernobyl nuclear disaster.

THE ECONOMY
Ukraine has 5% of global mineral reserves; metals account for around 40% of export earnings. Slow reform of land laws has held back the revival of agriculture. Political instability.

◆ **INSIGHT:** *Ukraine means "on the border," referring to its historic position on the edge of the old Russian Empire*

FACTFILE

OFFICIAL NAME: Ukraine
DATE OF FORMATION: 1991
CAPITAL: Kiev
POPULATION: 46.5 million
TOTAL AREA: 223,089 sq. miles (603,700 sq. km)
DENSITY: 199 people per sq. mile

LANGUAGES: Ukrainian*, Russian, Tatar
RELIGIONS: Christian (mainly Orthodox) 95%, other 5%
ETHNIC MIX: Ukrainian 78%, Russian 17%, other 5%
GOVERNMENT: Presidential system
CURRENCY: Hryvna = 100 kopiykas

United Arab Emirates

Bordering the Gulf on the northern coast of the Arabian Peninsula, the seven states of the United Arab Emirates form the Arab world's only working federation.

 GEOGRAPHY

Mostly flat, semiarid desert with dunes, salt pans, and occasional oases. Cities are watered by extensive irrigation systems.

 CLIMATE

Summers are humid, despite minimal rainfall. Sand-laden *shamal* winds blow in winter and spring.

 PEOPLE & SOCIETY

Emirians, who make up just a quarter of the population, are mostly Sunni Muslims of Bedouin descent, and largely city dwellers. In theory, women enjoy equal rights with men. Poverty is rare and there is no income tax. The 1970s oil boom encouraged the immigration of workers, mostly from Asia. Western expatriates are permitted a virtually unrestricted lifestyle. Islamism, however, is a growing force among the young.

THE ECONOMY

Major exporter of oil and natural gas. Dynamic Dubai has a free-trade zone and is a major financial center. Northern emirates are less developed. Most food and raw materials are imported, and water is scarce.

◆ **INSIGHT:** *Mina Jabal Ali, in Dubai, is the largest man-made port in the world*

500m/1640ft
200m/656ft
Sea Level

0   50 km
0   50 miles

DUBAI Emirate capital

FACTFILE

OFFICIAL NAME: United Arab Emirates
DATE OF FORMATION: 1971
CAPITAL: Abu Dhabi
POPULATION: 4.5 million
TOTAL AREA: 32,000 sq. miles (82,880 sq. km)
DENSITY: 139 people per sq. mile

LANGUAGES: Arabic*, Farsi, Indian and Pakistani languages, English
RELIGIONS: Muslim (mainly Sunni) 96%, Christian, Hindu, and other 4%
ETHNIC MIX: Asian 60%, Emirian 25%, other Arab 12%, European 3%
GOVERNMENT: Monarchy
CURRENCY: UAE dirham = 100 fils

United Kingdom

Separated from continental Europe by the English Channel, the United Kingdom consists of Great Britain (England, Wales, and Scotland), a number of smaller islands, and Northern Ireland.

GEOGRAPHY

Rugged uplands dominate the landscape of Scotland, Wales, and northern England. All of the peaks in the United Kingdom over 4000 ft (1219 m) lie in highland Scotland. Known as the "backbone of England," the Pennine mountains run the length of northern England. Lowland England rises into several ranges of rolling hills, and there is an interconnected system of rivers and canals. Over 600 islands, mostly uninhabited, lie west and north of the Scottish mainland.

CLIMATE

Generally mild, temperate, and highly changeable. Rain is fairly well distributed throughout the year. The west is generally wetter than the east, and the south warmer than the north. Winter snow is common in upland areas.

PEOPLE & SOCIETY

The Welsh and Scottish nations remain recognizably distinct, and the creation of the Scottish Parliament and Welsh Assembly has given each country greater political autonomy. The future of devolved government in Northern Ireland remains problematic. People from other ethnic minorities, over half of whom were born in the UK, account for around 8% of the population. Asians and West Indians in most cities face deprivation and social stress; Asian women can be particularly isolated. In key areas such as policing, multiethnic recruitment has made little progress. Marriage is in decline. Over 40% of all births occur outside marriage, but most of them to cohabiting couples. Single-parent households account for almost a quarter of all families. Income inequality is greater now than in 1884 when records began.

FACTFILE

OFFICIAL NAME: United Kingdom of Great Britain and Northern Ireland
DATE OF FORMATION: 1707
CAPITAL: London
POPULATION: 59.7 million
TOTAL AREA: 94,525 sq. miles (244,820 sq. km)

DENSITY: 640 people per sq. mile
LANGUAGES: English*, Welsh*, other
RELIGIONS: Anglican 45%, other 39%, Catholic 9%, Presbyterian 4% Muslim 3%
ETHNIC MIX: White 92%, Asian 4%, Black 2%, mixed race 1%, other 1%
GOVERNMENT: Parliamentary system
CURRENCY: Pound sterling = 100 pence

United Kingdom

$ THE ECONOMY

World leader in financial services, pharmaceuticals, and defense industries. Strong multinationals. Precision engineering and high-tech industries, including biotechnology and telecommunications. Energy sector based on declining North Sea oil and gas reserves. Innovative in computer software development. Flexible working practices. Success in controlling inflation. Decline of manufacturing sector, particularly heavy industries and car manufacture, matched by rise in financial and other services. High levels of government and consumer debt. Nonparticipation in euro threatens former status as EU's largest recipient of inward investment, and has prompted some major investors to close UK factories. The government is wary of adopting the currency fearing popular hostility to more European integration.

◆ **INSIGHT:** *The UK has no formal written constitution, but a stable government system based on Parliament, which originated as a check on royal power in the 13th century*

1000m/3281ft
500m/1640ft
200m/656ft
Sea Level

0   100 km
0   100 miles

United States of America

Stretching across the most temperate part of North America, and with many natural resources, the US is the world's leading economic power and third-largest country.

GEOGRAPHY

The US has a varied topography. Forested mountains stretch from New England in the far northeast, giving way to lowlands and swamps in the extreme south. The central plains are dominated by the Mississippi–Missouri River system and the Great Lakes on the Canadian border. The Rocky Mountains in the west contain active volcanoes and drop to the coast across the earthquake-prone San Andreas Fault. The southwest is arid desert. Mountainous Alaska is mostly Arctic tundra.

CLIMATE

There are four main climatic zones. The north and east are continental and temperate, with heavy rainfall, warm summers, and cold winters. Florida and the Deep South are tropical and prone to hurricanes. The southwest is arid desert with searing summer heat and low rainfall. Southern California is Mediterranean, with hot summers and mild winters.

United States of America

◆ **INSIGHT:** *The United States of America has the world's oldest constitution. Drafted in 1787, it has operated continuously ever since, albeit with numerous amendments*

United States of America

INSIGHT: *By law, information collected in a United States census must remain confidential for 72 years*

PEOPLE & SOCIETY

Though the demographic, economic, and cultural dominance of the whites is firmly entrenched after almost 400 years of settlement, the ethnic balance is rapidly shifting. The Hispanic community is now the largest single minority, and is predicted to account for 25% of the population by 2050. Despite its growing size, it struggles to compete socially with the better established, and more politically sensitive black community. The original native Amerindians, meanwhile, were dispossessed in the 19th century and are now among the poorest people. Constitutionally, state and religion are clearly separated. Conservative Christianity, however, is increasingly dominant politically. Living standards are high, but bad diet and insufficient exercise have left over a third of Americans clinically obese.

THE ECONOMY

World's largest economy: well-established engineering and high-tech industries, huge resource base, global spread of US culture. Manufacturing is in decline as jobs are lost to low-wage economies. Imports are increasing despite weak US dollar, which now faces competition from the euro as the leading global currency. In 2001 a record nine-year boom came to an end, bringing large corporations crashing down and raising unemployment to new highs, in a serious economic downturn. Recovery efforts focused on promoting consumer spending, the engine which drives the whole US economy. Taxes have been slashed along with interest rates. A concurrent increase in government spending, however, notably on defense, the "war on terror," and the 2003 invasion of Iraq, has seen a huge budget surplus slump to a record deficit.

FACTFILE

OFFICIAL NAME: United States of America
DATE OF FORMATION: 1776
CAPITAL: Washington D.C.
POPULATION: 298 million
TOTAL AREA: 3,717,792 sq. miles (9,626,091 sq. km)
DENSITY: 84 people per sq. mile

LANGUAGES: English*, Spanish, other
RELIGIONS: Protestant 52%, Catholic 25%, other 19%, Muslim 2%, Jewish 2%
ETHNIC MIX: White 62%, Hispanic 13%, Black 13%, other 7%, Asian 4%, Native American 1%
GOVERNMENT: Presidential system
CURRENCY: US dollar = 100 cents

Uruguay

Situated in southeastern South America, Uruguay returned to civilian government in 1985, after 12 years of military rule. Most land is used for farming: Uruguay is a major wool exporter.

GEOGRAPHY

Low, rolling grasslands cover 80% of the country. Narrow coastal plain. Alluvial floodplain in southwest. Five rivers flow westward and drain into the Uruguay River.

CLIMATE

Temperate throughout the country. Warm summers, mild winters, and moderate rainfall.

PEOPLE & SOCIETY

Uruguayans are largely second- or third- generation Italians or Spaniards. Wealth derived from cattle ranching enabled the country to become the first welfare state in South America. Despite economic decline since the 1950s, a large, if less prosperous, middle class remains. Though a Roman Catholic country, Uruguay is liberal in its attitude to religion and all forms are tolerated.

THE ECONOMY

Wool, meat, and hides exported. Buoyant tourism. Return to economic growth after recession (1999–2002).

INSIGHT: *Uruguay's rich pastures are ideal for raising livestock; animal products bring in over 40% of export earnings*

200m/656ft
Sea Level

0   100 km
0   100 miles

FACTFILE

OFFICIAL NAME: Eastern Republic of Uruguay
DATE OF FORMATION: 1828
CAPITAL: Montevideo
POPULATION: 3.5 million
TOTAL AREA: 68,039 sq. miles (176,220 sq. km)

DENSITY: 52 people per sq. mile
LANGUAGES: Spanish*
RELIGIONS: Roman Catholic 66%, other 30%, Jewish 2%, Protestant 2%
ETHNIC MIX: White 90%, Mestizo 6%, Black 4%
GOVERNMENT: Presidential system
CURRENCY: Urug. peso = 100 centésimos

Uzbekistan

Sharing what is left of the Aral Sea with its northern neighbor, Kazakhstan, Uzbekistan lies on the ancient Silk Road between Asia and Europe. It is the most populous central Asian republic.

GEOGRAPHY
Arid and semiarid plains in much of the west. Fertile, irrigated farmland in the east lies below the peaks of the western Pamirs.

CLIMATE
Harsh continental climate. Summers can be extremely hot and dry; winters are cold.

PEOPLE & SOCIETY
Complex ethnic makeup. Ex-communists are in firm control, but traditional social patterns based on clan, religion, and region have reemerged. Constitutional measures aim to control the influence of Islam: activities against Islamists have drawn international condemnation. Most people live in the fertile east. Birthrates are high, and the status of women continues to be low.

THE ECONOMY
Oil, gas, and coal. Rich mineral deposits: major producer of uranium and gold, with one of the world's largest gold mines. Cotton is a key export. Dependent on grain imports.

◆ **INSIGHT:** *The Aral Sea has shrunk to less then half of the area it covered in the 1960s, due to diversion of rivers for irrigation*

FACTFILE
OFFICIAL NAME: Republic of Uzbekistan
DATE OF FORMATION: 1991
CAPITAL: Tashkent
POPULATION: 26.6 million
TOTAL AREA: 172,741 sq. miles (447,400 sq. km)
DENSITY: 154 people per sq. mile

LANGUAGES: Uzbek*, Russian, Tajik, Kazakh
RELIGIONS: Sunni Muslim 88%, Orthodox Christian 9%, other 3%
ETHNIC MIX: Uzbek 80%, other 6%, Russian 6%, Tajik 5%, Kazakh 3%
GOVERNMENT: Presidential system
CURRENCY: Som = 100 tiyin

Vanuatu

An archipelago of 82 islands and islets in the South Pacific, Vanuatu was ruled jointly by the UK and France from 1906 until independence in 1980. Politics is democratic but volatile.

GEOGRAPHY
Mountainous and volcanic, with coral beaches and dense rainforest. Cultivated land along the coasts.

CLIMATE
Tropical. Temperatures and rainfall decline from north to south.

PEOPLE & SOCIETY
Indigenous Melanesians form a majority. Ni-Vanuatu culture is traditional; local social and religious customs are strong, despite centuries of missionary influence. Subsistence farming and fishing are the main activities. 80% of the population live on the 12 main islands. Women have lower social status than men and payment of bride-price is common.

◆ **INSIGHT:** *With 105 indigenous tongues, Vanuatu has the world's highest per capita density of languages*

THE ECONOMY
Copra and cocoa exports are declining. Tourism is growing. Offshore banking rules have been tightened after international pressure.

FACTFILE

OFFICIAL NAME: Republic of Vanuatu
DATE OF FORMATION: 1980
CAPITAL: Port Vila
POPULATION: 211,000
TOTAL AREA: 4710 sq. miles (12,200 sq. km)
DENSITY: 45 people per sq. mile

LANGUAGES: Bislama*, English*, French*
RELIGIONS: Presbyterian 37%, other 25%, Anglican 15%, Roman Catholic 15%, traditional beliefs 8%
ETHNIC MIX: Melanesian 98%, European 1%, other 1%
GOVERNMENT: Parliamentary system
CURRENCY: Vatu = 100 centimes

Vatican City

The Vatican City, or Holy See, the seat of the Roman Catholic Church, is a walled enclave in the city of Rome, Italy. It is the world's smallest fully independent state.

GEOGRAPHY
The Vatican's territory includes ten other buildings in Rome, plus the papal residence. The Vatican Gardens cover half the City's area.

CLIMATE
Mild winters with regular rainfall. Hot, dry summers with occasional thunderstorms.

PEOPLE & SOCIETY
The Vatican has about 900 permanent inhabitants, including over 100 lay persons. It also employs thousands of lay staff. Citizenship can be acquired through stable residence and holding a position within the City. The reigning pope has supreme legislative and judicial powers, and holds office for life. Though the Vatican City is officially neutral, papal opinion has a great influence on the world's 1.1 billion Roman Catholics.

THE ECONOMY
Investments and voluntary contributions made by Catholics worldwide (known as Peter's Pence) are backed up by tourist revenue and the issue of Vatican stamps and coins.

◆ **INSIGHT:** *The Vatican City is the spiritual center for 17% of the world's population*

📖 FACTFILE

OFFICIAL NAME: State of the Vatican City

DATE OF FORMATION: 1929

CAPITAL: Vatican City

POPULATION: 921

TOTAL AREA: 0.17 sq. miles (0.44 sq. km)

DENSITY: 5418 people per sq. mile

LANGUAGES: Italian*, Latin*

RELIGIONS: Roman Catholic 100%

ETHNIC MIX: Cardinals are from many nationalities, but Italians form the largest group. The current pope is from Germany.

GOVERNMENT: Papal state

CURRENCY: Euro = 100 cents

Venezuela

Lying on the southern shores of the Caribbean, Venezuela was the first of Spain's colonies to seek independence. Despite large oil reserves, many Venezuelans still live in poverty.

 GEOGRAPHY

Andes Mountains and the Maracaibo lowlands in the northwest. Central grassy plains are drained by the Orinoco River system. Forested Guiana Highlands in the southeast.

 CLIMATE

Tropical. Hot and humid. Uplands are cooler. Orinoco plains are alternately parched or flooded.

 PEOPLE & SOCIETY

Venezuela is historically a "melting pot," with immigrants from Europe and all over Latin America. The few indigenous Amerindians live in remote areas. Venezuela has one of the most urbanized societies in the region, with most of its population living in the northern cities. President Chávez's left-wing rhetoric raises opposition within Venezuela from urban society, and from the US.

THE ECONOMY

Oil provides over 80% of export earnings. Vast reserves of coal, gold, and other minerals. Overmanned and often inefficient state sector. High inflation. Clampdown on tax evasion.

◆ **INSIGHT:** *Venezuela's Angel Falls is the world's highest waterfall at 3210 ft (979 m)*

FACTFILE

OFFICIAL NAME: Bolivarian Republic of Venezuela
DATE OF FORMATION: 1830
CAPITAL: Caracas
POPULATION: 26.7 million
TOTAL AREA: 352,143 sq. miles (912,050 sq. km)

DENSITY: 78 people per sq. mile
LANGUAGES: Spanish*, native languages
RELIGIONS: Roman Catholic 89%, Protestant and other 11%
ETHNIC MIX: Mestizo 69%, White 20%, Black 9%, Amerindian 2%
GOVERNMENT: Presidential system
CURRENCY: Bolívar = 100 céntimos

Vietnam

Situated on the western edge of the South China Sea, Vietnam is run as a single-party Communist state. Since 1986 the regime has pursued a liberal economic policy known as *doi moi*.

 GEOGRAPHY
A heavily forested mountain range separates the northern Red River delta lowlands from the Mekong River delta in the south.

 CLIMATE
Cool winters in north; south is tropical, with even temperatures.

 PEOPLE & SOCIETY
Ethnic Vietnamese dominate; the Chinese minority was viewed as a corrupt bourgeoisie by the victorious Communists after the war. Mountain-based minorities (*montagnards*) were also sidelined by the regime; tensions persist over the resettlement of the central highlands by lowlanders. Women play an active role in society.

◆ **INSIGHT:** *The 1962–1975 Vietnam War was the longest conflict of the 20th century*

THE ECONOMY
The potential for continued strong growth rests on a diverse resource base (including gas reserves), an educated workforce, and strong light industries.

FACTFILE

OFFICIAL NAME: Socialist Republic of Vietnam
DATE OF FORMATION: 1976
CAPITAL: Hanoi
POPULATION: 84.2 million
TOTAL AREA: 127,243 sq. miles (329,560 sq. km)

DENSITY: 670 people per sq. mile
LANGUAGES: Vietnamese*, Chinese, other
RELIGIONS: Nonreligious 81%, Buddhist 9%, Christian 7%, other 3%
ETHNIC MIX: Vietnamese 86%, other 10%, Tay 2%, Thai 2%
GOVERNMENT: One-party state
CURRENCY: Dông = 10 hao = 100 xu

Yemen

Located in southern Arabia, Yemen was formerly two countries: the People's Democratic Republic of Yemen (south and east) and the Yemen Arab Republic (northwest), were united in 1990.

GEOGRAPHY
Mountainous west with a fertile strip along the Red Sea. Arid desert and mountains elsewhere.

CLIMATE
Desert climate, modified by altitude, which affects temperatures by as much as 54°F (30°C).

PEOPLE & SOCIETY
Yemenis are almost entirely of Arab and Bedouin descent. The majority are Sunni Muslims, of the Shafi sect. In rural areas and in the north, tribalism and Islamic orthodoxy are strong and most women wear the veil. Foreigners have been subject to sporadic attacks and kidnappings. Tension continues to exist between the south, led by the cosmopolitan city of Aden, and the more conservative north.

THE ECONOMY
Instability deters investment. Considerable oil and gas reserves. Agriculture is the largest employer: coffee, cotton, livestock, and fish.

◆ INSIGHT: *Mokha, on the Red Sea, gave its name to the first coffee beans exported to Europe in the 1600s*

3000m/9843ft
2000m/6562ft
1000m/3281ft
500m/1640ft
200m/656ft
Sea Level

0   100 km
0   100 miles

FACTFILE
OFFICIAL NAME: Republic of Yemen
DATE OF FORMATION: 1990
CAPITAL: Sana
POPULATION: 21 million
TOTAL AREA: 203,849 sq. miles (527,970 sq. km)
DENSITY: 97 people per sq. mile

LANGUAGES: Arabic*
RELIGIONS: Sunni Muslim 55%, Shi'a Muslim 42%, Christian, Hindu, and Jewish 3%
ETHNIC MIX: Arab 99%, Afro-Arab, Indian, Somali, and European 1%
GOVERNMENT: Presidential system
CURRENCY: Yemeni rial = 100 fils

Zambia

Bordered to the south by the Zambezi River, Zambia lies at the heart of southern Africa. In 1991, it made a peaceful transition from single-party rule to multiparty democracy.

GEOGRAPHY

A high savanna plateau, broken by mountains in northeast. Vegetation mainly trees and scrub.

CLIMATE

Tropical, with three seasons: cool and dry, hot and dry, and wet. Southwest is prone to drought.

PEOPLE & SOCIETY

There are more than 70 different ethnic groups, but there are fewer ethnic tensions than in many African states. The largest group is the Bemba in the northeast. Other major groups are the Tonga in the south, the eastern Nyanja, and the Lozi in the west. There are also thousands of refugees, mostly from the DRC and Angola. A National Gender Policy was issued in 2000 to redress inequalities between the sexes. The standard of living has fallen in real terms since independence.

THE ECONOMY

After years of decline, world copper prices are rising and Zambia's output has increased. New agricultural exports have boomed: notably flowers.

INSIGHT: *Spray from Musi-o-Tunya (Victoria Falls) can be seen up to 20 miles away*

FACTFILE

OFFICIAL NAME: Republic of Zambia
DATE OF FORMATION: 1964
CAPITAL: Lusaka
POPULATION: 11.7 million
TOTAL AREA: 290,584 sq. miles (752,614 sq. km)
DENSITY: 41 people per sq. mile

LANGUAGES: Bemba, Tonga, Nyanja, Lozi, Lala-bisa, Nsenga, English*
RELIGIONS: Christian 63%, traditional beliefs 36%, Muslim and Hindu 1%
ETHNIC MIX: Bemba 34%, other 27%, Tonga 16%, Nyanja 14%, Lozi 9 %
GOVERNMENT: Presidential system
CURRENCY: Zamb. kwacha = 100 ngwee

Zimbabwe

Situated in southern Africa, Zimbabwe achieved independence from the UK in 1980. President Robert Mugabe, in power since then, has become increasingly authoritarian.

GEOGRAPHY

High plateaus in center bordered by Zambezi River in the north and Limpopo in the south. Rivers crisscross central area.

CLIMATE
Tropical, though moderated by the high altitude. Wet season November–March. Drought is common in the eastern highlands.

PEOPLE & SOCIETY

There are two main ethnic groups, Shona in the north and east, and Ndebele in the south. Shona outnumber Ndebele by four to one. Whites are generally far more affluent than blacks. Government efforts to redress this imbalance have become increasingly more aggressive. Economic mismanagement and international isolation has destroyed the economy and prices have rocketed.

THE ECONOMY
The broad-based economy is undermined by drought, budget deficits, unemployment, and massive inflation. Food is increasingly scarce.

INSIGHT: *The city of Great Zimbabwe, after which the country is named, was built in the 8th century, near Masvingo*

FACTFILE
OFFICIAL NAME: Republic of Zimbabwe
DATE OF FORMATION: 1980
CAPITAL: Harare
POPULATION: 13 million
TOTAL AREA: 150,803 sq. miles (390,580 sq. km)
DENSITY: 87 people per sq. mile

LANGUAGES: Shona, isiNdebele, English*
RELIGIONS: Syncretic Christian / traditional beliefs 50%, Christian 25%, traditional beliefs 24%, other 1%
ETHNIC MIX: Shona 71%, Ndebele 16%, other African 11%, White 1%, Asian 1%
GOVERNMENT: Presidential system
CURRENCY: Zimbabwe $ = 100 cents

Overseas territories

Despite the rapid process of global decolonization since World War II, around eight million people in more than 50 territories around the world continue to live under the protection of France, Australia, Denmark, the Netherlands, Norway, New Zealand, the UK, or the USA. These remnants of former colonial empires may have persisted for economic, strategic, or political reasons and are administered by the protecting country in a variety of ways.

AUSTRALIA

Australia's overseas territories have not been an issue since Papua New Guinea became independent in 1975. Consequently there is no overriding policy toward them.
Norfolk Island is inhabited by descendants of the HMS *Bounty* mutineers and more recent Australian migrants. Phosphate is mined on Christmas Island.

ASHMORE & CARTIER IS. *Ref: 124 A3*

STATUS: External territory
CLAIMED: 1931
CAPITAL: Not applicable
POPULATION: None
AREA: 2 sq miles (5.2 sq km)

CHRISTMAS ISLAND *Ref: 123 E5*

STATUS: External territory
CLAIMED: 1958
CAPITAL: The Settlement
POPULATION: 1493
AREA: 52 sq miles (135 sq km)

COCOS ISLANDS *Ref: 123 D5*

STATUS: External territory
CLAIMED: 1955
CAPITAL: Not applicable
POPULATION: 574
AREA: 5.5 sq miles (14 sq km)

CORAL SEA ISLANDS *Ref: 126 B4*

STATUS: External territory
CLAIMED: 1969
CAPITAL: Not applicable
POPULATION: 8 (Meteorologists)
AREA: 1.2 sq miles (3 sq km)

HEARD & MCDONALD IS. *Ref: 123 C7*

STATUS: External territory
CLAIMED: 1947
CAPITAL: Not applicable
POPULATION: None
AREA: 161 sq miles (417 sq km)

NORFOLK ISLAND *Ref: 124 D4*

STATUS: External territory
CLAIMED: 1774
CAPITAL: Kingston
POPULATION: 1828
AREA: 13 sq miles (34 sq km)

DENMARK

The Faeroe Islands have been under Danish administration since Queen Margreth I of Denmark inherited Norway in 1380. The Home Rule Act of 1948 gave the Faeroese control over all their internal affairs. Greenland first came under Danish rule in 1380. Denmark remains responsible for the island's foreign affairs.

Overseas territories

FAEROE ISLANDS *Ref: 65 F5*

STATUS: External territory
CLAIMED: 1380
CAPITAL: Tórshavn
POPULATION: 47,246
AREA: 540 sq miles (1399 sq km)

GREENLAND *Ref: 64 D3*

STATUS: External territory
CLAIMED: 1380
CAPITAL: Nuuk
POPULATION: 56,361
AREA: 840,000 sq miles (2,175,500 sq km)

FRANCE

France has developed economic ties with its *Territoires d'Outre–Mer*, thereby stressing interdependence over independence. Overseas *départements*, officially part of France, have their own governments. Territorial *collectivités* and overseas *territoires* have varying degrees of autonomy.

CLIPPERTON ISLAND *Ref: 135 F3*

STATUS: Dependency of French Polynesia
CLAIMED: 1935
CAPITAL: Not applicable
POPULATION: None
AREA: 2.7 sq miles (7 sq km)

FRENCH GUIANA *Ref: 41 H3*

STATUS: Overseas department
CLAIMED: 1817
CAPITAL: Cayenne
POPULATION: 199,509
AREA: 35,135 sq miles (91,000 sq km)

FRENCH POLYNESIA *Ref: 127 H4*

STATUS: Overseas country
CLAIMED: 1843
CAPITAL: Papeete
POPULATION: 260,000
AREA: 1608 sq miles (4165 sq km)

GUADELOUPE *Ref: 37 G4*

STATUS: Overseas department
CLAIMED: 1635
CAPITAL: Basse-Terre
POPULATION: 452,000
AREA: 687 sq miles (1780 sq km)

MARTINIQUE *Ref: 37 G4*

STATUS: Overseas department
CLAIMED: 1635
CAPITAL: Fort-de-France
POPULATION: 397,000
AREA: 425 sq miles (1100 sq km)

MAYOTTE *Ref: 61 G2*

STATUS: Territorial collectivity
CLAIMED: 1843
CAPITAL: Mamoudzou
POPULATION: 201,234
AREA: 144 sq miles (374 sq km)

NEW CALEDONIA *Ref: 126 D5*

STATUS: Overseas territory
CLAIMED: 1853
CAPITAL: Nouméa
POPULATION: 241,000
AREA: 7347 sq miles (19,100 sq km)

RÉUNION *Ref: 61 H4*

STATUS: Overseas department
CLAIMED: 1638
CAPITAL: Saint-Denis
POPULATION: 796,000
AREA: 970 sq miles (2500 sq km)

Overseas territories

ST PIERRE & MIQUELON
Ref: 21 G4
- **STATUS:** Territorial collectivity
- **CLAIMED:** 1604
- **CAPITAL:** Saint-Pierre
- **POPULATION:** 7026
- **AREA:** 93 sq miles (242 sq km)

WALLIS & FUTUNA
Ref: 127 E4
- **STATUS:** Overseas territory
- **CLAIMED:** 1842
- **CAPITAL:** Matā'Utu
- **POPULATION:** 16,025
- **AREA:** 106 sq miles (274 sq km)

NETHERLANDS

The country's two remaining territories were formerly part of the Dutch West Indies. Both are now self-governing, but the Netherlands remains responsible for their defense.

ARUBA *Ref: 37 E5*

- **STATUS:** Autonomous part of the Netherlands
- **CLAIMED:** 1634
- **CAPITAL:** Oranjestad
- **POPULATION:** 71,891
- **AREA:** 75 sq miles (194 sq km)

NETHERLANDS ANTILLES *Ref: 37 E5*

- **STATUS:** Autonomous part of the Netherlands
- **CLAIMED:** 1816
- **CAPITAL:** Willemstad
- **POPULATION:** 184,000
- **AREA:** 371 sq miles (960 sq km)

NEW ZEALAND

New Zealand's government has no desire to retain any overseas territories. However, the economic weakness of Tokelau, Niue, and the Cook Islands has forced it to remain responsible for their foreign policy and defense.

COOK ISLANDS *Ref: 127 G4*

- **STATUS:** Associated territory
- **CLAIMED:** 1901
- **CAPITAL:** Avarua
- **POPULATION:** 21,388
- **AREA:** 91 sq miles (235 sq km)

NIUE *Ref: 127 F5*

- **STATUS:** Associated territory
- **CLAIMED:** 1901
- **CAPITAL:** Alofi
- **POPULATION:** 2166
- **AREA:** 102 sq miles (264 sq km)

TOKELAU *Ref: 127 F3*
- **STATUS:** Dependent territory
- **CLAIMED:** 1926
- **CAPITAL:** Not applicable
- **POPULATION:** 1392
- **AREA:** 4 sq miles (10 sq km)

NORWAY

In 1920, 41 nations signed the Spits-bergen treaty recognizing Norwegian sovereignty over Svalbard. There is a NATO base on Jan Mayen. Bouvet Island is a nature reserve.

Overseas territories

BOUVET ISLAND *Ref: 49 D7*
STATUS: Dependency
CLAIMED: 1928
CAPITAL: Not applicable
POPULATION: None
AREA: 22 sq miles (58 sq km)

JAN MAYEN *Ref: 65 F3*
STATUS: Dependency
CLAIMED: 1929
CAPITAL: Not applicable
POPULATION: None
AREA: 147 sq miles (381 sq km)

PETER I. ISLAND *Ref: 136 A3*
STATUS: Dependency
CLAIMED: 1931
CAPITAL: Not applicable
POPULATION: None
AREA: 69 sq miles (180 sq km)

SVALBARD *Ref: 65 F2*
STATUS: Dependency CLAIMED: 1920
CAPITAL: Longyearbyen
POPULATION: 2701
AREA: 24,289 sq miles (62,906 sq km)

UNITED KINGDOM

The UK has the largest number of overseas territories. These are locally governed by a mixture of elected representatives and appointed officials.

ANGUILLA *Ref: 37 G3*

STATUS: Dependent territory
CLAIMED: 1650
CAPITAL: The Valley
POPULATION: 13,477
AREA: 37 sq miles (96 sq km)

ASCENSION ISLAND *Ref: 49 C5*
STATUS: Dependency of St Helena
CLAIMED: 1673
CAPITAL: Georgetown
POPULATION: 1177
AREA: 34 sq miles (88 sq km)

BERMUDA *Ref: 17 E6*

STATUS: Crown colony
CLAIMED: 1612
CAPITAL: Hamilton
POPULATION: 65,773
AREA: 20 sq miles (53 sq km)

BRITISH INDIAN OCEAN TERRITORY *Ref: 122 C4*

STATUS: Dependent territory
CLAIMED: 1814
CAPITAL: Diego Garcia
POPULATION: 4000
AREA: 23 sq miles (60 sq km)

BRITISH VIRGIN IS. *Ref: 37 F3*

STATUS: Dependent territory
CLAIMED: 1672
CAPITAL: Road Town
POPULATION: 23,098
AREA: 59 sq miles (153 sq km)

CAYMAN ISLANDS *Ref: 36 B3*

STATUS: Dependent territory
CLAIMED: 1670
CAPITAL: George Town
POPULATION: 45,436
AREA: 100 sq miles (259 sq km)

FALKLAND ISLANDS *Ref: 47 D7*

STATUS: Dependent territory
CLAIMED: 1832
CAPITAL: Stanley
POPULATION: 2967
AREA: 4699 sq miles (12,173 sq km)

Overseas territories

GIBRALTAR *Ref: 74 D5*

STATUS: Crown colony
CLAIMED: 1713
CAPITAL: Gibraltar
POPULATION: 27,928
AREA: 2.5 sq miles (6.5 sq km)

GUERNSEY *Ref: 71 D8*

STATUS: Crown dependency
CLAIMED: 1066
CAPITAL: St. Peter Port
POPULATION: 65,409
AREA: 25 sq miles (65 sq km)

ISLE OF MAN *Ref: 71 C5*

STATUS: Crown dependency
CLAIMED: 1765
CAPITAL: Douglas
POPULATION: 75,441
AREA: 221 sq miles (572 sq km)

JERSEY *Ref: 71 D8*

STATUS: Crown dependency
CLAIMED: 1066
CAPITAL: St. Helier
POPULATION: 91,084
AREA: 45 sq miles (116 sq km)

MONTSERRAT *Ref: 37 G4*

STATUS: Dependent
territory
CLAIMED: 1632
CAPITAL: Plymouth (uninhabitable)
POPULATION: 9439
AREA: 40 sq miles (102 sq km)

PITCAIRN ISLANDS *Ref: 125 G4*

STATUS: Dependent
territory
CLAIMED: 1887
CAPITAL: Adamstown POPULATION: 45
AREA: 18 sq miles (47 sq km)

ST HELENA *Ref: 49 D5*

STATUS: Dependent territory
CLAIMED: 1673
CAPITAL: Jamestown
POPULATION: 4299
AREA: 47 sq miles (122 sq km)

SOUTH GEORGIA & THE
SANDWICH ISLANDS *Ref: 49 C7*

STATUS: Dependent territory
CLAIMED: 1775 CAPITAL: Not applicable
POPULATION: None
AREA: 1387 sq miles (3592 sq km)

TRISTAN DA CUNHA *Ref: 49 D6*

STATUS: Dependency of St. Helena
CLAIMED: 1612 CAPITAL: Edinburgh
POPULATION: 276
AREA: 38 sq miles (98 sq km)

TURKS & CAICOS ISLANDS *Ref: 37 E2*

STATUS: Dependent territory
CLAIMED: 1766
CAPITAL: Cockburn Town
POPULATION: 21,152
AREA: 166 sq miles (430 sq km)

UNITED STATES

US Commonwealth territories
are self-governing incorporated
territories that are an integral part
of the US. Unincorporated territories
have varying degrees of autonomy.

AMERICAN SAMOA *Ref: 127 F4*

STATUS: Unincorporated
territory
CLAIMED: 1900
CAPITAL: Pago Pago
POPULATION: 57,794
AREA: 75 sq miles (195 sq km)

BAKER & HOWLAND ISLANDS
Ref: 127 E2
STATUS: Unincorporated territory
CAPITAL: Not applicable
CLAIMED: 1856 POPULATION: None
AREA: 0.5 sq miles (1.4 sq km)

GUAM *Ref: 126 B1*

STATUS: Unincorporated territory
CLAIMED: 1898
CAPITAL: Hagåtña
POPULATION: 172,000
AREA: 212 sq miles (549 sq km)

JARVIS ISLAND *Ref: 127 G2*
STATUS: Unincorporated territory
CLAIMED: 1856
CAPITAL: Not applicable
POPULATION: None
AREA: 1.7 sq miles (4.5 sq km)

JOHNSTON ATOLL *Ref: 125 E1*
STATUS: Unincorporated territory
CLAIMED: 1858
CAPITAL: Not applicable
POPULATION: None
AREA: 1 sq miles (2.8 sq km)

KINGMAN REEF *Ref: 127 F2*
STATUS: Administered territory
CLAIMED: 1856
CAPITAL: Not applicable
POPULATION: None
AREA: 0.4 sq miles (1 sq km)

MIDWAY ISLANDS *Ref: 134 D2*
STATUS: Administered territory
CLAIMED: 1867
CAPITAL: Not applicable
POPULATION: None
AREA: 2 sq miles (5.2 sq km)

NAVASSA ISLAND *Ref: 36 D3*
STATUS: Unincorporated territory
CLAIMED: 1856 CAPITAL: Not applicable
POPULATION: None
AREA: 2 sq miles (5.2 sq km)

NORTHERN MARIANA ISLANDS
Ref: 124 C1

STATUS: Commonwealth territory
CLAIMED: 1947
CAPITAL: Saipan POPULATION: 82,459
AREA: 177 sq miles (457 sq km)

PALMYRA ATOLL *Ref: 127 G2*
STATUS: Unincorporated territory
CLAIMED: 1898 CAPITAL: Not applicable
POPULATION: None
AREA: 5 sq miles (12 sq km)

PUERTO RICO *Ref: 37 F3*

STATUS: Commonwealth territory
CLAIMED: 1898
CAPITAL: San Juan
POPULATION: 4 million
AREA: 3515 sq miles (9104 sq km)

VIRGIN ISLANDS *Ref: 37 F3*

STATUS: Unincorporated territory
CLAIMED: 1917
CAPITAL: Charlotte Amalie
POPULATION: 108,605
AREA: 137 sq miles (355 sq km)

WAKE ISLAND *Ref: 124 D1*
STATUS: Unincorporated territory
CLAIMED: 1898
CAPITAL: Not applicable
POPULATION: 200
AREA: 2.5 sq miles (6.5 sq km)

International organizations

This listing provides acronym definitions for the main international organizations concerned with worldwide economics, trade, and defense, plus an indication of membership.

ASEAN
Association of Southeast Asian Nations
ESTABLISHED: 1967
MEMBERS: Brunei, Cambodia, Indonesia, Laos, Malaysia, Myanmar, Philippines, Singapore, Thailand, Vietnam

CIS
Commonwealth of Independent States
ESTABLISHED: 1991
MEMBERS: Arm., Az., Belarus, Georgia, Kaz., Kyrgy., Mold., Russia, Tajik., Ukraine, Uzbek.

COMM
The Commonwealth
ESTABLISHED: 1931; evolved out of the British Empire. Formerly known as the British Commonwealth of Nations.
MEMBERS: 53

EU
European Union
ESTABLISHED: 1965; formerly known as EEC (European Economic Community) and EC (Economic Community)
MEMBERS: Austria, Belg., Cyprus, Czech Rep., Denmark, Est., Fin., Fr., Ger., Greece, Hung., Ireland, Italy, Lat., Lith., Lux., Malta, Neth., Pol., Port., Slvka., Slvna., Spain, Swed., UK

G8
Group of 8
ESTABLISHED: 1994
MEMBERS: Canada, France, Germany, Italy, Japan, Russia, UK, US

IMF
International Monetary Fund
(UN agency)
ESTABLISHED: 1945 MEMBERS: 184

NAFTA
North American Free Trade Agreement
ESTABLISHED: 1994
MEMBERS: Canada, Mexico, US

NATO
North Atlantic Treaty Organization
ESTABLISHED: 1949 MEMBERS: Belg., Bulg., Canada, Czech Rep., Denmark, Est., France, Ger., Greece, Hung., Iceland, Italy, Lat., Lith., Lux., Neth., Norway, Poland, Port., Rom., Slovakia, Slovenia, Spain, Turkey, UK, US

OPEC
Organization of Petroleum Exporting Countries
ESTABLISHED: 1960
MEMBERS: Algeria, Indonesia, Iran, Iraq, Kuwait, Libya, Nigeria, Qatar, Saudi Arabia, United Arab Emirates, Venezuela

UN
United Nations
ESTABLISHED: 1945 MEMBERS: 192; all nations are represented, except Taiwan. The Vatican City has "observer status" only.

WTO
World Trade Organization
ESTABLISHED: 1995
MEMBERS: 146

Abbreviations

This glossary provides a comprehensive guide to the abbreviations used in this atlas.

abbrev. abbreviation
Afgh. Afghanistan
Amh. Amharic
anc. ancient
Ar. Arabic
Arm. Armenia/Armenian
Aus. Austria
Aust. Australia
Az. Azerbaijan

Bas. Basque
Bel. Belorussian
Belg. Belgium/Belgian
Bos. & Herz. Bosnia & Herzegovina
Bul. Bulgarian
Bulg. Bulgaria
Bur. Burmese

C Central
C. Cape
Cam. Cambodian
Cast. Castilian
Chin. Chinese
Cord. Cordillera (Sp. mts.)
Cz. Czech
Czech Rep. Czech Republic

D.C. District of Columbia
Dan. Danish
Dominican Rep. Dominican Republic

E East
Emb. Embalse
Eng. English
Eq. Guinea Equatorial Guinea
Est. Estonia/Estonian

Faer. Faeroese
Fin. Finland/Finnish
Flem. Flemish
Fr. France/French

Geo. Georgia
Geor. Georgian
Ger. Germany/German
Gk. Greek

Heb. Hebrew
Hung. Hungary/Hungarian

I. Island
Ind. Indonesia, Indonesian
Is. Islands
It. Italian

Kaz. Kazakhstan/Kazakh
Kep. Kepulauan (Ind. island group)
Kir. Kirghiz
Kor. Korean
Kurd. Kurdish
Kyrgy. Kyrgyzstan

L. Lake, Lago
Lat. Latvia
Latv. Latvian
Leb. Lebanon
Liech. Liechtenstein
Lith. Lithuania/Lithuanian
Lux. Luxembourg

m meters
Mac. Macedonia
Med. Sea Mediterranean Sea
Mon. Montenegro
Mold. Moldova
Mt. Mount/Mountain
Mts. Mountains

N North
N. Korea North Korea
Neth. Netherlands
NW Northwest
NZ New Zealand

P. Pulau (Ind. island)
Peg. Pegunungan (Ind. mountain range)
Per. Persian
Pol. Poland/Polish

Port. Portugal, Portuguese
prev. previously
R. River, Rio, Río
Res. Reservoir
Rom. Romania/Romanian
Rus. Russian
Russ. Fed. Russian Federation

S South
S. Korea South Korea
SA South Africa
SCr. Serbian and Croatian
Serb. Serbia
Slvka. Slovakia
Slvna. Slovenia
Som. Somali
Sp. Spanish
St, St. Saint
Str. Strait
Swed. Swedish
Switz. Switzerland
Tajik. Tajikistan
Th. Thai
Turk. Turkish
Turkm. Turkmen
Turkmen. Turkmenistan

U.A.E. United Arab Emirates
UK United Kingdom
Ukr. Ukrainian
Urug. Uruguayan
US United States of America
Uzb. Uzbek
Uzbek. Uzbekistan

var. variant
Vdkhr. Vodokhranilishche (Rus. reservoir)
Vdskh. Vodoskhovyshche (Ukr. reservoir)
Ven. Venezuela

W West
W. Sahara Western Sahara
Wel. Welsh

Yugo. Yugoslavia

Zamb. Zambian

A

Aabenraa Denmark 67 A8

Aachen Germany 76 A4

Aalborg Denmark 67 B7

Aalst Belgium 69 B5

Aba Nigeria 57 G5

Ābādān Iran 102 C4

Abadan Turkmenistan *prev.* Bezmein, Büzmeýin 104 B3

Abashiri Japan 112 D2

Abéché Chad 58 D3

Aberdeen Scotland, UK 70 D3

Aberdeen South Dakota, USA 25 E2

Aberdeen Washington, USA 26 A2

Aberystwyth Wales, UK 71 C6

Abhā Saudi Arabia 103 B6

Abidjan Côte d'Ivoire 56 D5

Abilene Texas, USA 29 F3

Abomey Benin 57 F4

Abu Dhabi *capital of* United Arab Emirates *var.* Abū Ẓaby 103 D5

Abuja *capital of* Nigeria 57 G4

Abū Ẓaby *see* Abu Dhabi

Acapulco Mexico 33 E5

Acaraí Mountains *mountain range* Brazil/Guyana 41 F3

Acarigua Venezuela 40 D1

Accra *capital of* Ghana 57 E5

Acklins Island *island* Bahamas 36 D2

Aconcagua, Cerro *peak* Argentina 46 B4

A Coruña *Cast.* La Coruña 74 C1

ACT *see* Australian Capital Territory

Adalia *see* Antalya

Adalia, Gulf of *see* Antalya Körfezi

'Adan Yemen *Eng.* Aden 103 B7

Adana Turkey *var.* Seyhan 98 D4

Adapazarı Turkey *var.* Sakarya 98 B2

Ad Dahnā' *desert* Saudi Arabia 103 C5

Ad Dakhla Western Sahara 52 A4

Ad Dawḥah *see* Doha

Addis Ababa *capital of* Ethiopia *Amh.* Ādīs Ābeba 55 C5

Adelaide Australia 131 B6

Adélie, Terre d' *territory* Antarctica 136 C4

Aden *see* 'Adan

Aden, Gulf of *sea feature* Indian Ocean 122 A3

Adige *river* Italy 78 C2

Ādīs Ābeba *see* Addis Ababa

Adıyaman Turkey 99 E4

Adriatic Sea Mediterranean Sea 78 D4

Aegean Sea Mediterranean Sea *Gk.* Aigaío Pélagos, *Turk.* Ege Denizi 87 D5

Aeolian Islands *see* Isole Eolie

Afghanistan *country* C Asia 104-105

Africa 50-51

Africa, Horn of *physical region* Ethiopia/Somalia 122 A3

Afyon Turkey *prev.* Afyonkarahisar 98 B3

Afyonkarahisar *see* Afyon

Agadez Niger 57 G3

Agadir Morocco 52 B2

Agassiz Fracture Zone *tectonic feature* Pacific Ocean 135 E4

Agen France 73 B6

Āgra India 116 D3

Agrigento Italy 79 C7

Agrinio Greece 87 B5

Aguarico *river* Ecuador/Peru 40 B4

Aguascalientes Mexico 32 D4

Ahaggar *mountains* Algeria *var.* Hoggar 53 E4

Ahmadābād India 116 C4

Ahvāz Iran 102 C4

Ahvenanmaa *see* Åland

Aigaío Pélagos *see* Aegean Sea

Aintab *see* Gaziantep

Aïr, Massif de l' *region* Niger 57 G2

Aix-en-Provence France 73 D6

Ajaccio Corse, France 73 E7

Ajdābiyā Libya 53 G2

Ajmer India 116 D3

Akaba *see* Al 'Aqabah

Akchâr *desert* Mauritania 56 C2

Akimiski Island *island* Canada 20 C3

Akita Japan 112 D3

Akjoujt Mauritania 56 C2

Akmola *see* Astana

Akmolinsk *see* Astana

Akpatok Island *island* Canada 21 E1

Akra Kanestron *see* Palioúri, Akrotírio

Akron Ohio, USA 22 D3

Aksai Chin *disputed region* China/India 108 B4

Aktau Kazakhstan *prev.* Shevchenko 96 A4

Akureyri Iceland 65 E4

Akyab *see* Sittwe

Alabama *state* USA 30 D3

Alacant *see* Alicante

Alajuela Costa Rica 34 D4

Alamogordo New Mexico, USA 28 D3

Åland *island group* Finland *Fin.* Ahvenanmaa 67 D6

Al 'Aqabah Jordan *var.* Akaba 101 B7

Alaska *state* USA 18

Alaska, Gulf of *sea feature* Pacific Ocean 16 C3

Alaska Range *mountain range* Alaska, USA 18 C3

Albacete Spain 75 E3

Alba Iulia Romania 90 B4

Albania *country* SE Europe 83

Albany Australia 129 B7

Albany Georgia, USA 31 E3

Albany New York, USA 23 F3

Albany Oregon, USA 26 A3

Albany *river* Canada 20 B3

Al Başrah Iraq *var.* Basra 102 C4

Al Baydā' Libya 53 G2

Albert, Lake *lake* Uganda/Dem. Rep. Congo 59 E5

Alberta *province* Canada 19 E4

Albi France 73 C6

Albuquerque New Mexico, USA 28 D2

Alcácer do Sal Portugal 74 C4

Aldabra Group *island group* Seychelles 61 G2

Aleg Mauritania 56 C3

Aleksandriya *see* Oleksandriya

Aleksandropol' *see* Gyumri

Aleksinac Serbia 82 E4

Alençon France 72 B3

Alessandria Italy 78 B2

Ålesund Norway 67 A5

Aleutian Basin *undersea feature* Bering Sea 134 D1

Aleutian Islands *islands* Alaska, USA 18 A3

Aleutian Trench *undersea feature* Pacific Ocean 134 D1

Alexander Island *island* Antarctica 136 A3

Alexandra New Zealand 133 B7

Alexandretta *see* İskenderun

Alexandria Egypt 54 B1

Alexandria Louisiana, USA 30 B3

Alexandroúpoli Greece 86 D3

Al Fāshir *see* El Fasher

Alföld *see* Great Hungarian Plain

Algarve *region* Portugal 74 C4

Algeciras Spain 74 D5

Algeria *country* N Africa 52-53

Alghero Italy 79 A5

Algiers *capital of* Algeria 52 D1

Al Ḩasakah Syria 100 D2

Al Ḩudaydah Yemen 103 B7

Al Ḩufūf Saudi Arabia 103 C5

Alicante Spain *Cat.* Alacant 75 F4

Alice Springs Australia 130 A4

Al Jawf Saudi Arabia 102 B4

Al Jazīrah *region* Iraq/Syria 100 E2

Al Jīzah *see* El Gîza

Al Karak Jordan 101 B6

Al Khalīl *see* Hebron

Al Khārijah *see* El Khârga

Al Khums Libya 53 F2

Al Khurṭūm *see* Khartoum

Alkmaar Netherlands 68 C2

Al Kufrah Libya 53 H4

Al Lādhiqīyah Syria *Eng.* Latakia 100 B3

Allahābād India 117 E4

Allenstein *see* Olsztyn

Allentown Pennsylvania, USA 23 F4

Alma-Ata *capital of* Kazakhstan *Rus./Kaz.* Almaty 96 C5

Al Madīnah Saudi Arabia *Eng.* Medina 102 A5

Al Mafraq Jordan 101 B5

Almalyk Uzbekistan *Uzb.* Olmaliq 105 E2

Al Manāmah *see* Manama

Al Marj Libya 53 G2

Almaty *see* Alma-Ata

Al Mawşil Iraq *Eng.* Mosul 102 B3

Almelo Netherlands 68 E3

Almería Spain 75 E5

Al Mukallā Yemen 103 C7

Alofi *capital of* Niue 127 F5

Alor, Kepulauan *island group* Indonesia 121 E5

Alps *mountain range* C Europe 62 D4

Al Qāhirah *see* Cairo

Al Qāmishlī Syria *var.* Kamishli 100 E1

Al Qunayṭirah Syria 100 B4

Altai Mountains *mountain range* C Asia 108 C2

Altamura Italy 79 E5

Altar, Desierto de *Desert* Mexico/USA *var.* Sonoran Desert 32 A1

Altay China 108 C2

Altay Mongolia 108 D2

Altun Shan *mountain range* China 108 C3

Alturas California, USA 26 B4

Alytus Lithuania *Pol.* Olita 89 B5

Amadeus, Lake *seasonal lake* Australia 129 E5

Amakusa-nada *island group* Japan 113 A6

Amami-Ō-shima *island* Japan 113 A8

Amarillo Texas, USA 29 E2

Amazon *river* South America 38 C3

Amazon Basin *region* C South America 42 D2

Ambanja Madagascar 61 G2

Ambarchik Russian Federation 97 G2

Ambato Ecuador 40 A4

Amboasary Madagascar 61 F4

Ambon Indonesia 121 F4

Ambositra Madagascar 61 G3

Ambriz Angola 60 B1

Amdo China 108 C4

Ameland *island* Netherlands 68 D1

American Falls Reservoir *Reservoir* Idaho, USA 26 E4

American Samoa *external territory* USA, Pacific Ocean 127 F4

Amersfoort Netherlands 68 D3

Amga *river* Russian Federation 95 F2

Amiens France 72 C3

Amīndivi Islands *island group* India 114 C2

Amirante Islands *island group* Seychelles 61 H1

Amman *capital of* Jordan 101 B5

Ammassalik Greenland *Dan.* Angmagssalik 64 D4

Ammochostos *see* Gazimağusa

Āmol Iran 102 C3

Amorgós *island* Greece 87 D6

Amritsar India 116 D2

Amsterdam *capital of* Netherlands 68 C3

Amsterdam Island *island* French Southern and Antarctic Territories 123 C6

Am Timan Chad 58 C3

Amu Darya *river* C Asia 104 D3

Amundsen Gulf *sea feature* Canada 19 E2

Amundsen Plain *undersea feature* Pacific Ocean 136 B4

Amundsen Sea Antarctica 97 G4

Amur *river* E Asia 97 G4 107 E1

Anabar *river* Russian Federation 95 E2

Anadolu Dağları *see* Doğu Karadeniz Dağlari

Anadyr' Russian Federation 97 H1

Anápolis Brazil 43 F4

Anatolia *region* SE Europe 85 G3

Anchorage Alaska, USA 18 C3

Ancona Italy 78 C3

Andalucía *region* Spain 74 D4

Andaman Islands *island group* India 115 H2 119 A5

Andaman Sea Indian Ocean 122 D3

Andes *mountain range* South America 39 B6

Andijon Uzbekistan *Rus.* Andizhan 105 F2

Andizhan *see* Andijon

Andorra *country* SW Europe 73 B6

Andorra la Vella *capital of* Andorra 73 B6

Ándros *island* Greece 87 D5

Andros Island *island* Bahamas 36 C1

Angara *river* C Asia 95 D3

Ángel de la Guarda, Isla *island* Mexico 32 B2

Angel Falls *see* Salto Ángel

Angeles Philippines 121 E1

Ángel, Salto *waterfall* Venezuela *Eng.* Angel Falls 41 F2

Ångermanälven *river* Sweden 66 C4

Angers France 72 B4

Anglesey *island* Wales, UK 71 C5

Angmagssalik *see* Ammassalik

Angola *country* C Africa 60

Angola Basin *undersea feature* Atlantic Ocean 49 D6

Angora *see* Ankara

Angoulême France 73 B5

Angren Uzbekistan 105 E2

Anguilla *external territory* UK, West Indies 37

Anhui *province* China *var.* Anhwei, Wan 111 C5

Anhwei *see* Anhui

Anjouan *island* Comoros 61 F2

Ankara *capital of* Turkey *prev.* Angora 98 C3

Annaba Algeria 53 E1

An Nafūd *desert region* Saudi Arabia 102 B4

An Najaf Iraq *see* Najaf 102 B4

Annapolis Maryland, USA 23 F4

Ann Arbor Michigan, USA 22 C3

Annecy France 73 D5

Anshan China 110 D4

Ansongo Mali 57 E3

Antakya Turkey *var.* Hatay 98 D4

Antalaha Madagascar 61 G2

Antalya Turkey *prev.* Adalia 98 B4

Antalya, Gulf of *see* Antalya Körfezi

Antalya Körfezi *sea feature* Mediterranean Sea *Eng.* Gulf of Antalya, *var.* Gulf of Adalia 98 B4

Antananarivo *capital of* Madagascar *prev.* Tananarive 61 G3

Antarctica 136

Antarctic Peninsula *peninsula* Antarctica 136 A2

Antequera Spain 74 D5

Anticosti, Île d' *island* Canada 21 F3

Antigua *island* Antigua & Barbuda 37 G3

Antigua & Barbuda *country* West Indies 37

Anti-Lebanon *mountains* Lebanon/Syria 100 B4

Antipodes Islands *island group* New Zealand124 D5

Antofagasta Chile 46 B2

Antsirañana Madagascar 61 G2

Antsohihy Madagascar 61 G2

Antwerp *see* Antwerpen

Antwerpen Belgium *Eng.* Antwerp 69 C5

Anyang China 110 C4

Aoga-shima *island* Japan 113 D6

Aomori Japan 112 D3

Aoraki *peak* New Zealand *var.* Cook, Mount 133 B6

Aosta Italy 78 A2

Aoukâr *Plateau* Mauritania 56 D3

Apeldoorn Netherlands 68 D3

Apennines *see* Appennino

Apia *capital of* Samoa 127 F4

Appalachian Mountains *mountain range* E USA 17 D5

Appennino *mountain range* Italy *Eng.* Apennines 78 C4

Apure *river* Venezuela 40 D2

Aqaba *see* Al 'Aqabah

Aqaba, Gulf of *sea feature* Red Sea *Ar.* Khalīj al 'Aqabah 101 A8

'Aqabah, Khalīj al *see* Aqaba, Gulf of

Āqchah Afghanistan *var.* Āqcheh 104 D3

Āqcheh *see* Āqchah

Arabian Basin *undersea feature* Indian Ocean 122 B3

Arabian Peninsula *peninsula* Asia 85 H5 94 B5 103 C5

Arabian Sea Indian Ocean 122 B3

Aracaju Brazil 43 H3

Arad Romania 90 B4

Arafura Sea Asia/Australasia 126 A4

Araguaia *river* Brazil 43 F3

Arāk Iran 102 C3
Araks see Aras
Arak's see Aras
Aral Sea inland sea
Kazakhstan/Uzbekistan 94 C3
Araouane Mali 57 E2
Ararat, Mount peak Turkey
var. Great Ararat, Turk.
Büyükağrı Dağı 94 F3
Aras river SW Asia Arm.
Arak's, Per. Rūd-e Aras, Rus.
Araks, Turk. Aras Nehri 99 G3
Aras Nehri see Aras
Arauca Colombia 40 C2
Arauca river
Colombia/Venezuela 40 C2
Arbīl Iraq Kurd. Hawlêr 102 B3
Arctic Ocean 18-19 137
Arda river Bulgaria/Greece
86 C3
Ardabīl Iran 102 C3
Ardennes region W Europe
69 D7
Arendal Norway 67 A6
Arensburg see Kuressaare
Arequipa Peru 42 B4
Arezzo Italy 78 C3
Argentina country S South
America 46-47
Argentine Basin undersea
feature Atlantic Ocean 49 B7
Argun river China/Russian
Federation 95 E3
Århus Denmark 67 A7
Arica Chile 46 B1
Arizona state USA 28 B2
Arkansas state USA 30 B1
Arkansas river C USA 17 C5
Arkhangel'sk Russian
Federation 92 C3 96 C2
Arles France 73 D6
Arlington Texas, USA 29 G3
Arlington Virginia, USA 23 E4
Arlon Belgium 69 D8
Armenia country SW Asia
99 G2
Armenia Colombia 40 B3
Armidale Australia 131 D5
Arnhem Netherlands 68 D4

Arnhem Land region Australia
128 E2
Arno river Italy 78 B3
Arran island Scotland, UK
70 C4
Ar Raqqah Syria 100 C2
Arras France 72 C3
Ar Riyāḍ see Riyadh
Ar Rub 'al Khālī desert Asia
Eng. Empty Quarter, Great
Sandy Desert 103 C6
Ar Rustāq Oman var. Rostak
103 D5
Artesia New Mexico, USA
28 D3
Artigas Uruguay 44 B4
Aru, Kepulauan island group
Indonesia 121 G5
Arua Uganda 55 B6
Aruba external territory
Netherlands, West Indies
37 E5
Arusha Tanzania 55 C7
Asad, Buḥayrat al Lake Syria
Eng. Lake Assad 100 C2
Asadābād Afghanistan 105 E4
Asahikawa Japan 112 D2
Asamankese Ghana 57 E5
Ascension island Atlantic
Ocean 49 C5
Ascoli Piceno Italy 78 C4
Aseb Eritrea var. Assab 54 D4
Ashburton New Zealand
133 C6
Asheville North Carolina, USA
31 E1
Aşgabat capital of
Turkmenistan prev.
Ashkhabad, Poltoratsk
104 C3
Ashkhabad see Aşgabat
Ashmore and Cartier Islands
Australian external territory
Indian Ocean 124 A3
Ash Shāriqah see Sharjah
Asia 94-95 106-107
Asmara capital of Eritrea Amh.
Asmera 54 C4
Asmera see Asmara
Assab see Aseb

As Salṭ Jordan var. Salt
101 B5
Assamakka Niger 57 F2
Assen Netherlands 68 E2
Assad, Lake see
Asad, Buḥayrat al
As Sulayyil Saudi Arabia
103 B6
As Suwaydā' Syria 101 B5
Astana country capital
Kazakhstan prev. Akmola,
Akmolinsk, Tselinograd, Kaz.
Aqmola. 96 C4
Astoria Oregon, USA 26 A2
Astrakhan' Russian Federation
93 B7
Astypálaia island Greece 87 D6
Asunción capital of Paraguay
44 B3
Aswân Egypt 54 B2
Asyût Egypt 54 B2
Atacama Desert desert Chile
46 B2
Atamyrat prev. Kerki.
Turkmenistan 104 D3
Aṭār Mauritania 56 C2
Atbara Sudan 54 C3
Athabasca, Lake lake Canada
19 F4
Athens capital of Greece Gk.
Athína, prev. Athinai 87 C5
Athens Georgia, USA 31 E2
Athína see Athens
Athínai see Athens
Athlone Ireland 71 B5
Ati Chad 58 C3
Atlanta Georgia, USA 30 D2
Atlantic City New Jersey, USA
23 F4
Atlantic Ocean 48-49
Atlantic-Indian Basin undersea
feature Indian Ocean 136 B1
Atlantic-Indian Ridge undersea
feature Atlantic Ocean 49 D7
Atlas Mountains mountain
range Morocco 52 C2
Aṭ Ṭafīlah Jordan 101 B6
Aṭ Ṭā'if Saudi Arabia 102 B6
Attapu Laos 119 E5
Attawapiskat Canada 20 C3

Balaton *lake* Hungary *var.* Lake Balaton, *Ger.* Plattensee 81 C7

Balaton, Lake *see* Balaton

Balbina, Represa *Reservoir* Brazil 42 D2

Baleares, Islas *island group* Spain *Eng.* Balearic Islands 75 H3

Balearic Islands *see* Baleares, Islas

Bali *island* Indonesia 120 D5

Balıkesir Turkey 98 A3

Balıkpapan Indonesia 120 D4

Balkanabat Turkmenistan *prev.* Nebitdag 104 B2

Balkan Mountains *mountain range* Bulgaria *Bul.* Stara Planina 86 C2

Balkhash Kazakhstan 96 C5

Balkhash, Lake *see* Balkhash, Ozero

Balkhash, Ozero *lake* Kazakhstan *Eng.* Lake Balkhash 94 C3

Ballarat Australia 131 C7

Balsas *river* Mexico 33 E5

Bălţi Moldova 90 D3

Baltic Port *see* Paldiski

Baltic Sea Atlantic Ocean 67 C7

Baltimore Maryland, USA 23 F4

Baltischport *see* Paldiski

Baltiski *see* Paldiski

Bamako *capital of* Mali 56 D3

Bambari Central African Republic 58 D4

Bamenda Cameroon 58 B4

Banaba *island* Kiribati *prev.* Ocean Island 127 E2

Bandaaceh Indonesia 120 A3

Banda, Laut *see* Banda Sea

Banda Sea *sea feature* Pacific Ocean *Ind.* Laut Banda 121 F4

Bandar-e ʿAbbās Iran 102 D4

Bandar-e Büshehr Iran 102 C4

Bandar Lampung Indonesia *prev.* Tanjungkarang 120 C4

Bandar Seri Begawan *capital of* Brunei 120 D3

Bandon Oregon, USA 26 A3

Bandundu Dem. Rep. Congo 59 C6

Bandung Indonesia 120 C5

Bangalore India 114 D2

Banggai, Kepulauan *island group* Indonesia 121 E4

Banghāzī Libya *Eng.* Benghazi 53 G2

Bangka *island* Indonesia 120 C4

Bangkok *capital of* Thailand *Th.* Krung Thep 119 C5

Bangladesh *country* S Asia 117

Bangor Northern Ireland, UK 71 B5

Bangor Maine, USA 23 G2

Bangui *capital of* Central African Republic 59 C5

Bani *river* Mali 56 D3

Banī Suwayf *see* Beni Suef

Banja Luka Bosnia & Herzegovina 82 B3

Banjarmasin Indonesia 120 D4

Banjul *capital of* Gambia 56 B3

Banks Island *island* Canada 19 E2

Banks Islands *island group* Vanuatu, Pacific Ocean 126 D4

Banks Peninsula *peninsula* New Zealand133 C6

Banks Strait *sea feature* Tasman Sea 131 C7

Banská Bystrica Slovakia *Ger.* Neusohl, *Hung.* Besztercebánya 81 C6

Bantry Bay *sea feature* Ireland 71 A6

Banyo Cameroon 58 B4

Banzare Seamounts *undersea feature* Indian Ocean 123 C7

Baotou China 109 F3

Baranavichy Belarus *Rus.* Baranovichi, *Pol.* Baranowicze 89 C6

Baranovichi *see* Baranavichy

Baranowicze *see* Baranavichy

Barbados *country* West Indies 37 H4

Barbuda *island* Antigua & Barbuda 37 G3

Barcaldine Australia 130 C4

Barcelona Spain 75 G2

Barcelona Venezuela 41 E1

Barcolod City Philippines 121 E2

Bareilly India 117 E3

Barentsburg Svalbard 65 F2

Barentsøya *island* Svalbard 65 G2

Barents Sea Arctic Ocean 137 H5

Bari Italy 79 E5

Barinas Venezuela 40 D2

Barisan, Pegunungan *mountains* Indonesia 120 B4

Barkly Tableland *plateau* Australia 130 B3

Barlavento, Ilhas de *island group* Cape Verde *var.* Windward Islands 56 A2

Bar-le-Duc France 72 D3

Barlee, Lake *lake* Australia 129 B 5

Barlee Range *mountain range* Australia 128 B4

Barnaul Russian Federation 96 D4

Barnstaple England, UK 71 C7

Barquisimeto Venezuela 40 D1

Barra *island* Scotland, UK 70 B3

Barranquilla Colombia 40 B1

Barrier Range *mountain range* Australia 131 C5

Barrow *river* Ireland 71 B6

Barstow California, USA 27 C7

Bartang *river* Tajikistan 105 F3

Bartica Guyana 41 G2

Baruun-Urt Mongolia 109 F2

Barwon River *river* Australia 131 D5

Barysaw Belarus *Rus.* Borisov 89 D5

Basarabeasca Moldova 90 D4

Basel Switzerland 77 B6

Basra *see* Al Başrah

Bassein Myanmar 118 A4

Basse-Terre *capital of* Guadeloupe 37 G4

Basseterre *capital of* St Kitts & Nevis 37 G3

Bass Strait *sea feature* Australia 131 C7

Bastia Corse, France 73 E7

Bastogne Belgium 69 D7

Bata Equatorial Guinea 58 A5

Batangas Philippines 121 E2

Bătdâmbâng Cambodia 119 D5

Bath England, UK 71 D6

Bathurst Canada 21 F4

Bathurst Island *island* Australia 128 D2

Bathurst Island *island* Canada 19 F2

Bāṭin, Wādī al *dry watercourse* Asia 102 C4

Batman Turkey *var.* İluh 99 E4

Batna Algeria 53 E1

Baton Rouge Louisiana, USA 30 B3

Batticaloa Sri Lanka 115 E3

Bat'umi Georgia 99 F2

Bauru Brazil 44 D2

Bavarian Alps *mountains* Austria/Germany 77 C6

Bayamo Cuba 36 C2

Bayan Har Shan *mountain range* China 108 D4

Bayanhongor Mongolia 108 D2

Bay City Michigan, USA 22 C3

Baydhabo Somalia 55 D6

Baykal, Ozero *lake* Russian Federation *Eng.* Lake Baikal 95 E3

Bayonne France 73 A6

Baýramaly Turkmenistan 104 C3

Bayrūt *see* Beirut

Beaufort Sea Arctic Ocean 137 F2

Beaufort West South Africa 60 D5

Beaumont Texas, USA 29 H4

Beauvais France 72 C3

Béchar Algeria 52 C2

Be'ér Sheva' Israel 101 A6

Beijing *capital of* China *var.* Peking 110 C4

Beira Mozambique 61 E3

Beirut *capital of* Lebanon *var.* Beyrouth, Bayrūt 100 B4

Beja Portugal 74 C4

Béjaïa Algeria 53 E1

Bek-Budi *see* Karshi

Békéscsaba Hungary 81 D7

Belarus *country* E Europe *var.* Belorusia 89

Belau *see* Palau

Belcher Islands *islands* Canada 20 C2

Beledweyne Somalia 55 D5

Belém Brazil 43 F2

Belfast Northern Ireland, UK 71 B5

Belfort France 72 E4

Belgaum India 114 C1

Belgium *country* W Europe 69

Belgorod Russian Federation 93 A5

Belgrade *capital of* Serbia *SCr.* Beograd 82 D3

Belitung, Pulau *island* Indonesia 120 C4

Belize *country* Central America 34

Belize City Belize 34 C1

Belle Île *island* France 72 A4

Belle Isle, Strait of *sea feature* Canada 21 G3

Bellevue Washington, USA 26 B2

Bellingham Washington, USA 26 B1

Bellingshausen Sea Antarctica 136 A3

Bello Colombia 40 B2

Bellville South Africa 60 C5

Belmopan *capital of* Belize 34 C1

Belo Horizonte Brazil 45 F1

Belorussia *see* Belarus

Belostok *see* Białystok

Beloye More Arctic Ocean *Eng.* White Sea 63 F1

Belyy, Ostrov *island* Russian Federation 137 H4

Bend Oregon, USA 26 B3

Bendery *see* Tighina

Bendigo Australia 131 C7

Benevento Italy 79 D5

Bengal, Bay of *sea feature* Indian Ocean 122 D3

Bengbu China 111 D5

Benghazi *see* Banghāzī

Bengkulu Indonesia 120 B4

Benguela Angola 60 B2

Beni *river* Bolivia 42 C4

Benidorm Spain 75 F4

Beni Mellal Morocco 52 C2

Benin *country* N Africa *prev.* Dahomey 57

Benin, Bight of *sea feature* W Africa 57 F5

Benin City Nigeria 57 F5

Beni Suef Egypt *var.* Banī Suwayf 54 B1

Ben Nevis *mountain* Scotland, UK 70 C3

Benue *river* Cameroon/Nigeria 57 G4

Beograd *see* Belgrade

Berat Albania 83 D6

Berbera Somalia 54 D4

Berbérati Central African Republic 58 C5

Berdyans'k Ukraine 91 G4

Bereket Turkmenistan *prev.* Gazandzhyk, *var.* Kazandzhik, *Turkm.* Gazanjyk 104 B2

Berezina *see* Byerazino

Bergamo Italy 78 B2

Bergen Norway 67 A5

Bergse Maas *river* Netherlands 68 D4

Bering Sea Pacific Ocean 134 D1

Bering Strait *sea feature* Bering Sea/Chukchi Sea 134 D1

Berkeley California, USA 27 B6

Berlin *capital of* Germany 76 D3

Bermejo *river* Argentina 46 D2

Bermuda *external territory* UK, Atlantic Ocean 48 B3

Bern *capital of* Switzerland *Fr.* Berne 77 B7

Berne see Bern
Berner Alpen *mountain range*
Switzerland 77 B7
Bertoua Cameroon 59 B5
Besançon France 72 D4
Besztercebánya see Banská
Bystrica
Bethlehem West Bank 101 A5
Beyrouth see Beirut
Béziers France 73 C6
Bezmein see Abadan
Bhamo Myanmar 118 B2
Bhāvnagar India 116 C4
Bhōpal India 116 D4
Bhutan *country* S Asia 117
Biak, Pulau *island* Indonesia
121 G4
Białystok Poland *Rus.* Belostok
80 E3
Biel Switzerland 77 B7
Bielefeld Germany 76 B4
Bielitz-Biala see Bielsko-Biała
Bielsko-Biała Poland *Ger.*
Bielitz-Biala 81 C5
Bié Plateau *upland* Angola
51 C6
Bighorn Mountains *mountains*
C USA 24 C2
Bignona Senegal 56 B3
Big Spring Texas, USA 29 E3
Bihać Bosnia & Herzegovina
82 B3
Bihār *state* India 117 F3
Bijelo Polje Montenegro 82 D4
Bikāner India 116 C3
Bila Tserkva Ukraine 91 E2
Bilbao Spain 75 E1
Billings Montana, USA 24 C2
Bilma, Grand Erg de *desert*
Niger 57 G3
Biloela Australia 130 D4
Biloxi Mississippi, USA
30 C3
Biltine Chad 58 D3
Binghamton New York, USA
23 F3
Birāk Libya 53 F3
Birātnagar Nepal 117 F3
Birmingham England, UK 71 D6

Birmingham Alabama, USA
30 D2
Bîr Mogreïn Mauritania 56 C1
Birsen see Biržai
Biržai Lithuania *Ger.* Birsen
88 C3
Biscay, Bay of *sea feature*
Atlantic Ocean 62 C4
Bishkek *capital of* Kyrgyzstan
prev. Frunze, Pishpek 105 F2
Bishop California, USA 27 C6
Biskra Algeria 53 E2
Bismarck North Dakota, USA
25 E2
Bismarck Archipelago *island
group* Papua New Guinea
126 B3
Bismarck Sea *sea* Pacific Ocean
124 B2
Bissau *capital of* Guinea-Bissau
56 B4
Bitola Macedonia 83 E6
Bitterroot Range *mountains*
NW USA 26 D2
Biwa-ko *lake* Japan 113 C5
Bizerte Tunisia 53 E1
Bjelovar Croatia 82 B2
Bjørnøya *Island* N Norway *Eng.*
Bear Island 65 G3
Black Drin *river*
Albania/Macedonia 83 D5
Black Forest see Schwarzwald
Black Hills *mountains* C USA
24 D3
Blackpool England, UK 71 D5
Black River *river* China/Vietnam
118 D3
Black Sea Asia/Europe 63 F4
Black Volta *river* Ghana/Côte
d'Ivoire 57 E4
Blackwater *river* Ireland
71 A6
Blagoevgrad Bulgaria 86 C3
Blagoveshchensk Russian
Federation 97 G4
Blanca, Bahía *sea feature*
Argentina 39 D5
Blanche, Lake *lake* Australia
131 B5
Blantyre Malawi 61 E2

Blenheim New Zealand 133 D5
Blida Algeria 52 D1
Bloemfontein South Africa
60 D4
Blois France 72 C4
Bloomington Indiana, USA
22 C4
Bluefields Nicaragua 35 E3
Blue Mountains *mountains* W
USA 26 C2
Blue Nile *river* Ethiopia/Sudan
54 C4
Blumenau Brazil 44 D3
Bo Sierra Leone 56 C4
Boa Vista Brazil 42 D1
Boa Vista *island* Cape Verde
56 A3
Bobo-Dioulasso Burkina 56 D4
Bobruysk see Babruysk
Boca de la Serpiente see
Serpent's Mouth, The
Bochum Germany 76 B4
Bodø Norway 66 C3
Bodrum Turkey 98 A4
Bogor Indonesia 120 C5
Bogotá *capital of* Colombia
40 B3
Bo Hai *sea feature* Yellow Sea
110 D4
Bohemian Forest *region*
Germany 77 D5
Bohol Sea *Sea* Philippines
121 E2
Boise Idaho, USA 26 D3
Boké Guinea 56 C4
Bokhara see Buxoro
Bol Chad 58 B3
Bolivia *country* C South
America 42-43
Bologna Italy 78 C3
Bolton England, UK 71 D5
Bolzano Italy *Ger.* Bozen 78 C2
Boma Dem. Rep. Congo 59 B7
Bombay see Mumbai
Bomu *river* Central African
Republic/Dem. Rep. Congo
59 D5
Bongo, Massif des *upland*
Central African Republic
58 D4

Bongor Chad 58 C3

Bonn Germany 76 B4

Boosaaso Somalia 54 E4

Borås Sweden 67 B7

Bordeaux France 73 B5

Borger Texas, USA 29 E2

Borisov see Barysaw

Borlänge Sweden 67 C6

Borneo island SE Asia 120-121

Bornholm island Denmark 67 C8

Bosanski Šamac Bosnia & Herzegovina 82 C3

Bosna river Bosnia & Herzegovina 82 C3

Bosna I Hercegovina, Federacija Admin. region republic Bosnia and Herzegovina 82 C4

Bosnia & Herzegovina country SE Europe 82-83

Bosporus sea feature Turkey Turk. İstanbul Boğazi 98 B2

Bossangoa Central African Republic 58 C4

Bosten Hu Lake China 108 C3

Boston Massachusetts, USA 23 G3

Bothnia, Gulf of sea feature Baltic Sea 67 C5

Botoşani Romania 90 C3

Botswana country southern Africa 60

Bouar Central African Republic 58 C4

Bougainville Island island Papua New Guinea 126 C3

Bougouni Mali 56 D4

Boulder Colorado, USA 24 C4

Boulogne-sur-Mer France 72 C2

Bourges France 72 C4

Bourgogne region France Eng. Burgundy 72 D4

Bourke Australia 131 C5

Bournemouth England, UK 71 D7

Bouvet Island external territory Norway, Atlantic Ocean 49 D7

Bowen Australia 130 D3

Bowling Green Kentucky, USA 22 C5

Bozeman Montana, USA 24 B2

Bozen see Bolzano

Brač island Croatia 82 B4

Bradford England, UK 71 D5

Braga Portugal 74 C2

Bragança Portugal 74 C2

Brahmaputra river Asia 117 G3

Brăila Romania 90 D4

Brainerd Minnesota, USA 25 F2

Brandon Canada 19 F5

Brasília capital of Brazil 43 F4

Braşov Romania 90 C4

Bratislava capital of Slovakia Ger. Pressburg, Hung. Pozsony 81 C6

Bratsk Russian Federation 97 E4

Braunau am Inn Austria 77 D6

Braunschweig Germany Eng. Brunswick 76 C4

Brazil country South America 42-43

Brazil Basin undersea feature Atlantic Ocean 49 C5

Brazilian Highlands upland Brazil 43 G4

Brazos river SW USA 29 G3

Brazzaville capital of Congo 59 B6

Breda Netherlands 68 C4

Bregenz Austria 77 B7

Bremen Germany 76 B3

Bremerhaven Germany 76 B3

Brescia Italy 78 B2

Breslau see Wrocław

Brest Belarus Pol. Brześć nad Bugiem, prev. Brześć Litewski, Rus. Brest-Litovsk 89 B6

Brest France 72 A3

Brest-Litovsk see Brest

Bretagne region France Eng. Brittany 72 A3

Brezhnev see Naberezhnyye Chelny

Bria Central African Republic 58 D4

Bridgetown capital of Barbados 37 H4

Brig Switzerland 77 B5

Brighton England, UK 71 E7

Brindisi Italy 79 E5

Brisbane Australia 131 E5

Bristol England, UK 71 D6

British Columbia province Canada 18-19

British Indian Ocean Territory external territory UK, Indian Ocean 122 C4

British Isles islands W Europe 70-71

British Virgin Islands external territory UK, West Indies 37

Brittany see Bretagne

Brno Czech Republic Ger. Brünn 81 B5

Broken Arrow Oklahoma, USA 29 G1

Broken Hill Australia 131 B6

Broken Ridge undersea feature Indian Ocean 123 D6

Bromberg see Bydgoszcz

Brooks Range mountains Alaska, USA 18 D2

Brookton Australia 129 B6

Broome Australia 128 C3

Brownfield Texas, USA 29 E2

Brownsville Texas, USA 29 G5

Bruges see Brugge

Brugge Belgium Fr. Bruges 69 A5

Brunei country E Asia 120 D3

Brünn see Brno

Brunswick Georgia, USA 31 E3

Brunswick see Braunschweig

Brusa see Bursa

Brussel see Brussels

Brussels capital of Belgium Fr. Bruxelles, Flem. Brussel 69 C6

Brüx see Most

Bruxelles see Brussels

Bryan Texas, USA 29 G3

Bryansk Russian Federation 93 A5 96 A2

Brześć Litewski see Brest

Brześć nad Bugiem see Brest

Bucaramanga Colombia 40 C2

Buchanan Liberia 56 C5

Bucharest *capital of* Romania 90 C5

Budapest *capital of* Hungary 81 C6

Budweis *see* České Budějovice

Buenaventura Colombia 40 B3

Buenos Aires *capital of* Argentina 46 D4

Buenos Aires, Lago *lake* Argentina/Chile 47 B6

Buffalo New York, USA 23 E3

Bug *river* E Europe 90 C1

Bujumbura *capital of* Burundi *prev.* Usumbura 55 B7

Bukavu Dem. Rep. Congo 59 E6

Bukhara *see* Buxoro

Bulawayo Zimbabwe 60 D3

Bulgan Mongolia 109 E2

Bulgaria *country* E Europe 86

Bumba Dem. Rep. Congo 59 D5

Bunbury Australia 129 B6

Bundaberg Australia 130 E4

Bunia Dem. Rep. Congo 59 E5

Buraydah Saudi Arabia 103 B5

Burē Ethiopia 54 C4

Burgas Bulgaria 86 E2

Burgos Spain 75 E2

Burgundy *see* Bourgogne

Burketown Australia 130 B3

Burkina *country* W Africa 57

Burlington Iowa, USA 25 G4

Burlington Vermont, USA 23 F2

Burma *see* Myanmar

Burnie Tasmania 131 C8

Burns Oregon, USA 26 C3

Bursa Turkey *prev.* Brusa 98 B3

Burtnieku Ezers *lake* Latvia 88 C3

Buru, Pulau *island* Indonesia 121 E4

Burundi *country* C Africa 55

Busselton Australia 129 B7

Butembo Dem. Rep. Congo 59 E5

Buton, Pulau *Island* Indonesia 121 E4

Butte Montana, USA 24 B2

Butuan Philippines 121 F2

Buxoro Uzbekistan *var.* Bokhara, *Rus.* Bukhara 104 D2

Büyükağrı Dağı *see* Ararat, Mount

Buzău Romania 90 C4

Büzmeýin *see* Abadan

Bydgoszcz Poland *Ger.* Bromberg 80 C3

Byerazino *river* Belarus *Rus.* Berezina 89 D6

Byzantium *see* İstanbul

C

Caazapá Paraguay 44 C3

Cabanatuan Philippines 121 E1

Cabimas Venezuela 40 C1

Cabinda *exclave* Angola 60 B1

Cabot Strait *sea feature* Atlantic Ocean 21 G4

Čačak Serbia 82 D4

Cáceres Spain 74 D3

Cachoeiro de Itapemirim Brazil 45 F1

Cadiz Philippines 121 E2

Cádiz Spain 74 D5

Caen France 72 B3

Cagayan de Oro Philippines 121 F2

Cagliari Italy 79 A5

Cahors France 73 B5

Cairns Australia 130 D3

Cairo *capital of* Egypt *Ar.* Al Qāhirah, *var.* El Qâhira 54 B1

Čakovec Croatia 82 B2

Calabar Nigeria 57 G5

Calabria *region* Italy 79 D6

Calafate *see* El Calafate

Calais France 72 C2

Calais Maine, USA 23 H1

Calama Chile 46 B2

Calbayog Philippines 121 F2

Calcutta *see* Kolkata

Caldas da Rainha Portugal 74 B3

Caldwell Idaho, USA 27 C3

Caleta Olivia Argentina 47 C6

Calgary Canada 19 E5

Cali Colombia 40 A3

Calicut India *var.* Kozhikode 114 C2

California *state* USA 26–27

California, Golfo de *sea feature* Pacific Ocean *Eng.* California, Gulf of 32 B2 123 F2

Callabonna, Lake *lake* Australia131 B5

Callao Peru 42 A3

Caltanissetta Italy 79 C7

Camagüey Cuba 36 C2

Cambodia *country* SE Asia *Cam.* Kampuchea 119

Cambridge England, UK 71 E6

Cambridge New Zealand132 D2

Cameroon *country* W Africa 58–59

Campbell Plateau *undersea feature* Pacific Ocean 134 C5

Campeche Mexico 33 G4

Campeche, Bahía de *sea feature* Mexico *Eng.* Gulf of Campeche 33 G4

Campina Grande Brazil 43 H3

Campinas Brazil 45 E2

Campo Grande Brazil 44 C1

Campos Brazil 45 F2

Canada *country* North America 16–17

Canada Basin *undersea feature* Arctic Ocean *var.* Laurentian Basin 137 F2

Canadian River *river* SW USA 29 E2

Çanakkale Turkey 98 A3

Çanakkale Boğazı *see* Dardanelles

Canarias, Islas *islands* Spain *Eng.* Canary Islands 50 A2

Canary Basin *undersea feature* Atlantic Ocean 48 C4

Canary Islands *see* Canarias, Islas

Canaveral, Cape *coastal feature* Florida, USA 31 F4

Chittagong Bangladesh 117 G4

Chitungwiza Zimbabwe 60 D3

Choluteca Honduras 34 C3

Choma Zambia 60 D3

Chona *river* Russian Federation 95 E2

Chon Buri Thailand 119 C5

Ch'ŏngjin North Korea 110 E3

Chongqing *province* China *var.* Chungking 111 B5

Chonos, Archipiélago de los *island group* Chile 47 B6

Chornobyl' Ukraine *Rus.* Chernobyl' 91 E1

Choûm Mauritania 56 C2

Choybalsan Mongolia 109 F2

Christchurch New Zealand 133 C6

Christmas Island *external territory* Australia, Indian Ocean 122 C5

Christmas Island *see* Kiritimati

Christmas Ridge *undersea feature* Pacific Ocean 125 F1

Chuan *see* Sichuan

Chubut *river* Argentina 47 B6

Chudskoye Ozero *see* Peipus, Lake

Chui *see* Chuy

Chukchi Plain *undersea feature* Arctic Ocean 137 F2

Chukchi Sea Arctic Ocean *Rus.* Chukotskoye More 137 F1

Chukotskoye More *see* Chukchi Sea

Chula Vista California, USA 27 C8

Chulym *river* Russian Federation 94 D3

Chumphon Thailand 119 C6

Chungking *see* Chongqing

Chuquicamata Chile 46 B2

Chur Switzerland 77 B7

Churchill Canada 19 G4

Chuuk Islands *island group* Micronesia 126 B1

Chuy Brazil *var.* Chuí 44 C5

Cienfuegos Cuba 36 B2

Cieza Spain 75 F4

Cilacap Indonesia 120 C5

Cincinnati Ohio, USA 22 C4

Cirebon Indonesia 120 C5

Ciudad Bolívar Venezuela 41 E2

Ciudad del Este Paraguay 44 C3

Ciudad de México *see* Mexico City

Ciudad Guayana Venezuela 41 E2

Ciudad Juárez Mexico 32 C1

Ciudad Obregón Mexico 32 B2

Ciudad Ojeda Venezuela 40 C1

Ciudad Real Spain 75 E3

Ciudad Valles Mexico 33 E3

Ciudad Victoria Mexico 33 E3

Clarence *river* New Zealand 133 C5

Clarion Fracture Zone *tectonic feature* Pacific Ocean 125 G1

Clarksville Tennessee, USA 30 D1

Clearwater Florida, USA 31 E4

Clermont Australia 130 D4

Clermont-Ferrand France 73 C5

Cleveland Ohio, USA 22 D3

Clipperton Fracture Zone *tectonic feature* Pacific Ocean 125 G2

Clipperton Island *external territory* France, Pacific Ocean 135 F3

Cloncurry Australia 130 C3

Clovis New Mexico, USA 29 E2

Cluj-Napoca Romania 90 B3

Clutha *river* New Zealand 133 B7

Coast Ranges *mountain range* W USA 26 A5

Coats Island *island* Canada 20 C1

Coats Land *physical region* Antarctica 136 B2

Coatzacoalcos Mexico 33 G4

Cobán Guatemala 34 B2

Cochabamba Bolivia 42 C4

Cochin India *var.* Kochi 114 D3

Cochrane Canada 20 C4

Cochrane Chile 47 B6

Coco *river* Honduras/Nicaragua 34 D2

Cocos Basin *undersea feature* Indian Ocean 122 D4

Cocos Islands *external territory* Australia, Indian Ocean 122 D5

Cod, Cape *coastal feature* NE USA 23 G3

Coeur d'Alene Idaho, USA 26 C2

Coffs Harbour Australia 131 E6

Coihaique Chile 47 B6

Coimbatore India 114 D3

Coimbra Portugal 74 C3

Colchester England, UK 71 E6

Colmar France 72 E4

Cologne *see* Köln

Colombia *country* N South America 40-41

Colombo *capital of* Sri Lanka 115 E4

Colón Panama 35 F4

Colón, Archipiélago de *see* Galapagos Islands

Colorado *state* USA 24 C4

Colorado *river* USA 16 B5

Colorado *river* Argentina 47 C5

Colorado Plateau *upland region* S USA 28 B1

Colorado Springs Colorado, USA 24 D4

Columbia South Carolina, USA 31 F2

Columbia *river* NW USA 26 C1

Columbus Georgia, USA 30 D3

Columbus Mississippi, USA 30 C2

Columbus Nebraska, USA 25 E4

Columbus Ohio, USA 22 D4

Comayagua Honduras 34 C2

Comilla Bangladesh 117 G4

Communism Peak *peak* Tajikistan *Rus.* Pik Kommunizma, *prev.* Stalin Peak, Garmo Peak 105 F3

Como, Lago di *lake* Italy 78 B2

Comodoro Rivadavia Argentina 47 C6

Comoros *country* Indian Ocean 61

Conakry *capital of* Guinea 56 C4

Concepción Chile 47 B5

Concepción Paraguay 44 B2

Conchos *river* Mexico 32 C2

Concord New Hampshire, USA 22 G2

Concordia E Argentina 46 D3

Congo *country* C Africa 59

Congo *river* C Africa *var.* Zaire 51 C5

Congo Basin *drainage basin* C Africa 59 C5

Congo, Democratic Republic of *country* C Africa 59

Connecticut *state* USA 23 G3

Constance, Lake *river* C Europe 77 B6

Constantine Algeria 53 E1

Constantinople *see* İstanbul

Constanţa Romania 90 D5

Coober Pedy Australia 131 A5

Cook, Mount *see* Aoraki

Cook Islands *external territory* New Zealand, Pacific Ocean 127 G4

Cook Strait *sea feature* New Zealand 133 D5

Cooktown Australia 130 D2

Cooma Australia 131 D7

Coos Bay Oregon, USA 26 A3

Cootamundra Australia 131 D6

Copenhagen *capital of* Denmark 67 B7

Copiapó Chile 46 B3

Coppermine *see* Kuglukutuk

Coquimbo Chile 46 B3

Corabia Romania 90 B5

Coral Sea Pacific Ocean 130 E3

Coral Sea Islands *external territory* Australia, Coral Sea 130 E3

Corantijn *see* Courantyne

Cordillera Cantábrica *mountain range* Spain 74 D1

Córdoba Argentina 46 C3

Córdoba Spain 74 D4

Cordova Alaska, USA 18 D3

Corfu *see* Kérkyra

Corinth *see* Kórinthos

Corinth, Gulf of *see* Korinthiakós Kólpos

Corinto Nicaragua 34 C3

Cork Ireland 71 B6

Corner Brook Canada 21 G3

Coro Venezuela 40 D1

Coronel Oviedo Paraguay 44 C2

Corpus Christi Texas, USA 29 G5

Corrib, Lough *lake* Ireland 71 A5

Corrientes Argentina 46 D3

Corse *island* France *Eng.* Corsica 73 E7 84 D2

Corsica *see* Corse

Çorum Turkey 98 D2

Corvallis Oregon, USA 26 A3

Cosenza Italy 79 D6

Costa Blanca *coastal region* Spain 75 F4

Costa Brava *coastal region* Spain 75 H2

Costa Rica *country* Central America 34-35

Côte d'Ivoire *country* W Africa *Eng.* Ivory Coast 56 D4

Cottbus Germany 76 D4

Council Bluffs Iowa, USA 25 F4

Courantyne *river* Guyana /Suriname *var.* Corantijn 41 G3

Courland Lagoon *sea feature* Baltic Sea 88 B4

Coventry England, UK 71 D6

Covilhã Portugal 74 C3

Cowan, Lake *lake* Australia 129 C6

Cozumel, Isla de *island* Mexico 33 H3

Cracow *see* Kraków

Craiova Romania 90 B5

Cremona Italy 78 B2

Cres *island* Croatia 82 A3

Crescent City California, USA 26 A4

Crete *see* Kríti

Crete, Sea of Mediterranean Sea *Gk.* Kritikó Pélagos 87 D7

Crimea *see* Krym

Cristóbal Panama 48 A4

Croatia *country* SE Europe 82

Croker Island *island* Australia 128 E2

Crotone Italy 79 E6

Crozet Basin *undersea feature* Indian Ocean 123 B6

Crozet Islands *island group* Indian Ocean 123 B7

Crystal Brook Australia 131 B6

Cuanza *river* Angola 60 B2

Cuba *country* West Indies 36

Cubango *see* Okavango

Cúcuta Colombia 40 C2

Cuenca Ecuador 40 A5

Cuenca Spain 75 E3

Cuernavaca Mexico 33 E4

Cuiabá Brazil 43 E4

Culiacán Mexico 32 C3

Cumaná Venezuela 41 E1

Cumberland Maryland, USA 23 E4

Cunene *river* Angola/Namibia 60 B3

Cunnamulla Australia 131 C5

Curicó Chile 46 B4

Curitiba Brazil 44 D3

Cusco Peru *prev.* Cuzco 42 B4

Cuttack India 117 F5

Cuxhaven Germany 76 B3

Cuyuni *river* Guyana/Venezuela 41 F2

Cuzco *see* Cusco

Cyclades *see* Kykládes

Cymru *see* Wales

Cyprus *country* Mediterranean Sea 98 C5

Czechoslovakia *see* Czech Republic *or* Slovakia

Czech Republic *country* C Europe 80-81

Częstochowa Poland *Ger.* Tschenstochau 80 C4

Człuchów Poland 80 C3

D

Dacca see Dhaka

Dagden see Hiiumaa

Dagö see Hiiumaa

Dagupan Philippines 121 E1

Da Hinggan Ling *mountain range* China *Eng.* Great Khingan Range 109 G1

Dahomey see Benin

Dakar *capital of* Senegal 56 B3

Đakovo Croatia 82 C3

Dalain Hob China 108 D3

Dalaman Turkey 98 B4

Dalandzadgad Mongolia 109 E3

Đa Lat Vietnam 119 E5

Dalby Australia 131 D5

Dalian China 110 D4

Dallas Texas, USA 29 G3

Dalmacija *region* Croatia 82 B4

Daly Waters Australia 128 E3

Damän India 116 C5

Damas see Damascus

Damascus Syria *var.* Esh Sham, *Fr.* Damas, *Ar.* Dimashq 100 B4

Dampier Australia 128 B4

Damxung China 108 C5

Đa Nâng Vietnam 119 E4

Dandong China 110 D4

Daneborg Greenland 65 E3

Danghara Tajikistan 105 E3

Danmarksstraedet see Denmark Strait

Danube *river* C Europe 63 E4

Danville Virginia, USA 23 E5

Danzig see Gdańsk

Danzig, Gulf of 76 C2 *Gulf* Poland 80 C2

Dar'ā Syria 101 B5

Dardanelles *sea feature* Turkey *Turk.* Çanakkale Boğazı 98 A2

Dar es Salaam Tanzania 55 C7

Darfur *Cultural region* Sudan 54 A4

Darhan Mongolia 109 E2

Darien, Gulf of *sea feature* Caribbean Sea 35 G5

Darling *river* Australia 131 C6

Darmstadt Germany 77 B5

Darnah Libya 53 H2

Dartmoor *region* England, UK 71 C7

Dartmouth Canada 21 F4

Darwin Australia 128 D2

Dashhowuz see Daşoguz

Datong China 110 C4

Daugava see Western Dvina

Daugavpils Latvia *Ger.* Dünaburg, *Rus.* Dvinsk 88 D4

Dāvangere India 114 D2

Davao Philippines 121 F3

Davao Gulf *gulf* Philippines 121 F3

Davenport Iowa, USA 25 G3

David Panama 35 E5

Davie Ridge *undersea feature* Indian Ocean 123 A5

Davis Indian Ocean 136 D3

Davis Strait *sea feature* Atlantic Ocean 64 C3

Dayr az Zawr Syria 100 D3

Dayton Ohio, USA 22 C4

Daytona Beach Florida, USA 31 F4

Dead Sea *salt lake* SW Asia *Ar.* Al Bahr al Mayyit, Bahrat Lūt, *Heb.* Yam HaMelah 101 B5

Death Valley *valley* W USA 27 C6

Deatnu *river* Finland/Norway 66 D2

Debrecen Hungary *prev.* Debreczen, *Ger.* Debreczin 81 D6

Debreczen see Debrecen

Debreczin see Debrecen

Decatur Illinois, USA 22 B4

Deccan *plateau* India 106 B3 115 D1

Děčín Czech Republic *Ger.* Tetschen 80 B4

Dej Romania 90 B3

Delaware *state* USA 23 F4

Delémont Switzerland 77 A7

Delft Netherlands 68 C4

Delfzijl Netherlands 68 E1

Delhi India 116 D3

Del Rio Texas, USA 29 F4

Demchok *disputed region* China/India *var.* Dêmqog 108 B3

Demopolis Alabama, USA 30 C2

Dêmqog see Demchok

Denali see Mount McKinley

Denham Australia 129 A5

Den Helder Netherlands 68 C2

Denizli Turkey 98 B4

Denmark *country* NW Europe 67

Denmark Strait *sea feature* Greenland/Iceland *var.* Danmarksstraedet 65 D4

Denpasar Indonesia 120 D5

Denton Texas, USA 29 G2

Denver Colorado, USA 24 D4

Dera Ghāzi Khān Pakistan 116 C2

Derby England, UK 71 D6

Derg, Lough *lake* Ireland 71 B6

Desê Ethiopia 54 C4

Deseado *river* Argentina 47 C6

Des Moines Iowa, USA 25 F3

Despoto Planina see Rhodope Mountains

Dessau Germany 76 D4

Detroit Michigan, USA 22 D4

Deutschendorf see Poprad

Deva Romania 90 B4

Deventer Netherlands 68 D3

Devollit, Lumi i *river* Albania 83 D6

Devon Island *island* Canada 19 F2

Devonport Tasmania, Australia 131 C8

Dezfūl Iran 102 C3

Dhaka *capital of* Bangladesh *var.* Dacca 117 G4

Dhanbād India 117 F4

Dhrepanon, Ákra see Drépano, Akrotírio

Diamantina Fracture Zone
tectonic feature Indian Ocean
123 E6

Dickinson North Dakota, USA
24 D2

Diekirch Luxembourg 69 D7

Dieppe France 72 C3

Digul *River* Indonesia 121 H5

Dijon France 72 D4

Dikson Taymyrskiy (Dolgano-
Nenetskiy) Russian Federation
137 H4

Dili *capital of* East Timor 121 F5

Dilling Sudan 54 B4

Dilolo Dem. Rep. Congo 59 D8

Dimashq *see* Damascus

Dimitrovo *see* Pernik

Dinant Belgium 69 C7

Dinaric Alps *mountains* Bosnia
& Herzegovina/Croatia 82 B4

Diourbel Senegal 56 B3

Dirē Dawa Ethiopia 55 D5

Dirk Hartog Island *island*
Australia 129 A5

Disappointment, Lake *salt lake*
Australia 128 C4

Dispur India 117 G3

Divinópolis Brazil 45 F1

Diyarbakır Turkey 99 E4

Dkaraganda *see* Zhezkazgan

Djambala Congo 59 B6

Djibouti *country* E Africa 54

Djibouti *capital of* Djibouti *var.*
Jibuti 54 D4

Dnieper *river* E Europe 63 F4

Dniester *river* Moldova/Ukraine
90 D3

Dnipropetrovs'k Ukraine 91 F3

Dobele Latvia *Ger.* Doblen
88 C3

Doberai, Jazirah *Peninsula*
Indonesia 121 G4

Doblen *see* Dobele

Doboj Bosnia & Herzegovina
82 C3

Dobrich Bulgaria 86 E1

Dodecanese *see* Dodekánisa

Dodekánisa *islands* Greece
Eng. Dodecanese 87 E6

Dodge City Kansas, USA 25 E5

Dodoma *capital of* Tanzania
55 C7

Doğu Karadeniz Dağları
mountains Turkey *var.*
Anadolu Dağları 99 E2

Doha *capital of* Qatar *Ar.* Ad
Dawḩah 103 C5

Dolisie Congo 59 B6

Dolomites *see* Dolomitiche,
Alpi

Dolomitiche, Alpi *mountains*
Italy *Eng.* Dolomites 78 C2

Dolores Argentina 46 C4

Dolores Hidalgo Mexico 33 E4

Dominica *country* West Indies
37

Dominican Republic *country*
West Indies 37

Don *river* Russian Federation
93 B6 96 A3

Donegal Bay *sea feature*
Ireland 71 A5

Donets *river* Russian
Federation/Ukraine 93 A6

Donets'k Ukraine 91 G3

Dongguan China 111 C6

Dongola Sudan 54 B3

Donostia *see* San Sebastián

Dordogne *river* France 73 B5

Dordrecht Netherlands 68 C4

Dorpat *see* Tartu

Dortmund Germany 76 B4

Dothan Alabama, USA 30 D3

Douai France 72 D3

Douala Cameroon 59 A5

Douglas UK 71 C5

Douglas Arizona, USA 28 C3

Dourados Brazil 44 C2

Douro *river* Portugal/Spain *Sp.*
Duero 74 C2

Dover England, UK 71 E7

Dover Delaware, USA 23 F4

Drakensberg *mountain range*
Lesotho/South Africa 60 D5

Drake Passage *sea feature*
Atlantic Ocean/Pacific Ocean
39 C8

Dráma Greece 86 C3

Drammen Norway 67 B6

Drau *river* C Europe *var.* Drava
77 D7 82 C3

Drava *river* C Europe *var.* Drau
81 C7

Drépano, Akrotírio *coastal
feature* Greece *var.*
Dhrepanón Ákra 86 C4

Dresden Germany 76 D4

Drina *river* Bosnia &
Herzegovina/Serbia 82 D4

Drobeta-Turnu Severin
Romania *prev.* Turnu Severin
90 B4

Dronning Maud Land *region*
Antarctica 137 B1

Druskieniki *see* Druskininkai

Druskininkai Lithuania *Pol.*
Druskieniki 89 B5

Dubayy United Arab Emirates
103 D5

Dubăsari Moldova 90 D3

Dubawnt *river* Canada 19 F4

Dubbo Australia 131 D6

Dublin *capital of* Ireland 71 B5

Dubrovnik Croatia 83 C5

Dubuque Iowa, USA 25 G3

Duero *river* Portugal/Spain
Port. Douro 74 D2

Dugi Otok *island* Croatia 82 A4

Duisburg Germany 76 A4

Dulan China 108 D4

Duluth Minnesota, USA 25 F2

Dumfries Scotland, UK 70 C4

Düna *see* Western Dvina

Dünaburg *see* Daugavpils

Dundalk Ireland 71 B5

Dundee Scotland, UK 70 D3

Dunedin New Zealand 133 B7

Dunkerque France *Eng.*
Dunkirk 72 C2

Dunkirk *see* Dunkerque

Duqm Oman 103 E6

Durango Mexico 32 D3

Durango Colorado, USA 24 C5

Durazno Uruguay 44 C5

Durban South Africa 60 E4

Durham North Carolina, USA
31 F1

Durrës Albania 83 C5

Dushanbe *capital of* Tajikistan *var.* Dyushambe, *prev.* Stalinabad 105 E3

Düsseldorf Germany 76 A4

Dutch Harbor Alaska, USA 18 B3

Dutch West Indies *see* Netherland Antilles

Dvinsk *see* Daugavpils

Dyushambe *see* Dushanbe

Dzaudzhikau *see* Vladikavkaz

Dzhalal-Abad Kyrgyzstan *Kir.* Jalal-Abad 105 F2

Dzhambul *see* Taraz

Dzhezkazgan *see* Zhezkazgan

Dzvina *see* Western Dvina

E

Eagle Pass Texas, USA 29 F4

East Cape *coastal feature* New Zealand 132 E2

East China Sea Pacific Ocean 111 E5

Easter Fracture Zone *tectonic feature* Pacific Ocean 135 G4

Easter Island *island* Pacific Ocean 135 F4

Eastern Ghats *mountain range* India 117 B5

Eastern Sierra Madre *see* Sierra Madre Oriental

East Falkland *island* Falkland Islands 47 D7

East Indiaman Ridge *undersea feature* Indian Ocean 23 D5

East Indies *island group* Asia 122 E4

Eastmain *river* Canada 20 D3

East Pacific Rise *undersea feature* Pacific Ocean 135 F4

East Siberian Sea *see* Vostochno-Sibirskoye More

East St Louis Illinois, USA 22 B4

East Timor *country* SE Asia 121

East Novaya Zemlya Trench *var.* Novaya Zemlya Trench. *Undersea feature* Kara Sea 137 H4

Eau Claire Wisconsin, USA 22 A2

Ebolowa Cameroon 59 B5

Ebro *river* Spain 75 F2

Ecuador *country* NW South America 40

Ede Netherlands 68 D3

Ede Nigeria 57 F4

Edgeøya *island* Svalbard 65 G2

Edinburgh Scotland, UK 70 C4

Edirne Turkey 98 A2

Edmonton Canada 19 E5

Edward, Lake *lake* Uganda/Dem. Rep. Congo 59 E6

Edwards Plateau *upland* S USA 29 F4

Efate *island* Vanuatu *prev.* Sandwich Island 122 D4

Effingham Illinois, USA 22 B4

Eforie-Sud Romania 90 D5

Egadi, Isole *island group* Italy 79 B6

Ege Denizi *see* Aegean Sea

Eger *see* Ohře

Egypt *country* NE Africa 54

Eighty Mile Beach *beach* Australia 128 C3

Eindhoven Netherlands 69 D5

Eisenstadt Austria 77 E6

Eivissa *see* Ibiza

Elat Israel 101 A7

Elazig Turkey 99 E3

Elba, Isola d' *island* Italy 78 B4

Elbasan Albania 83 D6

Elbe *river* Czech Republic/Germany 81 B5

Elbing *see* Elbląg

Elbląg Poland *Ger.* Elbing 80 D2

El'brus *peak* Russian Federation 93 A7

El Calafate Argentina *var.* Calafate 47 B7

Elche Spain *Cat.* Elx 75 F4

Elda Spain 75 F4

Eldoret Kenya 55 C6

Eleuthera *island* Bahamas 36 C1

El Fasher Sudan *var.* Al Fāshir 54 A4

El Geneina Sudan 54 A4

Elgin Scotland, UK 70 C3

El Giza Egypt *var.* Al Jīzah 54 B1

El Hank *cliff* Mauritania 56 D1

Elista Russian Federation 93 B6

El Khalîl *see* Hebron

El Khârga Egypt *var.* Al Khārijah 54 B2

Elko Nevada, USA 27 D5

Ellensburg Washington, USA 26 B2

Ellesmere Island *island* Canada 19 F1

Ellsworth Land *region* Antarctica 136 A3

El Minya Egypt 54 B2

Elmira New York, USA 23 E3

El Mreyyé *desert* Mauritania 56 D2

El Obeid Sudan 54 B4

El Paso Texas, USA 28 D3

El Puerto de Santa María Spain 74 D5

El Qâhira *see* Cairo

El Salvador *country* Central America 34

Eltanin Fracture Zone *tectonic feature* Pacific Ocean 135 E5

El Tigre Venezuela 41 E2

Elx *see* Elche

Ely Nevada USA 27 D5

Emden Germany 76 B3

Emerald Australia 130 D4

Emmen Netherlands 68 E2

Empty Quarter *see* Ar Rub' al Khali

Ems *river* Germany/Netherlands 76 B3

Encarnación Paraguay 44 C3

Enderbury Island *atoll* Kiribati 136 C2

Enderby Land *region* Antarctica 136 C2

French Guiana *external territory* France, N South America 11

French Polynesia *external territory* France, Pacific Ocean 135 E3

French Southern and Antarctic Territories *French overseas territory* Indian Ocean *Fr.* Terres Australes et Antarctiques Françaises 123 C7

Fresnillo Mexico 32 D1

Fresno California, USA 27 B6

Frome, Lake *salt lake* Australia 131 B5

Frunze *see* Bishkek

Fu-chien *see* Fujian

Fuerte Olimpo Paraguay 44 B1

Fuerteventura *island* Spain 52 A3

Fuhkien *see* Fujian

Fujian *province* China *var.* Fu-chien, Fuhkien, Fukien, Min 111 D6

Fukien *see* Fujian

Fukui Japan 113 C5

Fukuoka Japan 113 A6

Fukushima Japan 112 D4

Fulda Germany 77 C5

Fünfkirchen *see* Pécs

Fushun China 110 D3

Furnas, Represa de *Reservoir* Brazil 45 E1

Fuxin China 110 D3

Fujian China *prev.* Linchuan 111 D6

FYR Macedonia *see* Macedonia

G

Gaalkacyo Somalia 55 E5

Gabès Tunisia 53 E2

Gabon *country* W Africa 59

Gaborone *capital of* Botswana 60 D4

Gabrovo Bulgaria 86 D2

Gadsden Alabama, USA 30 D2

Gaeta, Golfo di *sea feature* Italy 79 C5

Gafsa Tunisia 53 E2

Gagnoa Côte d'Ivoire 56 D5

Gagra Georgia 99 E1

Gairdner, Lake *lake* Australia 131 B6

Galapagos Fracture Zone *tectonic feature* Pacific Ocean 135 F3

Galapagos Islands *islands* Ecuador, Pacific Ocean *var.* Tortoise Islands, *Sp.* Archipiélago de Colón 135 G3

Galapagos Rise *undersea feature* Pacific Ocean 135 G3

Galaţi Romania 90 D4

Galesburg Illinois, USA 22 B4

Galicia *region* Spain 74 C1

Galilee, Sea of *see* Tiberias, Lake

Galle Sri Lanka 115 E4

Gallego Rise *undersea feature* Pacific Ocean 135 F3

Gallipoli Italy 79 E5

Gällivare Sweden 66 D3

Gallup New Mexico, USA 28 C2

Galveston Texas, USA 29 G4

Galway Ireland 71 A5

Gambia *country* W Africa 56

Gambia *River* Africa 56 C3

Gambier, Îles *island group* French Polynesia 135 E4

Gan *see* Gansu

Gan *see* Jiangxi

Gäncä Azerbaijan *Rus.* Gyandzha, *prev.* Kirovabad, Yelisavetpol 99 G2

Gand *see* Gent

Gander Canada 21 H3

Gandia Spain 75 F3

Ganges *river* S Asia 116 F4

Ganges Fan *Undersea feature* Bay of Bengal 122 D3

Ganges, Mouths of the *wetlands* Bangladesh/India 117 G4

Gangtok India 117 G3

Gansu *province* China *var.* Gan, Kansu 111 B5

Gao Mali 57 E3

Gaoual Guinea 56 C4

Gar China 108 A4

Garagum Kanaly *canal* Turkmenistan *prev.* Karakumskiy Kanal 104 C3

Garagum *desert* Turkmenistan *var.* Kara Kum, Karakumy 104 C2

Garda, Lago di *lake* Italy 78 B2

Gardiz Afghanistan 105 E4

Garissa Kenya 55 C6

Garmo Peak *see* Communism Peak

Garonne *river* France 73 B5

Garoowe Somalia 55 E5

Garoua Cameroon 58 B4

Gary Indiana, USA 22 B3

Gaspé Canada 21 F4

Gastonia North Carolina, USA 31 E1

Gävle Sweden 67 C5

Gaya India 117 F4

Gaza Gaza Strip 101 A6

Gazandzhyk *see* Bereket

Gazanjyk *see* Bereket

Gaza Strip *disputed territory* SW Asia 101 A6

Gaziantep Turkey *prev.* Aintab 98 D4

Gazimağusa Cyprus *var.* Famagusta *Gk.* Ammochostos 98 C5

Gdańsk Poland *Ger.* Danzig 80 C2

Gdingen *see* Gdynia

Gdynia Poland *Ger.* Gdingen 80 C2

Gedaref Sudan 54 C4

Geelong Australia 131 C7

Gëkdepe *see* Gökdepe

Gemena Dem. Rep. Congo 59 C5

General Eugenio A. Garay Paraguay 44 A1

General Santos Philippines 121 F3

Geneva *see* Genève

Geneva, Lake *lake* France/Switzerland *Fr.* Lac Léman, *var.* Le Léman, *Ger.* Genfer See 77 A7

Genève Switzerland *Eng.* Geneva 77 A7

Genfer See *see* Geneva, Lake

Genhe China 109 F1

Genk Belgium 69 D5

Genoa *see* Genova

Genoa Italy *see* Genoa 78 B3

Genova Italy *Eng.* Genoa 78 B3

Genova, Golfo di *sea feature* Italy 78 B3

Gent Belgium *Fr.* Gand, *Eng.* Ghent 69 B5

Geok-Tepe *see* Gökdepe

George South Africa 60 D5

George V Land *physical region* Antarctica 136 C4

Georgenburg *see* Jurbarkas

George Town *capital of* Cayman Islands 36 B3

Georgetown *capital of* Guyana 41 G2

George Town Malaysia 120 B3

Georgia *country* SW Asia 99 F2

Georgia *state* USA 31 E3

Gera Germany 76 C4

Geraldton Australia 129 A5

Gereshk Afghanistan 104 D5

Germany *country* W Europe 76-77

Gerona *see* Girona

Getafe Spain 75 E3

Gettysburg Pennsylvania, USA 23 E4

Gevgelija Macedonia 83 E6

Ghana *country* W Africa 57

Ghanzi Botswana 60 C3

Ghardaïa Algeria 52 D2

Gharyān Libya 53 F2

Ghaznī Afghanistan 105 E4

Ghent *see* Gent

Gibraltar *external territory* UK, SW Europe 74 D5

Gibson Desert *desert region* Australia 128 C4

Gijón Spain *var.* Xixón 74 D1

Gilbert Islands *see* Tungaru

Gilbert River *river* Australia 130 C3

Gillette Wyoming, USA 24 C3

Gingin Australia 129 B6

Girin *see* Jilin

Girne Cyprus *var.* Kyrenia 98 C5

Girona Spain *var.* Gerona 75 G2

Gisborne New Zealand 132 E3

Giurgiu Romania 90 C5

Gjirokastër Albania 83 D6

Gjøvik Norway 67 B5

Glasgow Scotland, UK 70 C4

Gleiwitz *see* Gliwice

Glendale Arizona, USA 28 B2

Glendive Montana, USA 24 D2

Gliwice Poland *Ger.* Gleiwitz 81 C5

Gloucester England, UK 71 D6

Glubokoye *see* Hlybokaye

Gobi *desert* China/Mongolia 108 D3

Godāveri *river* India 106 B3 115 E1

Godoy Cruz Argentina 46 B4

Godthåb *see* Nuuk

Godwin Austin, Mount *see* K2

Goiânia Brazil 43 F4

Gökdepe Turkmenistan *prev.* Geok-Tepe, *prev.* Gëkdepe 104 B3

Golan Heights *disputed territory* SW Asia 100 B4

Gold Coast *coastal region* Australia 131 E5

Goldingen *see* Kuldīga

Golmud China 108 D4

Goma Dem. Rep. Congo 59 E6

Gomel' *see* Homyel'

Gómez Palacio Mexico 32 D2

Gonaïves Haiti 36 D3

Gonder Ethiopia 54 C4

Gongola *river* Nigeria 57 G4

Good Hope, Cape of *coastal feature* South Africa 60 C5

Goondiwindi Australia 131 D5

Goose Lake *lake* W USA 26 B4

Goré Chad 58 C4

Gorē Ethiopia 55 C5

Gore New Zealand 133 B7

Gorgān Iran 102 D3

Gorki *see* Horki

Gor'kiy *see* Nizhniy Novgorod

Gorlovka *see* Horlivka

Gorontalo Indonesia 121 E4

Gorzów Wielkopolski Poland *Ger.* Landsberg 80 B3

Gospić Croatia 82 B3

Gosford Australia 131 D6

Gostivar Macedonia 83 D5

Göteborg Sweden 67 B7

Gotel Mountains *mountain range* Nigeria 57 G4

Gotland *island* Sweden 67 C7

Gotō-rettō *island group* Japan 113 A6

Göttingen Germany 76 C4

Gouda Netherlands 68 C4

Gough Island *external territory* UK, Atlantic Ocean 49 D7

Gouin, Réservoir *Reservoir* Canada 20 D4

Gouré Niger 57 G3

Governador Valadares Brazil 43 G4 45 F1

Gozo *island* Malta 79 C7

Grafton Australia 131 E5

Grampian Mountains *mountains* Scotland, UK 70 C3

Granada Nicaragua 34 D3

Granada Spain 75 E4

Gran Canaria *island* Spain 52 A3

Gran Chaco *region* C South America 38 C4 44 A2 46 D2

Grand Bahama *island* Bahamas 36 C1

Grand Banks *undersea feature* Atlantic Ocean 48 B3

Grand Canyon *valley* SW USA 28 B1

Grande, Rio *river* Brazil 45 E1

Grande, Rio *River* Mexico/USA 17 B6

Grande Comore *island* Comoros 61 F2

Grande Prairie Canada 19 E4

Grand Erg Occidental *desert region* Algeria 52 D2

Grand Erg Oriental *desert region* Algeria/Tunisia 53 E3

Grand Falls Canada 21 G3

Grand Forks North Dakota, USA 25 E1

Grand Junction Colorado, USA 24 C4

Grand Rapids Michigan, USA 22 C3

Graudenz see Grudziądz

Graz Austria 77 E7

Great Abaco island Bahamas 36 C1

Great Ararat see Ararat, Mount

Great Australian Bight sea feature Australia 128 C5

Great Barrier Island island N NZ 132 D2

Great Barrier Reef coral reef Coral Sea 130 C4

Great Basin region USA 26 D4

Great Bear Lake lake Canada 19 E3

Great Dividing Range mountain range Australia 130-131

Great Exhibition Bay inlet New Zealand 132 C1

Great Wall of China ancient monument China 110 C4

Greater Antarctica region Antarctica 136 C3

Greater Antilles island group West Indies 36 C3

Great Exuma Island island Bahamas 36 C2

Great Falls Montana, USA 24 B1

Great Hungarian Plain plain SE Europe Hung. Alföld 81 D7

Great Inagua island Bahamas 36 D2

Great Khingan Range see Da Hinggan Ling

Great Lakes, The lakes N America see Erie, Huron, Michigan, Ontario, Superior 17 C5

Great Nicobar island India 115 H3

Great Plain of China region China 106 E2

Great Plains region N America 16-17 C5

Great Rift Valley valley E Africa/SW Asia 55 C6

Great Salt Desert see Kavīr, Dasht-e

Great Salt Lake salt lake Utah, USA 24 B3

Great Sand Sea desert region Egypt/Libya 53 H3

Great Sandy Desert desert Australia 128 C4

Great Sandy Desert see Ar Rub' al Khali

Great Slave Lake lake Canada 19 E4

Great Victoria Desert desert Australia 129 C5

Greece country SE Europe 86-87

Green Bay Wisconsin, USA 22 B2

Greenland external territory Denmark, Atlantic Ocean var. Grønland 64

Greenland Sea Atlantic Ocean 65 F2

Greenock Scotland, UK 70 C4

Greensboro North Carolina, USA 31 F1

Greenville South Carolina, USA 31 E2

Grenada country West Indies 37 G5

Grenoble France 73 D5

Greymouth New Zealand 133 B5

Grey Range mountain range Australia 130 C3

Grimsby England, UK 71 E5

Groningen Netherlands 68 E1

Grønland see Greenland

Groote Eylandt island Australia 130 B2

Grootfontein Namibia 60 C3

Grosseto Italy 78 B4

Grosskanizsa see Nagykanizsa

Groznyy Russian Federation 93 B7 96 A4

Grudziądz Poland Ger. Graudenz 80 C3

Grünberg in Schlesien see Zielona Góra

Guadalajara Mexico 32 D4

Guadalcanal island Solomon Islands 124 C3

Guadalquivir river Spain 74 D4

Guadeloupe external territory France, West Indies 37 G4

Guadiana river Portugal/Spain 74 C4

Gualeguaychú Argentina 46 D4

Guam external territory USA, Pacific Ocean 126 B1

Guanare Venezuela 40 D1

Guanare river Venezuela 40 D2

Guangdong province China var. Kuang-tung, Kwangtung, Yue 111 C6

Guangxi autonomous region China var. Kwangsi 111 B6

Guangzhou China Eng. Canton 111 C6

Guantánamo Cuba 36 D3

Guaporé River Bolivia/Brazil 32 D3

Guarapuava Brazil 44 D3

Guatemala country Central America 34

Guatemala undersea feature Pacific Ocean 135 G3

Guatemala City capital of Guatemala 34 B2

Guaviare river Colombia 40 D3

Guayaquil Ecuador 40 A4

Guayaquil, Golfo do sea feature Ecuador/Peru 40 A5

Guernsey island Channel Islands 71 D8

Güney Dogu Toroslar mountain range SE Turkey 99 F3

Guiana Highlands upland N South America 38 C2

Guider Cameroon 58 B4

Guimarães Portugal 74 C2

Guinea country W Africa 56

Guinea, Gulf of sea feature Atlantic Ocean 49 D5

Guinea-Bissau country W Africa 56

Guiyang China 111 B6

Guizhou *province* China *var.* Kuei-chou, Kweichow, Qian 111 B6

Gujarāt *state* India 116 C4

Gujrānwāla Pakistan116 C2

Gujrāt Pakistan 116 C2

Gulf, The *sea feature* Arabian Sea *var.* Persian Gulf 122 B2

Gulfport Mississippi, USA 30 C3

Gulu Uganda 55 B6

Gumbinnen *see* Gusev

Gunnbjørn Fjeld *mountain* Greenland 64 D4

Gurbantünggüt Shamo *desert* China 108 C2

Guri, Embalse de *Reservoir* Venezuela 41 E2

Gusau Nigeria 57 F3

Gusev Kaliningrad, Russian Federation *prev.* Gumbinnen 88 B4

Gushgy *see* Serhetabat

Guwāhāti India 117 G3

Guyana *country* NE South America 41

Gwalior India 116 D3

Gyandzha *see* Gäncä

Gyangzê China 108 C5

Győr Hungary *Ger.* Raab 81 C6

Gyumri Armenia *Rus.* Kumayri, *prev.* Leninakan, Aleksandropol' '99 F2

Gyzylarbat *see* Serdar

H

Ha'apai Group *islands* Tonga 127 F5

Haapsalu Estonia *Ger.* Hapsal 88 C2

Haarlem Netherlands 68 C3

Haast New Zealand 133 B6

Hachijō-jima *island* Japan 113 D5

Hachinohe Japan 112 D3

Hadejia *river* Nigeria 57 G3

Ḥaḍramawt *Mountain range* Yemen 103 C7

Hagåtña Guam 126 B1

Hague, The *see* 's-Gravenhage

Haicheng China 110 D4

Haifa Israel *Heb.* Ḥefa 85 G4

Ḥā'il Saudi Arabia 102 B4

Hailar China 109 F1

Hainan *island* China *var.* Hainan Dao 106 D3 111 C8

Hainan *province* China *var.* Qiong 111 C7

Hainan Dao *see* Hainan Dao

Hai Phong Vietnam 118 D3

Haiti *country* West Indies 36

Hajdarken *see* Khaydarkan

Hakodate Japan 112 D3

Ḥalab Syria 100 B2

Ḥalānīyāt, Juzur al *Island group* Oman 103 D6

Halden Norway 67 B6

Halfmoon Bay New Zealand 133 A7

Halifax Canada 21 F4

Halle Germany 76 C4

Hallein Austria 77 D7

Halls Creek Australia 128 D3

Halmahera, Pulau *island* Indonesia 121 F3

Halmahera Sea *Sea* Indonesia 121 F4

Halmstad Sweden 67 B7

Hamada Japan 113 B5

Hamadān Iran 102 C3

Ḥamāh Syria 100 B3

Hamamatsu Japan 113 C5

Hamar Norway 67 B5

Hamburg Germany 76 C3

Hämeenlinna Finland 67 D5

HaMelah, Yam *see* Dead Sea

Hamersley Range *mountain range* Australia 128 B4

Hamhŭng North Korea 110 E4

Hami China 108 C3

Hamilton Canada 20 D5

Hamilton New Zealand 132 D3

Hamm Germany 76 B4

Hammerfest Norway 66 D2

Handan China 110 C4

HaNegev *desert region* Israel *Eng.* Negev 101 A6

Hangayn Nuruu *mountain range* Mongolia 108 D2

Hangzhou China 111 D5

Hannover Germany *Eng.* Hanover 76 B4

Hanoi *capital of* Vietnam 118 D3

Hanover *see* Hannover

Hanzhong China 111 B5

Hapsal *see* Haapsalu

Ḥaraḍ Yemen 103 C5

Harare *capital of* Zimbabwe 61 E3

Harbin China 110 E3

Hargeysa Somalia 55 D5

Hari *river* Indonesia 120 B4

Harīrūd *river* C Asia 104 D4

Harper Liberia 56 D5

Harrisburg Pennsylvania, USA 23 E4

Harstad Norway 66 C2

Hartford Connecticut, USA 23 G3

Har Us Nuur *lake* Mongolia 108 C2

Hasselt Belgium 69 D5

Hastings New Zealand 132 E4

Hastings Nebraska, USA 24 E4

Hatay *see* Antakya

Hatteras, Cape *coastal feature* North Carolina, USA 31 G1

Hattiesburg Mississippi, USA 30 C3

Hat Yai Thailand 119 C7

Hauraki Gulf *gulf* New Zealand 132 D2

Havana *capital of* Cuba *Sp.* La Habana 36 B2

Havelock North Carolina, USA 31 G1

Havre Montana, USA 24 C1

Havre-Saint-Pierre Canada 21 F3

Hawaii *state* USA 135 E2

Hawaiian Islands *islands* USA 125 F1

Hawaiian Ridge *undersea feature* Pacific Ocean 134 D2

Hawera New Zealand 132 D4

Hawke Bay *bay* New Zealand 132 E4

Hawlēr *see* Arbil

Hawthorne Nevada, USA 27 C6

Hay River Canada 19 E4

Hays Kansas, USA 25 E4

Hazar Turkmenistan *prev.* Cheleken 104 A2

Heard & McDonald Islands *islands* Indian Ocean 123 C7

Hebei *province* China *var.* Hopeh, Hopei, Ji; *prev.* Chihli 110 C4

Hebron West Bank *var.* Al Khalīl, El Khalil, *Heb.* Hevron 101 D7

Heerenveen Netherlands 68 D2

Heerlen Netherlands 69 D6

Hefa Israel *prev.* Haifa 101 A5

Hefei China 111 D5

Hei *see* Heilongjiang

Heidelberg Germany 77 B5

Heilbronn Germany 77 B5

Heilongjiang *province* China *var.* Hei, Hei-lung-chiang 110 E3

Hei-lung-chiang *see* Heilongjiang

Helena Montana, USA 24 B2

Hells Canyon *valley* Idaho/Oregon USA 26 C3

Helmand *river* Afghanistan 104 C5

Helmond Netherlands 69 D5

Helsingborg Sweden 67 B7

Helsinki *capital of* Finland 67 D6

Henan *province* China *var.* Honan, Yu 111 C5

Hengduan Shan *mountain range* China 111 A6

Hengelo Netherlands 68 E3

Hengyang China 111 C6

Henzada Myanmar 118 A4

Herāt Afghanistan 104 C4

Hermansverk Norway 67 A5

Hermosillo Mexico 32 B2

Herning Denmark 67 A7

Heywood Islands *island group* Australia 128 C3

Hiiumaa *island* Estonia *Ger.* Dagden, *Swed.* Dagö 88 C2

Hildesheim Germany 76 C4

Hilversum Netherlands 68 C3

Himalayas *mountain range* S Asia 106 B2

Himora Ethiopia 54 C4

Ḥimṣ Syria 100 B3

Hinchinbrook Island *island* Australia 130 D3

Hindu Kush *mountain range* C Asia 105 E4

Hiroshima Japan 113 B5

Hitachi Japan 112 D4

Hjørring Denmark 67 A7

Hlybokaye Belarus *Rus.* Glubokoye 89 D5

Hobart Tasmania 131 C8

Hobbs New Mexico, USA 29 E3

Hô Chi Minh Vietnam *var.* Ho Chi Minh City, *prev.* Saigon 119 E6

Ho Chi Minh City *see* Hô Chi Minh

Hodeida *see* Al Ḥudaydah

Hoek van Holland Netherlands 68 B4

Hoggar *see* Ahaggar

Hohe Tauern *mountain range* Austria 77 C7

Hohhot China 109 F3

Hokitika New Zealand 133 B5

Hokkaidō *island* Japan 112 D2

Holguín Cuba 36 C2

Holland *see* Netherlands

Hollabrunn Austria 77 E6

Holon Israel 101 A5

Holyhead Wales, UK 71 C5

Hombori Mopti, Mali 57 E3

Homyel' Belarus *Rus.* Gomel' 89 E7

Honan *see* Henan

Honduras *country* Central America 34–35

Honduras, Gulf of *sea feature* Caribbean Sea 34 C2

Hønefoss Norway 67 B6

Hông Gai Vietnam 118 E3

Hong Kong China *var.* Xianggang 111 C6

Honiara *capital of* Solomon Islands 126 C3

Honshū *island* Japan 112 D3

Hoorn Netherlands 68 C2

Hopa Turkey 99 E2

Hopedale Canada 21 F2

Hopeh *see* Hebei

Hopei *see* Hebei

Hopkinsville Kentucky, USA 22 B5

Horki Belarus *Rus.* Gorki 89 E5

Horlivka Ukraine *Rus.* Gorlovka 90 G3

Horn, Cape *see* Hornos, Cabo

Hornos, Cabo *Eng* Cape Horn *coastal feature* Chile 47 C8

Horsham Australia 131 B7

Hospitalet *see* L'Hospitalet de Llobregat

Hot Springs Arkansas, USA 30 B2

Houston Texas, USA 29 G4

Hovd Mongolia 108 C2

Hövsgöl Nuur *lake* Mongolia 108 D1

Hradec Králové Czech Republic *Ger.* Königgrätz 81 B5

Hrodna Belarus *Rus.* Grodno 89 B5

Huacho Peru 42 A3

Huainan China 111 D5

Huambo Angola 60 B2

Huancayo Peru 42 B3

Huang He *river* China *Eng.* Yellow River 110 C4

Huánuco Peru 42 B3

Huaraz Peru 42 B3

Hubei *province* China 111 C5

Hubli India 114 C2

Hudson *river* NE USA 23 F3

Hudson Bay *sea feature* Canada 16 C4

Hudson Strait *sea feature* Canada 19 H3

Huê Vietnam 118 E4

Huehuetenango Guatemala 34 B2

Huelva Spain 74 C4
Huesca Spain 75 F2
Hughenden Australia 130 C4
Hull see Kingston upon Hull
Hulun Nur lake China 109 F1
Humboldt river W USA 27 C5
Hunan province China var. Xiang 111 C6
Hungarian Plain plain C Europe 85 E2
Hungary country C Europe 81
Huntington Beach California, USA 27 C8
Huntington West Virginia, USA 22 D5
Huntsville Alabama, USA 30 D2
Hurghada Egypt 54 B2
Huron, Lake lake Canada/USA 22 D2
Hurunui river New Zealand 133 C5
Húsavík Iceland 65 E4
Huvadhu Atoll island Maldives 114 C5
Hvar island Croatia 82 B4
Hyargas Nuur lake Mongolia 108 D2
Hyderābād India 114 D1 116 B3
Hyères, Îles d' islands France 73 D6

I

Iaşi Romania 90 D3
Ibadan Nigeria 57 F4
Ibagué Colombia 40 B3
Ibarra Ecuador 40 A4
Iberian Peninsula peninsula SW Europe 84 B3
Ibérico, Sistema Mountain range Spain 75 F2
Ibiza island Spain Cat. Eivissa 75 G4
Ica Peru 42 B4
İçel see Mersin
Iceland country Atlantic Ocean 65 E4
Idaho state USA 26

Idaho Falls Idaho, USA 26 E3
Idfu Egypt 54 B2
Idlib Syria 100 B2
Ieper Belgium Fr. Ypres 69 A6
Ifôghas, Adrar des upland Mali var. Adrar des Iforas 57 F2
Iforas, Adrar des see Ifôghas, Adrar des
Iglau see Jihlava
Iglesias Italy 79 A5
Iguaçu River Argentina/Brazil 44 C3
Iguîdi, 'Erg Desert Algeria/Mauritania 56 D1
Ihosy Madagascar 61 G4
Iisalmi Finland 66 E4
IJssel river Netherlands 68 D3
IJsselmeer lake Netherlands prev. Zuider Zee 68 D2
Ikaría island Greece 87 D5
Iki island Japan 113 A6
Ilagan Philippines 121 E1
Ilebo Dem. Rep. Congo 59 C6
Ili River China/Kazakhstan 94 D3
Ilhéus Brazil 43 F2
Iligan Philippines 121 F2
Illapel Chile 46 B3
Illinois state USA 22 B4
Iloilo Philippines 121 E2
Ilorin Nigeria 57 F4
Iluh see Batman
Imatra Finland 67 E5
Imperatriz Brazil 43 F2
Imperia Italy 78 A3
Impfondo Congo 59 C5
Imphāl India 117 H4
Independence Missouri, USA 25 F4
India country S Asia 114-115, 116-117
Indian Ocean 122-123
Indiana state USA 22 C4
Indianapolis Indiana, USA 22 C4
Indigirka river Russian Federation 95 F3
Indonesia country SE Asia 120-121
Indonesian Borneo see Kalimantan
Indore India 116 D4

Indus river S Asia 116 C1
Indus Cone see. Indus Fan
Indus Fan var. Indus Cone. Undersea feature Arabian Sea 122 B3
Indus, Mouths of the wetlands Pakistan 116 B4
Ingolstadt Germany 77 C6
Inguri see Enguri
Inhambane Mozambique 61 E4
Inn river C Europe 77 D6
Innaanganeq headland Greenland 64 C1
Inner Hebrides islands Seychelles 61 H1
Inner Mongolia autonomous region China 109 F3
Innsbruck Austria 77 C7
I-n-Sâkâne, Erg Desert Mali 57 E2
I-n-Salah Algeria 52 D3
Insein Myanmar 118 B4
Inukjuak Canada 20 D2
Inuvik Canada 19 E3
Invercargill New Zealand 133 A7
Investigator Ridge undersea feature Indian Ocean 122 D4
Ioánnina Greece 86 A4
Iónia Nisiá island group Greece Eng. Ionian Islands 87 A5
Ionian Islands see Iónia Nisiá
Ionian Sea Mediterranean Sea 87 A6
Íos island Greece 87 D6
Iowa state USA 25 F3
Ipoh Malaysia 120 B3
Ipswich England, UK 71 E6
Iqaluit Canada 19 H3
Iquique Chile 46 B1
Iquitos Peru 42 B2
Irákleio Greece 87 D7
Iran country SW Asia 102-103
Iranian Plateau upland Iran 102 D4
Irapuato Mexico 33 E4
Iraq country SW Asia 102

Irbid Jordan 101 B5

Ireland *country* W Europe 70-71

Irian Jaya *see* Papua

Irish Sea British Isles 71 C5

Irkutsk Russian Federation 97 E4

Iron Mountain Michigan, USA 22 B2

Ironwood Michigan, USA 22 B1

Irrawaddy *river* Myanmar 118 B2

Irrawaddy, Mouths of the *wetlands* Myanmar 118 A4

Irtysh *River* Asia 94 C3

Iruña *see* Pamplona

Ishim *River* Kazakhstan/Russian Federation 94 C3

Isiro Dem. Rep. Congo 59 E5

İskenderun Turkey *Eng.* Alexandretta 98 D4

Iskŭr *river* Bulgaria 86 C1

Iskŭr, Yazovir *Reservoir* Bulgaria 86 C2

Islay *island* Scotland, UK 70 B4

Islāmābād *capital of* Pakistan 116 C1

Ismaila *see* Ismā'īlīya

Ismā'īlīya Egypt *Eng.* Ismaila 54 B1

Isna Egypt 54 B2

Isparta Turkey 98 B4

Israel *country* SW Asia 100-101

Issyk-Kul, Ozero *lake* Kyrgyzstan 105 G2

İstanbul Turkey *var.* Stambul, *prev.* Constantinople, Byzantium, *Bul.* Tsarigrad 98 B2

İstanbul Boğazi *see* Bosporus

Itabuna Brazil 43 G4

Itagüí Colombia 40 B2

Italy *country* S Europe 78-79

Ittoqqortoormiit Greenland 65 E3

Iturup *island* Japan/Russian Federation (disputed) 112 E1

Ivanhoe Australia 131 C6

Ivano-Frankivs'k Ukraine 90 C2

Ivanovo Russian Federation 92 B4

Ivittuut Greenland 64 B4

Ivory Coast *see* Côte d'Ivoire

Ivujivik Canada 20 D1

Iwaki Japan 112 D4

Izabal, Lago de *lake* Guatemala 34 C2

Izhevsk Russian Federation 93 C5 96 B3

İzmir Turkey *prev.* Smyrna 98 A3

İzmit Turkey *var.* Kocaeli 98 B2

Izu-shotō *island group* Japan 113 D6

J

Jabal ash Shifā *desert* Saudi Arabia 102 A4

Jabalpur India 116 E4

Jackson Mississippi, USA 30 C2

Jacksonville Florida, USA 31 E3

Jacksonville Texas, USA 29 G3

Jacmel Haiti 36 D3

Jaén Spain 75 E4

Jaffna Sri Lanka 115 E3

Jagdaqi China 109 G1

Jiangxi *province* China 111 C6

Jaipur India 116 D3

Jajce Bosnia & Herzegovina 82 C4

Jakarta *capital of* Indonesia 120 C5

Jakobstad Finland 66 D4

Jakobstadt *see* Jēkabpils

Jalālābād Afghanistan 105 E4

Jalal-Abad *see* Dzhalal-Abad

Jalandhar India 116 D2

Jalapa *see* Xalapa

Jamaame Somalia 55 D6

Jamaica *country* West Indies 36

Jamālpur Bangladesh 117 G4

Jambi Indonesia 120 B4

James Bay *sea feature* Canada 20 C4

Jammu & Kashmir *disputed region* India/Pakistan 116 D2

Jāmnagar India 116 B4

Jan Mayen *external territory* Norway, Arctic Ocean 65 F3

Japan *country* E Asia 112-113

Japan, Sea of Pacific Ocean 112 B3

Jarvis Island *external territory* USA, Pacific Ocean 125 F2

Java *see* Jawa

Java Sea Pacific Ocean *var.* Laut Jawa 120 D4

Java Trench *undersea feature* Indian Ocean 122 D4

Jawa *island* Indonesia *var.* Java 120 C5

Jawa, Laut *see* Java Sea

Jayapura Indonesia 121 H4

Jaz Mūrīān, Hāmūn-e *lake* Iran 102 E4

Jedda *see* Jiddah

Jefferson City Missouri, USA 25 G4

Jēkabpils Latvia *Ger.* Jakobstadt 88 C4

Jelgava Latvia *Ger.* Mitau 88 C3

Jember Indonesia 120 D5

Jena Germany 76 C4

Jenin *var.* Janīn, Jinīn; *anc.* Engannim. West Bank 101 D6

Jérémie Haiti 36 D3

Jerevan *see* Yerevan

Jericho West Bank 101 B5

Jerid, Chott el *salt lake* Africa 84 D4

Jersey *island* Channel Islands 71 D8

Jerusalem *capital of* Israel 101 B5

Jhelum Pakistan 116 C2

Ji *see* Hebei

Ji *see* Jilin

Jiangsu *province* China *var.* Chiang-su, Kiangsu, Su 111 D5

Jiangxi *province* China *var.* Chiang-hsi, Gan, Kiangsi 111 C6

Jiaxing Zhejiang, China 111 D5

Jibuti *see* Djibouti

Jiddah Saudi Arabia *Eng.* Jedda 103 A5

Jiftlik Post West Bank 101 D7

Jihlava Czech Republic *Ger.*
Iglau 81 B5

Jilin *province* China *var.* Chi-lin,
Girin, Ji, Kirin 110 E3

Jilin China 110 E3

Jīma Ethiopia 55 C5

Jin *see* Shanxi

Jinan China 111 C4

Jingdezhen China 111 D5

Jinhua China 111 D5

Jining China 109 F3

Jinotega Nicaragua 34 D3

Jinsha Jiang *river* China 108 D5

Jinzhou China 110 D4

Jīzān Saudi Arabia 103 B6

João Pessoa Brazil 43 H3

Jodhpur India 116 C3

Joensuu Finland 67 E5

Johannesburg South Africa
60 D4

Johnston Atoll *US
unincorporated territory*
Pacific Ocean 125 E1

Johor Bahru Malaysia 120 C3

Joinville Brazil 44 D3

Joliet Illinois, USA 22 B3

Jönköping Sweden 67 B7

Jonquière Canada 21 E4

Jordan *country* SW Asia
100-101

Jordan *river* SW Asia 101 B5

Joseph Bonaparte Gulf *gulf*
Australia 128 D2

Jos Plateau *upland* Nigeria
57 G4

Juan Fernandez, Islas *islands*
Chile 46 A4

Juàzeiro Brazil 43 G3

Juàzeiro do Norte Brazil 43 G3

Juba Sudan 55 B5

Júcar *river* Spain 75 E3

Judenburg Austria 77 D7

Juigalpa Nicaragua 34 D3

Juiz de Fora Brazil 43 G5 45 F2

Juneau Alaska, USA 18 D4

Junín Argentina 46 D4

Jura *mountains*
France/Switzerland 77 A7

Jura *island* Scotland, UK 70 B4

Jurbarkas Lithuania *Ger.*
Jurburg, *var.* Georgenburg
88 B4

Jurburg *see* Jurbarkas

Juruá *river* Brazil/Peru 42 C2

Juticalpa Honduras 34 D2

Jutland *see* Jylland

Juventud, Isla de la *island*
Cuba 36 B2

Jylland *peninsula* Denmark
Eng. Jutland 67 A7

Jyväskylä Finland 67 D5

K

K2 *peak* China/Pakistan *Eng.*
Mount Godwin Austen 116 D1

Kaachka *see* Kaka

Kaakhka *see* Kaka

Kabale Uganda 55 B6

Kabinda Dem. Rep. Congo 59 D7

Kābol *see* Kabul

Kabul *capital of* Afghanistan
Per. Kābol 105 E4

Kachch, Gulf of *sea feature*
Arabian Sea 116 B4

Kachch, Rann of *wetland*
India/Pakistan *var.* Rann of
Kutch 116 B4

Kadugli Sudan 54 B4

Kaduna Nigeria 57 G4

Kaédi Mauritania 56 C3

Kâghet *Physical region*
Mauritania 56 D1

Kagoshima Japan 113 A6

Kahramanmaraş Turkey *var.*
Marash, Maraş 98 D4

Kai, Kepulauan *island group*
Indonesia 121 G4

Kaifeng China 111 C5

Kaikohe New Zealand 132 C2

Kaikoura New Zealand 133 C5

Kainji Reservoir *Reservoir*
Nigeria 57 F4

Kairouan Tunisia 53 E1

Kaiserslautern Germany
77 B5

Kaitaia New Zealand 132 C2

Kajaani Finland 66 E4

Kaka Turkmenistan *prev.*
Kaahka, *var.* Kaachka 104 C3

Kakhovka Ukraine 91 F4

Kakhovs'ka Vodoskhovyshche
Reservoir Ukraine 91 F3

Kalahari Desert *desert*
southern Africa 60 C4

Kalamariá Greece 86 C3

Kalámata Greece 87 B6

Kalāt Afghanistan 104 D5

Kalbarri Australia 129 A5

Kalemie Dem. Rep. Congo 59
E7

Kalgoorlie Australia 129 C6

Kalimantan *geopolitical region*
Indonesia *Eng.* Indonesian
Borneo 120 D4

Kaliningrad *external territory*
Russian Federation 96 A2

Kaliningrad Kaliningrad,
Russian Federation *prev.*
Königsberg 88 A4

Kalinkavichy Belarus *Rus.*
Kalinkovichi 89 D7

Kalinkovichi *see* Kalinkavichy

Kalisch *see* Kalisz

Kalispell Montana, USA 24 B1

Kalisz Poland *Ger.* Kalisch
80 C4

Kalmar Sweden 67 C7

Kalpeni Island *island* India
114 C3

Kama *river* Russian Federation
92 D4

Kamchatka *peninsula* Russian
Federation 97 H3

Kamchiya *river* Bulgaria 86 E2

Kamina Dem. Rep. Congo 59 D7

Kamishli *see* Al Qāmishlī

Kamloops Canada 19 E5

Kampala *capital of* Uganda
55 B6

Kâmpóng Cham Cambodia
119 D6

Kâmpóng Chhnăng Cambodia
119 D5

Kâmpóng Saôm Cambodia
119 D6

Kâmpôt Cambodia 119 D6

Kampuchea *see* Cambodia

Kam"yanets'-Podil's'kyy
Ukraine 90 C3

Kananga Dem. Rep. Congo 59 D7

Kanazawa Japan 112 C4

Kandahār Afghanistan *var.* Qandahār 104 D5

Kandi Benin 57 F4

Kanivs'ke Vodoskhovyshche *Reservoir* Ukraine 91 E2

Kandy Sri Lanka 115 E3

Kanestron, Ákra *see* Palioúri, Akrotírio

Kangaroo Island *island* Australia 131 B7

Kangertittivaq *region* Greenland 64 E3

Kangikajik *headland* Greenland 65 E4

Kanjiža Serbia 82 D2

Kankan Guinea 56 D4

Kano Nigeria 57 G4

Kānpur India *prev.* Cawnpore 117 E3

Kansas *state* USA 24-25

Kansas City Kansas, USA 25 F4

Kansas City Missouri, USA 25 F4

Kansk Russian Federation 97 E4

Kansu *see* Gansu

Kaohsiung Taiwan 111 D7

Kaolack Senegal 56 B3

Kapfenberg Austria 77 E7

Kaposvár Hungary 81 C7

Kapsukas *see* Marijampolė

Kapuas *river* Indonesia 120 D4

Kara-Balta Kyrgyzstan 105 F2

Karabük Turkey 98 C2

Karāchi Pakistan 116 B4

Karaganda Kazakhstan 96 C4

Karakol Kyrgyzstan *prev.* Przheval'sk 105 G2

Kara Kum *see* Garagum

Karakumskiy Kanal *see* Garagum Kanaly

Karakumy *see* Garagum

Karamay China 108 C2

Karamea Bight *gulf* New Zealand 133 C5

Karasburg Namibia 60 C4

Kara Sea *see* Karskoye More

Karditsa Greece 86 B4

Kariba, Lake *lake* Zambia/Zimbabwe 60 D3

Karimata, Selat *strait* Indonesia 120 C4

Karkinits'ka Zatoka *sea feature* Black Sea 91 E4

Karl-Marx-Stadt *see* Chemnitz

Karlovac Croatia 82 B3

Karlovy Vary Czech Republic *Ger.* Karlsbad 81 A5

Karlsbad *see* Karlovy Vary

Karlskrona Sweden 67 C7

Karlsruhe Germany 77 B5

Karlstad Sweden 67 B6

Karnātaka *state* India 114 C1

Kárpathos *island* Greece 87 E7

Kars Turkey 99 F2

Karshi Uzbekistan *prev.* Bek-Budi, *Uzb.* Qarshi 104 D3

Karskoye More Arctic Ocean *Eng.* Kara Sea 137 N3

Kasai *river* Dem. Rep. Congo 59 C6

Kasama Zambia 61 E2

Kaschau *see* Košice

Kāshān Iran 102 C3

Kashi China 108 A3

Kasongo Dem. Rep. Congo 59 E6

Kassa *see* Košice

Kassala Sudan 54 C4

Kassel Germany 76 B4

Kastamonu Turkey 98 C2

Katanning Australia 129 B6

Katerini Greece 86 B4

Katha Myanmar 118 B2

Katherine Australia 128 E2

Kathmandu *capital of* Nepal 117 F3

Katsina Nigeria 57 G3

Katowice Poland 81 C5

Kauen *see* Kaunas

Kaunas Lithuania *Ger.* Kauen, *Pol.* Kowno, *Rus.* Kovno 88 B4

Kavadarci Macedonia 82 E5

Kavála Greece 86 C3

Kavaratti Island *island* India 114 C3

Kavīr, Dasht-e *Salt pan* Iran 102 D3

Kawasaki Japan 113 D5

Kayan *river* Indonesia 120 D3

Kayes Mali 56 C3

Kayseri Turkey 98 D3

Kazakhstan *country* C Asia 96

Kazan' Russian Federation 96 B3

Kazandzhik *see* Bereket

Kazanlŭk Bulgaria 86 D2

Kecskemét Hungary 81 D7

Kediri Indonesia 120 D5

Keetmanshoop Namibia 60 C4

Kefallonía *island* Greece *Eng.* Cephalonia 87 A5

Keá *see* Tziá

Kelang *see* Klang

Kelmė Lithuania 88 B4

Kelowna Canada 19 E5

Kemerovo Russian Federation 96 D4

Kemi Finland 66 D4

Kemi *river* Finland 66 D3

Kemijärvi Finland 66 D3

Kendari Indonesia 121 E4

Këneurgench *see* Köneürgench

Kénitra Morocco 52 C2

Kennewick Washington, USA 26 C2

Kenora Canada 20 A3

Kentucky *state* USA 22 C5

Kenya *country* E Africa 55

Kerala *state* India 114 D3

Kerch Ukraine 91 G4

Kerguelen *island group* Indian Ocean 123 C7

Kerguelen Plateau *undersea feature* Indian Ocean 123 C7

Kerki *see* Atamyrat

Kérkira *see* Kérkyra

Kérkyra Greece 86 A4

Kérkyra *island* Greece *prev.* Kérkira, *Eng.* Corfu 86 A4

Kermadec Islands *island group* Pacific Ocean 125 E4

Kermadec Trench *undsea feature* Pacific Ocean 125 E4

Kermān Iran *var.* Kirman 102 D4

Kermānshāh Iran *prev.* Bākhtarān 102 C3

Kerulen *river* China/Mongolia 109 E2

Ketchikan Alaska, USA 18 D4

Key West Florida, USA 31 E5

Khabarovsk Russian Federation 97 G4

Khanka, Lake *lake* China/Russian Federation 110 E3

Khankendy *see* Xankändi

Kharkiv Ukraine *Rus.* Khar'kov 91 G2

Khar'kov *see* Kharkiv

Khartoum *capital of* Sudan *var.* Al Khurṭūm 54 B4

Khāsh Iran 102 E4

Khaskovo Bulgaria 86 D2

Khaydarkan Kyrgyzstan *var.* Khaydarken, Hajdarken 105 E2

Khaydarken *see* Khaydarkan

Kherson Ukraine 91 E4

Kheta *river* Russian Federation 94 D2

Khios *see* Chíos

Khirbet el 'Aujā et Tahtā West Bank 101 D6

Khmel 'nyts'kyy Ukraine 90 D2

Khodzhent *see* Khŭjand

Khojend *see* Khŭjand

Khokand *see* Qo'qon

Kholm Afghanistan 105 E3

Khon Kaen Thailand 118 C4

Khorog *see* Khorugh

Khorugh Tajikistan *Rus.* Khorog 105 F3

Khouribga Morocco 52 C2

Khudzhand *see* Khŭjand

Khŭjand Tajikistan *var.* Khodzhent, Khojend, *Rus.* Khudzhand *prev.* Leninabad 105 E2

Khulna Bangladesh 117 G4

Khvoy Iran 102 B3

Kiangsi *see* Jiangxi

Kiangsu *see* Jiangsu

Kičevo Macedonia 83 D5

Kiel Germany 76 C2

Kielce Poland 80 D4

Kiev *capital of* Ukraine *Ukr.* Kyyiv 91 E2

Kiffa Mauritania 56 C3

Kigali *capital of* Rwanda 55 B6

Kigoma Tanzania 55 B7

Kikládhes *see* Kyklades

Kikwit Dem. Rep. Congo 59 C6

Kilimanjaro *peak* Tanzania 55 C7

Kilkis Greece 86 B3

Killarney Ireland 71 A6

Kimberley South Africa 60 D4

Kimberley Plateau *upland* Australia 128 D3

Kindia Guinea 56 C4

Kindu Dem. Rep. Congo 59 D6

King Island *island* Australia 131 C7

Kingissepp *see* Kuressaare

Kingman Reef *external territory* USA, Pacific Ocean 125 F2

King Sound *sound* Australia 128 C3

Kingsport Tennessee, USA 31 E1

Kingsville Texas, USA 29 G5

Kingston Canada 20 C5

Kingston *capital of* Jamaica 36 C3

Kingston upon Hull England, UK *var.* Hull 71 E5

Kingstown St Vincent & The Grenadines 36 G4

King William Island *island* Canada 19 F3

Kinneret, Yam *see* Tiberius, Lake

Kinshasa *capital of* Dem. Rep. Congo *prev.* Léopoldville 59 B6

Kirghizia *see* Kyrgyzstan

Kiribati *country* Pacific Ocean 127

Kirin *see* Jilin

Kiritimati *island* Kiribati *var.* Christmas Island 127 G2

Kirkenes Norway 66 F2

Kirklareli Turkey 98 A2

Kirksville Missouri, USA 25 F4

Kirkūk Iraq 102 B3

Kirkwall Scotland, UK 70 C2

Kirman *see* Kermān

Kirov Russian Federation 92 C4 96 B3

Kirovabad *see* Gäncä

Kirovakan *see* Vanadzor

Kirovohrad Ukraine 91 E3

Kiruna Sweden 66 C3

Kisangani Dem. Rep. Congo *prev.* Stanleyville 59 D5

Kishinev *see* Chişinău

Kismaayo Somalia 55 D6

Kisumu Kenya 55 C6

Kitakyūshū Japan 113 A5

Kitami Japan 112 D2

Kitchener Canada 20 C5

Kitwe Zambia 60 D2

Kivu, Lake *lake* Rwanda/Dem. Rep. Congo 55 B6 59 E6

Kızıl Irmak *river* Turkey 98 C2

Kizyl-Arvat *see* Serdar

Kladno Czech Republic 81 A5

Klagenfurt Austria 77 D7

Klaipėda Lithuania *Ger.* Memel 88 B4

Klamath Falls Oregon, USA 26 B4

Klang Malaysia *var.* Kelang 120 B2

Ključ Bosnia & Herzegovina 82 B3

Knin Croatia 82 B4

Knoxville Tennessee, USA 31 E1

Knud Rasmussen Land *region* Greenland 64 D1

Kōbe Japan 113 C5

Koblenz Germany 77 B5

Kobryn Belarus 89 B6

Kocaeli *see* İzmit

Kočani Macedonia 83 E5

Kōchi Japan 113 B6

Kochi *see* Cochin

Kodiak Alaska, USA 18 C3

Kodiak Island *island* Alaska, USA 18 C3

Koedoes *see* Kudus

Kohīma India 117 H3
Kohtla-Järve Estonia 88 D2
Kokand *see* Qo'qon
Kokchetav Kazakhstan 96 C4
Kokkola Finland 66 D4
Koko Nor *see* Qinghai
Koko Nor *see* Qinghai Hu
Kokshaal-Tau *mountain range* Kyrgyzstan 105 G2
Kola Peninsula *see* Kol'skiy Poluostrov
Kolguyev, Ostrov *island* Russian Federation 92 D2
Kolhumadulu Atoll *island* Maldives 114 C5
Kolka Latvia 88 C3
Kolkata India *var.* Calcutta 117 F4
Köln Germany *Eng.* Cologne 76 B4
Kol'skiy Poluostrov *peninsula* Russian Federation *Eng.* Kola Peninsula 63 F1 92 C2
Kolwezi Dem. Rep. Congo 59 D8
Kolyma *river* Russian Federation 95 G2
Kommunizma, Pik *see* Communism Peak
Komoé *river* Côte d'Ivoire 57 E4
Komotini Greece 86 D3
Komsomol'sk-na-Amure Russian Federation 97 G4
Kondoz Afghanistan *var.* Kondūz, Kunduz, Qondūz 105 E3
Kondūz *see* Kondoz
Köneürgench Turkmenistan *prev.* Kunya-Urgench, *prev.* Këneurgench 104 C2
Kong Christian IX Land *region* Greenland 64 D4
Kong Christian X Land *region* Greenland 64 E3
Kong Frederik VI Kyst *region* Greenland 64 C4
Kong Frederik VIII Land *region* Greenland 64 E2
Kong Frederik IX Land *region* Greenland 64 C3

Kong Karls Land *island group* Svalbard 65 G2
Kong Oscar Fjord *fjord* Greenland 65 E3
Konia *see* Konya
Königgrätz *see* Hradec Králové
Königsberg *see* Kaliningrad
Konispol Albania 83 D7
Konjic Bosnia & Herzegovina 82 C4
Konya Turkey *prev.* Konia 98 C4
Kopaonik *mountains* Serbia 83 D4
Koper Slovenia 77 D8
Koprivnica Croatia 82 B2
Korçë Albania 83 D6
Korčula *island* Croatia 82 B4
Korea Bay *bay* China/North Korea 110 D4
Korea Strait *sea feature* Japan/South Korea 110-111 E5
Korinthiakós Kólpos *sea feature* Greece *Eng.* Gulf of Corinth 87 B5
Kórinthos Greece *Eng.* Corinth 87 B5
Kōriyama Japan 113 D4
Korla China 108 C3
Koror *see* Oreor
Korosten' Ukraine 90 D1
Kortrijk Belgium 69 A6
Kos *island* Greece 87 E6
Kosciusko, Mount *peak* Australia 131 D7
Košice Slovakia *Ger.* Kaschau, *Hung.* Kassa 81 D6
Köslin *see* Koszalin
Kosovo *province* Serbia 83 D5
Kosovska Mitrovica Serbia 82 D4
Kosrae *island* Micronesia 126 C2
Kossou, Lac de *lake* Côte d'Ivoire 56 D4
Kostanay Kazakhstan *var.* Kustanay 96 C4
Kostyantynivka Ukraine 91 G3
Koszalin Poland *Ger.* Köslin 80 B2

Kota India 116 D4
Kota Bharu Malaysia 120 B3
Kota Kinabalu Malaysia 120 D3
Kotka Finland 67 E5
Kotlas NW Russia 92 C4
Kotuy *river* Russian Federation 95 E2
Koudougou Burkina 57 E4
Kourou French Guiana 41 H2
Kousséri Cameroon 58 B3
Kouvola Finland 67 E5
Kovel' Ukraine 90 C1
Kovno *see* Kaunas
Kowno *see* Kaunas
Kozáni Greece 86 B4
Kozhikode *see* Calicut
Kra, Isthmus of *coastal feature* Myanmar/Thailand 119 B6
Kragujevac Serbia 82 D4
Krakau *see* Kraków
Kraków Poland *Eng.* Cracow, *Ger.* Krakau 81 D5
Kraljevo Serbia 82 D4
Kranj Slovenia 77 D7
Krasnodar Russian Federation 93 A6
Krasnovodsk *see* Türkmenbaşy
Krasnoyarsk Russian Federation 96 D4
Krasnyy Luch Ukraine 91 H3
Kremenchuk Ukraine 91 F2
Kremenchuts'ke Vodoskhovyshche *Reservoir* Ukraine 91 E2
Krems an der Donau Austria 77 E6
Kretinga Lithuania *Ger.* Krottingen 88 B3
Krichev *see* Krychaw
Krishna *river* India 114 C1
Kristiansand Norway 67 A6
Kristianstad Sweden 67 B7
Kriti *island* Greece *Eng.* Crete 87 C7
Kritikó Pélagos *see* Crete, Sea of
Krivoy Rog *see* Kryvyy Rih
Krk *island* Croatia 82 A3
Kroonstad South Africa 60 D4
Krottingen *see* Kretinga

Krung Thep see Bangkok
Kruševac Serbia 83 E4
Krušné Hory see Erzgebirge
Krychaw Belarus *Rus.* Krichev 89 E6
Kryms'kyy Pivostriv *peninsula* Ukraine *var.* Crimea 90 F4
Kryvyy Rih Ukraine *Rus.* Krivoy Rog 91 E3
Kuala Lumpur *capital of* Malaysia 120 B3
Kuala Terengganu Malaysia 120 B3
Kuang-tung see Guangdong
Kuantan Malaysia 120 C3
Kuba see Quba
Kuching Malaysia 120 C3
Kuçovë Albania *prev.* Qyteti Stalin 83 D6
Kudus Indonesia *prev.* Koedoes 120 D5
Kuei-chou see China Guizhou
Kugluktuk Canada *prev.* Coppermine 19 E3
Kuito Angola 60 C2
Kuji Tajikistan *Rus.* Kulyab 105 E3
Kulyab see Kŭlob
Kum see Qom
Kuma *river* Russian Federation 93 B7
Kumamoto Japan 113 B6
Kumanovo Macedonia 83 E5
Kumasi Ghana 57 E5
Kumayri see Gyumri
Kumo Nigeria 57 G4
Kumon Range *mountain range* Myanmar 118 B1
Kunashir *island* Japan/Russian Federation (disputed) 112 E1
Kunduz see Kondoz
Kunja-Urgenč see Köneürgench
Kunlun Mountains see Kunlun Shan
Kunlun Shan *mountain range* China *Eng.* Kunlun Mountains 106 B4

Kunming China 111 B6
Kununurra Australia 128 D3
Kupang Indonesia 120 E5
Kür see Kura
Kura *river* Azerbaijan/Georgia *Az.* Kür 99 G2
Kurashiki Japan 113 B5
Kurdistan *region* Turkey 99 F4
Küre Dağları *mountains* Turkey 98 C2
Kuressaare Estonia *prev.* Kingissepp, *Ger.* Arensburg 88 C2
Kurgan–Tyube see Qŭrghonteppa
Kurile Islands *islands* Pacific Ocean 112 E1
Kurile Trench *undersea feature* Pacific Ocean 134 C2
Kurnool India 114 D2
Kushiro Japan 112 E2
Kushka see Serhetabat
Kustanay see Kostanay
Kütahya Turkey *prev.* Kutaiah 98 B3
Kutaiah see Kütahya
K'ut'aisi Georgia 99 F2
Kutch, Rann of see Kachch, Rann of
Kuujjuaq Canada 21 E2
Kuujjuarapik Canada 20 D2
Kuusamo Finland 86 E3
Kuwait *country* SW Asia 102 C4
Kuwait City *capital of* Kuwait 102 C4
Kuytun China 108 C2
Kvitøya *island* Svalbard 65 G1
Kwangju South Korea 111 E4
Kwango *river* Dem. Rep. Congo 59 C7
Kwangtung see Guangdong
Kweichow see Guizhou
Kyklades *island group* Greece *prev.* Kikládhes, *Eng.* Cyclades 87 D6
Kyrenia see Girne
Kyrgyzstan *country* C Asia *var.* Kirghizia 105
Kýthira *island* Greece 87 B6

Kyushu-Palau Ridge *undersea feature* Pacific Ocean 124 B1
Kyyiv see Kiev
Kyyivs'ke Vodoskhovyshche *Reservoir* Ukraine 91 E1
Kyōto Japan 113 C5
Kyūshū *island* Japan 113 B6
Kyzylorda Kazakhstan 96 B5

--- L ---

Laâyoune Western Sahara 52 B3
Labé Guinea 56 C4
Laborca see Laborec
Laborec *river* Slovakia *Hung.* Laborca 81 E5
Labrador *region* Canada 21 F2
Labrador Sea Atlantic Ocean 64 B5
Laccadive Islands see Lakshadweep
La Ceiba Honduras 34 D2
Lachlan River *river* Australia 131 C6
La Coruña see A Coruña
La Crosse Wisconsin, USA 22 A2
Ladoga, Lake see Ladozhskoye Ozero
Ladozhskoye Ozero *lake* Russian Federation *Eng.* Lake Ladoga 92 B3
Ladysmith Wisconsin, USA 22 A2
Lae Papua New Guinea 126 B3
La Esperanza Honduras 34 C2
Lafayette Louisiana, USA 30 B3
Laghouat Algeria 52 D2
Lagos Nigeria 57 F5
Lagos Portugal 74 C4
Lagouira Western Sahara 52 A4
La Grande Oregon, USA 26 C3
La Habana see Havana
Lahore Pakistan 116 C2
Laï Chad 58 C4
Laila see Laylá
Lajes Brazil 44 D3
Lake Charles Louisiana, USA

Lake District *region* England, UK 71 C5

Lakewood Colorado, USA 24 D4

Lakshadweep *island group* India *Eng.* Laccadive Islands 114 B2

La Ligua Chile 46 B4

La Louvière Belgium 69 B6

Lambaré Paraguay 44 B3

Lambaréné Gabon 59 B6

Lamía Greece 86 B4

Lancaster England, UK 71 D5

Lancaster California, USA 27 C7

Lancaster Sound *sea feature* Canada 19 F2

Landsberg *see* Gorzów Wielkopolski

Land's End *coastal feature* England, UK 71 C7

Landshut Germany 77 D6

Lang Son Vietnam 118 D3

Länkäran Azerbaijan *Rus.* Lenkoran' 99 H3

Lansing Michigan, USA 22 C3

Lanzarote *island* Spain 52 B3

Lanzhou China 110 B4

Laon France 72 D3

La Oroya Peru 42 B3

Laos *country* SE Asia 118

La Palma *island* Spain 52 A3

La Paz *capital* of Bolivia 42 C4

La Paz Mexico 32 B3

La Pérouse Strait *sea feature* Japan 112 D1

Lapland *region* N Europe 66 C3

La Plata Argentina 46 D4

Lappeenranta Finland 67 E5

Laptev Sea *see* Laptevykh, More

Laptevykh, More Arctic Ocean *Eng.* Laptev Sea 97 F2

L'Aquila Italy 78 C4

Laramie Wyoming, USA 24 C4

Laredo Texas, USA 29 F5

La Rioja Argentina 46 C3

Lárisa Greece 86 B4

Lärkäna Pakistan 116 B3

Larnaca Cyprus *var.* Larnaka, Larnax 98 C5

Larnaka *see* Larnaca

Larnax *see* Larnaca

La Rochelle France 72 B4

La Roche-sur-Yon France 72 B4

La Romana Dominican Republic 36 E3

Las Cruces New Mexico, USA 28 D3

Las Piedras Uruguay 44 C5

La Serena Chile 46 B3

La Spezia Italy 78 B3

Las Tablas Panama 35 F5

Las Vegas Nevada, USA 27 D7

Latakia *see* Al Lādhiqīyah

Latvia *country* NE Europe 88

Launceston Tasmania 131 C8

Laurentian Basin *see* Canada Basin

Laurentian Mountains *upland* Canada 16 C4

Lausanne Switzerland 77 A7

Laut, Pulau *prev.* Laoet. *Island* Indonesia 120 D4

Laval France 72 B4

Lawton Oklahoma, USA 29 F2

Laylá Saudi Arabia 103 C5

Lazarev Sea *sea* Antarctica 136 B2

Lebanon *country* SW Asia 100–101

Lebu Chile 47 B5

Lecce Italy 79 E5

Leduc Canada 19 E5

Leeds England, UK 71 D5

Leeuwarden Netherlands 68 D1

Leeward Islands *see* Sotavento, Ilhas de

Lefkáda *island* Greece *prev.* Levkás 87 A5

Lefkoşa *see* Nicosia

Lefkosia *see* Nicosia

Legaspi *see* Legazpi City

Legazpi City Philippines *var.* Legaspi 120 E2

Legnica Poland *Ger.* Liegnitz 80 B4

Le Havre France 72 B3

Leicester England, UK 71 D6

Leiden Netherlands 68 C3

Leipzig Germany 76 D4

Lek *river* Netherlands 68 C4

Le Léman *see* Geneva, Lake

Lelystad Netherlands 68 D3

Léman, Lac *see* Geneva, Lake

Le Mans France 72 B4

Lemesos *see* Limassol

Lemnos *see* Límnos

Lena *river* Russian Federation 97 F3

Leninabad *see* Khŭjand

Leninakan *see* Gyumri

Leningrad *see* St Petersburg

Leninsk *see* Tŭrkmenabat

Lenkoran' *see* Länkäran

León Mexico 33 E4

León Nicaragua 34 C3

León Spain 74 D1

Léopoldville *see* Kinshasa

Lepel' *see* Lyepyel'

Le Puy France 73 C5

Lérida *see* Lleida

Lerwick Scotland, UK 70 D1

Lesbos *see* Lésvos

Leshan China 111 B5

Leskovac Serbia 82 E4

Lesotho *country* southern Africa 60

Lesser Antarctica *region* Antarctica 134 B3

Lesser Antilles *island group* West Indies 37 G4

Lésvos *island* Greece *Eng.* Lesbos 86 B4

Lethbridge Canada 19 E5

Leti, Kepulauan *island group* Indonesia 121 F5

Leuven Belgium 69 C6

Leverkusen Germany 76 A4

Levin New Zealand 132 D4

Levkás *see* Lefkáda

Lewis *island* Scotland, UK 70 B2

Lewiston Idaho, USA 26 C2

Lewiston Maine, USA 23 G2

Lexington Kentucky, USA 22 C5

Lower California *see* Baja California

Lower Hutt New Zealand

Loxa *see* Loksa

Loyauté, Îles *island group* New Caledonia 126 D5

Loznica Serbia 82 C3

Lu *see* Shandong

Luanda *capital of* Angola 60 B1

Luanshya Zambia 60 D2

Lubango Angola 60 B2

Lubbock Texas, USA 29 E2

Lübeck Germany 76 C3

Lublin Poland *Rus.* Lyublin 80 E4

Lubny Ukraine 91 F2

Lubumbashi Dem. Rep. Congo 59 E8

Lucapa Angola 60 C1

Lucena Philippines 120 E2

Lučenec Slovakia *Hung.* Losonc, *Ger.* Losontz 81 D6

Lucerne *see* Luzern

Lucknow India 117 E3

Lüderitz Namibia 60 C4

Ludhiāna India 116 D2

Lugano Switzerland 77 B7

Lugo Spain 74 C1

Luhans'k Ukraine 91 H3

Luleå Sweden 66 D4

Lumsden New Zealand 133 A7

Lüneburg Germany 76 C3

Luninyets Belarus 89 C6

Luoyang *var.* Honan, Lo-yang. China 110 C4

Lusaka *capital of* Zambia 60 D2.

Lushnjë Albania 83 D6

Lüt, Baḥrat *see* Dead Sea

Luts'k Ukraine 90 C1

Luxembourg *country* W Europe 69 D8

Luxembourg *capital of* Luxembourg 69 D8

Luxor Egypt 54 B2

Luzern Switzerland *Fr.* Lucerne 77 B7

Luzon *island* Philippines 121 E1

Luzon Strait *sea feature* Philippines/Taiwan 107 E3

L'viv Ukraine *Rus.* L'vov 90 C2

L'vov *see* L'viv

Lyepyel' Belarus *Rus.* Lepel' 89 D5

Lyon France 73 D5

Lyublin *see* Lublin

M

Ma'ān Jordan 101 B6

Maas *see* Meuse

Maastricht Netherlands 69 D6

Macao *external territory* Portugal, E Asia *var.* Macau 111 C7

Macapá Brazil 43 F1

Macau *see* Macao

Macdonnell Ranges *mountains* Australia 130 A4

Macedonia *country* SE Europe officially Former Yugoslav Republic of Macedonia, *abbrev.* FYR Macedonia 83

Maceió Brazil 43 H3

Machala Ecuador 40 A5

Mackay Australia 130 D4

Mackay, Lake *lake* Australia 128 D4

Mackenzie *river* Canada 19 E4

Mackenzie Bay *sea feature* Atlantic Ocean 136 D3

Macleod, Lake *lake* Australia 128 A4

Mâcon France 72 D5

Macon Georgia, USA 31 E2

Madagascar *country* Indian Ocean 61

Madagascar Basin *undersea feature* Indian Ocean 123 B5

Madagascar Plateau *undersea feature* Indian Ocean 123 A6

Madang Papua New Guinea 126 B3

Madeira *river* Bolivia/Brazil 42 D2

Madeira *island group* Portugal 52 A2

Madhya Pradesh *state* India 117 E4

Madison Wisconsin, USA 22 B3

Madiun *prev.* Madioen. Indonesia 120 D5

Madona Latvia *Ger.* Modohn 88 D3

Madras *see* Chennai

Madre de Dios *river* Bolivia/Peru 42 C3

Madrid *capital of* Spain 75 E3

Madurai India 114 D3

Magadan Russian Federation 97 G3

Magallanes *see* Punta Arenas

Magallanes, Estrecho de *see* Magellan, Strait of

Magdalena *river* Colombia 40 B2

Magdeburg Germany 76 C4

Magelang Indonesia 120 C5

Magellan, Strait of *sea feature* S South America *Sp.* Estrecho de Magallanes 47 B8

Maggiore, Lake *lake* Italy/Switzerland 78 B2

Mahajanga Madagascar 61 G3

Mahalapye Botswana 60 D4

Mahanādi *river* India 117 F5

Mahārāshtra *state* India 116 D5

Mahé *island* Seychelles 61 H1

Mahilyow Belarus *Rus.* Mogilëv 89 E6

Mährisch-Ostrau *see* Ostrava

Maicao Colombia 40 C1

Maiduguri Nigeria 57 H4

Maimana *see* Meymaneh

Maine *state* USA 23 G1

Maine, Gulf of *gulf* USA 23 G2

Mainz Germany 77 B5

Maio *island* Cape Verde 56 A3

Maíz, Islas del *islands* Nicaragua 35 E3

Majorca *see* Mallorca

Majuro *island* Marshall Islands 126 D1

Makarska Croatia 82 B4

Makarov Basin *undersea feature* Arctic Ocean 137 G3

Makassar Indonesia *prev.* Ujungpandang 121 E4

Makassar Strait *strait* Indonesia 120 D4

Makeyevka *see* Makiyivka

Makhachkala Russian Federation 93 B7 96 A4

Makiyivka Ukraine *Rus.* Makeyevka 91 G5

Makkah Saudi Arabia *Eng.* Mecca 103 A5

Makkovik Canada 21 F2

Malabo *capital of* Equatorial Guinea 59 A5

Malacca, Strait of *sea feature* Indonesia/ Malaysia 106 C4 119 C8 120 B3

Maladzyechna Belarus *Rus.* Molodechno, *Pol.* Molodezno 89 D5

Málaga Spain 74 D5

Malakal Sudan 55 B5

Malang Indonesia 120 D5

Malanje Angola 60 C2

Malatya Turkey 99 E3

Malawi *country* southern Africa 61

Malay Peninsula *peninsula* Malaysia/Thailand 119 D8

Malaysia *country* Asia 120

Malden Island *atoll* Kiribati 125 F2

Maldives *country* Indian Ocean 114 C4

Male' *capital of* Maldives 114 C4

Malekula *island* Vanuatu 124 D3

Mali *country* W Africa 57

Malindi Kenya 55 C7

Mallorca *island* Spain *Eng.* Majorca 75 H3

Malmö Sweden 67 B7

Malta *country* Mediterranean Sea 79 C8

Malta Montana, USA 24 C1

Malta Channel *sea feature* Mediterranean Sea 79 C7

Maluku *island group* Indonesia *var.* Moluccas 107 E4 121 F4

Maluku, Laut Pacific Ocean *Eng.* Molucca Sea 121 F4

Mamberamo *river* Indonesia 121 H4

Mamoudzou *capital of* Mayotte 61 G2

Man, Isle of *island* UK 71 C5

Manado Indonesia 121 F3

Managua *capital of* Nicaragua 34 D3

Manama *capital of* Bahrain *Ar.* Al Manāmah 103 C5

Mananjary Madagascar 61 G3

Manaus Brazil 42 D2

Manchester England, UK 71 D5

Manchester New Hampshire, USA 23 G2

Manchurian Plain *plain* E Asia 107 E1

Mandalay Myanmar 118 B3

Mangalia Romania 90 D5

Mangalore India 114 C2

Manicouagan, Réservoir *Reservoir* Canada 21 E3

Manihiki *atoll* Cook Islands 125 F3

Maniitsoq Greenland 64 C3

Manila *capital of* Philippines 121 E1

Manisa Turkey *prev.* Saruhan 98 A3

Manitoba *province* Canada 19 G4

Manizales Colombia 40 B3

Manjimup Australia 129 B7

Mannar Sri Lanka 115 E3

Mannar, Gulf of *sea feature* Indian Ocean 114 D3

Mannheim Germany 77 B5

Manono Dem. Rep. Congo 59 E7

Mansel Island *island* Canada 20 C1

Mansfield Ohio, USA 22 D4

Manta Ecuador 40 A4

Mantes-la-Jolie France 72 C3

Mantova Italy *Eng.* Mantua 78 B2

Mantua *see* Mantova

Manurewa New Zealand 132 D3

Manzhouli China 109 F1

Mao Chad 58 B3

Maoke, Pegunungan *mountains* Indonesia 121 H4

Maputo *capital of* Mozambique 61 E4

Mar, Serra do *mountains* Brazil 38 D4

Maracaibo Venezuela 40 C1

Maracaibo, Lago de *inlet* Venezuela 40 C1

Maracay Venezuela 40 D1

Maradi Niger 57 F3

Marāgheh Iran 102 C3

Marajó, Ilha de *island* Brazil 43 F2

Marañón *river* Peru 42 B2

Maraş *see* Kahramanmaraş

Marash *see* Kahramanmaraş

Marbella Spain 74 D5

Marble Bar Australia 128 B4

Mar Chiquita, Laguna *salt lake* Argentina 46 C3

Mardān Pakistan 116 C1

Mar del Plata Argentina 47 D5

Mardin Turkey 99 E4

Margarita, Isla de *island* Venezuela 41 E1

Mārgow, Dasht-e- *desert* Afghanistan 104 C5

Mariana Trench *undersea feature* Pacific Ocean 124 B1 126 B1

Marías, Islas *islands* Mexico 32 C4

Maribor Slovenia 77 E7

Marie Byrd Land *region* Antarctica 136 B4

Mariehamn Finland 67 D6

Marijampolė Lithuania *prev.* Kapsukas 88 B4

Marília Brazil 44 D2

Maringá Brazil 44 D2

Marion, Lake *lake* South Carolina, USA 31 F2

Mariscal Estigarribia Paraguay 44 B2

Maritsa *river* SE Europe 86 D3

Mariupol' Ukraine *prev.*
Shdanov 91 G3

Marka Somalia 55 D6

Marmara, Sea of *see* Marmara
Denizi

Marmara Denizi Turkey *Eng.*
Sea of Marmara 98 B2

Marne *river* France 72 D3

Marotiri *Island group* French
Polynesia 125 F4

Maroua Cameroon 58 B3

Marowijne *river* French
Guiana/Suriname 41 H3

Marquesas Fracture Zone
tectonic feature Pacific Ocean
125 G3

Marquesas Islands *island group*
French Polynesia *Fr.* Îles
Marquises 125 G3

Marquette Michigan, USA
22 B1

Marquisas, Îles *see* Marquesas
Islands

Marrakech Morocco *Eng.*
Marrakesh 52 C2

Marrawah Australia 131 C8

Marree Australia 131 B5

Marsala Italy 79 C6

Marseille France 73 D6

Marshall Islands *country* Pacific
Ocean 126-127

Martin Slovakia *prev.*
Turčiansky Svätý Martin, *Ger.*
Sankt Martin, *Hung.*
Turócszentmárton 81 C5

Martinique *external territory*
France, West Indies 37

Mary Turkmenistan *prev.* Merv
104 C3

Maryborough Australia 131 E5

Maryland *state* USA 23 F4

Masai Steppe *grassland*
Tanzania 55 C7

Mascarene Basin *undersea
feature* Indian Ocean 123 B5

Mascarene Islands *island group*
Indian Ocean 61 H4

Mascarene Plain *undersea
feature* Indian Ocean 123 B5

Mascarene Plateau *undersea
feature* Indian Ocean 123 B5

Maseru *capital of* Lesotho
60 D4

Mas-ha Bank 101 D6

Mashhad Iran *var.* Meshed 100
E3

Masindi Uganda 55 B6

Maṣīra, Jazirat *Island* Oman
103 E6

Maṣīrah, Khalīj *bay* Oman
103 E6

Mason City Iowa, USA 25 F3

Masqaṭ *see* Muscat

Massachusetts *state* USA
23 G3

Massawa Eritrea 54 C4

Massif Central *upland* France
73 C5

Massoukou Gabon 59 B6

Masterton New Zealand
133 D5

Matadi Dem. Rep. Congo 59 B7

Matagalpa Nicaragua 34 D3

Matamoros Mexico 33 E2

Matanzas Cuba 36 B2

Matara Sri Lanka 115 E4

Mataram Indonesia 120 D5

Mataró Spain 75 G2

Mato Grosso *upland* Brazil
43 E3

Matosinhos Portugal 74 C2

Matsue Japan 113 B5

Matsuyama Japan 113 B5

Matterhorn *peak*
Italy/Switzerland 77 B7

Maturín Venezuela 41 E1

Maun Botswana 60 D3

Mauritania *country* W Africa 56

Mauritius *country* Indian
Ocean 61 H4 123 B5

Mayaguana *island* Bahamas
36 D2

Mayfield New Zealand 133 C6

Mayotte *external territory*
France, Indian Ocean 61 G2

Mayyit, Al Baḥr al *see* Dead Sea

Mazār-e Sharif Afghanistan
104 D3

Mazatlán Mexico 32 C3

Mažeikiai Lithuania 88 B3

Mazury *region* Poland 80 D3

Mazyr Belarus *Rus.* Mozyr'
89 D7

Mbabane *capital of* Swaziland
61 E4

Mbaké Senegal 56 B3

Mbala Zambia 61 E1

Mbale Uganda 55 C6

Mbandaka Dem. Rep. Congo
59 C5

Mbeya Tanzania 55 B8

Mbuji-Mayi Dem. Rep. Congo
59 D7

McKinley, Mount *peak* Alaska,
USA *var.* Denali 18 C3

Mead, Lake *lake* SW USA
28 A1

Mecca *see* Makkah

Mechelen Belgium 69 C5

Mecklenburger Bucht *bay*
Germany 76 C2

Medan Indonesia 120 B3

Medellín Colombia 40 B2

Médenine Tunisia 53 F2

Medford Oregon, USA 26 A4

Medina *see* Al Madīnah

Mediterranean Sea Atlantic
Ocean 84-85

Meekatharra Australia 129 B5

Meerut India 116 D3

Megísti *island* Greece 98 B4

Mek'elē Ethiopia 54 C4

Mekong *river* SE Asia 106 D3

Mekong, Mouths of the
wetlands Vietnam 119 D6

Melanesia *region* Pacific Ocean
126 C3

Melanesian Basin *undersea
feature* Pacific Ocean 134 C3

Melbourne Australia 131 C7

Melbourne Florida, USA 31 F4

Melghir, Chott *Salt lake* Algeria
53 E2

Melilla *external territory* Spain,
N Africa 52 C1

Melitopol' Ukraine 91 F4

Melo Uruguay 44 C4

Melville Island *island* Australia
128 E2

Melville Island *island* Canada 19 E2

Memel *see* Klaipėda

Memel *see* Neman

Memphis Tennessee, USA 30 C1

Mendaña Fracture Zone *tectonic feature* Pacific Ocean 135 G3

Mende France 73 C6

Mendeleyev Ridge *undersea feature* Arctic Ocean 137 G2

Mendocino Fracture Zone *tectonic feature* Pacific Ocean 134 D2

Mendoza Argentina 46 B4

Menengiyn Tal *plain* Mongolia 109 F2

Menongue Angola 60 C2

Menorca *island* Spain *Eng.* Minorca 75 H3

Metairie Louisiana, USA 30 C3

Mentawai, Kepulauan *island group* Indonesia 120 B4

Meppel Netherlands 68 D2

Merced California, USA 27 B6

Mercedes Uruguay 44 B5

Mergui Myanmar 119 B5

Mergui Archipelago *island chain* Myanmar 119 B6

Mérida Mexico 33 H3

Mérida Spain 74 D3

Mérida Venezuela 40 C2

Meridian Mississippi, USA 30 C2

Merredin Australia 129 B6

Mersin Turkey *var.* İçel 98 C4

Meru Kenya 55 C6

Merv *see* Mary

Mesa Arizona, USA 28 B2

Meshed *see* Mashhad

Messina Italy 79 D6

Messina, Stretto di *sea feature* Ionian Sea/Tyrrhenian Sea 79 D7

Mestre Italy 78 C2

Meta *river* Colombia/Venezuela 40 C2

Metković Croatia 82 C4

Metz France 72 E3

Meuse *river* W Europe *var.* Maas 72 D3

Mexicali Mexico 32 A1

Mexico *country* North America 32-33

México, Golfo de *see* Mexico, Gulf of

Mexico, Gulf of *sea feature* Atlantic Ocean/Caribbean Sea 48 A4

Mexico City *capital of* Mexico *Sp.* Ciudad de México 33 E4

Meymaneh Afghanistan *var.* Maimana 104 D4

Mezen' *river* Russian Federation 92 D3

Miami Florida, USA 31 F5

Miami Beach Florida, USA 31 F5

Mianyang China 111 B5

Michigan *state* USA 22 C2

Michigan, Lake *lake* USA 17 C5

Micronesia *country* Pacific Ocean 126 B2

Micronesia *region* Pacific Ocean 126

Mid Atlantic Ridge *undersea feature* Atlantic Ocean 48 B4

Middelburg South Africa 60 D5

Middle Andaman *island* India 115 G2

Middlesbrough England, UK 71 D5

Mid-Indian Basin *undersea feature* Indian Ocean 122 C4

Mid-Indian Ridge *undersea feature* Indian Ocean 123 C5

Midland Texas, USA 29 E3

Mid-Pacific Mountains *var.* Mid-Pacific Seamounts. *Undersea feature* Pacific Ocean 124 C1

Mid-Pacific Seamounts *see* Mid-Pacific Mountains

Midway Islands *US territory* Pacific Ocean 134 D2

Mikhaylovka Russian Federation 93 B6

Milagro Ecuador 40 A4

Milan *see* Milano

Milano Italy *Eng.* Milan 78 B2

Mildura Australia 131 C6

Millennium Island *island* Kiribati *prev.* Caroline Island 127 H3

Miles Australia 131 D5

Miles City Montana, USA 24 C2

Milford Haven Wales, UK 71 C6

Milford Sound New Zealand 133 E6

Milford Sound *inlet* New Zealand 133 A6

Milos *island* Greece 87 B6

Milwaukee Wisconsin, USA 22 B3

Min *see* Fujian

Minatitlán Mexico 33 G4

Minch, The *Strait* Scotland, UK 70 C3

Mindanao *island* Philippines 121 F2

Mindoro *island* Philippines 121 E2

Mindoro Strait *sea feature* South China Sea/Sulu Sea 121 E2

Mingäçevir Azerbaijan *Rus.* Mingechaur 99 G2

Mingechaur *see* Mingäçevir

Minho *river* Portugal/Spain *Sp.* Miño 74 C2

Minicoy Island *island* India 114 C3

Minneapolis Minnesota, USA 23 F2

Minnesota *state* USA 25 F2

Miño *river* Portugal/Spain *Port.* Minho 74 C1

Minorca *see* Menorca

Minot North Dakota, USA 24 D1

Minā' Qābūs Oman 122 B3

Minsk *capital of* Belarus 89 C5

Minto, Lake *lake* Canada 20 D2

Miranda de Ebro Spain 75 E1

Mirim, Lake *see* Mirim Lagoon

Mirim Lagoon *lagoon* Brazil/Uruguay *var.* Mirim, Lake 44 C5

Mirtóo Pelagos *sea feature* Mediterranean Sea 87 C6

Miskitos Cayos *islands* Nicaragua 35 E2

Miskolc Hungary 81 D6

Mişrātah Libya 53 F2
Mississippi *state* USA 30 C2
Mississippi *river* USA 16 C5
Mississippi Delta *wetlands* USA 30 C4
Missoula Montana, USA 24 B2
Missouri *state* USA 25 G4
Missouri *river* USA 17 C5
Mistassini, Lake *lake* Canada 20 D3
Mitau *see* Jelgava
Mitchell S Dakota, USA 25 E3
Mitchell River *river* Australia 130 C3
Mitilíni Greece 86 D4
Mito Japan 112 D4
Mitumba, Monts *Mountain range* Dem. Rep. Congo 59 E7
Miyazaki Japan 113 B6
Mjøsa *lake* Norway 67 B5
Mljet *island* Croatia 83 C5
Mmabatho South Africa 60 D4
Mo Norway 66 C3
Mobile Alabama, USA 30 C3
Moçambique Mozambique 61 F2
Mocímboa da Praia Mozambique 61 F2
Mocoa Colombia 40 B4
Mocuba Mozambique 61 F2
Modena Italy 78 B3
Modesto California, USA 27 B6
Modohn *see* Madona
Modriča Bosnia & Herzegovina 82 C3
Mogadiscio *see* Mogadishu
Mogadishu *capital of* Somalia *Som.* Muqdisho, *It.* Mogadiscio 55 D6
Mogilëv *see* Mahilyow
Mohéli *island* Comoros 61 F2
Mo i Rana Norway 66 C3
Mojave California, USA 27 C7
Mojave Desert *desert* W USA 27 C7
Moldavia *see* Moldova
Molde Norway 67 A5
Moldova *country* E Europe *var.* Moldavia 90

Molodechno *see* Maladzyechna
Molodeczno *see* Maladzyechna
Molotov *see* Perm
Moluccas *see* Maluku
Molucca Sea *see* Maluku, Laut
Mombasa Kenya 55 C7
Monaco *country* W Europe 73 E6
Monclova Mexico 33 E2
Moncton Canada 21 F4
Mongo Chad 58 C3
Mongolia *country* NE Asia 108-109
Monroe Louisiana, USA 30 B2
Monrovia *capital of* Liberia 56 C5
Mons Belgium 69 B6
Montague Seamount *undersea feature* Atlantic Ocean 45 H1
Montana *state* USA 24 C2
Montauban France 73 C6
Mont Blanc *peak* France/Italy 62 D4
Mont-de-Marsan France 72 B6
Monte Cristi Dominican Republic 37 E3
Montego Bay Jamaica 36 C3
Montenegro *Country* SE Europe 83 D5
Monterey California, USA 27 B6
Montería Colombia 40 B2
Montero Bolivia 42 D4
Monterrey Mexico 33 E2
Montes Claros Brazil 43 G4
Montevideo *capital of* Uruguay 44 C5
Montgomery Alabama, USA 30 D2
Monthey Switzerland 77 A7
Montpelier Vermont, USA 23 F2
Montpellier France 73 C6
Montréal Canada 21 E4
Montserrat *external territory* UK, West Indies 37
Monywa Myanmar 118 A3
Monza Italy 78 B2
Moora Australia 129 B6

Moore, Lake *lake* Australia 129 B6
Moorhead Minnesota, USA 25 E2
Moosonee Canada 20 C3
Mopti Mali 57 E3
Morava *river* C Europe 82 E4
Moravská Ostrava *see* Ostrava
Moray Firth *inlet* Scotland, UK 70 C3
Moree Australia 131 D5
Morelia Mexico 33 E4
Morena, Sierra *mountain range* Spain 74 D4
Morghāb *river* Afghanistan/Turkmenistan 104 D4
Morioka Japan 112 D3
Mornington Abyssal Plain *undersea feature* Pacific Ocean 135 G5
Morocco *country* N Africa 52
Morogoro Tanzania 55 C7
Mörön Mongolia 108 D2
Morondava Madagascar 61 F3
Moroni *capital of* Comoros 61 F2
Morotai, Pulau *island* Indonesia 121 F3
Morova *river* Poland 80 C6
Morris Jesup, Kap *headland* Greenland 65 E1
Moscow *capital of* Russian Federation *Rus.* Moskva 92 B4 96 B3
Mosel *river* W Europe *Fr.* Moselle 77 A5
Moselle *river* W Europe *Ger.* Mosel 72 E4
Mosgiel New Zealand 133 B7
Moshi Tanzania 55 C7
Moskva *see* Moscow
Mosquito Coast *coastal region* Nicaragua 35 E3
Moss Norway 67 B6
Mossendjo Congo 59 B6
Mossoró Brazil 43 H2
Most Czech Republic *Ger.* Brüx 80 A4

Mostaganem Algeria 52 D1
Mostar Bosnia & Herz. 82 C4
Mosul *see* Al Mawṣil
Motril Spain 75 E5
Motueka New Zealand 133 C5
Moulins France 72 C4
Moulmein Myanmar 118 B4
Moundou Chad 58 C4
Mount Gambier Australia
131 B7
Mount Isa Australia 130 B4
Mount Magnet Australia 129 B5
Mount Vernon Illinois, USA
22 B5
Mouscron Belgium 69 A6
Moyobamba Peru 42 B2
Moyu China 108 B2
Mozambique *country*
SE Africa 61
Mozambique Channel *sea feature* Indian Ocean 61 F3
Mozyr' *see* Mazyr
Mpika Zambia 61 E2
Mtwara Tanzania 55 C8
Muang Không Laos 119 D5
Muang Xaignabouri *see*
Xaignabouri
Mudanjiang China 110 E3
Mufulira Zambia 60 D2
Mugla Turkey 98 A4
Mulhouse France 72 E4
Mull *island* Scotland, UK 70 B3
Muller, Pegunungan *mountains*
Indonesia 120 C3
Multān Pakistan 116 C2
Mumbai India *var.* Bombay
117 C5
München Germany *Eng.*
Munich 77 C6
Muncie Indiana, USA 22 C4
Munich *see* München
Münster Germany 76 B4
Muqdisho *see* Mogadishu
Mur *river* C Europe 77 E7
Murchison River *river* Australia
129 B5
Murcia Spain 75 F4
Mureş *river* Hungary/Romania
81 D7

Murfreesboro Tennessee, USA
30 D1
Murgab Tajikistan 105 F3
Murgap *river* Turkmenistan
var. Murghab 104 C3
Murghab *see* Murgap
Müritz *lake* Germany 76 D3
Murmansk Russian Federation
92 C2 96 C1
Murray *river* Australia 131 B6
Murray Fracture Zone *tectonic
feature* Pacific Ocean 135 E2
Murray Ridge *Undersea feature*
Arabian Sea 122 B3
Murwillumbah Australia 131 E5
Murzuq Libya 53 F3
Muş Turkey 99 F3
Muscat *capital of* Oman *Ar.*
Masqaṭ 103 E5
Musgrave Ranges *mountain
range* Australia 129 D5
Musters, Lago *lake* Argentina
46 C6
Mu Us Shadi *Desert* China
109 E3
Mvonioälv *river*
Finland/Sweden 66 D3
Mwanza Tanzania 55 B6
Mwene-Ditu Dem. Rep. Congo
59 D7
Mweru, Lake *lake* Dem. Rep.
Congo/Zambia 59 D7
Myanmar *country* SE Asia *var.*
Myanmar 118-119
Mykolayiv Ukraine *Rus.*
Nikolayev 91 E4
Mykonos *island* Greece 87 D5
Mysore India 114 D2
Mzuzu Malawi 61 E2
Naberezhnyye Chelny Russian

N

Federation *prev.* Brezhnev
93 C5
Nablus West Bank *var.* Nābulus,
Heb. Shekhem 101 D6
Nābulus *see* Nablus
Nacala Mozambique 61 F2

Naga Philippines 120 E2
Nagano Japan 112 C4
Nagasaki Japan 113 A6
Nägercoil India 114 D3
Nagorno-Karabakh *region*
Azerbaijan 99 G2
Nagoya Japan 113 C5
Nägpur India 116 D4
Nagqu China 108 C5
Nagykanizsa Hungary *Ger.*
Grosskanizsa 81 C7
Nagyszombat *see* Trnava
Naha Japan 113 A8
Nain Canada 21 F2
Nairobi *capital of* Kenya 55 C6
Najaf *see* An Najaf
Najrān Saudi Arabia 103 B6
Nakamura Japan 113 B6
Nakhichevan' *see* Naxçivan
Nakhon Ratchasima Thailand
119 C5
Nakhon Sawan Thailand
119 C5
Nakhon Si Thammarat Thailand
119 C6
Nakuru Kenya 55 C6
Nal'chik Russian Federation
96 A4
Namangan Uzbekistan 105 E2
Nam Co *lake* China 108 C4
Nam Đinh Vietnam 118 D3
Namib Desert *desert* Namibia
60 B3
Namibe Angola 60 B2
Namibia *country* southern
Africa 60
Nampa Idaho, USA 24 C3
Namp'o North Korea 110 E4
Nampula Mozambique 61 F2
Namur Belgium 69 C6
Nanchang China 111 D5
Nancy France 72 D3
Nänded India 116 D5 114 D1
Nanjing China 111 D5
Nanning China 111 B6
Nanortalik Greenland 64 C5
Nansen Basin *undersea feature*
Arctic Ocean 137 G4
Nantes France 72 B4

Napier New Zealand 132 E4
Naples *see* Napoli
Napo *river* Ecuador/Peru 42 B2
Napoli Italy *Eng.* Naples 79 D5
Narbonne France 73 C6
Nares Strait *sea feature* Canada/Greenland 64 C1
Narew *river* Poland 80 E3
Narmada *river* India 116 D4
Narva Estonia 88 E2
Narva *river* Estonia/Russian Federation 88 E2
Narva Bay *sea feature* Gulf of Finland *Est.* Narva Laht, *Rus.* Narvskiy Zaliv 88 E2
Narva Laht *see* Narva Bay
Narvik Norway 66 C3
Narvskiy Zaliv *see* Narva Bay
Naryn Kyrgyzstan 105 G2
Näshik India 116 C5
Nashville Tennessee, USA 30 D1
Nâsir, Buheiret *see* Nasser, Lake
Nassau *capital of* Bahamas 36 C1
Nasser, Lake *reservoir* Egypt *var.* Nâsir, Buheiret 54 B2
Natal Brazil 43 H3
Natal Basin *Undersea feature* Indian Ocean 123 A5
Natitingou Benin 57 E4
Naturaliste Plateau *undersea feature* Indian Ocean 123 E6
Nauru *country* Pacific Ocean 126 D3
Navapolatsk Belarus *Rus.* Novopolotsk 89 D5
Navassa Island *external territory* USA, West Indies 36 D3
Navoiy Uzbekistan *Uzb.* Nawoly 104 D2
Nawäbshäh Pakistan 116 B3
Nawoly *see* Navoiy
Naxçivan Azerbaijan *Rus.* Nakhichevan' 99 G3
Náxos *island* Greece 87 D6
Nazaret *see* Nazerat
Nazca Peru 42 B4
Nazerat Israel *Eng.* Nazareth 101 A5

Nazrēt Ethiopia 55 C5
Nazwá Oman 103 E5
N'Dalatando Angola 60 B2
Ndélé Central African Republic 58 C4
N'Djamena *capital of* Chad 58 B3
Ndola Zambia 60 D2
Nebitdag *see* Balkanabat
Nebraska *state* USA 24-25 E3
Neches *river* S USA 29 H3
Neckar *river* Germany 77 B5
Necochea Argentina 47 D5
Neftezavodsk *see* Seýdi
Negēlē Ethiopia 55 C5
Negev *see* HaNegev
Negro, Río *river* Argentina 47 C5
Negro, Río *river* Brazil/Uruguay 44 C4
Negro, Río *river* N South America 40 C1
Neiva Colombia 40 B3
Nellore India 115 E2
Neman *river* NE Europe *Bel.* Nyoman, *Lith.* Nemunas, *Ger.* Memel, *Pol.* Niemen 88 B4
Nemunas *see* Neman
Nemuro Japan 112 E2
Nepal *country* S Asia 117
Neris *river* Belarus/Lithuania *Bel.* Viliya, *Pol.* Wilja 88 C4
Ness, Loch *lake* Scotland, UK 70 C3
Netherlands *country* W Europe *var.* Holland 68-69
Netherlands Antilles *external territory* Netherlands, West Indies *prev.* Dutch West Indies 37 E5
Netze *see* Noteć
Neubrandenburg Germany 76 D3
Neuchâtel, Lac de *lake* Switzerland 77 A7
Neumünster Germany 76 C2
Neuquén Argentina 47 C5
Neusiedler See *lake* Austria/Hungary 77 E6

Neusohl *see* Banská Bystrica
Neutra *see* Nitra
Nevada *state* USA 26-27
Nevers France 72 C4
Nevşehir Turkey 98 C3
New Amsterdam Guyana 41 G2
Newark New Jersey, USA 23 F3
New Britain *island* Papua New Guinea 126 B3
New Brunswick *province* Canada 21 F4
New Caledonia *external territory* France, Pacific Ocean 126 C5
New Caledonia *island* Pacific Ocean 124 D3
New Caledonia Basin *undersea feature* Pacific Ocean 124 D4
Newcastle Australia 131 D6
Newcastle upon Tyne England, UK 70 D4
New Delhi *capital of* India 116 D3
Newfoundland & Labrador *province* Canada 21 F2
Newfoundland *island* Canada 21 G3
Newfoundland Basin *undersea feature* Atlantic Ocean 48 B3
New Georgia Islands *island group* Solomon Is 126 C3
New Guinea *island* Pacific Ocean 126 B3
New Hampshire *state* USA 23 G2
New Haven Connecticut, USA 23 G3
New Ireland *island* Papua New Guinea 126 C3
New Jersey *state* USA 23 F4
Newman Australia 128 B4
New Mexico *state* USA 28-29
New Orleans Louisiana, USA 30 C3
New Plymouth New Zealand 132 D3
Newport Oregon, USA 26 A3
Newport News Virginia, USA 23 F5

North Uist *island* Scotland, UK 70 B3

Northwest Territories *territory* Canada 19 E3

Norway *country* N Europe 66-67

Norwegian Sea Arctic Ocean 137 G5

Norwich England, UK 71 E6

Noteć *river* Poland *Ger.* Netze 80 C3

Nottingham England, UK 71 D6

Nottingham Island *island* Hudson Strait 20 D1

Nouâdhibou Mauritania 56 B2

Nouakchott *capital of* Mauritania 56 B2

Nouméa *capital of* New Caledonia 126 D5

Nova Gradiška Croatia 82 C3

Nova Iguaçu Brazil 43 F5 45 F2

Novara Italy 78 B2

Nova Scotia *province* Canada 21 F4

Novaya Zemlya *islands* Russian Federation 137 H4

Novaya Zemlya Trench *see* East Novaya Zemlya Trench

Novi Sad Serbia 82 D3

Novokuznetsk Russian Federation *prev.* Stalinsk 96 E4

Novopolotsk *see* Navapolatsk

Novosibirsk Russian Federation 96 D4

Novosibirskiye Ostrova *islands* Russian Federation *Eng.* New Siberian Islands 95 F1

Novo Urgench *see* Urgench

Novyy Margilan *see* Fargʻona

Nsanje Malawi 61 E3

Nsawam Ghana 57 E5

Nubian Desert *desert* Sudan 54 B3

Nuʻeima West Bank 101 D7

Nuevo Laredo Mexico 33 E2

Nukuʻalofa *capital of* Tonga 127 F5

Nukus Uzbekistan 104 C2

Nullarbor Plain *region* Australia 129 D6

Nunap Isua Island *coastal region* Greenland *var.* Uummannaruaq *Dan.* Kap Farvel 64 C5

Nunavut *Territory* Canada 19 F3

Nunivak Island *island* Alaska, USA 18 B2

Nuoro Italy 79 A5

Nuremberg *see* Nürnberg

Nürnberg Germany *Eng.* Nuremberg 77 C5

Nusa Tenggara *islands* East Timor / Indonesia 120 E5

Nuuk Greenland *var.* Godthåb 64 C4

Nyainqêntanglha Shan *mountain range* China 108 D5

Nyala Sudan 54 A4

Nyasa, Lake *lake* E Africa 51 D5

Nyeri Kenya 55 C6

Nyima China 108 C4

Nyíregyháza Hungary 81 E6

Nyitra *see* Nitra

Nykøbing Denmark 67 B8

Nyköping Sweden 67 C6

Nyngan Australia 131 D6

Nyoman *see* Neman

—————— O ——————

Oakland California, USA 27 B6

Oakley Kansas, USA 25 E4

Oamaru New Zealand 133 B7

Oaxaca Mexico 33 F5

Obʻ *river* Russian Federation 96 D4

Oban Scotland, UK 70 C4

Obihiro Japan 112 D2

Obo Central African Republic 58 D4

Oceania 124-125

Ocean Island *see* Banaba

Oceanside California, USA 27 C8

Ochamchira *see* Ochʻamchʻire

Ochʻamchʻire Georgia *Rus.* Ochamchira 99 E1

Ödenburg *see* Sopron

Odense Denmark 67 B7

Oder *river* C Europe 80 C4

Odesa Ukraine *Rus.* Odessa 91 E4

Odessa *see* Odesa

Odessa Texas, USA 29 E3

Odienné Côte d'Ivoire 56 D4

Oesel *see* Saaremaa

Ofanto *river* Italy 79 D5

Offenbach Germany 77 B5

Ogaden *plateau* Ethiopia 55 D5

Ogallala Nebraska, USA 24 D4

Ogbomosho Nigeria 57 F4

Ogden Utah, USA 24 B3

Ogdensburg New York, USA 23 F2

Oger *see* Ogre

Ogre Latvia *Ger.* Oger 88 C3

Ogulin Croatia 82 B3

Ohio *state* USA 22 D4

Ohio *river* N USA 22 B5

Ohrid Macedonia 83 D6

Ohrid, Lake *lake* Albania/Macedonia 83 D6

Ohře *river* Czech Republic/ Germany *Ger.* Eger 81 A5

Ōita Japan 113 B6

Okavango *river var.* Cubango southern Africa 60 C3

Okavango Delta *wetland* Botswana 60 C3

Okayama Japan 113 B5

Okazaki Japan 113 C5

Okeechobee, Lake *lake* Florida, USA 31 E4

Okhotsk Russian Federation 97 G3

Okhotsk, Sea of Pacific Ocean 134 C1

Okinawa *island* Japan 113 A8

Oki-shotō *island group* Japan 113 B5

Oklahoma *state* USA 29 F1

Oklahoma City Oklahoma, USA 29 F2

Okushiri-tō *island* Japan 112 C2

Pishpek see Bishkek

Pistyan see Piešťany

Pitcairn Islands *external territory* UK, Pacific Ocean 125 G4

Piteå Sweden 66 D4

Pitești Romania 90 C4

Pittsburgh Pennsylvania, USA 23 E4

Piura Peru 42 A2

Pivdennyy Bug *river* Ukraine 91 E3

Plasencia Spain 74 D3

Plata, Rio de la *river* Argentina/Uruguay *var.* River Plate 44 B5 46 D4

Plate, River see Plata, Rio de la

Platte *river* C USA 25 E4

Plattensee see Balaton

Plenty, Bay of *bay* New Zealand 132 E3

Pleven Bulgaria 86 C1

Płock Poland 80 D3

Ploiești Romania 90 C4

Plovdiv Bulgaria *Gk.* Philippopolis 86 C2

Plungė Lithuania 88 B4

Plymouth *capital of* Montserrat 37 G3

Plymouth England, UK 71 C7

Plzeň Czech Republic *Ger.* Pilsen 81 A5

Po *river* Italy 78 B2

Pocatello Idaho, USA 26 E4

Po Delta *wetland* Italy 78 C3

Podgorica *capital of* Montenegro 83 C5

Pohnpei Island *island* Micronesia 126 C2

Pointe-Noire Congo 59 B6

Poitiers France 72 B4

Poland *country* E Europe 80-81

Polatsk Belarus 89 D5

Pol-e Khomrī Afghanistan 105 E4

Poltava Ukraine 91 F2

Poltoratsk see Aşgabat

Polynesia *region* Pacific Ocean 127

Pomeranian Bay *bay* Germany/Poland 80 B2

Pompano Beach Florida, USA 31 F5

Ponca City Oklahoma, USA 29 G1

Pondicherry India 115 E2

Ponta Grossa Brazil 44 D2

Pontevedra Spain 74 C1

Pontianak Indonesia 120 C4

Poona see Pune

Poopó, Lake *lake* Bolivia 42 C5

Popayán Colombia 40 B3

Poprad Slovakia *Ger.* Deutschendorf 81 D5

Porbandar India 116 B4

Pori Finland 67 D5

Porsgrunn Norway 67 B6

Portalegre Portugal 74 C3

Port Angeles Washington, USA 26 A1

Port Arthur Texas, USA 29 H4

Port Augusta Australia 131 B6

Port-au-Prince *capital of* Haiti 36 D3

Port Blair India 115 G2

Port Douglas Australia 130 D3

Port Elizabeth South Africa 60 D5

Port-Gentil Gabon 59 A6

Port Harcourt Nigeria 57 F5

Port Hardy Canada 18 D5

Port Hedland Australia 128 B4

Portland Australia 131 B7

Portland Maine, USA 23 G2

Portland Oregon, USA 26 B2

Port Lincoln Australia 131 A6

Port Louis *capital of* Mauritius 61 H4

Port Macquarie Australia 131 E6

Port Moresby *capital of* Papua New Guinea 126 B3

Porto Portugal *Eng.* Oporto 74 C2

Porto Alegre Sao Tome and Principe 44 D4

Port-of-Spain *capital of* Trinidad & Tobago 37 G5

Porto-Novo *capital of* Benin 57 F5

Porto Velho Brazil 42 C3

Portoviejo Ecuador 40 A4

Port Said Egypt 54 B1

Portsmouth England, UK 71 D7

Port Sudan Sudan 54 C3

Portugal *country* SW Europe 74

Port-Vila *capital of* Vanuatu 126 D5

Porvenir Chile 47 B7

Posadas Argentina 46 E3

Posen see Poznań

Pöstyén see Piešťany

Potenza S Italy 79 D5

P'ot'i Georgia 99 E2

Potosí Bolivia 42 C5

Potsdam Germany 76 D4

Póvoa de Varzim Portugal 74 C2

Powder *river* N USA 24 C2

Powell, Lake *lake* SW USA 24 B5

Poza Rica Mexico 33 F4

Poznań Poland *Ger.* Posen 80 C3

Pozo Colorado Paraguay 44 B2

Pozsony see Bratislava

Prag see Prague

Prague *capital of* Czech Republic *Cz.* Praha, *Ger.* Prag 81 B5

Praha see Prague

Praia *capital of* Cape Verde 56 A3

Prato Italy 78 B3

Pratt Kansas, USA 25 E5

Preschau see Prešov

Prescott Arizona, USA 28 B2

Presidente Prudente Brazil 44 D2

Prešov Slovakia *Ger.* Eperies, *var.* Preschau, *Hung.* Eperjes 81 D5

Prespa, Lake *lake* SE Europe 83 D6 86 A3

Presque Isle Maine, USA 23 G1

Pressburg see Bratislava

Preston England, UK 71 D5

Pretoria *see* Tshwane
Préveza Greece 86 A4
Prijedor Bosnia & Herzegovina
82 B3
Prilep Macedonia 83 E5
Prince Albert Canada 19 F5
Prince Edward Island *province*
Canada 21 F4
Prince Edward Islands *island
group* South Africa 123 A7
Prince George Canada 19 E5
Prince of Wales Island *island*
Canada 19 F2
Prince Rupert Canada 18 D4
Princess Charlotte Bay *bay*
Australia 130 C2
Princess Elizabeth Land *region*
Antarctica 136 C3
Principe *island* Sao Tome &
Principe 59 A5
Pripet *river* Belarus/Ukraine
90 C1
Pripet Marshes *wetlands*
Belarus/Ukraine 90 C1
Priština Serbia 83 D5
Prizren Serbia 83 D5
Prome Myanmar 118 A4
Prossnitz *see* Prostějov
Prostějov Czech Republic *Ger.*
Prossnitz 81 C5
Provence *region* France 73 D6
Providence Rhode Island, USA
23 G3
Providencia, Isla de *island*
Colombia 35 E3
Provo Utah, USA 24 B4
Prudhoe Bay Alaska, USA
18 D2
Przheval'sk *see* Karakol
Pskov Russian Federation
92 A4
Pskov, Lake *lake*
Estonia/Russian Federation
Est. Pihkva Järv, *Rus.*
Pskovskoye Ozero 88 D3
Pskovskoye Ozero
see Pskov, Lake
Ptich' *see* Ptsich
Ptsich *river* Belarus *Rus.* Ptich'
89 D6

Pucallpa Peru 42 B3
Puebla Mexico 33 F4
Pueblo Colorado, USA 22 D4
Puerto Aisén Chile 47 B6
Puerto Barrios Guatemala
34 C2
Puerto Carreño Colombia
40 D2
Puerto Cortés Honduras
34 C2
Puerto Deseado Argentina
47 C6
Puerto Maldonado Peru
42 C4
Puerto Montt Chile 47 B5
Puerto Natales Chile 47 B7
Puerto Plata Dominican
Republic 37 E3
Puerto Princesa Philippines
120 E2
Puerto Rico *external territory*
USA, West Indies 37 F3
Puerto San Julián Argentina
47 C7
Puerto Suárez Bolivia 42 D4
Puerto Vallarta Mexico 32 D4
Pula Croatia 82 A3
Pune India *prev.* Poona 114 C1
Puno Peru 42 C4
Punta Arenas Chile *prev.*
Magallanes 47 B7
Puntarenas Costa Rica 34 D4
Purmerend Netherlands
68 C3
Purus *river* Brazil/Peru 42 C3
Pusan South Korea 110 E4
Putrajaya *capital of* Malaysia
120 B3
Putumayo *river* NW South
America 38 B3
Pyapon Myanmar 118 B4
Pyarnu *see* Pärnu
Pyinmana *capital of* Myanmar
118 B3
Pyongyang *capital of* North
Korea 110 E4
Pyramid Lake *lake* Nevada,
USA 27 C5
Pyrenees *mountain range* SW
Europe 62 C4

Q

Qaanaaq Greenland *var.* Thule
64 D1
Qâbatiya West Bank 101 D7
Qaidam Pendi *basin* China
108 D4
Qalqilya West Bank 101 D7
Qamdo China 108 D5
Qandahār *see* Kandahār
Qaqortoq Greenland 64 C4
Qara Qum *see* Karakumy
Qarshi *see* Karshi
Qasigiannguit Greenland 64 C3
Qatar *country* SW Asia 103 D5
Qattara Depression *see*
Qaṭṭâra, Monkhafad el
Qaṭṭâra, Monkhafad el *desert
basin* Egypt *Eng.* Qattara
Depression 54 A1
Qena Egypt 54 B2
Qeqertarsuaq Greenland 64 B3
Qeqertarsuaq *island* Greenland
64 B3
Qian *see* Guizhou
Qilian Shan *mountain range*
China 108 D4
Qimusseriarsuaq *bay* Greenland
64 C2
Qingdao China 110 D4
Qinghai *province* China *var.*
Chinghai, Koko Nor, Qing,
Tsinghai 108 D4
Qinghai Hu *lake* China *var.*
Koko Nor 108 D4
Qingzang Gaoyuan *plateau*
China *Eng.* Plateau of Tibet
110 A4
Qiong *see* Hainan
Qiqihar China 110 D3
Qira China 108 B4
Qitai China 108 C3
Qom Iran *var.* Kum 102 C3
Qondūz *river* Afghanistan
105 E4
Qondūz *see* Kondoz
Qo'qon Uzbekistan *prev.*
Kokand, *var.* Khokand, 105 E2
Quba Azerbaijan *Rus.* Kuba
99 H2

Québec Canada 21 E4
Québec *province* Canada 20 D3
Queen Charlotte Islands *islands* Canada 18 D4
Queen Charlotte Sound *sea feature* Canada 18 D5
Queen Elizabeth Islands *islands* Canada 19 F1
Queensland *state* Australia 130 C4
Queenstown New Zealand 133 B6
Quelimane Mozambique 61 E3
Querétaro Mexico 33 E4
Quetta Pakistan 116 B2
Quezaltenango Guatemala 34 B2
Quibdó Colombia 40 B2
Quimper France 72 A3
Qui Nhon Vietnam 119 E5
Qing *see* Qinghai
Quito *capital of* Ecuador 40 A4
Qürghonteppa Tajikistan *Rus.* Kurgan–Tynbe 105 E3
Qyteti Stalin *see* Kuçovë

R

Raab *see* Győr
Raab *see* Rába
Rába *river* Austria/Hungary *Ger.* Raab 81 C7
Rabat *capital of* Morocco 52 C2
Race, Cape *coastal feature* Canada 21 H4
Rach Gia Vietnam 119 D6
Radom Poland 80 D4
Radviliškis Lithuania 88 C4
Ragusa Italy 79 D7
Rahīmyār Khān Pakistan 116 C3
Raipur India 117 E5
Rājahmundry India 115 E1
Rājasthān *state* India 116 C3
Rājkot India 116 C4
Rājshāhi Bangladesh 117 G4

Rakaia *river* New Zealand 133 C6
Rakvere Estonia *Ger.* Wesenberg 88 D2
Raleigh North Carolina, USA 31 F1
Ralik Chain *islands* Marshall Islands 126 D1
Râmnicu Vâlcea Romania *prev.* Rîmnicu Vîlcea 90 B4
Ramallah West Bank 101 D7
Ramree Island *island* Myanmar 118 A3
Rancagua Chile 46 B4
Rānchi India 117 F4
Randers Denmark 67 A7
Rangiora New Zealand 133 C6
Rangitikei *river* New Zealand 132 D4
Rangoon *capital of* Myanmar *Bur.* Yangon 118 B4
Rankin Inlet Canada 19 G3
Rapid City South Dakota, USA 24 D3
Rarotonga *island* Cook Islands 127 G5
Rasht Iran 102 C3
Ratak Chain *islands* Marshall Islands 126 D1
Ratchaburi Thailand 119 C5
Rat Islands *island group* Alaska, USA 18 A2
Raukumara Range *mountain range* New Zealand 132 E3
Rauma Finland 67 D5
Ravenna Italy 78 C3
Rāwalpindi Pakistan 116 C1
Rawson Argentina 47 C6
Razgrad Bulgaria 86 D1
Reading England, UK 71 D6
Rebecca, Lake *lake* Australia 129 C6
Rebun-tō *island* Japan 112 D1
Rechytsa Belarus 89 D7
Recife Brazil 43 H3
Recklinghausen Germany 76 G4
Red Deer Canada 19 E5
Redding California, USA 27 B5
Red River *river* S USA 30 B3

Red River *river* China/ Vietnam 118
Red Sea Indian Ocean 122 A3
Reefton New Zealand 133 C5
Regensburg Germany 77 C5
Reggane Algeria 52 D3
Reggio di Calabria Italy 79 D6
Reggio nell' Emilia Italy 78 B3
Regina Canada 19 F5
Rehoboth Namibia 60 C4
Reichenberg *see* Liberec
Reid Australia 129 D6
Reims France *Eng.* Rheims 72 D3
Reindeer Lake *lake* Canada 17 C4
Reni Ukraine 90 D4
Rennes France 72 B3
Reno Nevada, USA 27 B5
Resistencia Argentina 46 D3
Reşiţa Romania 90 B4
Resolute Canada 19 F2
Réunion *external territory* France, Indian Ocean 123 B5
Reus Spain 75 G2
Reutlingen Germany 77 B6
Reval *see* Tallinn
Revel *see* Tallinn
Revillagigedo, Islas *island* Mexico 32 B4
Rey, Isla del *island* Panama 35 F5
Reykjavík *capital of* Iceland 65 E5
Reynosa Mexico 33 E2
Rēzekne Latvia *Ger.* Rositten, *Rus.* Rezhitsa 88 D4
Rezhitsa *see* Rēzekne
Rheims *see* Reims
Rhine *river* W Europe 62 D3
Rhode Island *state* USA 23 G3
Rhodes *see* Ródos
Rhodope Mountains *mountain range* Bulgaria/Greece *Gk.* Orosirá Rodópis, *Bul.* Despoto Planina 86 C3
Rhône *river* France/Switzerland 62 C4
Ribeirão Preto Brazil 45 E1

Sabadell Spain 75 G2
Sabah *cultural region* Borneo 120 D3
Sab'atayn, Ramlat *as desert* Yemen 103 C7
Sabhā Libya 53 F3
Sabzevār Iran 102 D3
Sacramento California, USA 27 B6
Ṣa'dah Yemen 103 B6
Sado *island* Japan 112 C4
Safi Morocco 52 B2
Saginaw Michigan, USA 22 C3
Sahara *desert* N Africa 50 B3
Sahel *region* W Africa 50 B3
Saïda Lebanon *anc.* Sidon 100 B4
Saidpur Bangladesh 117 G3
Saigon *see* Hô Chi Minh
Saimaa *lake* Finland 67 E5
Saint-Brieuc France 72 A3
Saint Catherines Canada 20 D5
Saint-Chamond France 73 D5
St Christopher & Nevis *see* St Kitts & Nevis
St Cloud Minnesota, USA 25 F2
St-Denis *capital of* Réunion 61 H4
Saintes France 72 B5
Saint-Étienne France 73 D5
Saint George Australia 131 D5
St. George's *capital of* Grenada 37 G5
St Helena *external territory* UK, Atlantic Ocean 49 D5
St Helier Jersey 71 D8
Saint-Jean, Lake *lake* Canada 21 E4
Saint John Canada 21 F4
St John's *country capital* Antigua and Barbuda 37 G3
Saint John's Canada 21 H3
St Joseph Missouri, USA 25 F4
St Kitts & Nevis *country* West Indies *var.* St Christopher & Nevis 37
St.-Laurent-du-Maroni French Guiana 41 H2

Saint Lawrence *river* Canada 21 E4
Saint Lawrence, Gulf of *sea feature* Canada 21 F3
St. Lawrence Island *island* Alaska, USA 18 C2
Saint-Lô France 73 B3
Saint Louis Senegal 56 B3
St Louis Missouri, USA 25 G4
St Lucia *country* West Indies 37
Saint-Malo France 72 B3
Saint-Nazaire France 72 B4
Saint Paul Minnesota, USA 25 F2
St-Paul, Île *island* French Southern and Antarctic Territories 123 C6
St Peter Port *capital of* Guernsey 71 D8
St Petersburg Russian Federation *Rus.* Sankt-Peterburg, *prev.* Leningrad, Petrograd 92 B3 96 B2
St Petersburg Florida, USA 31 E4
Saint Pierre & Miquelon *external territory* France, Atlantic Ocean 21 G4
St Vincent, Cape *see* São Vicente, Cabo de
St Vincent & The Grenadines *country* West Indies 37
Saipan *island country capital* Northern Mariana Islands 124 B1
Sakākah Saudi Arabia 102 B4
Sakakawea, Lake *lake* North Dakota, USA 24 D2
Sakarya *see* Adapazarı
Sakhalin *island* Russian Federation 97 H4
Sal *island* Cape Verde 56 A2
Salado *river* Argentina 46 C3
Şalālah Oman 103 D6
Salamanca Spain 74 D2
Sala y Gómez *island* Chile, Pacific Ocean 135 F4
Saldus Latvia *Ger.* Frauenburg 88 B3
Salekhard Russian Federation 96 D3

Salem India 114 D2
Salem Oregon, USA 26 A3
Salerno Italy 79 D5
Salerno, Golfo di *sea feature* Italy 79 D5
Salihorsk Belarus *Rus.* Soligorsk 89 C6
Salima Malawi 61 E2
Salinas California, USA 27 B6
Salisbury England, UK 71 D7
Salisbury Island *island* Canada 20 D1
Salonica *see* Thessaloniki
Salso *river* Italy 79 C7
Salt *see* As Salt
Salta Argentina 46 C2
Saltillo Mexico 33 E2
Salt Lake City Utah, USA 24 B4
Salto Uruguay 44 B4
Salton Sea *lake* California, USA 27 D8
Salvador Brazil 43 G4
Salween *river* SE Asia 111 A6
Salzburg Austria 77 D6
Salzgitter Germany 76 C4
Samara Russian Federation 93 C6 96 B3
Samarinda Indonesia 121 E4
Samarkand Uzbekistan 104 D2
Sambre *river* Belgium 69 B7
Samoa *country* Pacific Ocean 127 F4
Sambor Croatia 82 B3
Sámos *island* Greece 87 D5
Samothrace *see* Samothráki
Samothráki *island* Greece *Eng.* Samothrace 86 D3
Samsun Turkey 98 D3
Samui, Ko *island group* Thailand 119 C6
San *river* Poland 81 E5
Saña Peru 42 A3
Sana *capital of* Yemen *var.* Ṣan'ā' 103 B7
Sanandaj Sinneh. Iran 102 C3
San Andrés, Isla de *island* Colombia 35 E3
San Angelo Texas, USA 29 F3
San Antonio Chile 46 B4

Sardegna *island* Italy *Eng.*
Sardinia 79 A5

Sardinia *see* Sardegna

Sarema *see* Saaremaa

Sargasso Sea Atlantic Ocean
48 B4

Sargodha Pakistan 116 C2

Sarh Chad 58 C4

Sārī Iran 102 D3

Saruhan *see* Manisa

Sasebo Japan 113 A6

Saskatchewan *province*
Canada 19 F5

Saskatchewan *river* Canada
19 F5

Saskatoon Canada 19 F5

Sassandra River Côte d'Ivoire 56
D5

Sassari Italy 79 A5

Satu Mare Romania 90 B3

Saudi Arabia *country* SW Asia
102-103

Sault Sainte Marie Canada
20 C4

Sault Sainte Marie Michigan,
USA 22 C1

Saurimo Angola 60 C2

Sava *river* SE Europe 82 C3

Savannah Georgia, USA
31 F3

Savannah *river* SE USA 31 E2

Savissivik Greenland 64 C2

Savona Italy 78 A3

Savu Sea *sea* Indonesia 120 E5

Şawqirah Oman 103 D6

Saýat Turkmenistan 104 D3

Sayhūt Yemen 103 D7

Saynshand Mongolia 109 E2

Say 'ūn Yemen 103 C6

Scandinavia *geophysical region*
Europe 48 D2

Schaffhausen Switzerland
77 B6

Schaulen *see* Šiauliai

Schefferville Canada 21 E2

Scheldt *river* W Europe 69 B5

Schiermonnikoog *island*
Netherlands 68 D1

Schneidemühl *see* Piła

Schwäbische Alb *mountains*
Germany 77 B6

Schwarzwald *Forested
mountain region* Germany
Eng. Black Forest 77 B6

Schwerin Germany 76 C3

Scilly, Isles of *islands* UK 71 B7

Scotia Sea Atlantic Ocean
136 A1

Scotland *national region* UK 70

Scottsbluff Nebraska, USA
24 D3

Scottsdale Arizona, USA 28 B2

Scranton Pennsylvania, USA
23 F3

Scutari, Lake *lake*
Albania/Montenegro 83 C5

Seddon New Zealand 133 C5

Seattle Washington, USA 26 B2

Ségou Mali 56 D3

Segovia Spain 75 E2

Segura *river* Spain 75 E4

Seikan Tunnel *tunnel* Japan
112 D3

Seinäjoki Finland 67 D5

Seine *river* France 72 C3

Selfoss Iceland 65 E5

Semara *see* Smara

Semarang Indonesia 120 D4

Semipalatinsk Kazakhstan 96
D4

Sendai Japan 112 D4

Senegal *country* W Africa 56

Senegal *river* Africa 56 C3

Sên, Stœng *river* Cambodia
119 D5

Seoul *capital of* South Korea
Kor. Sŏul 110 E4

Sept-Iles Canada 21 F3

Seraing Belgium 69 D6

Seram, Pulau *island* Indonesia
121 F4

Serbia *country* SE Europe
82 D3

Serdar Turkmenistan *prev.*
Gyzylarbat, *prev.* Kizyl-Arvat
104 B2

Serhetabat Turkmenistan *prev.*
Gushgy, Kushka
104 C4

Serov Russian Federation 96 C3

Serpent's Mouth, The *sea
feature* Trinidad &
Tobago/Venezuela *Sp.* Boca
de la Serpiente 41 F1

Serra do Mar *mountains* Brazil
44 A3

Sérres Greece 86 C3

Setesdal *valley* Norway 67 A6

Sétif Algeria 53 E1

Setúbal Portugal 74 C4

Seul, Lake *lake* Canada 20 A3

Sevana Lich *lake* Armenia
99 G2

Sevastopol' Ukraine 91 F5

Severn *river* Canada 20 B3

Severn *river* England/Wales, UK
71 D6

Severnaya Dvina *river* Russian
Federation *Eng.* Northern
Dvina 92 C3

Severnaya Zemlya *island group*
Russian Federation 137 H3

Sevilla Spain *Eng.* Seville
74 D4

Seville *see* Sevilla

Seychelles *country* Indian
Ocean 61 122 B4

Seydhisfjördhur Iceland 65 E4

Seýdi Turkmenistan *prev.*
Neftezavodsk 104 D2

Seyhan *see* Adana

Sfax Tunisia 53 F2

's-Gravenhage *capital of*
Netherlands *Eng.* The Hague
68 B3

Shaan *see* Shaanxi

Shaanxi *province* China *var.*
Shaan, Shan-hsi, Shaanxi
Sheng, Shenshi, Shensi
111 C5

Shaanxi Sheng *see* Shaanxi

Shache China 108 A3

Shackleton Ice Shelf *ice feature*
Antarctica 136 D3

Shandong *province* China *var.*
Lu, Shantung 110 D4

Shanghai China 111 D5

Shangrao China 111 D6

Shan-hsi *see* Shaanxi

Shannon *river* Ireland 71 B5

Tangiers *see* Tanger

Tangra Yumco *lake* China 108 B5

Tangshan China 110 D4

Tanimbar Islands *see* Tanimbar, Kepulauan

Tanimbar, Kepulauan *island group* Indonesia *Eng.* Tanimbar Islands 121 F5

Tanjungkarang *see* Bandar Lampung

Tan-Tan Morocco 52 B3

Tanzania *country* E Africa 55

Taoudenni Mali 57 E2

Tapa Estonia *Ger.* Taps 88 D2

Tapachula Mexico 33 G5

Tapajós *river* Brazil 43 E2

Taps *see* Tapa

Ṭarābulus Tripoli, Lebanon

Ṭarābulus al-Gharb *see* Tripoli, Libya

Taranto Italy 79 E5

Taranto, Golfo di *sea feature* Mediterranean Sea 79 E5

Tarapoto Peru 42 B2

Tarawa *island* Kiribati 127 E2

Taraz Kazakhstan *prev.* Dzhambul, Zhambyl 96 C5

Tarbes France 73 B6

Tarcoola Australia 131 A5

Târgovişte Romania *prev.* Tîrgovişte 90 C4

Târgu Mureş Romania *prev.* Tîrgu Mureş 90 C4

Tarija Bolivia 42 C5

Tarim Basin *basin* China 108 B3

Tarim He *river* China 108 B3

Tarn *river* France 73 C6

Tarnów Poland 81 D5

Tarragona Spain 75 G2

Tarsus Turkey 98 D4

Tartu Estonia *prev.* Yur'yev, *var.* Yurev, *Ger.* Dorpat 88 D3

Ṭarṭūs Syria 100 B3

Tashauz *see* Daşoguz

Tashkent *capital* of Uzbekistan *var.* Taškent, *Uzb.* Toshkent 105 E2

Taškent *see* Tashkent

Tasman Bay *inlet* New Zealand 132 C4

Tasmania *state* Australia 131 C8

Tasman Basin *undersea feature* Tasman Sea 124 D5

Tasman Plateau *undersea feature* Pacific Ocean 124 C5

Tasman Sea Pacific Ocean 134 C4

Tassili-n-Ajjer *desert plateau* Algeria 53 E4

Tatabánya Hungary 81 C6

Tatar Pazardzhik *see* Pazardzhik

Taubaté Brazil 43 F5 45 E4

Taumarunui New Zealand 132 D3

Taunggyi Myanmar 118 B3

Taunton England, UK 71 D7

Taupo New Zealand 132 D3

Taupo, Lake *lake* New Zealand 132 D3

Tauragė Lithuania 88 B4

Tauranga New Zealand 132 D3

Taurus Mountains *mountain range* Turkey *see* Toros Dağları 94 D4

Tavoy Myanmar 119 B5

Tawau Malaysia 120 D3

Taymyr, Ozero *lake* Russian Federation 97 E2

Taymyr, Poluostrov *peninsula* Russian Federation *Eng.* Taymyr Peninsula 97 E2

Taymyr Peninsula *see* Taymyr, Poluostrov

Tbilisi *capital* of Georgia *Geor.* T'bilisi, *prev.* Tiflis 99 F2

Te Anau New Zealand 133 A7

Te Anau, Lake *lake* New Zealand 133 A7

Tedzhen *see* Tejen

Tegal Indonesia 120 C5

Tegucigalpa *capital* of Honduras 34 C2

Teheran *see* Tehrān

Tehrān *capital* of Iran *prev.* Teheran 102 C3

Tehuacán Mexico 33 F4

Tehuantepec, Golfo de *sea feature* Mexico 33 G5

Tejen Turkmenistan *prev.* Tedzhen 104 C3

Tejo *see* Tagus

Te Kao New Zealand 131 C1

Tekirdağ Turkey *It.* Rodosto 98 A2

Te Kuiti Waikato, New Zealand 132 D3

Tel Aviv-Yafo Israel 101 A5

Teles Pires *river* Brazil 43 E3

Tell Atlas *plateau* Africa 84 C3

Telschen *see* Telšiai

Telšiai Lithuania *Ger.* Telschen 88 B4

Temuco Chile 47 B5

Ténéré *physical region* Niger 57 G2

Tenerife *island* Spain 52 A3

Tennant Creek Australia 130 A3

Tennessee *state* USA 31 C1

Tennessee *river* SE USA 31 C1

Tepelenë Albania 83 D6

Tepic Mexico 32 D4

Teplice Czech Republic *Ger.* Teplitz, *prev.* Teplice-Šanov, *Ger.* Teplitz-Schönau 80 A4

Teplice-Šanov *see* Teplice

Teplitz *see* Teplice

Teplitz-Schönau *see* Teplice

Teraina *island* Kiribati 127 G3

Teresina Brazil 43 G2

Termez Uzbekistan 105 E3

Terneuzen Netherlands 69 B5

Terni Italy 78 C4

Ternopil' Ukraine *Rus.* Ternopol' 90 C2

Ternopol' *see* Ternopil'

Terrassa Spain 75 G2

Terre Haute Indiana, USA 22 B4

Terres Australes et Antarctiques Françaises *see* French Southern and Antarctic Territories

Terschelling *island* Netherlands 68 C1

Teruel Spain 75 F3

Teseney Eritrea 54 C4

Tessalit Mali 57 E2
Tete Mozambique 61 E3
Tétouan Morocco 52 C1
Tetovo Macedonia 83 D5
Tetschen see Děčín
Tevere river Italy 78 C4
Texas state USA 28-29 F3
Texarkana Arkansas, USA 30 A2
Texas City Texas, USA 29 G4
Texel island Netherlands 68 C2
Thailand country SE Asia 118-119
Thailand, Gulf of sea feature South China Sea 119 C6
Thames river England, UK 71 D6
Thar Desert desert India/Pakistan 116 C3
Tharthār, Buḩayrat ath lake Iraq 102 B3
Thásos island Greece 86 C3
Thaton Myanmar 118 B4
Theiss see Tisza
Thermaic Gulf see Thermaïkós Kólpos
Thermaïkós Kólpos sea feature Greece Eng. Thermaic Gulf 86 B4
Thessaloníki Greece var. Salonica 86 B3
The Valley dependent territory capital Anguilla 37 G5
Thimphu capital of Bhutan 117 G3
Thionville France 72 E3
Thompson Canada 19 F4
Thorn see Toruń
Thorshavn see Tórshavn
Thracian Sea Greece Gk. Thrakikó Pélagos 86 C3
Thrakikó Pélagos see Thracian Sea
Three Kings Islands island group New Zealand 132 C1
Thule see Qaanaaq
Thunder Bay Canada 20 B4
Thuner See lake Switzerland 77 B7
Thurso Scotland, UK 70 C2
Tianjin China var. Tientsin 110 D4

Tiberias, Lake lake Israel var. Sea of Galilee, Heb. Yam Kinneret, Ar. Bahrat Tabariya 101 B5
Tibesti mountains Chad/Libya 50 C3
Tibet autonomous region China Chin. Xizang 108 C5
Tibet, Plateau of see Qingzang Gaoyuan
Tienen Belgium 69 C6
Tien Shan mountain range C Asia 105 G2
Tientsin see Tianjin
Tierra del Fuego island Argentina/Chile 47 C8
Tiflis see Tbilisi
Tighina Moldova prev. Bendery 90 D4
Tigris river SW Asia 94 B4
Tijuana Mexico 32 A1
Tiki Basin undersea feature Pacific Ocean 135 E3
Tiksi Russian Federation 97 F2
Tilburg Netherlands 68 C4
Timaru New Zealand 133 B6
Timişoara Romania 90 A4
Timmins Canada 20 C4
Timor island Indonesia 121 F5
Timor Sea Indian Ocean 121 F5
Tindouf Algeria 52 B3
Tínos island Greece 87 D5
Tirana capital of Albania 83 D6
Tiraspol Moldova 90 D4
Tîrgovişte see Târgovişte
Tîrgu Mureş see Târgu Mureş
Tirol region Austria var. Tyrol 77 C7
Tiruchchirāppalli India 114 D3
Tisa see Tisza
Tisza river E Europe Ger. Theiss, Cz./Rom./SCr. Tisa 81 D6
Titicaca, Lake lake Bolivia/Peru 42 C4
Tlemcen Algeria 52 D2
Toamasina Madagascar 61 G3
Toba, Danau lake Indonesia 120 B3

Tobago island Trinidad and Tobago 37 G5
Toba Kākar Range mountains Pakistan 116 B2
Tobruk see Ţubruq
Tocantins river Brazil 43 F3
Tocopilla Chile 46 B2
Togo country W Africa 57 E4
Tokat Turkey 98 D3
Tokelau external territory New Zealand, Pacific Ocean 127 F3
Tokmak Kyrgyzstan 105 F2
Tokuno-shima island Japan 113 A8
Tokushima Japan 113 B5
Tokyo capital of Japan 113 D5
Toledo Spain 75 E3
Toledo Ohio, USA 22 C3
Toledo Bend Reservoir Reservoir S USA 29 H3
Toliara Madagascar 61 E3
Tol'yatti prev. Stavropol' Russian Federation 93 C5
Tomakomai Japan 112 D2
Tombouctou Mali 57 E3
Tombua Angola 60 B2
Tomini, Gul of sea feature Indonesia 121 E4
Tomsk Russian Federation 96 D4
Tonga country Pacific Ocean 127
Tongatapu island Tonga 125 E3
Tongking, Gulf of sea feature South China Sea var. Gulf of Tonkin 111 B7
Tongliao China 109 G2
Tongtian He river China 108 C4
Tonkin, Gulf of see Tongking, Gulf of
Tônle Kông river Cambodia/Vietnam 118 E5
Tônlé Sap lake Cambodia 119 D5
Tonopah Nevada, USA 27 C6
Toowoomba Australia 131 D5
Topeka Kansas, USA 25 F4
Top Springs Australia 130 A3
Torino Italy Eng. Turin 78 A2

Turan Lowland *lowland*
Turkmenistan/Uzbekistan *var.*
Turan Plain, *Rus.* Turanskaya
Nizmennost' 104 C2

Turan Plain *see* Turan Lowland

Turanskaya Nizmennost' *see*
Turan Lowland

Turčiansky Svätý Martin *see*
Martin

Turin *see* Torino

Turkana, Lake *lake*
Ethiopia/Kenya *var.* Lake
Rudolf 50 D4 55 C5

Turkey *country* SW Asia 98-99

Türkmenabat Turkmenistan
prev. Chardzhev, *Rus.*
Chardzhou, *prev.* Leninsk,
Turkm. Chärjew 104 D3

Türkmenbaşy Turkmenistan
prev. Krasnovodsk 104 A2

Turkmenistan *country* C Asia 104

Turks & Caicos Islands *external
territory* UK, West Indies 37

Turku Finland 67 D5

Turnagain, Cape *headland* New
Zealand 151 E4

Turnhout Belgium 69 C5

Turnu Severin *see* Drobeta-
Turnu Severin

Turócszentmárton *see* Martin

Turpan China 108 C3

Turtkul' *see* To'rtko'l

Türtkül *see* To'rtko'l

Tuscany *see* Toscana

Tuvalu *country* Pacific Ocean
127

Tuxtla Mexico 33 G5

Tuz Gölü *lake* Turkey 98 C3

Tuzla Bosnia & Herz. 82 C3

Tver' Russian Federation 92 B4

Twin Falls Idaho, USA 26 D4

Tyler Texas, USA 29 G3

Tyre *see* Soûr

Tyrnau *see* Trnava

Tyrol *see* Tirol

Tyrrhenian Sea Mediterranean
Sea 78 C4

Tyup Kyrgyzstan 105 G2

Tziá *island* Greece *prev.* Kéa
87 C5

U

Ubangi *river* C Africa 59 C5

Uberaba Brazil 43 F5 45 E1

Uberlândia Brazil 43 F5 45 E1

Ubon Ratchathani Thailand
119 D5

Ucayali *river* Peru 42 B3

Uchkuduk Uzbekistan *Uzb.*
Uchquduq 104 D2

Uchquduq *see* Uchkuduk

Udine Italy 78 C2

Udon Thani Thailand 118 C4

Uele *river* Dem. Rep. Congo
58 D5

Ufa Russian Federation 96 B3

Uganda *country* E Africa 55

Uíge Angola 60 B1

Ujungpandang *see* Makassar

Ukhta Russian Federation 92 D4

Ukiah California, USA 27 A5

Ukmergė Lithuania 88 C4

Ukraine *country* E Europe
90-91

Ulaanbaatar *see* Ulan Bator

Ulaangom Mongolia 108 C2

Ulan Bator *capital of* Mongolia
var. Ulaanbaatar 109 E2

Ulan-Ude Russian Federation
97 E4

Ullapool Scotland, UK 70 C3

Ulm Germany 77 C6

Ulster *region* Ireland/UK 71 B5

Ulungur Hu *lake* China 108 C2

Uluru *peak* Australia *var.* Ayers
Rock 129 E5

Ul'yanovsk Russian Federation
93 C5

Umeå Sweden 66 D4

Umnak Island *island* Alaska,
USA 18 B3

Una *river* Bosnia &
Herzegovina/Croatia 82 B3

Unalaska Island *island* Alaska,
USA 18 B3

Ungava, Péninsule d' *peninsula*
Canada 20 D1

Ungava Bay *sea feature*
Canada 21 E1

United Arab Emirates *country*
SW Asia 103 D5

United Kingdom *country* NW
Europe 70-71

United States of America
country North America
16-17

Uppsala Sweden 67 C6

Ural *river* Kazakhstan/Russian
Federation 96 B4

Ural Mountains *mountain
range* Russian Federation
var. Ural'skiy Khrebet,
Ural'skiye Gory 92-93

Ural'sk Kazakhstan 96 B3

Ural'skiy Khrebet *see* Ural
Mountains

Ural'skiye Gory *see* Ural
Mountains

Urfa *see* Şanlıurfa

Urganch *see* Urgench

Urgench Uzbekistan *prev.* Novo
Urgench, *Uzb.* Urganch
104 C2

Uroševac Serbia 83 D5

Ŭroteppa Tajikistan 105 E2

Uruapan Mexico 33 E4

Uruguaiana Brazil 44 B4

Uruguay *country* SE South
America 44

Uruguay *river* S South America
46 D3

Urumchi *see* Ürümqi

Ürümqi China *prev.* Urumchi
108 C3

Usa *river* Russian Federation
92 D3

Uşak Turkey *prev.* Ushak 98 B3

Ushak *see* Uşak

Ushuaia Argentina 47 C8

Ust'-Chaun Russian Federation
97 G1

Ustica, Isola de *island* Italy 79
C6

Ústí nad Labem Czech Republic
Ger. Aussig 80 A4

Ust'-Kamchatsk Russian
Federation 97 H2

Ust'-Kamenogorsk Kazakhstan
96 D5